WORKING
ABROAD

BDO Expatriate Services

Make the most of tax planning opportunities – structure your affairs before you leave

For international tax and social security planning, please call **Stephen Asher** on **0207 486 5888** or email the expatriate services team on **expat@bdo.co.uk**

Alternatively, for more information regarding the range of expatriate services provided by BDO International, please turn to our corporate profile on page < >.

www.bdo.co.uk

BDO Stoy Hayward

About BDO Stoy Hayward

We are the UK member firm of BDO, a multinational accounting organisation, which since 1963 has grown to be the fifth largest in the world with:

2,142 Partners
25,118 Staff
More than 600 offices in over 100 countries
World-wide fee income of US$3 billion

BDO International is well placed to serve both individuals with global taxation, social security and immigration issues and multinational businesses in the UK and overseas. We also provide a comprehensive range of audit, assurance, corporate finance and taxation services.

BDO Stoy Hayward's global expatriate services

Tax, immigration, social security and pension issues for expatriates are often far more complex than for most. When being assigned overseas, you need to consider whether you will cope with the different tax and social security issues arising in various countries and their implications. You must ensure you have the appropriate work permit and visa in place before commencing the assignment.

You must also consider your continuing home country obligations if, for example, you will be letting your house or if you have other UK sources of income.

At BDO Stoy Hayward, our dedicated team of expatriate tax and immigration specialists offers tailored service and an in-depth understanding of the issues facing employees working, or planning to work, overseas.

Reducing the burden of international tax and social security compliance

Complying with unfamiliar and constantly changing tax legislation in foreign countries is a daunting task for any employee looking to work, or currently working abroad. BDO Stoy Hayward can remove this burden by ensuring that all host obligations are met as well as providing ongoing tax advice in the UK. Our services include:

- pre-departure planning meetings and briefings with executives to deal with home country issues and any pre-assignment tax planning
- arrival meetings in the host country to familiarise executives with the tax implications of their assignments
- dealing with all home and host country tax returns and filing obligations in order to keep responsibilities up to date and avoid interest and penalties
- hypothetical tax calculations and Inland Revenue documentation
- payroll issues
- liaison with and necessary tax documentation for tax authorities worldwide

- social security advice
- stock option and share scheme advice
- advice on the implications of being a non-UK resident landlord
- pension planning advice
- double taxation treaty advice
- high level international tax planning
- immigration, work permit and visa advice.

For expatriates repatriating or moving on to their next assignment, timely advice can also prevent needless tax liabilities arising.

Reducing the cost of international assignments

Effective planning for expatriate executives relies on extensive, accessible knowledge of the home and host country tax law. Using our global network we can ensure that assignment costs are kept to a minimum. BDO Stoy Hayward can offer:

- reviews of company and expatriate policies and remuneration packages. It is important for compensation packages to be carefully structured in order to ensure tax efficiency for both the employer and assignee
- tax equalisation and protection mechanisms to deal with varying tax exposure for employees worldwide
- immigration/work permit advice for long-term and short-term assignments around the world.

Planning points

There are many planning opportunities for employees working abroad, below are just a few to consider:

- **Secondment length** affects both employer and employee tax and social security obligations, and the type of visa or work permit the employee is eligible for
- It is important to consider the **start date of an assignment**. By moving it forward or backwards, tax savings can be maximised
- **The structure of the compensation package** can, in certain countries, minimise tax and social security costs, for instance by substituting benefits for a proportion of salary.
- Always consider **reporting obligations**. Even when there are no tax paymentobligations, there are sometimes reporting obligations. If these are ignored the penalties can be high
- In some host countries, **employer pension contributions** are taxable and employee contributions are not deductible, therefore planning is essential
- Does the employee qualify for a work permit, or does the employer qualify as a sponsor for a work permit application.

Contact us

For further information on the services BDO Stoy Hayward can offer to expatriates and their employers, please call Amanda Sullivan on **020 7893 3442** or email **expat@bdo.co.uk**

Rosetta Stone (**www.rosettastone.co.uk**), the world's leading self study language learning company, has invested heavily over recent years to keep at the forefront of advances in technology and education. Rosetta Stone's Dynamic Immersion method works by stimulating the natural learning process we all experienced as children and the same experience you'll face as you immerse yourself into your new home abroad.

Rosetta Stone is distinguished from other language learning material by its ability to fulfill the promise of true, interactive, multimedia language learning. With their unique Dynamic Immersion method, thousands of real-life colour images convey the meaning of each spoken and written phrase. Speech recognition develops pronunciation and fluency while dictation builds proficiency in syntax and spelling.

By providing instantaneous feedback within a carefully sequenced structure, new languages are learned without memorisation, without translation and without studying the rules of grammar. The result is natural and effective learning, replicating the way we learned our first language as a child. Learners of all ages start at the very beginning and surprise themselves with success. They learn quickly and love it.

As you prepare, or start to think about living or working abroad, consider the benefits of using Rosetta Stone to get a great head start on the local language before you arrive. From the first day, you'll understand directions, set appointments, shop and get yourself to the office with confidence. Start removing the barriers to success by learning a new language with Rosetta Stone today.

For more information call us today on **0800 310 1829** *or go to* **www.rosettastone.co.uk**

Dream Job...Nightmare Move!

Starting a new job can be daunting at the best of times. Couple this with issues and complications that are associated with relocating to a new country i.e. culture, regulations, forms and languages. The dream of working and living abroad can start off as a nightmare.

However the awarding winning website **Helpiammoving.com** has now added an overseas section to their web site **www.Helpiammovingoverseas.com** tailored specifically for people moving and relocating abroad. Packed full of free and independent advice, the web site aims to point people moving abroad in the right direction, making life and the whole process of moving as straight forward as possible. Written by an ex removal company owner Helpiammovingoverseas.com aims to give totally unbiased independent advice from a trade perspective and experience rather than just hearsay.

Helpiammovingoverseas.com offers hints & tips, useful contacts, pet shipping, F.A.Q's, links to customs & embassies, lists of removal companies, glossary of terms, countdown days to moving, checklists and advice on everything you will need when moving and relocating abroad. What is the difference between a full container, compared to only having a part container load? Should you pack yourself or have the removal team pack for you? What are the issues involved with using a part load service in Europe? These are just some of the questions that you can find the answers to.

Within the web site you can also find a free moving quote request service, fill out one of our forms with the details of your move and this is then forwarded on to five removal companies that cover your area and are specifically dedicated to Overseas (Deep Sea) and European relocation. Helpiammoving.com do not take a cut or commission from any removal work and so you the 'mover' receives a fair and competitive price.

"After all the complications of selling your house, the actual job of moving is often neglected and a big headache. The key to a stress-free move abroad are the 2 'P's, Planning and Preparation. Planning a move abroad is very different from a domestic move. You must allow a lot more time and will need to be even more organised" says Andrew Scholey, Founder of Helpiammoving.com

Helpiammoving.com is solely dedicated to moving house allowing it to concentrate and give accurate advice on only one topic, moving! Helpiammoving is not run by a Removal / Self Storage Company or Trade Association, and so is able to offer unbiased advice.

These are just some of the many comments we have had from visitors:

"What a brilliant website! This is exactly what I have been looking for."

"I heard about your web site from radio 2 and that I found it very useful for last minute tips to check I hadn't forgotten anything. As both my fiancé and I have either been in the forces or grown up in forces families, we are both experienced at moving, but we still got some ideas. Thanks for a useful web site."

"I found the whole thing very useful and was reassured that I was not over fussing about how much there is to do or how important it is to be organised."

"This is a very useful web site congratulations on the standard of your information."

"What a joy to find such a comprehensive guide. I looked through as my daughter is moving abroad shortly."

WORKING ABROAD

THE COMPLETE GUIDE TO OVERSEAS EMPLOYMENT

27TH EDITION

JONATHAN REUVID

BDO Stoy Hayward

PPP HEALTHCARE

KOGAN PAGE

London and Philadelphia

First published in 1977
Twenty-seventh edition 2006

Kogan Page Limited
120 Pentonville Road
London N1 9JN
United Kingdom
www.kogan-page.co.uk

Kogan Page US
525 South 4th Street, #241
Philadelphia PA 19147
USA

Every effort has been made to ensure information in this book is up to date at the time of printing. Where no revisions to country profiles were received from individual embassies, the text from the 26th edition has sometimes been used.

ISBN 0 7494 4644 7

British Library Cataloguing in Publication Data

A CIP record for this book is available from the British Library.

Library of Congress Cataloging-in-Publication Data

Reuvid, Jonathan.
  Working abroad : the complete guide to overseas employment. — 27th ed. / Jonathan Reuvid.
    p. cm.
  Rev. ed. of: Working abroad / Godfrey Golzen and Margaret Stewart. 2nd ed. 1979.
  Includes bibliographical references and index.
  ISBN 0-7494-4644-7
  1. British–Employment—Foreign countries—Handbooks, manuals, etc. 2. Employment in foreign countries—Handbooks, manuals, etc. I. Golzen, Godfrey, 1930—Working abroad. II. Title.
HF5549.5.E45G64 2006
331.702—dc22
                        2006017487

Typeset by Saxon Graphics Ltd, Derby
Printed and bound by Thanet Press Ltd, Margate

Whatever view you wake up to

AXA PPP healthcare is right there with you

Resident expatriate or local national... working, travelling or retired: when you're living abroad you deserve quality healthcare from a well grounded company that really knows their way around the world of private health!

AXA PPP healthcare has an International Health Plan to suit your needs. Join us and you can rely on quick, easy access to private medical treatment; a choice of hospitals; emergency evacuation or repatriation; plus an English-speaking health information line that's on call for you around-the-clock.

All claims are assessed for eligibility against both the terms and conditions of the chosen product and any individual exclusions placed on your policy at joining.

For healthcare insurance you can trust – anywhere in the world – join us now and get two months cover free
Call +44(0)1892 508791 quoting reference WA2006 or visit
www.axappphealthcare.com/media

PPP HEALTHCARE

Be Life Confident

the world health service

"I feel **happy** because I can **reduce the cost** of my health care cover"

Do you want to be able to pay more towards the cost of your claim to save money on the cost of your cover? *To get the feeling, there's only one number to call.

THE QUEEN'S AWARDS
FOR ENTERPRISE:
INTERNATIONAL TRADE
2005

BUPA
International

Reduce your cost with optional deductibles on our Lifeline scheme

Call +44 (0) 1273 208181
www.bupa-intl.com

Your calls will be recorded and may be monitored.
*Available for Individual Lifeline schemes.

Contents

Part Five: Country Profiles and Personal Taxation
(* denotes countries with personal taxation profiles)

If you work overseas, you might like to know that we do too

International personal banking from a British bank.

When your work takes you abroad, we can help take care of your finances. A multi-currency banking service. Fast, easy access to your money. And personal relationship managers who are there for you.

However far your job takes you, we make sure your finances are never left behind.

ⓘ Any questions? Just contact us.

Call: +44 (0)1624 638000
and quote Working Abroad Guide

Fax: +44 (0)1624 615408

Email: newaccs@lloydstsb-offshore.com

Web: www.lloydstsb-offshore.com/international

Lloyds TSB
International

OXFORD BILINGUAL DICTIONARIES – ONE THING YOU REALLY CAN'T AFFORD TO LEAVE BEHIND...

Whether you are planning a short period abroad or are leaving the UK permanently, an Oxford bilingual dictionary is an indispensable item for your suitcase.

As well as capturing the up-to-date character of the language, Oxford bilingual dictionaries provide a wide range of additional features to ease your transition into a new culture. These include:

- Calendars of local events, holidays and festivals
- Clear layout to find information fast
- In-text notes on life and culture
- Information on text messaging
- Example emails, postcards, CVs add practical communication help
- Guides to effective communication with model letters

Oxford publishes bilingual dictionaries at every level, in over 50 different languages, from Arabic to Urdu, French to Japanese, Polish to Thai, and there are resources to suit every need: from complete beginners and refresher learners, to advanced students and professional translators.

Oxford dictionaries offer more than just excellence in language reference; they are dynamic passports to other cultures. By capturing the idiomatic, colloquial, spoken, and written character of the language, and featuring phrasefinders, correspondence guides, and cultural information, Oxford dictionaries get to the heart of the language and provide practical help in getting to grips with a new culture.

For further information on the right dictionary to suit your needs visit:
www.askoxford.com/languages

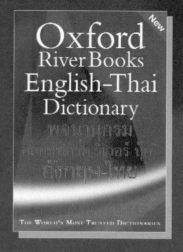
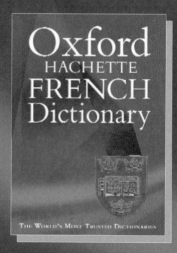

Acknowledgements

Over the years many individuals and organisations have helped us with information and advice on various aspects of working and living abroad, and in updating information for successive editions. We wish to extend our thanks to the European Council of International Schools; Val Vardy and Mike Langley of Towers Perrin; Chris Maddock, Amanda Sullivan and their colleagues BDO Stoy Hayward LLP; David Roberts of Lloyds TSB Bank; the members of foreign embassies and high commissions in London and the press offices of various government departments (particularly DSS, DfES, HM Customs) who have helped in the revision of the text; and readers who have written in with criticisms, information and suggestions.

Reward yourself. The British Council takes an active interest in the welfare and careers of its teachers and there are many other rewards for teaching English abroad. Discovering and engaging with other cultures makes all our teachers richer people. If you would like more information about a rewarding career teaching English as a Foreign Language, please e-mail us on teacher.vacancies@britishcouncil.org, telephone 020 7389 4931 or visit our website at **http://trs.britishcouncil.org**

BRITISH
COUNCIL

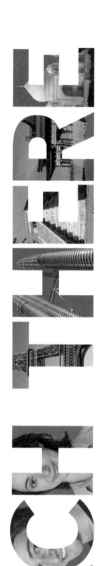

Demand for understanding English is vast. Get back to school!

One of the most rewarding ways to experience a foreign country is to work as an English teacher. Suddenly you're no longer a tourist – you're a valuable part of your students' lives, giving them access to the world's media and information.

The British Council has a network of teaching centres in over 100 cities worldwide. We teach English to children and adults at all levels, and special courses for companies – such as airlines, hotels, petroleum workers and journalists, and public services including lawyers and the military. For all these students we need imaginative and inspiring teachers.

Teachers working for the British Council need a degree in any subject and a qualification in English language teaching, such as the Cambridge CELTA or Trinity College TESOL certificate. These qualifications are taught in several different countries and in the UK. Have a look at the websites at the end of this article to see where.

We only recruit teachers who have at least two years teaching experience after training, but many other language schools have opportunities for newly qualified teachers. Working for a British Council school, teachers benefit from very good terms and conditions and lots of encouragement to develop professionally. Contracts are usually for two years in any one city.

We are a non-political organisation concerned with building lasting relationships. The lessons we teach and learn endure through political and economic upheavals, and our teachers are thoroughly engaged in our public diplomacy role. To find out more about us, or how to become a Teacher of EFL, please visit our website **http://trs.britishcouncil.org**

Useful websites:
Cambridge ESOL **www.cambridgeesol.org**
Trinity College London **www.trinitycollege.co.uk**
Professional TEFL jobseekers site **www.tefl.com**
Helpful resource for all things TEFL **www.cactustefl.com**

Introduction

THE JOB OUTLOOK FOR UK EXPATRIATES

Although British expatriates are still highly regarded abroad and their salary rates are competitive against labour recruited from the United States and the Western European states other than the 10 countries which joined the European Union (EU) on 1 May 2004, overseas job markets for British knowledge workers and managers have become increasingly tough. However, US and European contractors still turn to the United Kingdom to recruit skilled workers for their overseas projects at salary rates not necessarily below those demanded by their own nationals. This type of contract is normally lucrative in salary terms for the UK national and has the added advantage that the contractor frequently provides good living and contractual conditions.

The ability to earn significant salaries overseas, together with the chance to avoid UK taxes, sounds like Utopia. However, the expatriate worker is faced with a new set of problems. Many of these will be outside work and will involve his or her family and social life. Working abroad requires a substantial adjustment in attitudes towards work and life in general. The ability to adapt to the new environment is absolutely essential, together with a willingness to make the best of things as they are in the new surroundings. Attempting to change the new surroundings to your own country's way of life is bound to be frustrated and to result in the resentment of the host country.

Lucrative overseas employment can solve many problems and may seem like the answer to a prayer. But it also creates human problems that may result in broken marriages, ruined careers and disturbed children. In accepting a job overseas you are taking a substantial risk and you should calculate how big the risk is in your particular case. Very often you will find that there is a direct correlation between risk and salary. For example, working for a major company such as British Aerospace in Saudi Arabia, with the benefit of a more secure environment at work and company housing, ought to carry much less risk than working for a Saudi company. The rate of pay offered may be very different, with the Saudi company offering much higher pay, but the security and facilities which British Aerospace provide would not be available. However, even working for British Aerospace will not stop or cure all the problems caused by working overseas. It will also not give workers immunity if they break the laws of the host country; nor, as we are all too well aware, does it provide immunity from acts of international terrorism.

People work overseas for many different reasons and are motivated by so many different things. It is difficult to believe anyone who says that money is not one of the major incentives. The duration of overseas employment is also varied. Some people just work a one- or two-year contract to help pay off the mortgage, or to produce the capital to start a business. However, such short-term contracts attract many applications and usually tend to be taken up by 'permanent expatriates' – those people who have spent much of their working lives abroad.

The risks of working overseas for extended periods were enhanced by a Court of Appeal decision (24 January 2004), which said that rights contained in the 1996 Employment Rights Act were designed to cover 'employment in Great Britain'.

The unfair dismissal rights of expat workers has been a grey area of employment law, particularly since a section of the 1996 Act was repealed without replacement more than three years ago. Hitherto, judges had ruled that employees working abroad should be able to pursue unfair dismissal claims in the UK if their employment had a 'substantial connection' with Great Britain, a much looser interpretation, which the Court of Appeal said that it did not accept. Further cases will continue to establish the parameters for the definition of 'employment in Great Britain'.

Increasingly, though, employers are looking to replace expatriation with short-term assignments, often to train suitably qualified local nationals on the job, or even commuting to locations, where practically possible. New technology has encouraged such changes and the introduction of 'virtual assignments' has meant that professionals can manage projects from their own country, with regular visits to their international office. While this might avoid the problems traditional models of expatriation face – such as the upheaval of family and home – an entirely new set of problems arise, such as the burden of frequent travel, which will also be investigated further on in this book.

Career development is another common reason for working abroad and is particularly important for those working in multinational and international companies, government bodies, banks and organisations with large export markets.

An expatriate returning to the UK faces as many adjustments to life and work as he or she does in going out to an overseas job. Picking up the threads of a career in the UK can be extremely difficult and overseas experience is not always regarded favourably. Employers with no previous experience in overseas work themselves may think that you are returning from a very alien environment with outdated technology and human relations practices no longer acceptable in the EU, and doubt your ability to cope with new technology and life in the UK.

Recruiting organisations need to find workers who can perform a specified job in an overseas environment. It is easy to find candidates who can do the job in a British environment but only a small proportion can survive and succeed overseas. Their second task is to ensure that any applicant they select is aware of all the problems and difficulties he or she is likely to encounter in the country where he or she is going to work. They do not want the candidate to be surprised by conditions when he or she arrives, resulting in a premature termination of contract. This is bad for the individual and may affect his or her future employment prospects. It is bad for the company since it is very disruptive and involves them in substantial replacement costs. It is also bad for the recruitment agent since it undermines the confidence of the client company, which can turn totally against the idea of using British workers.

Given that you have decided, after careful consideration of your family and your career, to find work overseas, you will need to identify the best way of achieving this, and to decide in which overseas countries you wish to work. Working in the Middle East is very different from working in Africa, which is also poles apart from working in the United States, Europe or the Far East. Carrying out research on your host country before departure will help, and the resource section at the back of this book will help get you started on this. However, more often than not it is not until you arrive in your new home that the differences in work and home environment, and whether or not you will be able to fit in comfortably, will become apparent.

CHANGES IN OVERSEAS JOB MARKETS

The overall number of jobs for UK expatriates has declined significantly in the past 15 years. Before that the jobs most affected were for unskilled, semi-skilled, clerical and administrative workers, many of which are now filled by workers from South East Asia and the Indian sub-continent where wage rates are much lower, or outsourced where possible to the same locations. Initially, there was a knock-on effect in some of the more senior positions traditionally filled by US workers, which were switched to less costly British labour. However, even high-wage professional jobs are now migrating to low-cost countries as a result of the trend towards global outsourcing in service industries.

This trend has been strongest in IT services, particularly in call centre activities related to commercial and investment banking and other service industries where there is a high usage of information technology systems management and data transactions. India, with its pool of well-educated, English-speaking workers, is at the forefront of these developments, together with Australia, Malaysia, Singapore and, increasingly, China. South Africa, too, is offering opportunities for offshore relocation. As the migration of white-collar work moves up the value chain from call centre operators to occupations such as equity research, accounting, computer programming and chip design, there is a clear threat to domestic jobs employing those skills. There may be limited opportunities for British expats in the short term in setting up and managing these service facilities but salaries are unlikely to be more than 10–20 per cent above current UK rates. Of course, the ability to avoid tax and deductions from salary and the receipt of free accommodation and other benefits may still make such contracts financially attractive.

Other movements in overseas job markets have taken place nearer to home. On 1 May 2004 the EU was enlarged from 15 to 25 members with the long-awaited accession of Cyprus, the Czech Republic, Estonia, Hungary, Latvia, Lithuania, Malta, Poland, Slovakia and Slovenia. At one level opportunities for British managers in professional firms and foreign-invested enterprises are declining as local management skills and experience grow. However, for those seeking employment or considering a change of residence to any of those countries, the level playing field of EU membership will apply in terms of employment law and social services.

Another trend that has become noticeable since the eight Central and East European states, such as Poland, joined the EU is that of well-educated and skilled nationals from those countries taking up work in the UK to gain experience and to enjoy the benefit of higher wages and salaries before returning home to take up jobs domestically. This temporary migration does nothing to increase job opportunities abroad for British citizens.

FAMILY CONSIDERATIONS

Perhaps the most fundamental question an expatriate must resolve is whether he or she is going to take up a post on an unaccompanied status or whether he or she is looking for accompanied postings. Many people who apply for overseas jobs have not thought out the problems and have not reached a family agreement on the type of posting required. One of the major irritations affecting international recruiters is that some candidates apply for single-status jobs and then at the final interview state they are only prepared to accept an accompanied status situation. This results in a complete waste of time and money for both parties and is guaranteed to reduce your chances of getting employment through that agent.

Before you even decide to apply for an overseas job you must discuss and agree with your family the status of posting that you are prepared to take, the countries you would want to work in, and the minimum remuneration and benefits package you will accept. Only when you have decided these points are you in a position to start making job applications. Furthermore, many dual-income couples will need to investigate job opportunities for an accompanying partner in the new location, as many are no longer prepared to give up their own career for the sake of a foreign sojourn. The issues affecting the 'trailing spouse' are fully discussed in Chapter 6.

USING TECHNOLOGY

Advances in communications technology have certainly made the expatriate's life easier. Keeping in contact with colleagues, friends and family can be done with ease. If you haven't already done so, become acquainted with the internet. This has become an invaluable aid for the international community and provides quick and cheap global communication. It also provides excellent information on any subject you care to think of, including country-specific information, job opportunities, government advice and so on. The impact of the internet on the expatriate community is acknowledged and where possible website addresses for relevant information are included. For this edition, where there are no websites available we have included the postal address and telephone number instead. However, website addresses change frequently, as does the content, and we are unable to take responsibility for the accuracy of these contact details. Once you are on the right track using the links provided by many websites it should prove a worthwhile and fruitful journey, arming you with the information required to settle into your foreign assignment.

THE EMPLOYER'S PERSPECTIVE

Chapter 2 focuses on the development of internationally mobile employee (IME) strategy, employment policies and the administration of IMEs. This chapter primarily addresses companies with international business operations, which are engaged in the assignment of employees to overseas appointments for varying periods.

If you are not in the position of working for a company that may offer you overseas employment and do not expect to do so, you may prefer to omit this chapter from your reading. However, if you are considering company employment in an overseas operation the chapter may provide some understanding of the corporate mindset and the kinds of conditions and benefits that you may be offered.

You will note that multinationals today are looking hard at the high costs of their globally mobile staff and may be taking less generous attitudes towards benefits.

CONCLUSION

The rewards of working abroad can be high and usually offer the chance to make significant savings. The amount of your savings depends largely on the location chosen and your attitude to life abroad.

Perhaps the expatriate who finds life the most difficult is the married person with teenage children, since in many countries secondary education is either unavailable or extremely expensive. The alternative of a UK boarding school is also expensive, and tends to break up the family unit.

We strongly recommend that if you are seriously contemplating a job overseas you should research the job market very carefully. You should try to decide whether you have the ability to survive and succeed overseas and whether, where appropriate, your family can also adapt to the new lifestyle. Once you have made this decision honestly, you must identify the countries that offer the rewards and conditions you require and then identify the companies that might offer you employment.

NEW CONTRIBUTORS

There are two new professional contributions to this twenty-seventh edition of *Working Abroad*, and several significantly revised contributions. I am grateful to Malcolm Harrison and Adrian Turner for their comprehensive update of the 'Letting and insuring your home while abroad' sections of Chapter 4 and to AXA PPP healthcare for its additions to the text of Chapter 8.

Gavin Watkins of Towers Perrin has updated Chapter 2 for changes to global employment practice, and Jonathan Wix of the Teacher Recruitment section of the British Council has updated the information on Teaching English as a Foreign Language in Chapter 1, and his section for Chapter 6 – Partner Issues, which was first published in our last edition. Likewise, Neill Ransom of Chelstoke International has updated his section for Chapter 7 on the criteria for selecting schools abroad.

Lloyds TSB Bank has again contributed the sections on financial planning for expatriates leaving the UK, living abroad and planning to return.

For this edition BDO Stoy Hayward, our main collaborator, has again authored Chapter 3 and the checklists in Part Two detailing the effects on personal taxation of working abroad. BDO has also revised extensively its personal taxation briefings for expatriates moving to the many countries in which it practises, and the information provided on immigration procedures.

In Part Five, the number of countries surveyed has expanded from 47 to 60 and more recent detailed information on the economies of each country is provided.

Part One:

Job Opportunities and the Employer's Perspective

1 Independent Job Opportunities

It is difficult, if not impossible, to form any precise idea of the number of UK citizens currently working overseas. Despite the flood of human resource statistics which flows from Whitehall, there is no central register of expatriates. The broad trend can, however, be adduced by examining people's intentions, looking at the range of jobs on offer, and the numbers of applications for particular posts. The peak was probably reached about 30 years ago, before rising unemployment in many countries, political uncertainties in the Middle East and Africa and perhaps more optimism about prospects at home combined to make people more cautious. Moreover, reductions in UK income tax rates tended to reduce financial incentives to work and live overseas.

However, expatriate employment, though continuing to be an attractive prospect to UK jobseekers, is no longer the Klondike it used to be. At present only the most intrepid and seasoned expatriates would consider taking up postings in most Middle East and some African countries. Economic and political problems have affected the expatriate job markets in Africa and Latin America, and opportunities for non-Chinese speakers in China or Hong Kong following China's accession to the World Trade Organisation are increasingly limited. Multinational company appointments in China are now filled mainly by those with Chinese as a second (or first) language or with young, internationally educated Chinese people who have returned home. Compensating factors are a continuing demand in specific areas of employment, notably in the financial and retail service sectors, and the growth in short-term contracts.

This shading off has been accompanied by a trend towards greater stability in salaries, as well as some degree of uniformity in the remuneration packages being offered by different employers for comparable jobs, as competition for expatriate labour diminishes. In many parts of the world remuneration in sterling terms has only risen by the level of UK inflation.

Opportunities have diminished more markedly at technician and supervisory levels, because of competition from qualified personnel in developing countries who are prepared to accept much lower salaries, and also because of the gradual emergence of skilled workers among local nationals as the fruits of training schemes come on-stream. On the other hand, at more senior grades the relatively low level of British executive salaries by international standards continues to make UK managers an attractive proposition – especially those who are prepared to be reasonably flexible about working and living conditions. The typical US expatriate employee will often expect to take with him or her the standard of living associated with an executive lifestyle in the United States. Consequently, many senior jobs go to British or European personnel.

FINDING A JOB ABROAD

So how do you set about trying to find a job abroad? Both new and old forms of media provide ample opportunities for jobseekers looking from their home country. And for the brave, there is always the choice of turning up on spec to search out job opportunities in the chosen destination, although this approach is no longer recommended.

Newspapers

Not only the nationals and the Sunday newspapers but also the trade press carry overseas job advertisements. Graduates can look in annual career directories for details of overseas employers. It stands to reason that any employer wishing to recruit UK personnel will advertise in the UK press, but there is another good reason why the 'overseas vacancies' pages are worth scanning: they give a very good indication of the going rates of salary and benefits in particular parts of the world. Indeed, even if you have been made an offer without having replied to an advertisement, it is worth looking closely at these pages over a few issues to make sure that the remuneration package being put to you is in line with market rates.

However, if you are actually looking for a job, do not just confine your reading to the ads. It is worth reading any news and features

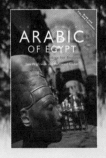

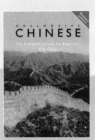

that relate to the countries you are interested in. Not only will news of general or specific developments – a new type of industry opening up, for instance – give you background information that might be very useful in an interview, but it might also in itself be a source of job leads. Indeed, if you can read the papers in the language of the country you would like to work in, so much the better. They will go into potential job-lead information in more depth and, of course, they contain job advertisements. How useful these are likely to be to the British jobseeker depends somewhat on the country in which the paper is published. In the Far East, for instance, employers would almost exclusively be looking for locals when advertising in a local paper. But in the EU, a response from a suitably qualified EU national might well produce a positive result. Quite a number of European countries are involved in projects in the Middle East and in other resource-rich countries where English is the dominant language. In those cases, some think in terms of putting UK nationals on location as well as their own people.

Apart from the major newspapers, some countries have also developed their equivalent of career publications. Published every two weeks, *Overseas Jobs Express*, 20 New Road, Brighton, Sussex BN1 1UF (tel: 01273 699777, fax: 01273 699778) carries international recruitment advertising and provides information and news about working abroad. This excellent paper costs £75 a year, or £29.95 for three months. *Overseas Jobs Express* also publishes several books, including *Finding a Job in Canada* and *Finding a Job in Australia*, both £9.95, as well as a number of titles for young people wanting to live and work abroad.

There are also a number of news-sheets which are advertised from time to time, but some of them, it must be said, are fly-by-night operations and you would be ill-advised to part with your money without seeing a sample copy or to subscribe for more than six months at a time.

The internet

One of the most effective ways of looking for a job abroad is to search the wide range of websites offering information for jobseekers. There are a number of ways in which the internet can help and *Online Job Hunting – Great Answers to Tough Questions* by Martin Yate and Terra Dourlain (published by Kogan Page) is a good source of help. Useful categories include:

☐ Careers libraries in schools, colleges and universities.
☐ Professional associations and journals.
☐ People doing the job you are interested in. You can 'talk' to people via the internet using a service such as Internet Relay Chat.
☐ Job advertisements, job descriptions and person specifications.
☐ Employers and employment agencies in the industries to which your skills and experience are relevant.
☐ Promotional organisations.

Many large employers have job advertisements and descriptions for every area of work and provide application forms online. Interesting sites are listed in the directory at the back of this book, but two good examples of employer websites can be found at Shell International on www.shell.com and Hewlett-Packard on www.jobs.hp.com. Another invaluable resource is The Monster Board, which has information and sites in Canada, Australia, Belgium and The Netherlands on www.monster.com. Most large employers have sites and they are well worth a visit to assess what kinds of international opportunities are available. The advantages of carrying out a job search on the internet are as follows:

☐ The main sources of information on vacancies are unchanged. However, they are made more accessible to all by means of the web.
☐ Searching for vacancies on the web should be quicker and more effective than by other means. Dedicated search tools make finding appropriate jobs in newspapers and with agencies quick and straightforward.
☐ There are simple ways of arranging to be notified of suitable vacancies by e-mail.
☐ Some employers encourage and facilitate speculative applications via their websites.
☐ CV databases enable you to make your skills and abilities known to a large audience of potential employers.
☐ Web-based vacancy searches should enhance, not replace, other means of job hunting.

Source: *Net That Job!* **Irene Krechowiecka**

FINDING A JOB ON SPEC

Possible sources of job information are, of course, legion and they change constantly. Apart from keeping a close watch on the papers, as good a move as any is to get in touch with trade associations connected to the country in which you are interested or local chambers of commerce there. They will not be able to give you any job leads as such, unless you are very lucky, but they can usually give you lists of firms or other organisations that have a particularly close connection with the UK. Preliminary leads of this nature are essential if you are going to a country to look for a job on spec, and, except in the EU, you should never state this as your intention when entering a country. In most places now you need to have a job offer from a local employer in order to get a work permit, so you should always state that you are entering as a visitor, whatever your subsequent intention might be. It must be said, however, that some countries do not permit turning a visitor's visa into a work permit – that is something you will have to check on, discreetly, before you go.

In general, however, going abroad on spec to find a job is not a good idea. Even in the EU, where it is permitted, some jobseekers have had unhappy experiences unless they are in a 'hot' area such as electronics. By far the best plan is to get interviews lined up before you go or at least get some expressions of interest from potential employers – they will probably not commit themselves to more than that from a distance, even if there is a job possibility. To do more might put them under an embarrassing moral obligation when you turn up on their doorstep, having spent a lot of time and money to get there.

British jobseekers now have greater access to vacancies in Europe with the introduction of the EURES (European Employment Services) computer network, which provides jobseekers with free information and guidance on current opportunities throughout the EU. The database includes up-to-date information on living and working conditions in other member states. In Britain, anyone interested in working abroad can access the EURES database, and obtain advice from a Euroadviser, via their local Jobcentre. The International Job Search Advice unit of the Employment Service produces a useful information booklet *Working Abroad*, as well as a series of guides entitled *Working in...*, concerning specific countries. These deal with entry requirements, information sources, benefits, liabilities, taxation, state of the market and cultural notes. The unit also holds information on work overseas in specific professions. Write with your details to International Job Search Advice, 6th Floor, Whitehall II, Whitehall Quay, Leeds LS1 4HR (tel: 0113 309 8090) or visit www.jobcentreplus.gov.uk. Alternatively, consult the linked website www.eures-jobs.com on which job vacancies across the EU are advertised and you can post your CV and details.

Further useful information on the EU and its members can be accessed via Public Information Relays (PIR), European Documentation Centres (EDC) and Euro Info Centres (EIC) set up in libraries or at regional government offices or Business Links. Contact your local library for details of your nearest source of EU information.

Writing on-spec letters to potential employers is a subject that is well covered elsewhere. In essence what you have to do is address yourself to something that you have identified as being the employer's need or possible need – this is where researching the background on the internet and elsewhere and looking for job leads comes into play. For instance, if you have read in *Der Spiegel* or in *Frankfurter Allgemeine Zeitung* of a German firm being awarded a large contract in the Middle East, it is likely that they will respond in some way, provided your letter demonstrates that you have relevant skills and experience. Even if they intend advertising the job, the fact that you have taken an intelligent interest in their activities will count in your favour. It is rarely worthwhile advertising in the situations wanted column, though writing to headhunters is a good move, especially if you are qualified to work in one of the fields in current demand, such as financial services and retailing. Letters should be kept short and your CV should not exceed two pages – highlighting and quantifying achievements, rather than just listing posts you have held. With technical jobs you may have to show that your knowledge of the field is up to date with current developments, especially in areas where things are changing rapidly.

When a job is actually advertised, the interview will probably be in London, or your fare will be paid if you are called upon to travel abroad. Here again, the rules for replying to an advertisement are no different from those relating to UK employers: read the text carefully and frame your reply and organise your CV in such a way as to show that you meet the essential requirements of the job. As one Canadian employer put it recently, paraphrasing, no doubt, John F Kennedy's much quoted presidential address, 'The question to ask is not what I can gain from moving to your company, but what your company (or organisation or school) can gain from me.'

If you need to arrange your own travel, companies such as The Visaservice, 2 Northdown Street, London N1 9BG; tel: 020 7833 2709; 24-hour information line: 09068 343638; fax: 020 7833 1857, website: www.visaservice.co.uk specialises in processing applications for business, working-holiday and tourism visas and passports on your behalf, which is particularly useful for those living outside London, where most embassies and consulates are located. Most professions have specialist agencies to help find work both nationally and internationally, and these could be a first port of call. Non-professional jobs such as au-pairing or voluntary work are also well served and details are given further on in this chapter.

SPECIALIST AREAS

Engineers and technicians

These terms cover many grades of expatriate worker, from truck drivers and road builders to site supervisors and project directors. Many overseas companies, especially airlines and construction companies, recruit directly in the UK by advertising in UK newspapers. Examine all such offers carefully. Many companies will arrange for technicians going abroad to meet compatriots on leave, who can answer their questions.

However, this is one area where opportunities are now very limited indeed. Workers from countries such as Korea, the Philippines and Pakistan, or even China, now predominate at this end of the labour market.

At the top end of the scale, the Malla Technical Recruitment Consultancy at 77 Cornhill, London EC3V 3QQ (tel: 020 7556 1122, e-mail: recruit@malla.com, website: www.malla.com) has a register of international engineering experts on all subjects who are leased out on contract worldwide.

The professionally qualified

The professions and qualifications most in demand overseas are medicine, agriculture and food, process engineering, finance, civil engineering and construction. In general, positions in these areas can best be found through the companies themselves or through management consultants and headhunters (executive search consultants). Many consultants specialise in particular professions such as accountancy.

Some are on a small, specialist scale. An example of an international, multi-purpose agency is International Training and Recruitment Link Ltd (ITRL, 56 High Street, Harston, Cambridge CB2 5PZ; tel: 01223 875100, fax: 01223 875150, website: www.eurotech.org). ITRL recruit only for the Middle East, the Far East and North Africa. They are a major international training and recruitment agency specialising in executive, managerial, technical and scientific fields. They are particularly involved with construction, maintenance and operations, engineering, oil and petrochemicals, health care, hospitals, and general financial and commercial management.

People with professional qualifications will obviously consult their appropriate professional association or trade union. In the medical profession, jobs are usually found through advertisements in the medical press. BMA members are advised to contact the International Department at the British Medical Association (BMA House, Tavistock Square, London WC1H 9JP; tel: 020 7387 4499, fax: 020 7383 6400, website: www.bma.org.uk) for information and advice on working abroad. Most intending emigrants would prefer to work in North America and Australasia, but opportunities are limited. Within the EU there is recognition of medical qualifications. Remuneration is highest in Germany and Denmark, followed by France, Belgium and Luxembourg, with the UK towards the bottom of the scale. But there is unlikely to be much of a 'brain drain' to Europe since there is already a surplus of doctors in training there and the profession is becoming particularly overcrowded in Italy and Scandinavia. Indeed the reverse is true with the National Health Service actively recruiting doctors and dentists from the Central and Eastern European countries that are now EU members.

The developing countries, by contrast, are in urgent need of doctors and nurses. The average doctor/patient ratio in these countries is about 1:10,000 compared with 1:750 in the UK; in some areas it is as high as 1:80,000, with rural areas being almost completely neglected. The International Health Exchange (1 Great George Street, London SW1P 3AA; tel: 020 7233 1100, fax: 020 7233 3590, e-mail: info@ihe.org.uk, website: www.ihe.org.uk) helps provide appropriately trained health personnel for programmes in countries in Africa, Asia, the Pacific, Eastern Europe, Latin America and other areas seeking assistance. It maintains a register of health workers for those actively seeking work in developing countries and areas requiring humanitarian aid.

International demand for UK nurses has been reduced by radical health service reforms in many countries, but opportunities still exist, particularly in the United States and the Middle East, for those with sound, post-registration experience and qualifications. The International Office of the Royal College of Nursing, 20 Cavendish Square, London W1G 0RN; tel: 020 7409 3333, website: www.rcn.org.uk provides overseas employment advice to its members, and overseas vacancies appear in weekly nursing journals such as *Nursing Standard*, on sale at newsagents.

In the UK, the Department for Trade and Industry (DTI) provides information on the mutual recognition of professional qualifications at degree level and above and has overall responsibility for the operation of the UK Certificate of Experience Scheme, which is run by the British Chambers of Commerce on behalf of the DTI. The Department for Education and Skills (DfES) provides advice on qualifications below degree level.

Further information can be obtained from DTI at Bay 212, Kingsgate House, 66–74 Victoria Street, London SW1E 6SW; tel: 020 7215 5000, and from DfES at Room E4b, Moorfoot, Sheffield S1 4PQ; tel: 0870 000 2288, e-mail info@dfes.gsi.gov.uk for advice on international recognition of qualifications. Copies of the DTI/DfES publication *Europe Open for Professions* are available from either organisation.

Information on the Certificate of Experience Scheme is available from the Certification Unit, British Chambers of Commerce, Westwood House, Westwood Business Park, Coventry CV4 8HS; tel: 024 7669 5688.

Finally, one can get a direct comparison between any UK qualifications and those recognised in any EU country via the National Academic Recognition Information Centre (NARIC). However, you can only do this from abroad to the local jobcentre equivalent by asking to contact the local NARIC representative.

Business schools

For high-flyers, a possible route into the overseas job market is a course at one of the European business schools – either a short executive programme or a full-scale MBA. The latter course is in huge demand and is offered by a very large and ever-increasing number of schools worldwide, whether on a full-, part-time or distance-learning basis. The internet has also been adopted as a learning medium. However, one should weigh up its worth with care, given the effort, time and expense involved. A book and directory of business schools approved by the Association of MBAs is the annual *AMBA Guide to Business Schools* (FT/Pitman).

Another possibility lies with the Open University Business School, which offers a range of six-month courses on a distance-learning basis: OUBS Customer Relations Centre, PO Box 625, Milton Keynes MK1 1TY; tel: 01908 654321 (24 hrs).

The longest established European business school is INSEAD. Founded in 1959, today the school is widely recognised as one of the most influential business schools in the world. Its global scope and multicultural diversity make it the model for international management education. Located in Fontainebleau, France, INSEAD runs a 10-month MBA programme, a PhD programme and shorter executive development courses with a focus on general management in an international environment. Holders of the MBA can find jobs through the INSEAD Career Management Service. The emphasis is on international business management. Each year several hundred companies find that INSEAD is an excellent source for recruiting talented, multilingual and geographically mobile managers with high potential. Over one-third of graduates go on to start their own business sometime in their career. Students come from more than 50 countries with no single nationality dominating.

The majority of MBA students come as non-sponsored individuals. Various scholarships and loans are available. INSEAD is clearly a good investment for your future if you have the right background. Courses are taught in English but a fair knowledge of French is required. A third language is required in order to graduate and courses in German and Spanish are available. For further information contact INSEAD, MBA Admissions, Boulevard de Constance, F-77305 Fountainebleau Cedex; tel: +33 1 60 72 40 05, fax: +33 1 60 74 33 00.

Department for International Development

The Department for International Development (DfID) manages Britain's programme of aid to developing countries. The range of skills required under the programme is vast and constantly changing. Workers are drawn from a large number of backgrounds and professions such as agriculture, education and engineering.

The minimum requirement for most vacancies is usually a professional qualification and at least two to three years' relevant experience, including some in a developing country. A limited number of postgraduate study awards are also offered. Successful applicants are usually given assignments of up to two to three years as either a cooperation officer, employed by the DfID and 'on loan' to the overseas client government, or as a supplemented officer, under contract to the relevant government on local salary, with a supplement provided by the DfID to equal UK pay level.

Where the DfID needs immediate expert advice, consultants are used on appointments lasting from a few days to several months. Such assignments are open to both employed and self-employed specialists. The DfID also provides assistance to the United Nations and its specialist agencies (eg International Labour Office) in recruitment to field programmes, as well as the Junior Professional Officers Scheme.

For further information please write, enclosing a CV, to the Service and Resource Development Group, Room AH304, Department for International Development, Abercrombie House, Eaglesham Road, East Kilbride, Glasgow G75 8EA (tel: 01355 844000, fax: 01355 844099).

The British Council

The British Council (10 Spring Gardens, London SW1A 2BN; tel: 020 7930 8466, website: www.britishcouncil.org) promotes Britain abroad. It provides access to British ideas, talents and experience through education and training, books and periodicals, the English language, the arts, science and technology.

It is represented in 109 countries, 209 libraries and information centres and over 118 English language schools and has offices in 228 towns and cities. The Council provides an unrivalled network of contacts with government departments, universities, embassies, professional bodies and business and industry in Britain and overseas.

The British Council is an independent and non-political organisation. In developing countries it has considerable responsibilities for the DfID in the field of educational aid, and in recent years it has become involved in the design and implementation of education projects funded by international lending agencies such as the World Bank.

The Council also acts as an agent for governments and other employers overseas in recruiting for contract teaching and educational advisory posts in ministries, universities, training colleges and secondary and primary schools. The Council usually guarantees the terms of such posts and sometimes subsidises them. In these appointments it works closely with the DfID. Teachers are also recruited on contract for the Council's network of English language schools.

Vacancies include teacher trainers, curriculum designers and British studies specialists for posts in projects or for direct placement with overseas institutions. Candidates must be professionally qualified and have appropriate experience.

Appointments are usually for one or two years initially and often renewable by agreement. Vacancies are advertised in *The Times Educational Supplement*, *The Guardian* and other journals as appropriate.

Teaching English as a Foreign Language

EFL teachers are in demand in both the private and public education sectors abroad. Public sector recruiting is usually done by the government concerned through the British Council; private recruitment varies from the highly reputable organisation (such as International House) to the distinctly dubious. Most EFL teachers have a degree and/or teaching qualification. A Cambridge CELTA qualification will also be required. Most employers will accept the Trinity College London Certificate (TESOL) and their Diploma as equivalents of CELTA and DELTA (website: www.trinitycollege. co.uk). A four-week Cambridge Certificate in CELTA (Certificate in English Language Teaching to Adults) or the associated Diploma (DELTA) are available at International House in London and Hastings, and at a number of other centres. The University of Cambridge Local Examinations Syndicate (tel: 01223 553311) can provide comprehensive lists of the centres running courses leading to these awards, worldwide. Alternatively, the website www.cambridgeesol.org/centres/teach.htm has information on all training providers.

Bear the following points in mind when applying for an EFL post abroad:

- ☐ Will your travel expenses be paid? Some schools refund them on arrival or at the end of the contract.
- ☐ Is accommodation provided? If so, is it free or is the rent deducted from your salary? Is your salary sufficient to meet the deduction? If you find your own accommodation, are you helped to find it, especially if your knowledge of the local language is modest? Does the school lend you money to help pay the accommodation agency's fee and deposit? If the accommodation is provided, does it include hard or soft furnishing, and what should you bring with you?
- ☐ Contracts and work permits. Will you have a contract, how long for, and will the school obtain the permits to legalise your position in the country?
- ☐ Salary. Are you paid by the hour, week or month? If you are paid by the hour, is there a guaranteed minimum amount of teaching available for you? Do ensure that you can survive financially in the face of cancelled classes, bank strikes and numerous public holidays. Are there cost-of-living adjustments in countries with alarming inflation rates? Salaries are generally geared to local rates, but do make sure they are adequate. In sterling terms, one may earn a very low salary (in Rabat, for instance) yet enjoy a higher standard of living than a teacher earning double in Italy, or three times as much in Singapore.
- ☐ How many hours are you expected to teach? Be wary of employers who expect you to teach more than about 25 hours a week (remember you need additional time to prepare lessons). What paid leisure time do you expect? This is variable, but two weeks at both Easter and Christmas is fairly common.
- ☐ What type of student will you be teaching? Children or adults, those learning general English or English for special purposes (ESP)?
- ☐ What levels will you be teaching and what course books will be used? Will there be a director of studies to help you over any initial difficulties and provide some form of in-service training?

A knowledge of the local language is an asset; in some situations, it is absolutely essential. Without it, one's social contacts are restricted to the English-speaking community which, in some areas, is virtually non-existent.

Locating the vacancies

1. International House recruits teachers only for its own affiliated schools, of which there are 100 in 26 countries. Vacancies elsewhere can be seen on the IH noticeboard in the Staffing Unit, 106 Piccadilly, London W1V 9FL (tel: 020 7518 6999, fax: 020 7518 6998, e-mail: info@ihlondon.co.uk, website: www.ihlondon.com). Other major reputable EFL institutes that anyone looking for a job would do well to try are:

   - Bell (www.bell-centres.com)
   - English First (www.englishfirst.com)
   - InLingua (www.inLingua.com)
   - Linguarama (www.linguarama.com)
   - Regent (www.regent.org.uk)
   - Saxon Court (www.saxoncourt.com)
   - St Giles International (www.tefl.stgiles.com)

2. Advertisements appear in publications such as *The Times Educational Supplement* (Fridays) and *The Guardian* (Tuesdays). Of course many teachers are already overseas and can't get these newspapers. The international edition of *The Guardian* carries some advertisements, but many people look online: http://jobs.guardian.co.uk.

3. The British Council Central Management of Direct Teaching recruits EFL teachers for the British Council's Language Centres around the world. It can be contacted at 10 Spring Gardens, London SW1A 2BN (tel: 020 7389 4931, website: www.britishcouncil.org or via e-mail at teacher.vacancies@ britishcouncil.org). British Council vacancies are also advertised in the press. The British Council Overseas Appointments Services recruits for posts funded directly by overseas employers. It can be contacted at Bridgewater House, 58 Whitworth Street, Manchester M1 6BB; tel: 0161 957 7383.

4. The Centre for British Teachers, CfBT Education Services, 1 The Chambers, East Street, Reading RG1 4JD (tel: 0118 902 1621, fax: 0118 902 1736, e-mail: international@cfbt.com, website: www.cfbt.com) recruits teachers for English language teaching projects in Brunei, Oman and Turkey and educational specialists for consultancies on donor-funded projects in Eastern Europe, Africa, Asia and India.

5. If you want to learn more about English language teaching qualifications, Cactus Teachers are a helpful source of information

(www.cactusteachers.com). They specialise in advice on CELTA and the Trinity College Certificate.

Voluntary work

Those who are technically skilled or professionally qualified and who would like to share their skills with developing countries could apply to VSO (Voluntary Service Overseas). VSO has over 1,750 skilled people working in 58 countries: in Africa, Asia, the Caribbean, Eastern Europe and the Pacific. Placements are in education, health, natural resources, technical trades, engineering, business, communications and social development. Volunteers are aged from 20 to 70, usually 23–60, with no dependent children.

Accommodation and a modest living allowance are provided by the local employer. Flights, insurance and other allowances are provided by VSO. Posts are generally for two years, but many volunteers stay longer.

Working as a VSO volunteer is very much a two-way process; volunteers often feel that they learn more from the society and culture they are involved with than they can possibly contribute. For further information contact The Enquiries Unit, VSO, 317 Putney Bridge Road, London SW15 2PN, tel: 020 8780 7500, website: www.vso.org.uk.

Checklist: Independent job opportunities

1. Research professional and national media for overseas jobs.
2. Investigate opportunities on the internet and place your CV with databanks on the web.
3. Check out the possibilities of turning a visitor's visa into a work permit before you look for a job on spec.
4. Contact your trade or professional associations for overseas vacancies and guidance on employment conditions and what to expect.
5. Consider taking a qualification, such as an MBA, in a foreign business school as a way to open doors overseas.
6. Examine the pay and conditions of language schools.
7. Have realistic expectations of short-term work such as au-pairing or working on a kibbutz, and ensure that all details are given in writing before departure.

2 | Managing Internationally Mobile Employees

This chapter is primarily for organisations seeking guidance on the development of their human resource (HR) strategies and on reward packages for employees sent abroad, whether:

☐ on short- or longer-term assignments either as commuters or locally resident to support local business needs, for example to provide project skills or management expertise; or
☐ as permanent relocations to fulfil a particular local role; or
☐ as part of a globally mobile executive cadre who frequently move from country to country.

An understanding of the employer's perspective is also important to company managers and specialist skilled staff who are asked to work abroad in any of these capacities or for whom international experience is a prerequisite for career advancement into senior management positions. Individual readers who are not working now, or do not intend to work, in a corporate environment, may prefer to omit this chapter and go forward to Part Two.

PREPARING THE BUSINESS CASE

Who needs a mobile workforce?

The need to fill overseas appointments with managers or skilled staff selected from an employer's home base or another of its overseas operations, rather than with local nationals, can arise at any time. This applies equally to large multinational organisations and to smaller companies, whose activities have extended from the domestic market into as little as one overseas manufacturing location or a handful of export markets. The degree of globalisation may vary within the following continuum:

☐   from companies engaged in the export of goods and/or services only;
☐   to international companies (including those with loosely associated, autonomous operations in just a few locations);
☐   to multinationals with operations in a number of different countries in more than one region, having common business processes and systems (especially financial controls and IT);
☐   to global corporations covering most, if not all, developed and transition economies, with universal branding, integrated marketing and manufacturing strategies and centrally controlled financial, corporate planning and HR functions.

The background to this continuum is an unstoppable trend of globalisation that has been characterised as 'The continued and growing economic interdependence of countries, the increasing volume and variety of cross-border transaction' (International Monetary Fund, 1997 – *World Economic Outlook*).

Why have an IME policy?

The large organisations in the multinational and global categories will certainly have in place HR policies for the management of internationally mobile employees (IMEs).

Smaller organisations, whose IME requirements are occasional or sporadic, may be tempted to manage expatriate assignments on an *ad hoc* basis without articulating an IME strategy or reward policies. Besides being poor management practice, lack of clearly defined policy is dangerous and can lead to unwelcome outcomes.

For example, in the case of an international company that has decided to develop a new manufacturing operation involving a transfer of technology from the home plant, the only course of action may be to send a senior factory manager for a period of two to three years to handle the start-up and to develop a local management capability. An external appointment is not really feasible, because of the technology transfer, and there may be no more than one, or perhaps two candidates. In these circumstances the company's opportunistic decision to invest may be matched by the preferred or only candidate's equally opportunistic demands for the most favourable reward package that the employee can achieve. In the absence of an established reward policy, the company might find it impossible to resist the employee's more exorbitant demands and, worse still, the appointment risks setting a precedent that the company would not wish to repeat.

A familiar client scenario for Towers Perrin, the international human resource management consultancy, is that in which a new client describes an overseas appointment that it plans to make and asks 'How much do we need to pay?' Invariably, Towers Perrin's advice is for the client to take a step back and develop a business case for the assignment before considering the package. Necessary conditions for preparing the business case are that the client has already developed its business strategy and can analyse its motivation for making the appointment.

INTERNATIONALLY MOBILE EMPLOYEE (IME) STRATEGY

Who are the stakeholders?

A first step in the strategy development process is recognition by the corporate employer that there are four interested parties or players to each international staff transfer:

☐ the home country operation from which the employee is transferred;
☐ the host country operation to which the employee is transferred;
☐ the overall corporation and its group interest;
☐ the employee who is sent on assignment.

The interests of each player differ widely as Chart 2.1 demonstrates.

What are their issues?

The key issues concerning management of the home country and host country operations are self-explanatory; for both of these players the transfer of skilled and experienced employees is inevitably a disruptive event that will affect the smooth running of

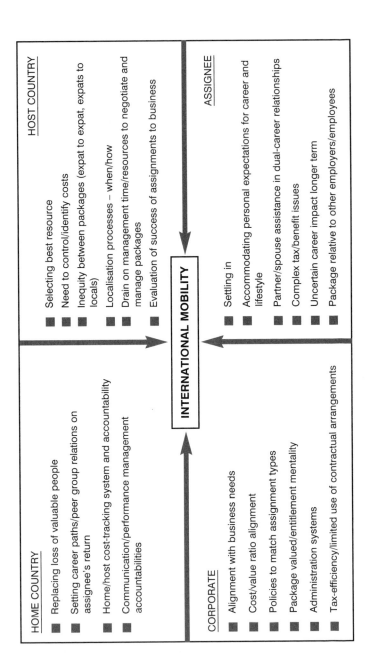

HOME COUNTRY

- Replacing loss of valuable people
- Setting career paths/peer group relations on assignee's return
- Home/host cost-tracking system and accountability
- Communication/performance management accountabilities

HOST COUNTRY

- Selecting best resource
- Need to control/identify costs
- Inequity between packages (expat to expat, expats to locals)
- Localisation processes – when/how
- Drain on management time/resources to negotiate and manage packages
- Evaluation of success of assignments to business

INTERNATIONAL MOBILITY

CORPORATE

- Alignment with business needs
- Cost/value ratio alignment
- Policies to match assignment types
- Package valued/entitlement mentality
- Administration systems
- Tax-efficiency/limited use of contractual arrangements

ASSIGNEE

- Settling in
- Accommodating personal expectations for career and lifestyle
- Partner/spouse assistance in dual-career relationships
- Complex tax/benefit issues
- Uncertain career impact longer term
- Package relative to other employers/employees

Chart 2.1 International mobility – the players and their issues

their local businesses. Similarly, for the assignee and his or her family the key concerns are clearly definable, although the order of importance attached to each issue will vary. The various issues are discussed separately in the sections that follow.

The corporate issues are necessarily more complex, involving the need to balance the interests of the home and host operations with overriding group interest, which include building and maintaining a cadre of effective, experienced and well-motivated IMEs. Particular attention is given to reward strategy, selection criteria and career management later in this chapter.

What are the business drivers?

The next step in strategic planning is to analyse the external reasons for deploying IMEs in terms of global business strategy, which drives organisational capabilities and requirements and, in turn, generates the need for mobility. In smaller, export-orientated companies the dominant international business motivation is likely to remain opportunism; for international companies the dominant focus will probably be business control and technology transfer in selected markets. For truly multinational companies, the international business focus becomes management of the group's portfolio of businesses while the global corporation, by definition, is focused on managing a worldwide business.

The organisation structures of these four types of company in the globalisation continuum follow their international business focus. Export-orientated companies are usually organised by function or division, but the next level of international companies relies on centralised core competencies with local coordination.

In multinational corporations the organisational balance shifts towards decentralised, nationally self-sufficient subsidiaries. Finally, the global corporation seeks to develop an integrated 'borderless' structure that fosters interdependence within a strong corporate culture.

What are the likely IME profiles?

These organisation requirements in turn determine the sourcing of key talent and the characteristics of international personnel expatriates. Export-orientated companies can only draw their IMEs from the headquarters country, which is their sole source of key talent. International companies may have a choice between their headquarters country and key operating countries to source mid-career executives and business specialists but the number of 'from-to' alternatives is likely to be limited.

Within multinationals, the alternative combinations drawn from developed operations countries or headquarters will grow and include younger executives who are given international exposure and experience within career development programmes.

In global corporations, IMEs are drawn from worldwide centres of excellence and include senior as well as mid-career executives with business specialist and developmental staff deployed in growing numbers in new markets.

Within these parameters, each company individually needs to define:

☐   the business need;
☐   the extent to which local managers can be used;
☐   at what levels and which functions international managers will perform.

What are the resourcing aims?

Following these definitions, the company will be able to set its HR policies for the development and deployment of IMEs. For example, one UK-based global corporation has ruled that top management positions in any country must be filled by local nationals with international experience.

Further examples, in contrast, are the diverse IME strategies of two automotive global corporations for their joint ventures in China. Volkswagen, the Chinese market leader in passenger car manufacture, has established a management structure in its Shanghai plants where Chinese and German managers work in parallel positions at each management level from general manager to departmental managers. All management responsibilities and decisions are taken on a partnership basis.

Fiat-Iveco took a quite different approach when developing their van manufacturing joint venture at an established Chinese factory in Nanjing. Over a two-year period, a total of some 200 Chinese employees were taken to Italy for six-month periods to be trained and work in an Iveco factory manufacturing similar vehicles. After the programme there were just two Italian managers left in Nanjing, one marketing expert and one manufacturing manager, both operating in largely mentoring roles. One by-product of the programme, surprising to visitors, is that the entire Chinese management team speaks fluent Italian.

Even in smaller international or export-orientated companies there are some functions that are almost always performed by expatriates from the headquarters country. Start-ups in a new territory or training to deliver skills in local markets inevitably involve expatriate management. In post-acquisition situations it is normal to import an expatriate general manager and financial controller, unless there is a long-established and successful local operation within the group from which the positions can be filled.

How are the IME categories defined?

Development of IME strategy also involves determining the different categories of IME and the types of people to be assigned. Expatriate assignments may be categorised by length of appointment – six months or less, perhaps, in the case of training local staff for skills or technology transfers; two to five years (which may even result in localisation at the end of the assignment) in the case of senior line management appointments. Appointees for these assignments are usually drawn from mid-career managers at sub-divisional board level and, in the case of technology transfer appointments, may include case-hardened older managers who may be at retirement age post-assignment.

There has been a growing trend towards so-called 'commuter' appointments where the IME travels from his or her base every week. Very often the commuting approach is adopted at the instigation of the appointee whose family are unwilling to move, and may not represent the employer's first choice for assignments of longer than six months. Although the considerable cost of moving a partner and family may be avoided, commuting generates many strains on the employee, both socially and on work performance, and may have an adverse effect on peer relationships with local managers who resent the apparent privilege and reduced involvement.

In multinationals and global corporations there is a further category of junior developmental IMEs who are being given early international experience both to load the pipeline of available talent and to cement organisational and cultural integration within the company. Junior developmental assignees are normally in their mid-20s to 30s, often without family commitments, possibly having single status.

Finally, in the global corporation there will be a cadre of career internationalists employed at headquarters level and drawn from any country within the span of the group's activities who are committed to moving from one international assignment to the next. They are the cultural glue of the organisation and the world is truly their oyster.

REWARD STRATEGY

In the light of the company's articulated IME strategy, management should now turn to determining reward strategy and compensation policies. In the case of the smaller company considering a single assignment to meet an *ad hoc* business opportunity, the IME strategy will assist in making the business case and fixing the reward package in terms of the confirmed need for an expatriate appointment and a reasoned cost/benefit analysis.

How to develop appropriate reward programmes?

A successful reward strategy encompasses much more than the compensation package, although that may be the key practical element in ensuring that the appointee, partner and family set off on the assignment with confidence and in a positive frame of mind. Towers Perrin typically work with organisations to develop a checklist of globally mobile programme components, each of which they discuss with their clients in order to determine the degree of significance. This will enable the company to prioritise the key elements of the reward programme, as:

1. critical to success;
2. important to be fair and equitable;
3. limited importance but cannot ignore.

An example of this Towers Perrin's matrix is reproduced overleaf as Chart 2.2 – *Relative importance of globally mobile programme components.* Towers Perrin work with the organisation to determine to what extent these different components should be given different

PROGRAMME COMPONENTS	SENIOR EXECUTIVES	HIGH POTENTIALS	CAREER INTER-NATIONALISTS	KEY REGIONAL/LOCAL EXECUTIVES	SKILL GAP TRANSFERS	REGIONAL TRANSFERS	DEVELOPMENTAL TRANSFERS
Career planning							
Base salary							
Short-term incentives							
Long-term incentives							
Retirement							
Health care							
Expatriate support services							
Special needs (tax, housing, education, spousal career)							
Flexibility							
Assimilation							
Next assignment support							
Communications							
Integration with corporate programmes							

KEY: 1. Critical to success   2. Important to be fair and equitable   3. Limited importance but cannot ignore

Chart 2.2 Relative importance of globally mobile programme components

priorities for the various categories of assignees that the company may potentially have, as shown in the chart.

If you are in the business of designing your company's reward strategy or a prospective candidate for an expatriate appointment, you may like to complete the matrix for relevant positions.

What are the key reward issues?

Paramount among the employer's reward strategy principles is the objective of moving the assignee's motivation from a package value/entitlement mindset towards a personal focus on career development through the acceptance of overseas assignments and/or an international career. This may be more difficult in the case of smaller companies where the range of opportunities for IMEs is limited, or inappropriate in the case of older managers for whom a single overseas assignment precedes retirement.

Indeed, retirement is a key issue in reward strategy and pension benefits are recognised as a major element in the compensation package. There is a natural fear on the part of many IMEs who are members of a pension plan in the home territory that their entitlements will be affected adversely by secondment to an overseas operation.

How to address retirement benefits

Here, as in many other areas of reward strategy, a flexible approach by the employer is required commensurate with the nature and duration of the assignment.

In the case of short-term or traditional two- to three-year assignments the best approach is to maintain the employee in the home pension plan. If the pension scheme rules do not permit membership during absence, the company might need to substitute an unfunded promise for the assignment period or enrol the IME in membership of the host operation pension plan (if there is one). As a last resort, the loss of future entitlement can be compensated for by extra basic pay. In the case of internationalist staff the most favoured alternatives are to enrol the IME in the home or host country or headquarters plan with unfunded top-up where a global standard has been promised or to enrol in the group international pension plan (if there is one). In fact, there is an increasing trend towards implementing international plans, sometimes established in an offshore location. Advantages of such plans include:

- [ ] continuity of retirement provision, regardless of where the IME works;
- [ ] security of benefits (depending on design and financing method);
- [ ] greater equity among IMEs of different nationalities and locations of employment;
- [ ] planned design, which can incorporate much more flexibility than local plans to address diverse employee needs;
- [ ] readier adaptability to any other wealth accumulation programmes for executives;
- [ ] potentially simpler administration than a multiplicity of local plans.

For IMEs who are transferred permanently, the preferred options are to enrol in the host plan for the whole period of service or retain membership of the home plan for all or part of past service and enrol in the host plan for future service.

Towers Perrin and Citco International Pension Services conducted a survey with 102 major multinationals in 13 countries in 2002 which updates their previous extensive study carried out in 2000. One-third of the new sample had operations in more than 40 countries, and the respondents together provided information on more than 30,000 IMEs.

Of these, around 70 per cent were traditional (long-term) transfers, 20 per cent were 'globalists' and the balance of 10 per cent were permanent transfers.

In the context of this chapter, the main survey findings were:

- [ ] The number of employees in each category is expected to increase over the next five years. The proportion of globalists has increased significantly, whereas traditional and permanent transfers form a smaller portion.
- [ ] Globalists are increasingly recognised as a separate group with separate needs. In particular, they are increasingly likely to have a separate international retirement package.
- [ ] 32 per cent of survey participants currently have an international retirement plan and 29 per cent of the remainder expect to have one in the next five years.
- [ ] Creating a consistent and simple approach towards IMEs and encouraging international mobility are the main motivations

for implementing an international retirement plan rather than cost reductions.

☐   Around 60 per cent of survey participants operate a defined contribution plan, of which 40 per cent have converted from defined benefit to defined contribution in the last 10 years. A further 19 per cent expect to change over within the next five years.

Other points of interest in the survey findings are that traditional transfers are still covered by the home country build-up package, predominantly based on a home country benefit design, while a larger proportion of companies (now 85 per cent) use the host country approach for permanent transfers.

What are the trends?

In addition to employer recognition of pension and other benefits as key parts of total reward, Towers Perrin identify five further trends:

☐   increasing emphasis on tailoring IME reward to business needs by matching segmentation of policies to the recognition of diversity;
☐   a movement towards performance-driven packages;
☐   some use of global/regional packages;
☐   simplification of allowance structures;
☐   stronger emphasis on employee communication and family support.

In the context of this book, the last two trends in the above list demand additional comment. Surveys of IMEs have shown that a flexible approach to the award and administration of allowances is a very important factor for expatriate employees.

Where the employer has no particular concerns other than cost, judgements can be left to the employer. For example, in the matter of family travel allowances, where the company provides for a home visit once a year, it might allow the option of disbursing an equivalent sum if the family decided to spend that time travelling in the region of the host country or elsewhere. Similarly, flexibility may be given to the removal allowances for moving home, setting up in new accommodation and returning home at the end of the assignment. For example, rather than disbursement against invoices up to a prescribed limit, the employer might consider a lump sum approach with, say, two-thirds paid up front and the balance on return.

Moreover, host housing provision typically forms an important (and costly) part of the overall package. Companies are now becoming more cautious of the need to control these costs and are offering cash allowances of a level to provide appropriate (but not luxurious) accommodation, which the IME then uses, or supplements, to meet the family's particular housing needs.

Changes to global employment practice

Large multinationals are considering alternative ways to meet their global employment needs, especially in developing countries and countries where they have particular skills requirements. These include:

- [ ] 'commuting' assignments (live in home country, work fully or partially in host country);
- [ ] seconding staff from home country (short duration);
- [ ] overseas postings of skilled staff from home country (longer duration);
- [ ] deployment of career globalists to the host country (no 'home' country);
- [ ] employing local staff in host country and providing onsite or external training;
- [ ] leasing skilled staff from an employment 'leasing' company.

The greater focus on distinguishing between expats, secondees, postings, career globalists, etc is not simply driven by tax and regulations. Fundamental HR approaches to reward and talent management are being applied to establish the most appropriate reward framework – including compensation, benefits, relocation expenses, cost of living adjustments and so on. Leasing companies provide a means of obtaining skilled staff without the responsibilities/liabilities that typically accompany employment.

In addition, certain large multinationals have indicated a shift in attitude in terms of which overseas appointments will be viewed in future as a 'career advancement' opportunity and a 'privilege/reward' and not as a career disadvantage requiring enhanced compensation and/or benefits. Clearly a company's ability to be able to take this approach will be very dependent on the nature of the country/city to which the individual is being posted.

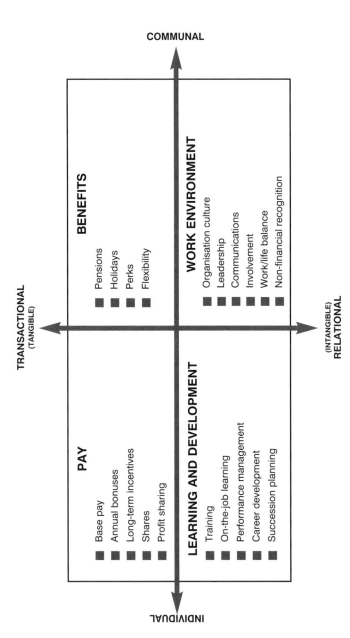

COMMUNAL

TRANSACTIONAL
(TANGIBLE)

INDIVIDUAL

(INTANGIBLE)
RELATIONAL

PAY

- Base pay
- Annual bonuses
- Long-term incentives
- Shares
- Profit sharing

BENEFITS

- Pensions
- Holidays
- Perks
- Flexibility

LEARNING AND DEVELOPMENT

- Training
- On-the-job learning
- Performance management
- Career development
- Succession planning

WORK ENVIRONMENT

- Organisation culture
- Leadership
- Communications
- Involvement
- Work/life balance
- Non-financial recognition

Chart 2.3 A total reward model

A further distinction that companies are making is in relation to the compensation and benefits structure for company-initiated appointments as opposed to employee-initiated transfers.

In summary, it is evident that companies are reviewing the relatively high costs of their globally mobile employees and are looking at alternatives.

Successful reward is not just about cash

Communication by the company with the assignee and his or her family both before and during the assignment is now recognised as an important factor in helping IMEs to prepare for the transfer and to settle in. Family support extends to helping the family investigate and decide on the most appropriate schooling for children and is focused strongly on helping partners to resolve dual-career issues. For partners who decide to step out from their home country careers for the period of the assignment, financial assistance is often given to obtain a job in the host country or to maintain professional education standards during absence from work. However, few if any companies would directly compensate the partner for loss of income during his or her absence.

Returning to the second item on the list of further trends identified by Towers Perrin, a corollary to the tailoring of IME reward to business needs is the absolute necessity that any diversity within the categories should be seen to be equitable and that there should be a justifiable logic for differentiation between categories.

In conclusion on the topic of reward strategy, Chart 2.3 on page 40 is a reproduction of Towers Perrin's total reward model for multinational and global corporations. Under a successful reward strategy, the tangible transactional elements of pay and benefits strengthen and are themselves supported by the intangible relational outcomes of individual learning and development and the communal work environment.

A summary of typical executive perquisites for 27 countries is provided in the Chart 2.4 at the end of this chapter.

SELECTION

We have already referred to the problems that international companies face when there is a dearth of candidates for an expatriate appointment. For multinationals and global corporations the solution lies in creating a talent pool from which IMEs can be selected as assignments arise. With this objective in mind, the company should assess incoming staff on their potential for international assignments when hiring.

Towers Perrin list the most common required competencies for international managers as:

- ☐ cultural sensitivity;
- ☐ interpersonal skills;
- ☐ listening;
- ☐ flexibility/adaptability;
- ☐ ability to learn;
- ☐ personal ambiguity tolerance;
- ☐ emotional stability;
- ☐ technical competencies.

Relationship and self-enhancement skills are placed ahead of technical skills and abilities.

What are the important selection criteria?

Of course, selection is a two-way process. Given the emphasis that employers now place on accommodating partner needs, companies understand that acceptance of an expatriate appointment is a collective family decision and have become mindful of the factors in expatriate partner suitability. Interestingly, Towers Perrin have found that employers and employees agree on the relative importance, in descending order, of the following characteristics, although in a recent survey a rather higher percentage of employers than employees mentioned each factor, except for language skills:

- ☐ family flexibility;
- ☐ personal resilience;
- ☐ personality;
- ☐ cultural sensitivity;
- ☐ interpersonal skills;
- ☐ international experience;
- ☐ employability;
- ☐ language skills.

Within the company the selection process for each appointment ideally involves the HR and finance functions and line management within the division to which the appointee will be assigned. However, the whole process of IME selection is a minefield as the following collection of facts and figures demonstrates:

☐ the cost of intended assignments is normally 2 to 3.5 times the home package;
☐ 40 per cent of international assignees (IAs) return early;*
☐ 97 per cent of IAs agree success is directly related to the happiness of their partner;
☐ 20 per cent of companies involve partners at the selection stage;**
☐ 25 per cent of businesses are looking at changing their selection procedures;**
☐ 50 per cent of IAs would like changes to be made to selection procedures.

Sources: * Kealey **CBI/Umist 1995

Towers Perrin believe that the overall global demand for IMEs may be shrinking as companies realise that they can do better with local employee development programmes, and that the internet revolution has made it easier to manage multinationals remotely, particularly in terms of financial controls, monitoring, technical input and consultancy advice. The increasing reluctance of companies to guarantee repatriation of IMEs to their home operations at the end of longer-term assignments may be symptomatic of this trend. There is also some evidence that the global trend towards outsourcing key functions has also impacted the incidence of expatriate placements.

CAREER MANAGEMENT

Managing careers and expectations is a crucial aspect of growing and maintaining a pool of talented IMEs. Unsuccessful placements and disaffected managers who believe that the organisation has reneged on its promises quickly taint the well of talent from which IMEs are drawn and developed. The objective of moving personal motivation from the compensation package to career fulfilment will only be achieved if there are sufficient case histories that demonstrate that the company cares about, plans and develops the careers of individuals.

Critical to manage career expectations

Succession planning is an important aspect of career management and in the field of international appointments it is normal to include in the expatriate assignee's job description participation in the task of identifying, selecting and training a replacement to ensure continuity.

Given that there are no prior commitments to job security in today's business world, it is normal for a contract of expatriate employment to specify the term of the appointment, to set out a procedure for discussing repatriation in the final 6 to 12 months of the appointment and to provide for an extended period of notice – say 6 months – in the event that a further appointment is not on offer.

Performance management is an integral part of HR best practice and career management, even if the reward package does not include an element of performance-related compensation. Annual appraisals including a review of personal performance against responsibilities and tasks and the joint setting of objectives for the next year are the norm among multinationals and global corporations, as well as some smaller companies. They are conducted either by group/home office management in the case of senior appointments or by regional or local management superiors.

For IMEs performance reviews may be an important point of contact with home country management colleagues but regular liaison throughout the year between home and host country with colleagues and peers is essential to the appointee's well-being and effectiveness.

IMPLEMENTATION/ONGOING ADMINISTRATION

Towers Perrin recommend that the process of managing international assignees should be fully integrated by the HR function responsible for administration. The process involves the following consecutive phases:

☐   profiling the assignment;
☐   screening, assessment and selection;

- [ ] pre-departure preparation;
- [ ] supporting and managing performance;
- [ ] pre-return (or next assignment) preparation;
- [ ] managing re-entry or next assignment;
- [ ] evaluation.

The transition phases are particularly stressful for the assignee and his or her family; companies experienced in expatriate placement are careful to provide as much information and administrative support as possible in handling the logistics of the move abroad and the family's return. In larger corporations the development of peer group family circles among other expatriates in the host country have been particularly helpful in acclimatising new arrivals to the unfamiliar environment and culture.

Good communication is critical to success

Transition, either return to the home country or localisation within the host country, may also involve some reduction in the compensation package. This is an issue that needs careful handling and communication. In some cases, companies may phase out the additional allowances or benefits over a period rather than withdraw them immediately.

Enhanced communication is an ongoing theme in the effective implementation of IME strategy, including handbooks and newsletters for family consumption and a company website giving full information on company policy in all HR areas. All too often company perceptions of IME satisfaction or dissatisfaction with aspects of IME reward strategy differ keenly from reality, as do employee perceptions of what the corporate strategy may really be. Such misconceptions are invariably rooted in communications failure.

Payroll and tax are other sensitive areas in IME administration. Very often companies prefer to keep the details of IME reward packages confidential from local host company operations and will continue to pay expatriates from the centre, making appropriate tax deductions. Some global and multinational corporations have chosen to form service companies that employ all IMEs and lease out their services to the operations to which they are assigned. In this way the individual remuneration details are hidden within an overall leasing charge. It is sometimes suggested that registration of such service companies in tax havens will reduce the taxation burden. However, this device is unlikely to benefit IME employees, who are generally taxed according to their place of domicile rather than employment.

The home base or headquarters should remain responsive to the daily needs of expatriate employees and their families. Cutting the umbilical cord between the employee and the home office generates insecurity and there ought to be at least one member of HR staff with responsibility for the welfare of IME expatriates who is able to provide a helpline service.

In summary, Towers Perrin remind the administrators of IME strategy of the main objectives for each stage in the expatriate cycle:

☐ *Pre-departure.* Create and sustain a sufficient and high-calibre demand pool for assignments.
☐ *On assignment.* Facilitate business delivery consistent with strategy and justify expatriate spend.
☐ *Package.* Provide competitive and comprehensive compensation and benefit programme to retain key staff.
☐ *Next assignment.* Integrate valuable assignment knowledge within the organisation to ensure continuity of the cycle.

Checklist: The employer's perspective

1. Avoid making expatriate appointments without preparing a business case first.
2. Identify where your company stands in the globalisation continuum.
3. Develop an IME strategy for your company.
4. Define your company's business need for IMEs, the extent to which local managers can be used and the levels and functions where IMEs will perform.
5. Define reward strategy and develop compensation policies according to your company's IME strategy to be equitable within and justifiable between job categories.
6. Move your IMEs motivation from a package value/entitlement mindset to focusing on career development.
7. Recognise that retirement is a key issue in reward strategy, particularly for older IMEs.
8. Simplify and allow flexibility of allowance structures.
9. Emphasise employee communication and family support.

10. Recognise the needs of dual-career partners.
11. Place relationship and self-enhancement skills ahead of technical skills in IME selection criteria.
12. Manage IME career development and plan for succession.

Checklist: Employment conditions

If you have been offered employment abroad, bear in mind that you will incur a whole range of expenses which would not arise if you were employed here. It is vital to consider these expenses and to check whether your remuneration package covers them, either directly or in the form of fringe benefits.

If you are going to work for a reputable international company, it will probably have a standard reward package that includes the fringe benefits that it is prepared to offer. But if your employer is new to, or inexperienced in, the game of sending people to work abroad (especially if he or she is a native of the country to which you are going and therefore possibly not aware of expatriates' standards in such matters as housing) here are some of the factors you should look at in assessing how good the offer really is.

To help you arrive at realistic, up-to-date answers to the following questions, it is worth trying to talk to someone who has recently worked in the country to which you are thinking of going, as well as reading the relevant sections in this book.

If you are discussing the terms of an executive appointment abroad you may find Chart 2.4 at the end of this chapter useful. Prepared by Towers Perrin it compares the executive perquisites that are commonly granted to executives of larger public companies in 26 locations around the world. More details from Towers Perrin's 'Worldwide Total Remuneration' may be found at www.towersperrin.com.

1. **Family**
   (a) Is your employer going to help your partner find a job or to identify other opportunities such as further education or voluntary work?
   (b) If your employer is not able to help your partner find work, do they have a policy of reimbursing for loss of income?
   (c) Is your partner involved in the briefing sessions provided by your employer before departure?

(d) Does your employer provide a support network for your partner?

(e) Will your employer provide details of schools?

(f) Do you have contacts provided by your employer to talk to before you move?

(g) Is your employer going to meet the cost of travel out from the UK for your family as well as yourself?

2. Accommodation

(a) Is your employer going to provide accommodation? If so:
   - ☐ Of what standard?
   - ☐ How soon will it be available after you arrive?
   - ☐ Is it furnished or unfurnished? If furnished, what will be provided in the way of furniture?

(b) If accommodation is not free, but there is a subsidy, is this assessed:
   - ☐ As an absolute sum? In this case, is it realistic in the light of current prices? If not, is there any provision to adjust it?
   - ☐ As a proportion of what you will actually have to pay?

(c) Who is going to pay for utilities (gas, water, electricity, telephone)?

(d) If there is no subsidy and accommodation is not free, are you sure your salary, however grand it sounds, is adequate? Do not accept the job unless you are sure about this.

(e) Will the employer subsidise or pay for you and your family's hotel bills for a reasonable period until you find somewhere to live? Is the figure realistic in the light of local hotel prices?

3. Removal assistance

(a) Will you be paid a disturbance allowance? Is it adequate to cover the cost of shipping (and, possibly, duty at the other end) for as many household and personal effects as you need? Will your eventual return to the UK as well as your departure be taken care of?

(b) What arrangements will be made:
   - ☐ To cover legal and other fees if you have to sell your UK home?
   - ☐ To cover the difference, if you have to let your UK home while you are away, between the rental income and such outgoings as insurance, mortgage interest and

agent's management? Will you be compensated for any legal expenses you incur, eg to get rid of an unsatisfactory tenant?

☐   To cover the cost of storing household effects?

4. Personal effects and domestic help

(a)   Will you be paid a clothing allowance, bearing in mind that you will need a whole new wardrobe if you are going to a hot country? Will it cover just your clothes, or those of your family as well?

(b)   Will your employer pay for or subsidise household items (eg air conditioning) that you will need in a hot climate and that are not included in an accommodation package?

(c)   Will your employer provide/subsidise the cost of domestic servants? If not, is your salary adequate to pay for them yourself, if they are necessary and customary in the country and at the level at which you are being employed?

(d)   Is a car going to be provided with the job – with or without driver?

(e)   Will the employer pay for or subsidise club membership and/or entrance fees?

(f)   Will you be paid an allowance for entertaining?

5. Leave entitlement

(a)   If your children attend UK boarding schools, what arrangements are there for them to join you in the holidays? Will the employer pay for their air fares and if so will this be for every holiday or only some of them? If the latter, can you arrange for them to be looked after at Christmas or Easter?

(b)   What arrangements are there for your own leaves? Does the employer provide return air fares to the UK or another country of your choice? Will these cover your family? And for how many holidays?

6. Personal finance

(a)   Will the employer pay for/subsidise all or any additional insurance premiums you may incur? In some countries (eg Saudi Arabia) it is advisable to insure your servants. The cost of motor vehicle insurance may be inordinately high because of poor roads and low driving standards.

    (b) If social security payments are higher than in the UK (eg in some EU countries), will your employer make up the difference?

    (c) Will the employer contribute to your medical expenses if free medical attention is not available or is inadequate?

7. **Salary**

    (a) If your salary is expressed in sterling, would you be protected against loss of local buying power in case of devaluation? Equally, if your salary is in local currency, would it be adjusted for a rise in sterling against that currency?

    (b) Is your salary in any way index-linked to the cost of living? How often are the effects of inflation taken into account in assessing and adjusting your current level of remuneration?

    (c) If there are any restrictions on remittances, is your employer prepared to pay a proportion of your salary into a UK bank or that of some other country with a freely negotiable currency?

8. **Language**

    (a) Will your employer contribute towards language teaching for you and/or your partner?

9. **Legal status**

    (a) Is the legal status of your appointment clear? If you are held to be your employer's sole or principal representative, you may be personally liable in some countries for any obligations incurred, eg the payment of corporate taxes or social security contributions.

    (b) Have all the terms of the job and the provisions of the remuneration package been confirmed in writing concerning the contract and conditions of employment subject to English law and, if not, do you or your advisers clearly understand how they should be interpreted should a dispute arise?

10. **Working for a foreign company**

    (a) If the job is with a foreign company, particularly a locally based one rather than a multinational, there are a number of points that need special attention:

        ☐ Are the duties of the job clearly spelt out in writing in a contract of employment?

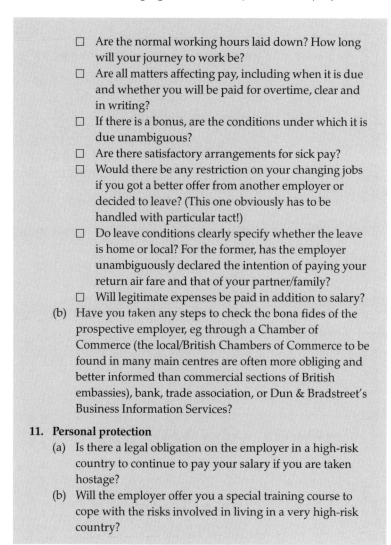

□ Are the normal working hours laid down? How long will your journey to work be?

□ Are all matters affecting pay, including when it is due and whether you will be paid for overtime, clear and in writing?

□ If there is a bonus, are the conditions under which it is due unambiguous?

□ Are there satisfactory arrangements for sick pay?

□ Would there be any restriction on your changing jobs if you got a better offer from another employer or decided to leave? (This one obviously has to be handled with particular tact!)

□ Do leave conditions clearly specify whether the leave is home or local? For the former, has the employer unambiguously declared the intention of paying your return air fare and that of your partner/family?

□ Will legitimate expenses be paid in addition to salary?

(b) Have you taken any steps to check the bona fides of the prospective employer, eg through a Chamber of Commerce (the local/British Chambers of Commerce to be found in many main centres are often more obliging and better informed than commercial sections of British embassies), bank, trade association, or Dun & Bradstreet's Business Information Services?

11. Personal protection

(a) Is there a legal obligation on the employer in a high-risk country to continue to pay your salary if you are taken hostage?

(b) Will the employer offer you a special training course to cope with the risks involved in living in a very high-risk country?

(Much of the content of this chapter was provided by Valerie Vardy and Mike Langley of Towers Perrin whose collaboration the authors gratefully acknowledge.)

Chart: Executive perquisites

Country	Annual Physical 1	Club Membership 2	Company Automobile 3	Entertainment Allowance 4	Extra Vacation 5	Financial Counselling 6	Housing Assistance 7	Low-Interest Loans 8	Mobile Telephone 9
Argentina	◑	○	●	○	●	◑	○	◑	●
Australia	●	○	●	◑	◑	●	○	○	●
Belgium	◑	◑	●	●	◑	○	○	○	◑
Brazil	●	◑	●	●	○	○	○	◑	◑
Canada	●	●	●	○	○	◑	○	○	●
China (Hong Kong SAR)	●	●	●	○	●	○	◑	◑	◑
China (Shanghai)	◑	○	◑	○	◑	○	◑	○	○
France	◑	◑	●	○	◑	○	◑	○	●
Germany	●	●	●	○	◑	○	◑	○	●
India	◑	◑	●	○	◑	○	●	●	●
Italy	◑	●	●	●	○	○	◑	◑	●
Japan	●	◑	●	◑	○	○	◑	◑	●
Malaysia	●	◑	●	○	○	○	○	◑	●
Mexico	●	○	●	○	○	○	○	○	◑
Netherlands	○	●	●	●	●	○	○	○	●
New Zealand	○	●	●	◑	○	○	○	○	●
Singapore	●	●	●	◑	◑	◑	◑	●	●
South Africa	●	●	●	●	●	○	○	○	●
South Korea	●	◑	●	◑	◑	○	○	○	◑
Spain	●	○	●	○	●	○	◑	●	●
Sweden	●	○	●	◑	◑	◑	○	○	●
Switzerland	○	●	●	◑	◑	◑	○	○	●
Taiwan	○	○	●	○	◑	◑	◑	○	○
United Kingdom	◑	○	◑	●	◑	●	○	○	◑
United States	◑	◑	◑	○	○	●	○	○	◑
Venezuela	●	●	●	○	○	○	○	◑	●

● Usually provided ◑ Sometimes provided ○ Rarely provided

Source: Towers Perrin '"Worldwide" Total Remuneration 2003–2004'

Chart 2.4 Executive perquisites

Part Two:

Managing Personal Finance

3 Domicile and Residence

When leaving the UK on secondment you must consider the impact on your residence and domicile status, as this will dictate how you are treated for taxation purposes during your assignment. The government has been undertaking a review of the domicile and residence law for some time and it is expected that a formal consultation paper will be issued. You should be aware that this might lead to changes that could take place while you are living abroad.

THE CONCEPTS

Domicile is a complex legal issue, but normally you are domiciled in the country in which you have your permanent home. The place of domicile is where you intend to reside indefinitely and the country to which you ultimately intend to return.

A domicile of origin is usually inherited from your father at birth (or from your mother, if either your parents did not marry or your father died before you were of legal age). Establishing a new domicile of choice is extremely difficult, and in the case of someone with a domicile in the UK is only achieved by emigrating permanently to another country with no intention of returning to the UK and by severing all ties with the UK.

Your residence status for tax purposes is determined by the facts and your intentions and is therefore likely to be affected by an overseas assignment. UK tax law distinguishes between 'residence' and 'ordinary residence'. Whereas residence is based on UK physical presence in each tax year, ordinary residence equates broadly to habitual residence and takes into account the individual's intentions and UK presence over the short and medium term.

UK nationals leaving the UK for an assignment abroad will remain UK resident for tax purposes unless the overseas employment contract and the absence abroad cover at least one complete UK tax year (6 April to 5 April). In addition, the individual's visits to the UK must not exceed 183 days in total in any one tax year or an average of 91 or more days per tax year averaged over a maximum of four years.

When working abroad you should always consider the host country's definition of residence and domicile. Most countries without a legal system inherited from the UK do not have the concept of 'domicile' as understood in the UK and may base domicile on factors such as the intention to reside long-term. Other countries may use the word 'domicile' or its equivalent in their language to mean no more than a place of abode.

Having a UK domicile and UK-resident status does not preclude you from becoming a resident or domiciliary of the host country under its domestic tax law. In these circumstances, double taxation may arise and complicate the situation.

THE IMPACT ON UK TAXATION

The expatriate who does not break UK residence

If you are domiciled in the UK and remain resident and ordinarily resident during your assignment, your liability to UK tax on your worldwide employment and investment income, capital gains and assets will continue. Capital gains tax and inheritance tax will be chargeable irrespective of the location of the relevant assets. Explained below is the way that the correct use of foreign tax credits, double tax treaties and effective planning can prevent double taxation and mitigate your overall exposure to taxation.

One advantage of remaining UK resident is that you remain eligible to contribute to tax-efficient investments like ISAs. However, being non-resident does not always result in losing your right to make tax-deductible pension contributions (see below).

The non-UK resident expatriate

A non-UK resident is taxable in the UK only on employment income relating to duties performed in the UK. If these UK duties are, however, merely incidental to the overseas duties (eg receiving instructions, reporting on progress, or up to 91 days each year of training during which no productive work is done), the earnings should not be liable to UK income tax.

Nevertheless, you may still be liable to UK income tax on employment income received while non-resident. This arises in the case of bonuses, termination payments and the exercise of unapproved stock options (if you were UK resident when the option was granted or the grant relates to UK duties). As these items are earned over a period of time, HM Revenue and Customs (HMRC) in the UK may tax the proportion of the income that relates to the period of UK residence and to any non-incidental duties performed in the UK when non-resident.

If you are not UK resident, income from your foreign investments is outside the scope of UK income tax. Even if you are UK resident, it will not be chargeable to UK tax if you are not UK domiciled and you do not bring any of the income into the UK. Income from UK investments such as rental income from UK property, dividends on UK shareholdings and interest on UK accounts will continue to be liable to UK income tax.

As regards departures from the UK after 16 March 1998, capital gains tax cannot normally be avoided by being non-UK resident at the time the gain arises. Individuals who have been resident or ordinarily resident in the UK during any part of four out of the previous seven tax years and leave the UK may be liable to capital gains tax in the year of their return on any gains made during their absence. A UK absence of five complete tax years or more, however, negates this rule. The rule also usually only applies to assets already held by the individual when he or she leaves the UK (so that gains on assets that are both acquired and disposed of during a shorter non-resident period can be tax-free). Note that the terms of a double tax treaty between the UK and the new country of residence may also override the UK charge. Specific professional advice should be sought if you might dispose of assets during your UK absence.

You should note that, subject to certain conditions, capital gains tax is not usually chargeable on the sale of your UK property if it has been your only or main residence. Advice should be obtained to ensure that maximum advantage is taken of this generous relief.

The assets of a UK domiciliary may be charged to UK inheritance tax on death or earlier transfer, irrespective of their location and the residence status of the individual. Individuals who are not UK domiciled should note the 'deemed domicile' provisions, which impose UK inheritance tax on their worldwide assets if they have been UK resident for 17 out of the last 20 tax years. Specialist advice should always be obtained before making any gifts, and an appropriate will is essential for all expatriates.

If you remain employed by the UK company or a group company while working abroad, you can continue to contribute, and to have employer contributions made, to your UK occupational pension scheme. This can normally continue for 20 years or longer with HMRC approval and provided that you intend to return to work in the UK. The non-UK consequences of maintaining a UK pension scheme should always be considered, as the employer contributions may be taxable in your host country.

It is also possible to continue making contributions to a personal pension plan (including one that is funded by your employer) for up to five UK tax years of non-residence, provided that certain conditions are met. Income tax relief will be given at source on your personal contributions at the basic rate (22 per cent) even if you do not have any UK-taxable income.

When you are non-resident in the UK, you will no longer be eligible to take out new tax-efficient investment schemes (such as ISAs) or to contribute to them, although you can continue to retain existing schemes. Tax relief on life assurance premiums on pre-March 1983 policies is also forfeited for your period of non-residence.

YOUR EMPLOYMENT PACKAGE

Employers have many options when considering how to structure an expatriate remuneration package. The decision is based on many factors, of which tax is just one. Set out below are the three main categories of expatriate package, and the type of expatriate to whom they are usually offered.

BDO Expatriate Services

Don't let your international assignment end at the airport by ensuring that local immigration requirements have been met

For immigration compliance and advice, please call **Surekha Kukadia** on **0207 486 5888** or email the expatriate services team on **expat@bdo.co.uk**

Alternatively, for more information regarding the range of expatriate services provided by BDO International, please turn to our corporate profile on page < >.

www.bdo.co.uk   **BDO Stoy Hayward**

Tax equalisation

The basic principle of equalisation is that the expatriate continues to pay the same amount of tax as would have been paid if he or she had continued working in the home country (on the home country package). Social security contributions may also be included in this calculation. The employer deducts an amount equal to the normal home country tax (hypothetical tax) from the employee's salary and then assumes responsibility for paying the individual's actual tax liability, wherever it arises.

The actual tax paid on behalf of the employee by the employer is, in itself, a taxable payment and must be grossed up. The employer meets any additional liability to tax in excess of the hypothetical tax, but equally will retain any tax savings that arise during the assignment. For example, an employer settling tax on behalf of an employee liable at 40 per cent actually has to pay UK tax at 100/40 (a 67 per cent effective rate), but is able to use the hypothetical tax withheld from the individual to fund this. There may also be tax savings from tax breaks in the home and host countries as a result of the assignment. Companies with large expatriate populations tend to use this method because it encourages mobility, since it provides expatriates with more certainty about their take-home pay.

Tax protection

This method can be less expensive for the employer, but can be more difficult to administer. The principle is that expatriates will pay no more tax than they would have done had they remained working in the home country. No hypothetical tax is withheld by the employer. Instead the individual pays the actual home and host country tax up to the amount of the normal home country tax liability. If the actual overall tax liability is higher, the employer will pay the excess. If there is a saving by comparison to the normal home country liability, the expatriate keeps it. Sometimes only part of the expatriate's earnings is tax protected, for example foreign accommodation costs paid by the company.

This method is often used by companies sending expatriates to countries with lower tax rates than the home country. It can discourage mobility, as it provides a financial incentive for assignees to move to low-tax countries from high-tax countries and to stay there.

Laissez-faire

This method does not involve the employer at all (apart from any responsibilities like employer's social security contributions). The individual is simply responsible for his or her own tax liability in the home and host countries. This may be beneficial if the overall tax rates on assignment are lower than the normal home country rates.

This method is often applied where the expatriate has requested the assignment, to career development assignments, by companies with little experience of international assignments, and by companies continually sending expatriates to countries that have no income tax or very low tax rates.

PLANNING POINTS

Timing

As explained above, UK non-residence is normally only achieved where a full-time overseas employment and the employee's UK absence cover a complete UK tax year. Thus, if the assignment was planned to begin on 20 April, you should consider bringing forward the date that the overseas employment commences and the UK departure date, so that they fall before 6 April.

There are tax reliefs for certain overseas assignments of two years or less, the details of which are set out below. HMRC will reject claims to relief from the date when there is a clear intention for the assignment to last more than two years or where the employee is under an employment contract with the company in the host location. Indicators such as work permits, social security certificates and assignment letters will be taken into account.

An overseas assignment that results in the individual being present in the host country for less than 184 days and during which he or she remains resident in the home country may provide the opportunity to avoid an income tax liability in the host country under the terms of a double taxation treaty. Remember that in most countries the tax year is the calendar year, so there may be scope for some planning on this point, although some tax treaties count the individual's days on a different basis to the tax year (see below).

If you are about to be granted share options, you should consider carefully whether it is preferable for you to be granted them before or after your UK departure. The option gains are likely to be taxable in either the home or host country (if not both) and your marginal tax rates in each country should be considered.

Non-contractual payments on termination of employment may be wholly or partly exempt from UK tax, if the employment involved periods of foreign service. You should seek advice if you receive such a payment, as the UK tax savings can be considerable but there may also be a foreign tax charge.

Avoiding double taxation

The UK has double tax treaties with numerous countries, which try to prevent double taxation of individual income and gains. There are also a few treaties that cover potential double taxation of capital assets. Although treaties vary and they should be examined in detail in every case, the rules for exemption of earnings from tax in the host country are normally:

☐ You must be UK resident under the definition in the treaty.
☐ You should not be present in the host country for more than 183 days (in the fiscal year, the calendar year or any 12-month period, depending on the treaty).
☐ You must remain employed by a business that is resident in the UK and that is not resident in the host country.
☐ The costs of your assignment must not be borne by a branch or permanent establishment of your employer in the host country (or, in some countries, by a subsidiary or parent company).

In some circumstances, double taxation is unavoidable. In these cases, the UK HMRC will normally reduce the UK tax by the foreign taxes paid on the double-taxed earnings, up to the amount of the UK tax otherwise payable.

Expatriate reliefs and allowances

Where an expatriate does not break UK residence, there are a number of tax reliefs that should not be overlooked. These include the following:

☐ For assignments that are not expected to exceed two years, a tax deduction can normally be claimed in respect of your additional living costs on the basis that you are working away from your normal workplace. The deduction can include the cost of the overseas accommodation and related costs, meals, travel and subsistence (but you must be prepared to produce receipts or other documentation to support your claim). Equally, if the employer reimburses these costs, HMRC will not normally tax them if they meet the conditions for the deduction. Alternatively, a tax-free, flat-rate allowance of £10 per night is available to cover incidental expenses when working abroad.

☐ For longer-term assignments, the following reimbursed expenses are normally not taxable in the UK:
  – qualifying relocation costs of up to £8,000, when leaving the UK and on returning from the assignment;
  – outbound and return travel costs for you and your family (including children under 18 at the start of the outward journey);
  – home leave travel for certain family members.

☐ All individuals who are Commonwealth or EEA nationals are entitled to a personal allowance that is deductible from their income taxable in the UK, as are nationals of certain other countries with which the UK has a double tax treaty regardless of whether they are resident or non-resident in the UK. This allowance is £4,895 for the 2005/6 UK tax year and £5,035 for the 2006/7 UK tax year.

Tax on investments

If you are going to become non-UK resident, you may consider moving your UK investments offshore prior to your departure. This can potentially avoid UK tax on income arising from those investments while you are on assignment (but note that there may be a tax charge in the host country).

Before you return to the UK, you should close down all interest-bearing overseas bank accounts before the date on which you resume UK residence, in order to avoid UK income tax on the interest credited while you are non-resident. If you close the accounts after you have resumed UK residence, the interest credited from the date UK residence resumed will be taxable in the UK.

Finally, you should be aware that the host country may tax your investment income during your assignment, in particular where the local rules tax residents on their worldwide income and gains.

CONCLUSION

The key issue in expatriate taxation is to plan in advance. You might be able to save yourself a substantial amount of tax by merely adjusting the terms of your assignment package, but this must be weighed up against the personal and commercial needs of your secondment.

Checklist: Tax aspects of leaving the UK

1. Plan ahead. Consult a tax professional to ensure that your remuneration package and investment portfolio have been structured tax-efficiently, from both a UK and host country perspective. Ideally, you should try to meet a UK adviser before you leave the UK, and a host country adviser on arrival in the new location.
2. Inform HMRC. File a UK HMRC departure form P85. Take care with the wording of your answers on this document, as it will form the basis of the HMRC's evaluation of your residence status during your assignment (and may therefore affect the amount of tax you will pay). If you intend to let your UK property while you are non-UK resident, you should complete a non-resident landlord form NRL1 so that your rent can be received without the requirement for the tenant or agent to withhold tax from the rent. Remember, you may be required to file arrival forms and annual documentation in the host country.
3. Inform your bank, building society and insurer. Even if you do not expect your UK bank interest to exceed your tax-free personal allowance, if you will be not ordinarily resident in the UK you can receive bank interest gross while overseas (ask for the form at the bank or building society). This will save you from having to file a tax return to obtain any refund of withholding tax. If you believe your UK-source income will exceed your tax-free personal allowance, you may wish to set up an offshore bank account so that your bank interest is not liable to UK tax. You should advise your insurer that you will be living and working abroad, as this may affect the cover under your life and household policies.
4. Notify your payroll department. In many cases, you will need to stay on the UK payroll in order to continue making UK pension and UK National Insurance (social security) contributions. If you expect to become non-UK resident, apply to HMRC for an NT (no tax) code to prevent withholding of tax (PAYE) from your salary.

BDO Expatriate Services

With your tax and social security compliance in hand, you will be free to focus on your assignment objectives

For tax and social security compliance services, please call **Stephen Asher** on **0207 486 5888** or email the expatriate services team on **expat@bdo.co.uk**

Alternatively, for more information regarding the range of expatriate services provided by BDO International, please turn to our corporate profile on page < >.

BDO Stoy Hayward

www.bdo.co.uk

If you are going to remain UK resident and expect to pay foreign tax on your earnings, you should apply for the foreign tax to be included in your PAYE code number or set against your UK PAYE by your payroll department, to avoid double tax during the year.

5. Inform your pension provider. Check whether you remain eligible to make tax-deductible contributions to your pension scheme.

6. File a UK tax return. The tax reliefs and allowances available to expatriate assignees must be claimed on your UK tax return. A repayment of UK tax may be due, as personal allowances are given in full for each tax year, even if you are only UK resident for part of the year.

7. Register in your host country. Do this on arrival and take appropriate professional advice to avoid the risk of large and unexpected tax bills at the end of the tax year.

Checklist: Tax aspects of returning to the UK

1. Plan ahead. Seek advice if you have made capital gains, received large payments such as termination payments, or have a complex investment portfolio. If you are considering exercising stock options you should seek advice on timing issues.

2. Close offshore accounts. To prevent the UK from taxing the accrued interest, ideally you should close the accounts in the tax year before the year in which you return to the UK.

3. Deregister with the host country. Ensure you have informed the appropriate authorities of your departure, to prevent any attempt to dispute your actual date of departure.

4. Register with HMRC. File an arrival form P86. This form will not only dictate your tax treatment from the date of your UK return date, but also validate your tax treatment during your absence.

4 Banking, Financial Planning and Asset Management

For most people, working abroad means a rise in income. For those in countries with a low rate of income tax, or, as is the case in some countries in the Middle East, without income tax, it may be the first chance they have had to accumulate a substantial amount of money, and this may indeed be the whole object of the exercise. Expatriates are therefore an obvious target for firms and individuals offering financial advice on such matters as tax, mortgages, insurance schemes, school fee funding, income building plans and stock and 'alternative' investments. Most of them are honest, but some are better than others, either in choosing investments wisely or in finding schemes that are most appropriate to the needs and circumstances of their client, or both. At any rate the expatriate with money to spend is nowadays faced with a wide variety of choices, ranging from enterprising local traders proffering allegedly valuable antiques, and fly-by-night operators selling real estate in inaccessible tropical swamps, to serious financial advisers and consultants. The internet might also help independently minded investors in remote locations, and provides another option.

It is estimated that 16 million UK expatriates now live all over the world, 95 per cent of them in Australia, Hong Kong, Canada, Spain, South Africa, New Zealand, Germany, Ireland, France, the United States, the UAE, Argentina, Cyprus, Italy and The Netherlands.

Some people will love their new environment and may stay on for longer than originally anticipated. Some may loathe it and can't wait to get back.

When moving to a country that has a totally different culture and way of life you will need to respect and adhere to differing traditions and customs. Not only will the language be 'alien' but so too will be the culture and the general way of life. Before you 'up sticks' you need to spend some time in methodical planning. After all, the key to any successful move is to be well prepared and organised. Limiting potential problems or issues will help you to settle in and adjust quickly to your new 'homeland'.

A good starting point is to research your destination so you know what to expect. There may be a 'British' or 'Expatriate' community where you are moving to, which will help you to understand what help and support is available to you and your family. Assistance may be available from your employer or more widespread support organisations.

OFFSHORE BANKING SERVICES

Awareness of offshore banking services is traditionally low within the UK, with many people asking their local banking branch to refer them to the relevant specialist department, logging on to the internet or relying on good quality money management media for guidance. Others may rely on word of mouth from a colleague who has already opened an offshore account. Good financial planning should start by establishing a sound offshore base for your finances before leaving the UK or country of residence.

Whichever bank you choose, you need to be reassured of its probity and expertise. A choice of currencies, 24-hour internet banking and telephone banking are probably minimum requirements. Lloyds TSB International, for example, has a long history of assisting international customers with all aspects of their financial planning. It established its International Account service over 15 years ago and is now helping tens of thousands of international customers. As well as having a first-class banking service that looks after all international banking requirements, it also offers customers investment and savings alternatives, provides international mortgage products and gives customers benefits that offer discounted rates on a variety of third-party services including health and travel insurance and a VIP airport lounge service. Lloyds TSB International can also help new and existing international customers before they go, while they are away and when they return to their normal country of residence, as it offers a tax referral service and provides in-depth country profiles, and the relationship management team are on hand to help with any enquiry you may have.

Whether you are taking up a new posting overseas and require a personal/business account, or you are retiring to sunnier climes, ensure that you make your banking arrangements in plenty of time. You can then concentrate on the real reason for the move, be that work or relaxation.

For more information regarding the International Account, log on to www.lloydstsboffshore.com/international or call 01624 638000 (+44 1624 638000).

ALTERNATIVES FOR INVESTING SURPLUS INCOME

There are really only three types of objectives in investment: growth, income, and growth with income. The choice of one main objective usually involves some sacrifice in regard to the other. A high degree of capital appreciation generally implies a lower level of income and vice versa. Growth with income is an ideal, but generally it means some growth with some income, not a maximisation of both. Ultimately, the objective is the preservation of capital in bad times and the increase of wealth in good ones, but your adviser cannot perform miracles. If he or she is lucky enough to catch the market in an upward phase, as in the case of the current equities 'bull' market, he or she may be able to show quick results, but normally investment is a process that pays off over a longer period and through the course of varying market cycles.

The prolonged 'bear' market in equities, which preceded the present bull market, exposed the fallibility of fund managers. Few foresaw the length or depth of the decline in equity prices, or reacted by switching their clients' funds into stable fixed-interest securities before heavy losses were incurred.

INVESTMENT THROUGH UK OR OFFSHORE MANAGED FUNDS

There are many investment opportunities in the offshore fund markets, from specialised funds in individual countries to international ones spread across many industries. There are equally many ways of investing: regular investments, lump-sum purchase of units, periodic and irregular investments. It is also possible to invest in commodity markets and there are specialists trading in gold, silver, diamonds, sapphires and metals generally. Another innovation is the currency fund, which regulates holdings of foreign exchange and aims to predict fluctuations in exchange rates.

Your consultant should be able not only to inform you of the various schemes available, but also to advise on the degree of risk, the quality of management available and the combination of investments most likely to achieve your aims.

For those who prefer the safety of banks or building society deposits, there is now a concession to non-residents – interest is paid without tax being deducted at source. However, you will have to inform your bank about your non-resident status. A building society may also require you to open a separate, non-resident account.

You may still be assessed for income tax on any interest earned in the year of your return to the UK. For this reason, there are a number of advantages in taking up the facilities that UK banks offer non-residents to open an account in one of the established tax havens, notably the Channel Islands and the Isle of Man.

In all cases, though, there are important tax considerations before you return to the UK. You should discuss these with your adviser at least six months before then, so that the necessary plans can be drawn up.

SCHOOL FEES PLANNING

There are many schemes available for school fees planning. These schemes aim to provide you with a tax-free income at a specified date for a predetermined length of time. They need not necessarily be used for educational purposes, and some readers may feel that if the employer is paying school fees, as is often the case, there is no need to take out such a policy. However, parents should bear in mind that it is highly advisable not to interrupt children's education, and taking out such a policy would obviously be a good way of ensuring that your child could go on with his or her education at the same school, even if your employment with that employer ended.

BASIC PLANNING POINTS

There are a number of basic planning points for expatriates to bear in mind, whatever their nationality of origin or place of work.

Two tax regimes

Usually there will be two tax regimes to consider: the home tax regime and the host tax regime. Almost invariably these will operate in different ways. The interaction between the two can be complex, but it is a vital part of sound financial planning.

Advice based on only the host or home country's rules is best avoided; what works in the UK may not work over there and vice versa. Therefore, potential British expats should read and understand the advice provided by BDO Stoy Hayward in Chapter 3 relating to the UK taxation aspects of working abroad and review carefully the summary in Part 5 of the taxation regime to which they plan to transfer provided by the local BDO Stoy Hayward associate office.

Fundamentals that do not change

While tax rules will vary from country to country, many of the fundamentals of financial planning apply across the globe. For example, it will always make sense to hold a rainy-day cash reserve in a readily accessible deposit account. For expatriates that might mean two cash reserves – one in their host currency and one in their home currency.

While being an expatriate may offer tax advantages, tax must not become the only reason for doing something. So, for example, investment decisions should firstly be made on investment grounds, with tax then being considered only in terms of the structuring of the investment, eg whether the chosen investment fund is set up onshore or offshore.

Regular professional reviews are vital

All financial plans must be reviewed regularly. Laws can change with great speed, rendering last year's tax-efficient plan this year's no-go area. The UK has seen plenty of examples of this in recent years, some of which have had a direct impact on expatriates. It is particularly important to review plans a year or so before returning home – if sufficient advance warning is available.

If in doubt, the expatriate should always seek professional advice. The combination of different legal and tax regimes can make what would be a simple matter for the ordinary UK employee subject to UK tax highly complex for the expatriate counterpart. As a general rule, only the larger financial and accountancy firms will possess the necessary expertise.

PLANNING FOR DEPARTURE FROM THE UK

The sooner the would-be expatriate takes professional advice on financial planning the better. There will usually be a number of decisions to be made and changes to be undertaken, all of which are best not handled hastily. These are covered in the following sections.

Dealing with the home

As a general rule, leaving a property empty while overseas is best avoided, as there will always be a concern about vandalism or occupation by squatters. From a financial planning viewpoint, an empty property is a poor use of capital. It will yield no income but continue to generate costs such as general maintenance and, probably, mortgage interest. If the home will not be occupied by family members while the employee is working overseas, the real choice is whether it should be sold or rented out.

The case for selling is that it removes the problem of looking after a property from a distance and clears an outstanding mortgage debt. Some people will prefer to sell rather than have strangers (ie tenants) in their home. Selling property will also produce a lump sum to invest, but this may create its own problems in terms of investment risk, as the money will normally be earmarked for future property purchase on return to the UK.

Conversely, the major advantage of renting out property is that it allows the expatriate to retain a foothold in the UK residential property market. There are plenty of cautionary tales of expatriates who sold up only to find that, on their return several years later, they could not afford to buy the equivalent of their former property because of price increases during their absence. The case for letting and insuring your house while you are away and some explanation on how to do this with professional advice are presented later in this chapter.

Pension benefits

In this area it is important to determine how the expatriate's employment will be structured. Will he or she be employed by the UK employer or will the contract of employment be moved to an overseas employer, possibly a subsidiary?

If the expatriate remains employed by the UK company, then the employee can remain in that employer's occupational pension scheme unless the transfer abroad is permanent. An expatriate working for an overseas employer may retain membership of his or her UK pension scheme, subject to a number of conditions specified by HMRC. The most notable of these is that the pension entitlement must be based on the remuneration that would have applied had the employment been in the UK.

Expatriates with personal pensions are less favourably treated. If they are not resident for tax purposes, then neither they nor their employer can make personal pension contributions in respect of their overseas earnings. This could mean that pension-linked life cover has to be cancelled. As already noted in Chapter 2, any remuneration package for the expatriate will need to take account of the pension position in terms of the impact on benefit entitlement and any foreign tax liabilities that might arise.

Ancillary employee benefits

Alongside pension rights, there will also be other benefit entitlements that need to be addressed as part of the expatriate's financial planning. The most significant of these is adequate private medical insurance, and the provision of expatriate medical cover is discussed in detail in Chapter 8. Permanent health insurance (income protection cover) should also be reviewed in the context of overseas employment.

Existing investments

As a broad rule, existing investments do not need to be disturbed ahead of departure from the UK, other than as part of normal financial planning:

☐ ISAs, SIPPs and TESSAs can continue to be held by non-UK residents with unchanged tax advantages, although it is only possible to make further eligible contributions to TESSAs while non-UK resident.
☐ Unit trusts, shares and life insurance policies can all be retained. Although these may give rise to a UK tax liability (at no more than the basic rate), for a non-UK resident what limited potential tax savings are available by moving offshore would probably be offset by the costs of sale and reinvestment.
☐ Deposit accounts are an exception to the general rule. A non-UK resident can request to receive interest without declaration of tax from UK bank and building society accounts. Strictly speaking such interest is not tax-free and would be taken into account by HMRC when considering how any claim to use personal allowances was applied. For this and other tax-related reasons, the normal advice is that the expatriate should open an offshore bank account – typically in the Channel Islands or Isle of Man – and close UK-based deposits. Interest from offshore accounts is paid gross and will be free of UK tax while the expatriate is non-UK resident.
☐ New investments ahead of departure should only be made after seeking professional advice. There may be opportunities to structure fresh investments to ensure that profits only arrive once the investor is free of UK tax liabilities.

FINANCIAL PLANNING WHILE OVERSEAS

Provided that the advance preparation has been satisfactory, the best financial planning action that the new expatriate can take in the first few months overseas is to do nothing. The reason for this is that it will take the new expatriate at least this period to adjust to the new life and pattern of expenditure. Once settled into a routine, the expatriate will be much more aware of what he or she can save on a regular basis.

Existing investments

A change introduced by the 1998 Budget significantly reduced the capital gains tax advantages of being an expatriate. As a general rule, for the expatriate who has been resident and UK ordinarily resident for at least four out of the seven tax years before departure overseas and who will be non-UK resident and not UK ordinarily resident for less than five tax years, any capital gains realised on investments held before leaving the UK will remain subject to UK capital gains tax. For these 'short-term' expatriates, the 1998 change limits the scope for realising large gains, as might for example have accrued from the exercise of share options. Even for the expatriate who expects to be abroad for five or more tax years, caution is necessary until the five-year point is reached; a premature return to the UK could occur for any number of reasons, including health, business or even war.

Income from UK shares and unit trusts will usually continue to be subject to UK tax, which will generally not be reclaimable. There may also be a liability in the host country, although this will often be reduced or eliminated as a result of double taxation agreements.

New investments

Aside from monies placed in Channel Island/Isle of Man deposit accounts (see above), professional advice should always be sought before making investments while overseas. Ideally the advice should be from a firm regulated in the UK by the Financial Services Authority (FSA). Any advice should take into account potential host-country tax liabilities – a point sometimes overlooked by UK-based advisers.

The obvious first port of call for new investments is the offshore financial centres, including Luxembourg, Bermuda and Dublin, as well as the islands closer to home. While certain offshore invest-ments can offer tax benefits to expatriates, these may be offset by higher charges than apply in the UK. Investments made while overseas will usually escape UK capital gains tax provided that gains are realised before the tax year of return to the UK.

Consideration must always be given to what happens to the investment on return to the UK because the tax-efficient investment for the non-UK resident can turn into a tax-inefficient investment for the UK resident. This can be a particular problem if an overseas employment is terminated at short notice.

Expatriates should avoid committing themselves to fixed-term savings contracts as a way of accumulating funds while non-resident. Lack of flexibility can be a serious drawback in many of these schemes, although they are heavily promoted.

Share options

The tax treatment of share options held by expatriates is a highly complex subject. For example, under an unapproved scheme, a UK tax liability will arise on exercise by a non-UK-resident employee if the option was granted when the employee was UK resident. Professional advice should be sought before any action is taken, including the initial grant of an option.

THE UK EXPATRIATE – PLANNING FOR RETURN

In an ideal world, every expatriate would spend the year before return to the UK putting his or her financial plans in order. In practice, there may be a last-minute rush, either because the expatriate was too busy with other matters or because the return home was earlier than originally intended.

Pre-return planning is as important as pre-departure planning. The aims should be to minimise the overall tax liabilities on investments before arrival in the UK, and to ensure that any new plans put in place are appropriate upon return to the UK. This will require professional advice, which should begin in the tax year before that in which the return to the UK will take place.

The planning will need to consider UK tax rules alongside host-country tax rules. It may be better to suffer UK tax – at a maximum rate of 40 per cent – rather than host-country tax. In some instances, it could even be worth spending a few days in a third country and realising profits at that interim stage, before becoming UK tax resident but after ceasing to be host-country tax resident.

For 'short-term' expatriates, there will only be scope to avoid UK capital gains tax on investments acquired while overseas, provided that they are not sold in the tax year of return to the UK. The old planning trick of 'bed and breakfast' – selling one day and buying back the next – to realise a gain but to retain the investment is no longer effective. However, the same result can be achieved if one spouse sells and the other buys.

If offshore deposit accounts are used, usually these should be closed immediately before return to the UK so that all interest is crystallised free of UK tax. UK deposit accounts will automatically give rise to taxable interest in the tax year of return, even if interest is paid before the date of physical return.

LETTING AND INSURING YOUR HOME WHILE ABROAD

Most home owners going to live abroad for a limited period will be looking for a tenant to live in their house or flat while they are away. There is, of course, an obvious alternative, which is to sell, but then there is the question of storage of your effects – the average storage charge for the contents of a typical three-bedroomed house will be £50–£60 per week – and, more to the point, the fact that when you do return to this country you will have no place of your own to go to. Even if you do not intend to return to the house you lived in when you come back, it may be advisable to retain ownership because your house represents a fairly inflation-indexed asset. Conversely, if you believe that the UK housing market in 2006 is so overheated that a collapse in house prices is likely while you are abroad, there is a strong case for selling up if you are leaving now.

The case for letting, as opposed to leaving your home empty, hardly needs to be put today when crime and vandalism are constantly in the headlines. The government, recognising the difficulties for owners leaving their homes and wishing to encourage the private landlord, introduced the 1988 Housing Act which came into force on 15 January 1989. This Act simplified the many provisions of the various Rent and Housing Acts from 1965 to 1988, and introduced the Assured Shorthold Tenancy (AST), making letting safer and easier. The 1988 Act was further amended by the 1996 Housing Act, making an AST the market 'default' type of tenancy agreement as long as certain criteria are met. An AST guarantees possession to a landlord at the end of a tenancy. Lettings to large companies where the occupier is a genuine employee being housed by the company temporarily are excluded from the Act and are simply contractual tenancies (referred to as Company Lets); these types of tenancy are quite common in bigger cities, particularly central London. It is not possible here to define the various differences between these two forms of tenancy. It should be noted that a letting to a member of the Diplomatic Corps based in the UK has some risks and complications. Generally a court order for possession can be executed but successfully imposing any type of monetary court order (for rent arrears or damages) can be very problematical as the individual would be outside the jurisdiction of British courts and may well have returned to his or her country of origin. It is essential, therefore, for the owner to obtain proper advice before deciding which form of tenancy to choose.

Assured shorthold tenancies

1. These can be for any length of time if both parties agree, although it is most common to start with either 6- or 12-month fixed-term tenancies. However, the landlord will not be able to seek a court order for possession before the end of 6 months unless there has been a breach of the tenancy agreement.
2. The rent will be a market rent, although the tenant may apply to the Rent Assessment Committee during the first 6 months if he or she feels it is too high. However, on the expiry of the original term, the owner is entitled to request the tenant to pay a higher rental and the tenant is not entitled to go back to the Rent Assessment Committee. It is common to have rent increase clauses within longer-term tenancy agreements.
3. Two months' notice has to be served that the landlord requires possession on a certain date (but not before the end of the fixed term); if the tenant refuses to leave, the courts must grant possession.

Additional and amended provisions (grounds) for a mandatory possession order have been included in the 1996 Act, such as two months' arrears of rent, and there are a number of discretionary grounds on which possession can be granted, even if the owner does not wish to return to the house. However, there is one specific disadvantage if the owner is unfortunate enough to have a tenant who refuses to leave when the owner wishes to reoccupy and the landlord then has to apply to court. The judicial system in the UK can occasionally take some time to operate and this can be particularly true if a local court happens to be busy. This unfortunately can extend the period needed before a possession order is granted by the court and owners would be well advised to take out one of the various insurance policies now available to cover hotel costs, legal fees, etc, and as a minimum to make sure that either alternative accommodation is temporarily available in the event of an earlier than expected return home, or alternatively ensure that the procedures for terminating the tenancy are instigated well before the projected date of return.

As must now be obvious to the reader, the complexity of the rules do nothing to encourage owners to attempt to let the property or manage their home themselves while away, and the need for an experienced property management firm becomes even more important than in the past. A solicitor might be an alternative but, although possibly more versed in the legal technicalities than a managing agent, he or she will not be in a position to market the house to the best advantage (if at all) and solicitors' practices do not usually have staff experienced in property management, able to carry out inspections, deal with repairs, arrange inventories and to handle the many and various problems that often arise.

Having obtained advice to ensure that you have the correct form of tenancy, you now need to find an experienced and reliable letting and management agent. Ideally, he or she should be a member of the Royal Institution of Chartered Surveyors (RICS), the Association of Residential Letting Agents (ARLA) or the National Association of Estate Agents (NAEA) specialising in property management who will be well versed in both the legal and financial aspects of the property market.

Property management

Property management is a rather specialised role and you should check carefully that the agent you go to can give you the service you need, that he or she is not just an accommodation broker, and that he or she is equipped to handle the letting, collection of rent and management of your property, as well as the more common kinds of agency work. Your solicitor should be able to advise you here, but to some extent you will have to rely on your own judgement of how ready and satisfactory the agent's answers are to the sort of questions you are going to want to ask. There are several specialised firms well equipped to deal with your affairs, but it is best to stick to members of RICS, ARLA and NAEA as they and their activities are all regulated by their professional bodies.

In the first place the agent you instruct should have a clear idea of the kind of tenant you expect for your property, and preferably be able to show you that he or she does have people on his or her books who are looking for rented accommodation of this kind. Obviously the rent and the tenant you can expect will vary with what you have to offer, and an agent who understands the local market well will be able to advise on what additional fixtures and equipment you need to install in order to maximise the rental value. A normal family house in a good area should attract someone like the executive of a multinational company who is in a similar, but reverse, position to your own: that is, someone working here on a contract basis for a limited period of time who may well provide a stable tenancy for the whole or a substantial part of your absence. A smaller house or flat would be more likely to attract a younger person who only wants the property for a limited period or who, at any rate, might be reluctant to accept a long-term commitment because of the possibility of a change in professional circumstances or marital status. Equally, if you are only going to be away for a shortish period like 6 to 12 months, you are going to be rather lucky to find a tenant whose needs exactly overlap with your absence. You will probably have to accept a slightly shorter period than your exact stay abroad.

For your part you should bear in mind that tenants, unlike house purchasers, are usually only interested in a property with almost immediate possession, but you should give the agent, wherever possible, at least four to six weeks' warning of your departure in order that interest may be built up by advertising, mailing out details, etc, over a period of time.

Rent

How much rent you can expect will also vary with what you have to offer and where it is, but the point to bear in mind is that rents are not usually subject to bargaining like the price of a house. Bargaining, if there is to be any, is more likely to occur over the terms of the lease, which are set out below. Do not, therefore, ask for an unrealistically high figure in the expectation that the tenant will regard this as a starting point for negotiation. Your agent, if he or she knows the job, will be able to advise you on the rental you should ask, though if you have not had previous dealings with him or her it might be advisable to ask the agent to give you some instances of rentals being achieved in the market for similar accommodation. An offer that is a bit less than you had hoped for, but from a good tenant, might be worth taking in preference to a better one from somebody who, for various reasons, looks more doubtful.

Terms of agreement

A property management agent should have, or be able to produce fairly quickly, a draft agreement to cover the specific situation of the overseas landlord. Member agents of the three professional bodies all have access to model agreements that take account of the various pieces of legislation and will have been drafted taking account of the Unfair Terms in Consumer Contract Regulations which impact heavily on what can and cannot be said in such agreements. You should show this to your solicitor, and how well it is drafted will again be a pointer to how effective the agent concerned is likely to be. The document should cover at least the following points:

1. The intervals of payment – monthly or quarterly – and the length of lease.
2. How much the tenancy deposit is to be and where it will be held, and the process for dealing with damages disputes at the end of the tenancy. (NB: from October 2006 the government is introducing legislation to protect tenancy deposits and any AST will have to include by law certain clauses about this.)
3. An undertaking by the tenant to take steps to reasonably maintain the garden.
4. An undertaking by the tenant to pay for telephone and other services from the commencement of the lease, including Council Tax.
5. An undertaking to allow the landlord, or the agent, access to the property (upon lawful notice) for inspection and repair; and two months before the expiry of the lease to allow him or her to take other prospective tenants or purchasers round the property.

6. A clause stating that the lease is terminated if any of the other clauses are broken, although the wording has to be carefully drafted to avoid invalidating the agreement.
7. What you, as landlord, are responsible for in the way of repairs: usually the maintenance of the structure and furnishings of the property together with anything left in the property (eg the central heating boiler). You can exclude some items, such as the television, from your responsibility, but generally the tenant is only liable for specific damage to items left in the house and not for their general maintenance. The government has tightened up safety laws in respect of gas appliances. In November 1994 the Gas Safety (Installation & Use) Regulations 1994 were introduced, forcing landlords to take greater responsibility for the safety of their tenants by regularly servicing and repairing any gas appliances through a British Gas or Corgi registered company. A landlord has to provide a tenant annually with a Gas Safety Record. Heavy penalties will be enforced for failing to comply.
8. Any special restrictions you want to impose: if, for example, your house is full of valuable antiques you may wish to specify 'no small children'.
9. Notice under Sections 47 and 48 of the Landlord and Tenant Act 1987. The former should be on all rent demands; the latter, notifying the tenant of an address in England or Wales at which notices can be served on the landlord, need only be served once on a tenant at the beginning of a tenancy.

Although the agreement is probably the central document in the transactions involved in letting your house, it does not bring to an end all the things you have to think about. For instance, there is the important matter of the contents insurance. Letting your home to a third party is probably not covered in your policy and you will have to notify your insurers (and the people who hold your mortgage) that this is what you are doing. In many instances, insurance companies will not insure the contents if the property is to be let and you will need to check carefully that you have cover and switch to another company if it becomes necessary. (This is covered in greater detail on pages 87–88, under Insurance.) At the same time you would be wise to check that the contents insurance covers the full value of what you have left in the house. This check could be combined with making a proper inventory of the contents, which is in any case essential before tenants move into a furnished property. Making an exact inventory is quite a time-consuming business and you should bear in mind that it will also have to be checked at the end of the lease, when you may not be there. There are several firms that provide a specialist inventory service at both ends of the lease, covering dilapidations as well as items actually missing, for quite a modest charge which, incidentally, is deductible from the tax due from the letting. Any good management agent should be able to put you on to one of them or will provide an in-house inventory service.

It is also essential that landlords are aware of important fire regulations that have come into force concerning the supply of furniture and furnishings when letting out accommodation. The Furniture (Fire) (Safety) Regulations 1988, introduced for all landlords on 1 January 1997, make it an offence to supply furniture which does not comply with the regulations concerning fire resistance. Essentially, it covers all upholstery and upholstered furnishings, including loose fittings and permanent or loose covers. These must comply with the following three tests, each of which measures the flame-retardant properties of the furnishings: Cigarette Test; Match Test; Ignitability Test. Heavy penalties will be enforced for failing to comply. Your managing agent should be able to provide details of exactly what furniture should be removed or replaced and when.

Finding the tenant and getting a signature on the agreement marks the beginning rather than the end of the property management firm's responsibilities. Broadly, these fall under two headings: the collection of rental and the management of the property. The rent is collected from the tenant, usually on a standing order basis, under the terms – monthly or quarterly – as set out in the agreement; and, in the event of persistent non-payment, the agent will instruct solicitors on your behalf to issue a County Court summons, or if you have taken out rental or legal insurance, the agent will contact the insurance company.

What can you expect from the agent?

The letting and residential managing agent should be regulated. Most commonly this means being a member of the Association of Residential Letting Agents, ARLA. This is the only professional body that is solely concerned with letting and renting and the management of residential property. To be a member of ARLA, the agent must be fully compliant with client accounts, professional indemnity insurance and the ARLA bonding scheme. Every ARLA member office must employ staff with relevant qualifications. Should it be felt that the agent has not performed satisfactorily, ARLA operates an independent redress system.

To check whether or not an agent is an ARLA member, or to find one, or for advice on letting your property or buying to let, visit www.arla.co.uk.

Management is a more complex subject, but an experienced property management agent should be able to supply you with a list of the services that he or she can undertake. It is, therefore, also a checklist of the kind of eventualities that may crop up in your absence which, broadly speaking, relate to the collection of rent, the payment of charges such as service charges and insurance, arrangements for repairs to the fabric of the building and its contents, garden maintenance, and forwarding mail.

Thus, apart from the basic business of collecting the rent, the agent can also pay, on your behalf, any charges on the property (eg, ground rent, water rates and insurance) that your contract with the tenant does not specify should be paid by him or her. There may also be annual maintenance agreements to pay in respect of items like central heating plant and the washing machine.

Then there is the question of what to do about repairs. As we have indicated earlier, whatever you manage to get the tenant to agree to take care of under the terms of the lease, there are certain responsibilities for maintenance and repair that you have to accept by virtue of your status as a landlord. If repairs are necessary, you will simply have to trust the agent to obtain fair prices for you.

On the other hand, except in the case of essential repairs that affect the tenant's legal rights of enjoyment of the property, you can ask your agent to provide estimates for having the work carried out, so that your approval must be obtained before the job is put in hand. Bear in mind, though, that in certain parts of the world the postal system may not be all that reliable. You may, therefore, find it a good idea to put a clause in the management contract giving the agent freedom to proceed with the best estimate if he or she does not hear from you within a specified period. For the same reason it is also wise to ask the agent to send you a formal acknowledgement of receipt of any special or new instructions you have given. An example of this might be an instruction to inspect the property at regular intervals.

To summarise, the responsibilities of a property management agent are as follows:

- ☐ collection of rent;
- ☐ day-to-day tenant liaison;
- ☐ general supervision of the property;
- ☐ payment of service charges and insurance;
- ☐ arranging repairs to the building and contents;
- ☐ payment of charges on the property;
- ☐ payment of maintenance agreements;
- ☐ obtaining prices/estimates for repairs.

Depending on how many concessions you have to make to the tenant to get him or her to sign the lease, there may be other articles for which repair and maintenance remain your responsibility. These may include the washing machine, TV and the deep freeze. Such responsibilities should be set out in the management contract and you should give the agent the details of any guarantees or maintenance contracts relating to them and photocopies of the actual documents for reference. If no such arrangements apply, you should list the manufacturers' names and the model number and age of each item so that the agent can get the manufacturer to send the repair people along equipped with the right spares.

It is very important that a third party, other than you and the tenant, should be in possession of all this information, particularly when there is likely to be more than one tenancy during your absence; and it is a competent management agent, rather than friends, relatives or even a solicitor, who will be best equipped in this case to find new tenants, to check their references, to draw up new agreements and supervise the handover of the tenancy.

Costs and tax

The costs of all these services vary according to the nature of the package you need. For example, the charge for letting and collection is usually 10 per cent of annual rental. In the case of management services, expect to find additional charges made (usually 5 to 7 per cent of the annual rent). These are reasonable fees for the quite considerable headaches involved. We have shown enough of them here to indicate that not only is it virtually impossible to administer a tenancy yourself from a distance, but also that these are not matters to be left to an amateur – friend or relative – however well intentioned. In real terms the agent's charges may be reduced because they are deductible against the tax levied in the UK against rental income.

Expatriates letting their homes also derive a further benefit in respect of capital gains tax. Generally, if you let your principal residence, when you come to sell it you can claim exemption from CGT only for those years in which you lived in it yourself. However, if you let it because you are absent abroad this does not apply, provided you come back to live in the house before you sell it.

Finally, in this context, it is worth pointing out that some mortgage lenders are now prepared to consider giving mortgages to expatriates for the purchase of a property in the UK *and* to allow them to lease that property for the period of their stay overseas. Up to 90 per cent of the purchase price is available at normal rates of interest. This is an attractive proposition for expatriates, particularly for young executives and professional people who have not yet bought a home in the UK but are earning a substantial income in, say, the Middle East, and for older expatriates perhaps thinking of a retirement home in the UK.

Some agencies supply details of the lenders offering this facility, or you could approach a lender directly and explain your position. Should you buy a house as an expatriate and then let it until you return, the earlier recommendation that you leave the management of the property to an experienced and competent agent still applies. If a UK property is bought purely as an investment, you would have to time its sale carefully to avoid liability for CGT.

Taxation is too complex a subject and varies considerably in its effects on the individual, preventing any practical advice being offered other than to state the importance of employing the services of an accountant in your absence, but it must be stressed that rent received in the UK is considered unearned income, and is subject to UK tax laws. A new scheme now operates whereby letting agents, or where there are no letting agents, tenants of a non-resident landlord, must deduct tax at the basic rate from the rental income, and pay tax quarterly to Her Majesty's Revenue and Customs. Those landlords who wish to receive their income with no tax deducted can apply to CNRL for approval. Forms are available from: CNRL (non-residents), St John's House, Merton Road, Bootle, Merseyside L69 9BB; tel: 0151 472 6208/6209.

Insurance

One important point that is often overlooked by people who let their house or flat is the necessity of notifying the insurers that a change of occupancy has taken place. Insurance policies only cover occupancy by the insured, not the tenants, though they can be extended to do so on payment of what is usually only a small premium. As many insurance companies will not cover properties that are or will be let, notifying the company concerned becomes essential.

What worries insurance companies much more is if the house is left unoccupied for any length of time. If you look at your policy you will see that it lapses if you leave your house empty for more than 30 days or so – a point that is sometimes forgotten by people who go away on extended holidays. If you are going abroad and leave the house empty – maybe because you have not yet succeeded in finding a tenant – the insurers will usually insist that you turn off the main services and that the premises are inspected regularly by a qualified person. That means someone like a letting agent, not a relative or friend. Even if you have let the house without an agent, it may still be advisable to get one to look after the place. A situation could easily occur where the tenant moves out, leaving the place empty and without satisfactory steps having been taken from an insurance point of view. Furthermore, if the worst happens and the house is broken into or damaged, it is imperative that the insurers are notified right away. The effects of damage can be made worse if they are not rapidly attended to, and insurers do not hold themselves responsible for anything that happens between the time the insured eventuality occurs and the time they are notified of it. For instance, if your house is broken into and, a few days later, vandals get in through a broken point of entry and cause further damage, you would not be covered for that second incident unless the insurers had been notified of the first break-in.

Valuable contents are best put into storage and insured there. Pickfords, for instance, charges a premium of 12.5 per cent of the storage charge, inclusive of insurance premium tax (IPT). For contents worth more than £25,000, a reduction may be possible. For very high-value items, safe deposit boxes are becoming popular, but from an everyday point of view, the important thing is to make sure you are insured for full values. If you insure contents for £15,000 and the insurer's assessors value them at £20,000 you will only get three-quarters of your claim. To keep insured values in line with rising costs, an index-linked policy would be the best buy for anyone contemplating a long stay abroad. A policy specially written for expatriates is available from Europea-IMG Ltd: the Weavers Homeowners Policy. It also offers expatriate motor insurance on private cars being used overseas. All insurance premiums are now subject to IPT.

Insuring at full value, incidentally, is equally important when it comes to insuring contents and personal belongings in your residence abroad. Many items will cost much more locally if you have to replace them than they did at the time they were originally bought. There are a few such policies available in the UK, or it may be possible to insure in the country concerned.

Finally, but most importantly, you should insure against legal and hotel costs when letting your house. Although in principle the legal instruments for quick repossession exist, events have shown that a bloody-minded tenant with a committed lawyer can spin things out to his or her advantage for almost an indefinite period. Premiums, which can be offset against rental income, are in the region of £85 a year.

Also recently introduced are rental protection policies, some providing limited cover at a relatively low premium, others covering the higher rental amounts, which are naturally more expensive. In addition, these policies will normally cover legal and other costs. However, due to the wide cover involved, the insurance companies usually insist on their own credit check and the employment of a managing agent, as well as the usual references.

The same companies will add, as an extra, buildings and/or contents cover when the property is let, often at rates that are competitive to the premiums charged when the property was owner-occupied.

Checklist: Financial planning and the expatriate

1. Check out your financial adviser's credentials.
2. Consider the pros and cons of offshore funds.
3. Check your life assurance policy to make sure that there are no restrictions about overseas living.
4. Consider tax-efficient ways to save for school fees.
5. If your company has a pension scheme in the country of residence, make sure you become acquainted with its rules and local legislation through your financial adviser.
6. Notify your financial adviser at least 12 months before the tax year of your return so that he or she can mitigate tax liabilities.

Checklist: Letting your home

1. Take professional advice about the most appropriate type of tenancy and the likely rental level, terms, etc.
2. Remember to take account of notice periods when planning your return.
3. Ask your property management agent to explain to you what kinds of people he or she has on the books.
4. Try to give the agent six to eight weeks warning prior to the rental date.
5. Seek advice from your solicitor concerning the agent's draft contract.
6. Inform your insurance company (and your mortage lender) of your intention to let your home and check that your contents insurance covers the full value of what you have left in the house.
7. Make a full inventory of the contents.
8. Ensure that your furniture complies with fire regulations.
9. Provide your agent with details of any guarantees or maintenance contracts.
10. Put valuable possessions into storage.
11. Consider insuring against legal and hotel costs.

The sections in this chapter on offshore banking are provided by Lloyds TSB Bank plc, and the editors express their thanks to the author, David Roberts, for use of the material.

Lloyds TSB
International Account benefits

Security

- Relationship with a respected British bank with a world-wide reputation built on trust.

- Secure and stable offshore centre.

- A subsidiary of Lloyds TSB Bank plc, which has an Aaa credit rating from Moody's.

Products

- **Sterling, US dollar or euro accounts:** The sterling account has chequebook facilities enabling cheques to be cleared through the UK clearing system.Interest paid on all sterling balances and on all currency balances over $/€2,000.

- **Debit cards:** The accounts come with a debit card. Cash withdrawals may be made of up to £500 per day on the sterling account, $/€750 on the currency accounts (provided there is enough money in your account) and purchase can be made wherever you see the Visa or Delta sign is displayed.

- **Savings accounts and investments:** A range of products is available including savings accounts, fixed term deposits and Money Market call accounts.

Service

- **International banking team:** Our dedicated relationship management team is experienced in dealing with the needs of international customers and is always available to help you.

- **Telephone banking:** Available 24 hours a day, 7 days a week.

- **Internet banking:** Available for sterling and currency accounts.

- **Shoreline:** Our quarterly magazine for international expatriates.

- **Overseas visits:** We operate an extensive visiting programme.

- **Interest without deduction of tax:** competitive tiered interest rates, paid monthly.

Other benefits

- **Introductions to tax advice and will writing specialists.**

- **American Express International Currency Charge Cards.**

- **Sentinel International:** card cancellation and replacement from anywhere in the world with one phone call.

- **Discounted travel and health insurance.**

- **Priority Pass:** Access to over 450 airport lounges worldwide and discounted membership fees.

- **Lifestyle service:** 24 hour concierge service to make life that little bit easier both at home and abroad.

- **Lloyds TSB Travel Service:** discounted holidays, city breaks, cruises and more.

- **Discounted UK airport car parking.**

- **Discounted weekend breaks.**

For further information, or to apply, please call or email us on:

Tel: +44 (0) 1624 638000

Email: newaccs@lloydstsb-offshore.com

Alternatively you can visit our website

www.lloydstsb-offshore.com/international

and download an application form

5 National Insurance, Benefits and Pensions

The desire to earn more money – and to pay less of it in tax and other deductions – looms large for many as a motive for going to work abroad. People who take this step are often temperamentally inclined to be strongly individualistic and self-reliant and, as such, many feel that they would rather fend for themselves when circumstances get difficult rather than rely on what they regard as 'state handouts'. Whatever the virtues of this attitude of mind may be, those who have it are more to be commended for their sense of independence than their common sense. The fact is that during your working life in the UK you will have made compulsory National Insurance contributions and you are therefore eligible for benefits in the same way as if you had paid premiums into a private insurance scheme; drawing a state benefit you are entitled to is no more taking a handout than making an insurance claim.

National Insurance has another feature in common with private insurance: you lose your entitlement to benefit if you fail to keep up your contributions, though the circumstances under which this would happen are different from, and more gradual than in, the private sector. Furthermore, you cannot immediately reactivate your eligibility for benefits in full if, your payments having lapsed for a period of time, you return to this country and once again become liable to make contributions. For instance, in order to qualify in full for a UK retirement pension you must have paid the minimum contribution for each year for at least 90 per cent of your working life. In the case of other benefits too, in order to qualify to get them, there must be a record of your having made a certain level of contributions in the two tax years governing that in which benefits are being claimed.

DSS AGENCIES

National Insurance provisions are handled by Executive Agencies of the Department of Social Security. The Contributions Agency deals with all contributions and insurability matters, while the Benefits Agency deals with all matters relating to social security benefits.

NI contribution matters for persons working abroad are handled by the Contributions Agency's International Services, Longbenton, Newcastle upon Tyne NE98 1YX; tel: 0845 915 4811. The International service can provide you with information on your National Insurance liability, voluntary contributions, retirement pension forecasts, health care and other benefits. Visit the website at www.inlandrevenue.gov.uk/nic/intserv/osc.htm. Matters relating to benefits are handled by the Benefit Agency's Pensions and Overseas Benefits Directorate at Newcastle upon Tyne NE98 1BA.

Leaflet NI 38, or for European Economic Area countries leaflet SA29, available from either Agency at Newcastle, or from a local social security office, sets out the basic conditions relating to National Insurance and benefits abroad.

LIABILITY FOR CONTRIBUTIONS WHILE ABROAD

If your employer in the UK sends you to work in another European Economic Area country or in a country with which the UK has a reciprocal agreement (these are listed in leaflet NI 38) for a period not expected to exceed that which is specified in the EC regulations *or* the reciprocal agreement (RA) involved, you will normally continue to be subject to the UK social security scheme for that period and you will be required to pay Class 1 contributions as though you were in the UK. (The specified period can vary between one year where the EC regulations apply and up to five years depending upon the reciprocal agreement involved.) If your employment unexpectedly lasts longer than 'the specified period', then for certain countries you may remain insured under the UK scheme with the agreement of the authorities in the country in which you are working. Your employer will obtain a certificate for you from the Contributions Agency, International Services, at Newcastle upon Tyne confirming your continued liability under the UK scheme, which you should present to the foreign authorities if required to confirm your non-liability under their scheme. This form, E101, is issued with European Health Cards which provide health care cover abroad for you and your family for the period of employment in another country.

If you are sent by your UK employer to an EU member state or to a country with which there is a reciprocal agreement in circumstances other than the above, eg for an initial period expected to exceed 12 months or for a period of indefinite duration, then normally you will cease to be liable to pay UK contributions from the date you are posted and will instead become liable to pay into the scheme of the country you are working in. Leaflet SA29 tells you about the European Community (EC) Regulations on social security and their effect on EU nationals. If you would like a copy of leaflet SA29 or would like more information, you can telephone or write to International Services. Alternatively you can get a copy of leaflet SA29 from your local social security office.

If you are sent by your employer to a country other than those in the EU or with which there is a reciprocal agreement you will be liable to pay Class 1 contributions for the first 52 weeks of your posting provided your employer has a place of business in the UK, you were resident in the UK immediately before you took up employment abroad, you remain 'ordinarily resident' in the UK while you are abroad and you are under UK retirement age (currently 60 for women and 65 for men). If you are self-employed you must obtain forms E101/E102/E128.

MAKING VOLUNTARY CONTRIBUTIONS

For non-EU and non-RA countries, when your period of liability for Class 1 contributions ends, you may wish to pay voluntary Class 3 contributions to the UK scheme in order to protect your UK retirement/widow's pension entitlement. We will deal with the mechanics of this later, but at this stage it should be pointed out that if you are going abroad for a British-based firm you will be liable to make the same contributions as if you were employed in this country up to a maximum earnings level of £645 per week (2006/2007 tax year). Your proportion of this contribution will be deducted from your salary, as if you were still working in the UK. Payment of these contributions for the first 52 weeks of your employment abroad will make you eligible to receive incapacity or unemployment benefit and, in the case of a woman, maternity allowance, under the usual conditions applicable to those benefits, on your return to the UK – even though this may be some years later – because Class 1 contributions will be deemed to have been paid in the tax year(s) relevant to your claim. This is subject to the proviso that you remained 'ordinarily resident' in the UK during your absence. If you did not intend to sever your connection with the UK when you went abroad, continuing ordinary residence will usually be accepted. To establish ordinary residence you may need to show that you maintained a home or accommodation in the UK or stored your furniture in the UK during your absence. To maintain entitlement to UK retirement pension or widow's benefits, however, it will usually be necessary to pay Class 3 contributions after the Class 1 period has expired although this may not be necessary for the balance of the year – April to April – in which Class 1 liability ceased. The Contributions Agency, International Services, Room BP1303, Longbenton, Newcastle upon Tyne NE98 1ZZ can advise you about this. Remember always to quote your National Insurance number and the country involved when you write.

Class 1 contributions are not payable at all in respect of employment abroad if your employer has no place of business in the UK. However, if you work for an overseas government or an international agency such as the UN, you will be able to pay your share of the Class 1 contribution for the first 52 weeks of your employment abroad and so qualify on return to the UK for the benefits named in the previous paragraph.

You may, of course, have been a self-employed person paying the Class 2 rate of £2.10 a week for the 2006/07 tax year. These contributions also cover a more limited range of benefits – Jobseeker's Allowance (previously unemployment benefit) and injury or death caused by an industrial accident or prescribed disease are excluded – but like Class 3 contributions, they can also be paid voluntarily if you go to work in an EU country or countries with which the UK has an RA agreement, provided you are gainfully occupied there. However, you *need not* pay Class 2 contributions just because you were self-employed before you went abroad. You can go to the voluntary Class 3 rate (which is £7.55 for the 2006/2007 tax year), but if you want to qualify for incapacity benefit when you return to the UK, provided you were employed abroad you can switch back to Class 2 payments for the two tax years governing the benefit year in which you are due to return. Advice for those who are self-employed is available from the National Insurance Contributions Office, Self-Employment Services, Benton Park View, Newcastle upon Tyne NE98 1ZZ, or by ringing the Helpline (0845 915 4515) and quoting your National Insurance number.

These rates and conditions apply, of course, as much to women as to men. The right of married women to pay reduced rate contributions has been phased out. If you get married while working abroad you should write to International Services for leaflet CA 13 which explains in more detail your National Insurance position as a married woman. A married woman may consider paying contributions in her own right (eg for retirement pension purposes). See leaflet NI 38.

Leaflet NI 38 contains a form at the back (CF 83) which should be filled in when you want to start making voluntary payments. You can pay by annual lump sum, by arranging for someone in the UK to make regular payments for you, or through direct debit if you have a bank or building society in the UK or Channel Islands.

Class 2 and Class 3 contributions can be paid before the end of the sixth tax year following the one in which they were due. However, although you have six years in which to pay there is a limited period in which to pay at the relevant year's contribution rates. International Services can advise you about this. Whatever method you choose it is important that your contributions are paid on time. For further information see leaflet CA07 – *Unpaid and late paid contributions*. Also see CF411 *How to protect your State Retirement Pension*.

GETTING NI BENEFITS ABROAD

Thus far we have only mentioned the range of benefits available to you once you return to the UK. But is there any way you can become eligible for benefits while still abroad? Generally, the answer is that you can only receive retirement pensions and widow's benefits, but there are important exceptions in the case of

EU countries and some others – a full list is given in leaflet NI 38 – with which the UK has reciprocal agreements. How those agreements affect you varies somewhat from country to country, but in essence they mean that the contributions you have paid in the UK count, for benefit purposes, as if you had paid them in the reciprocal agreement country, and vice versa. This is usually advantageous if you do become eligible for benefit while abroad because in relation to the cost of living – or even in absolute terms – UK benefits are lower than many foreign ones. You will, in general, have to pay contributions to the scheme of the country you are working in, so by the same token if you are going to a country with which the UK has a reciprocal agreement, you will have to decide if you want to pay voluntary contributions to the UK in order to maintain UK pension entitlement when you return here. The Contributions Agency can advise you on this. If you have not yet come under the scheme of a foreign country and are paying Class 1, 2 or 3 contributions to the UK while working abroad then, if you think you are eligible for benefit, you should write to the Benefits Agency, Pensions and Overseas Benefits Directorate immediately the contingency governing your claim arises. One important point to bear in mind in this case, though, is that if benefit can be paid, you will only get paid at the UK rate, not that of similar welfare schemes of the country in which you are living. In many cases the latter may be much more generous than UK rates; furthermore, UK rates may bear very little relationship to the cost of living abroad.

In this connection it is also worth pointing out that the UK is by no means the top of the world league table when it comes to the percentage of the pay packet taken up by contributions to social services. In many of the EU countries, in particular, it is significantly higher. This is an important detail to discuss with a prospective employer, because the 'social wage' and what you have to put in to get it obviously have a bearing on the real value of the remuneration package you are being offered.

THE NHS AND HEALTH CARE BENEFITS

In one important instance UK benefits are actually more generous than those of many other countries. We refer here to the UK National Health Service. But medical expenses incurred abroad are definitely not refunded by the NHS, which is only available to people living in this country; so, contrary to popular belief, you will no longer be able to get free NHS treatment in this country once you become permanently resident abroad. Many overseas countries do have reciprocal health agreements with the UK – once again a list is given on the HMRC site – but the services they provide are not exactly comparable with those of the British NHS. European Health Cards are available from the DSS or post offices and are essential documents in being able to access this reciprocal care. See also leaflet T5 – *Health Advice for Travellers Anywhere in the World*. The range of treatment provided free of charge varies considerably and it is advisable to take out private health insurance to cover eventualities where free medical attention is not, or is only partially, available. Leaflets giving information on the procedures you need to observe, both in the case of temporary spells and permanent residence abroad, are available from the Contributions Agency's International Services (tel: 0845 915 4811 or 44-191-225 4811 if calling from abroad).

CHILD BENEFITS WHILE WORKING ABROAD

There are various situations which, in different ways, affect your entitlement to receive child benefit while working abroad:

1. If you go abroad permanently, taking your children with you, your child benefits cease from the date of your departure. When you arrive in the new country you can only rely on that country's family benefit.
2. If you go to work in another EU country you will generally be insured under its social security legislation and so entitled to the local family allowances. If you are insured under another EU scheme but leave your children behind in Great Britain, you may still be entitled to family allowances from the EU country in which you are insured. If you remain insured under the Great Britain scheme, child benefit may still be payable whether your children are in Great Britain or with you. If your children are not with you, you would have to maintain them by at least the weekly rate of child benefit after the first 56 days. If your children live with you but your

spouse or partner is insured under another EU scheme, you will be entitled to local family allowances. However, you may be paid a 'supplement' equal to the difference between the local rate and the Great Britain rate of benefit if the Great Britain rate is higher.

3. If you have been sent abroad to work temporarily, for a period of not more than eight weeks, and you return within that time, benefit will continue to be paid whether or not you take your children with you. Child benefit orders cannot be cashed outside Great Britain, but you will be able to cash them when you return, provided each order is cashed within three months of the date stamped on it. After eight weeks of temporary absence, your eligibility for Great Britain child benefit ceases unless you happen to be in one of the reciprocal agreement countries.

4. You can also continue to be eligible for Great Britain child benefit, even after eight weeks of absence, if in the relevant tax year at least half your earnings from the employment which took you abroad are liable to United Kingdom income tax. However, in this case your entitlement cannot be decided until your tax liability has been assessed.

5. If a child is born abroad within eight weeks of the mother's departure from Great Britain and she is abroad only temporarily, child benefit may be paid from then until the end of the eight-week period of absence. If you wish to claim in these circumstances you should write to the Child Benefit Centre (Washington), PO Box 1, Newcastle upon Tyne NE88 1AA, quoting your child benefit number if you are already getting child benefit for another child.

6. Special rules exist in respect of serving members of the forces and civil servants; persons falling into these categories should consult their paying officer or Establishments Division.

Full details of these schemes, including the form CH 181(TO) which you have to fill in before your departure, are set out in leaflet CH 6, available from your local Social Security office. Alternatively, you can get a copy by writing to the Information Division, Leaflet Unit, Block 4, Government Buildings, Honeypot Lane, Stanmore, Middlesex HA7 1AY.

UNEMPLOYMENT BENEFITS FOR JOB HUNTERS WITHIN THE EU

Under EU law you can go jobseeking for up to three months in most EU countries, provided you have been registered as unemployed in the UK for four weeks before departure. You are entitled to receive Jobseeker's Allowance on the day of departure and you actually register for work in the new country. While you are in the other country, you can continue drawing UK Jobseeker's Allowance via the employment services of the country you are in provided you follow their control procedures.

You should inform your local unemployment benefit office *in person* of your intention well in advance of your departure, and obtain from them leaflet UBL 22. The Pensions and Overseas Benefits Directorate of the Benefits Agency will then issue the authorisation form E303 to you if you are going to France, Greece, Portugal, Spain, Germany or Italy and there is enough time before your departure. Otherwise, it will be sent to your address there. If you are going to another EU country, the form will be sent to a liaison office in the country concerned. Regardless of which country you are going to, ask your local unemployment benefits office to issue you with a letter of introduction. You should give this – and form E303 if you have it – to the employment services when registering for work in another EU country.

In practice, many EU countries have blocked this progressive move by putting obstacles in the way over such matters as residence permits – France is particularly bad in this respect – because the UK is not alone among European Union countries in having an unemployment problem. The good news is that if you do succeed in getting a job in an EU country, in some states not only are wages and salaries higher but so also are unemployment benefits. If you are unlucky enough to lose your 'new' job after being insurably employed under the social security scheme of an EU country, your previous UK insurance may be taken into account to help you become eligible for unemployment benefits which are very much higher than those in the UK.

All Jobcentres now handle vacancies in the EU and can give further details on relevant legislation and social welfare provisions. The Employment Service issues a useful leaflet on these matters, called *Working Abroad*, as well as others detailing conditions in individual countries.

UK PENSION SCHEMES AND THE EXPATRIATE

UK pension schemes have been affected by changes in the state provisions introduced since July 1988. Many pension experts think that employees of companies contracted in to the state scheme, known as SERPS, might be better advised to set up a personal pension scheme which the new legislation now allows them to do, on an individual basis. The value of such a step would depend on a wide variety of circumstances, such as age, whether the expatriate has taxable income in the UK, and if the employer has a contracted out pension scheme, just how good the benefits of its scheme are. Under the Welfare Reform and Pensions Act 1999, UK employers who do not provide either a final salary scheme with defined benefits or a money purchase pension under a defined contributions scheme are obliged to offer access to a stakeholder pension scheme. The issues are very complicated and you should seek advice from a reputable financial management firm with experience of expatriate problems.

Checklist: Working abroad and National Insurance

1. Contact both the Contributions Agency and the Benefit Agency for relevant literature on working abroad and National Insurance contributions.
2. Consider paying voluntary contributions to maintain your benefits entitlement on your return and organise payment through direct debit from your bank or building society while you are away.
3. Check to see if you are still entitled to be paid Child Benefit.
4. If you are looking for work and claiming Jobseeker's Allowance, inform your local unemployment benefits office well in advance of your departure.
5. Take advice on your pension scheme arrangements while working abroad.

Part Three:

Preparing the Family

6 Partner Issues

The success or failure of foreign assignments nowadays is more often than not affected by the family's willingness to relocate, and the pressures on an expatriate family should not be underestimated. Many families are organised around a dual-income couple with equal weight given to both careers. The problems of accommodating two careers, or for one partner to give up his or hers for the sake of the other, are considerable. Furthermore, there is less willingness to send children to boarding school and many employees are accompanied by both partner and offspring to a new location. Creating a fulfilling experience for both partner and children is the key to a successful assignment and this chapter looks at some of the ways in which this may be achieved.

COMPANY ATTITUDES

Enlightened organisations have accepted that the days when the partner was a 'wife', and that a wife did not work, are long gone. Unmarried and dual-earning couples are now frequently the case and, as such, the partner status has become an increasingly urgent problem to sort out. Many partners are unwilling to put their careers on hold. Furthermore, those that do will need help to turn the experience into a worthwhile venture if the employee is to complete the assignment.

It is perhaps no surprise that partners show reluctance to relocate. Relocation company ECA found that while 65 per cent of expatriates were accompanied by a partner on assignment, of the partners, 60 per cent had worked prior to the assignment but only 16 per cent worked during the assignment. It is quite reasonable to presume that a number of the 44 per cent who didn't work chose not to; however, it is also safe to assume that many would have liked to work, but were not given the opportunity to do so.

With this in mind, larger companies are beginning to recognise the need to provide support to partners. However, these are still a minority, for according to the ECA survey only 12 per cent of companies have established a uniform policy, and of that number, 35 per cent deal with partner careers on a case-by-case basis. Job searches, career counselling, network contacts and educational assistance are some of the ways in which these companies are trying to help partners. Table 6.1 shows the range of company assistance currently on offer or being considered by organisations.

However, companies with a long-established tradition of expatriation have also begun to develop strategies that see the partner included in the relocation process right from the very start, including the initial selection interview. The inclusion of the partner at this stage not only secures an understanding of his or her needs and expectations but gives a good indication of whether employees have thought through the impact a foreign assignment might have on their personal relationships.

Employees will have the support and structure of the company to help settle in to their new location. The partner, on the other hand, might well be giving up a job, and certainly a social network, to move to a foreign location without any structure or obvious objective.

Table 6.1   Assistance with partner careers

	Current practice (%)	Considering (%)
Networking contacts	50	10
Work permits	41	11
Education/training assistance	38	22
Career consultancy advice	33	18
Cost of career enhancement	25	12
Access to recruitment specialist	26	17
Arrange employment within company	24	10
Arrange employment with partner's company	6	3
Intra-company database/job swap	2	10

Source: ECA International

At the first interview we insist that they bring their partner with them. That has a number of messages. For a start, if an employee asks why their partner should attend, this immediately flashes a warning signal. Occasionally you get people who just haven't thought through the implications for their partner. In most cases, they have discussed it with their partner but have taken the view that 'it's my job, and I'll get it fixed up and find out what the implications are for you'. We turn it the other way round and say 'this is a deal between the two of you and us and it's only going to be as strong as the weaker of you. If we explain to you all the issues that may be involved, and you can discuss with equal amounts of information the implications for you, you can come to us together and raise your concerns and we will deal with them for you together'. We're talking to a team even though only one of them is likely to be working for us, particularly in a foreign assignment. The stresses and the pressures on the non-employee are potentially far greater.

John Thompson, PricewaterhouseCoopers

Recruiters like John Thompson of PricewaterhouseCoopers have recognised that it is a false economy not to try to help partners either to find a job or to have a local support network. Failed assignments are costly and many flounder on the trailing partner's desire to return home.

Elisabeth Marx has written about the problems faced by partners in *Breaking Through Culture Shock* and suggests that the pressures are twofold. First, couples experience major problems and crises on international assignments because of the unique situation they find themselves in. Faced with the unpredictability of their situation and having to depend on each other, they are without their social network and normal social controls. Furthermore, Marx points to the fact that in most cases the female partner has to deal with the challenges of settling into a new place. These include organising schooling for the children, sorting out a home and the daily basics, and supporting a partner through the early stages of a new job. Additionally, she will have to try to tap into a social network for the children, and for her and her partner. Add to this the possible demands of her new job, for those who have found one, and one can see why enlightened companies are keen to involve partners from the earliest stage.

Professor Cary Cooper has written extensively about the pressures on dual-income families, and occupational stress. He believes that companies can avoid problems by communicating honestly and inclusively with couples: 'It would seem reasonable that the spouse should be given the "option" to get involved in the decision-making and information-sharing process concerning any move that may impinge on the family. At the moment, organisations are contracting with one element of the family unit, but making decisions which radically affect the unit as a whole. By operating in this way they often cause conflict between the individual and his/her family' (Cooper and Lewis, *The Workplace Revolution*, Kogan Page).

FINDING WORK

The biggest problem for companies is in trying to find career opportunities for the partner in the new location. Apart from being able to find a suitable job to match up to the partner's skills in the new location, there are many parts of the world that will not allow couples to work on one work permit.

If you are a citizen of the European Union original 15 countries (ie live in Austria, Belgium, Denmark, Finland, France, Germany, Greece, Ireland, Italy, Luxembourg, The Netherlands, Portugal, Spain, Sweden or the United Kingdom) and you are being relocated within its borders, there are no such restrictions and partners are allowed to work without a permit.

Outside the European Union, however, work permits for EU citizens are hard to come by, as are permits for non-EU citizens to work in the European Union. In most cases work permits are provided only for the employee who has the backing of an international organisation and a specified job to go to. Dependants are generally allowed resident visas but the opportunity to work on their partner's permit is arbitrary and on the whole limited. For example, Australia allows dependants the right to work on an employee's permit, as does Sweden. Japan, on the other hand, allows part-time work. Islamic countries, such as Saudi Arabia, do not issue work permits to females unless they are in the teaching or nursing professions. Perhaps the most difficult country of all for which to obtain a work permit is the United States, which operates a rigorous immigration policy, unless the partner can show that he or she has unique and rare skills to offer.

Large companies are able to negotiate limited reciprocal arrangements on work permits with other countries, but these tend to be used up by employees. 'In some cases they can go with a joint work permit,' explains John Thompson, 'in other cases there is a real problem and virtually prohibitive because if you have an unmarried partner, for example, some countries will not give visas. They would not be recognised as a de facto spouse. In some cases we have to say, well, it won't work. As far as we are concerned their status is what it is and if they are going together as an established couple, provided the immigration authorities in the country we are dealing with recognise that, we will do so as well. But we have to look at the practicalities of what can be done.'

Given the difficulties, a few companies will try to find work within their own company for partners with appropriate skills and relocate them in their own right. Others might begin communication with a partner's company to see if there are possibilities for relocation to the same destination within their existing organisation. However, both these, as seen by the ECA survey results, are the least favoured options. Barry Page from Accenture points to further problems, caused by the changing workforce profile, in trying to relocate working partners. 'I have come across organisations where the spouse or partner has a more senior position than the employee and that creates more problems. Also, one cannot presume that the spouse or partner is a female either.'

Many companies find it easier to help partners obtain work permits in their own right rather than to try to do so as a dependant, and to do this have set up network systems and recruitment search facilities to help look for new opportunities. For example, Shell International has set up its OUTPOST website, www.shellspouseemployment.com, which provides information to partners who wish to work or develop their skills during and after expatriation. Others provide advice through a career consultancy agency for partners seeking jobs, and advice is given on academic and professional qualifications, and whether training is needed to pursue their career abroad. However, partners looking for work should also think about taking up some of the suggestions in Chapter 1, Independent Job Opportunities, in their search for a job in their own right. Further useful websites are listed at the back of this book.

It is quite possible to look for work once relocated and in situ. However, work permit restrictions might, once again, cause problems and it is worth finding out the situation before leaving for your foreign destination.

FROM EXPAT TO EXPERT

Jonathan Wix, Teacher Recruitment Section, British Council

Sooner or later, UK expats discover that they are not very far from a British Council library and information centre, and the spirit of Empire swells in their breast. But gone are the days when our libraries held the latest edition of *Horse and Hound* and 'Carry on Up the Khyber' videos for rental – these days our resources are carefully aimed at the local population and are selected to help us achieve our purpose of increasing appreciation for the contemporary UK's creativity and achievements and building mutually beneficial international relations.

Aside from the local population, plenty of expats are pleasantly surprised to find that when they join one of our libraries or Knowledge and Learning Centres they can borrow recent fiction, CDs and videos, as well as books or magazines on contemporary British politics, architecture and a range of subjects that give a window on contemporary Britain.

But not all the people who use our resources realise that some of our centres have up to 1,200 students at any one time taking English language courses. In the academic year 2004/5, 300,000 students learnt English in British Council centres worldwide. Across about 90 centres, our teachers taught a whopping 1.07 million class hours.

Some people know they want to teach English as a Foreign Language (EFL) abroad and make all the right moves early on, but a lot of people don't. For many good reasons, a large number of EFL teachers come to the profession later in life, and sometimes only through necessity or accident. If you find yourself with time on your hands in a foreign city, your ability to speak English at native fluency is potentially one of your greatest assets. Our teaching centre managers recognise that life experiences and diverse skills, combined with teaching ability, are valuable in the classroom and always appreciate what someone entering their second or third career has to offer. There is a particularly high demand for teachers who have the skills to manage a class of school-age children. If you've already taught children or had teacher training in the UK, then you have valuable skills for an EFL institute.

Teaching EFL used to be akin to missionary work. Now it's big business. In addition to offering regular classes for independent students, language institutes – including the British Council – bid for valuable contracts from corporate clients. When we win such a contract, we suddenly need more teachers, either to design and deliver the corporate lessons or to cover for staff teachers while they take it on themselves. Commercial realities mean the institutes that thrive are those that can be flexible in this way, and there is always a need for part-time or short-term teachers to work alongside full-time staff.

Managers who need part-time teachers will advertise locally – in the local English language press, and maybe on their own websites. But students at the better institutes are now used to being taught by experts, and the jobs will go to the best qualified candidates. Without some training, leading to a recognised qualification, your chances of working for a good employer are slim.

The best training courses are those that lead to qualifications that are recognised across the globe. Currently we use the Cambridge ESOL Certificate in English Language Teaching to Adults (CELTA) and the Trinity College London Certificate in Teaching English to Speakers of Other Languages (Cert. TESOL), or any course that is their equivalent, as one of our entry-level requirements for all recruits. You can take these courses in many different cities around the world. Go to the relevant websites for the provider locators. Some British Council centres offer the CELTA course, where your fellow trainees could be local ELT specialists from the state system or expat novices.

You don't have to be British to work for the British Council, but you do need to speak English to native ability in order to teach. If you don't have a UK passport, in some countries we would only be able to hire you on a local contract, but the work you do, your status and the rate of pay are the same as for teachers appointed from the UK. Hourly-paid part-time staff are only hired on local contracts, regardless of nationality. Far from being looked down on, some of our most expert and experienced teachers prefer to take only short-term or part-time contracts.

As long as there are enough paid hours in the week, part-time teachers are encouraged to take part in training and personal development, including assessments, as much as anyone else. The working hours are unconventional for most teachers, however. Since most students have day jobs they come for English lessons after work or at weekends. If you are looking after family or want to spend time with your partner who's working too, it's important to bear this in mind.

The typical student is someone in his or her early professional life who needs to learn English in order to get a better job or an international qualification, maybe with the aim of studying at a UK university. Although the majority of students will have a common cultural background, it's not unusual for a class to include students from several different countries. A typical class in Jordan, for example, could include people from Saudi Arabia, China and Belarus in addition to the Jordanians. Students are motivated and eager to share their culture as much as learn about others, and through learning English they are learning much more than when to use the present continuous – our teachers equip their students with skills and attitudes that make them international citizens.

With the skills and experience of an EFL teacher you can work pretty much all over the world. If you're not one when you start, it's not long before you become an international citizen yourself.

Websites:
British Council teacher recruitment: http://trs.britishcouncil.org
University of Cambridge ESOL qualifications:
www.cambridgeesol.org
Trinity College London ESOL qualifications:
www.trinitycollege.co.uk
Helpful resource for TEFL qualifications: www.cactusefl.com
Worldwide jobs in TEFL: www.tefl.com

FURTHER EDUCATION

If finding a job or obtaining a work permit proves too difficult, the time spent abroad might be a chance to explore other avenues. There are several options available to a trailing partner. For example, investigating educational opportunities in a new location could be one avenue for a trailing partner. Universities and business schools might offer an alternative structure and social network to a job. Furthermore, taking a local qualification might aid the process of finding a job in the new location. For example, INSEAD, the French Business School, provides a career service to holders of its MBA.

The internet is also becoming an invaluable educational tool. There is an increasing number of distance learning courses available through the web. As mentioned in Chapter 1, the Open University

Business School is one institution that is using electronic means to fully explore educational potential and offers a range of six-month courses on a distance learning basis. Professionals might also use this opportunity to take postgraduate professional qualifications. Professional associations and regulatory bodies will advise you on the availability of distance learning courses. Non-professional education might also be available. For example, learning the language of your host country will provide both practical help and intellectual stimulus.

NETWORKING AND CONSIDERING THE CHILDREN

An invaluable aid to partners is the network of contacts that an employee's company can provide before expatriation. This is not just a way to find out what the location is really like but also provides invaluable contacts on arrival. Shell International has recognised the importance of this and has set up a worldwide information network 'Outpost' of Shell expatriate families, which is run by volunteer Shell partners and spouses. Likewise, PricewaterhouseCoopers encourages contact with expatriates already in location and tries to link up non-working partners.

Once again, the internet has come into its own when considering the opportunities of contacting other expatriate partners. The plethora of websites for expat spouses is too numerous to mention here and is listed in the back of this book. However, apart from the Shell Spouse Centre at www.shellspouseemployment.com, there is also the *Electronic Telegraph's* expatriate website at www.telegraph.co.uk, Expat Resources for Spouses at www.thesun.org and Expat Forum at www.expatforum.com. Numerous nationality-, location- and occupation-specific forums also exist on the internet and, again, are listed at the back of the book. Furthermore, if your partner's company has not got an expat partner's website, it might also be a good time to enquire as to the possibilities of setting one up.

The focus of settling children in to a new country tends to be placed on schooling, and this will be dealt with in depth in the next chapter. However, it is also important to consider the effect that expatriation will have on their psychological and social development. Each child is, of course, uniquely different and will deal with new situations in his or her own way. For some children the opportunity to experience a new place and meet new people will be regarded as an adventure and will be welcomed. For others, it could be a profoundly disturbing experience, with family and friends disappearing from their daily lives. Older children will also present problems and before relocating it is worth considering how they might find living in a more restrictive or more liberal environment and what kind of freedoms they might expect in comparison to their home culture. Harsh punishments can be handed out for the use of 'soft' drugs and other such misdemeanours in many parts of the world. The example of the flogging of a US teenager for vandalism in Singapore should act as a warning. However, the advice remains consistent. As companies need to include partners in the decision-making process, so too children should be included in preparatory discussions and be given information about their new home. An inclusive process for the whole family might well ease some of the anxiety and stresses of relocation. Likewise, new technology might provide the answer to homesick children who can keep in contact with friends and family through the use of e-mail and the internet. As in other situations, children can act as conductors for the emotional highs and lows of a family and if there is tension and anxiety surrounding the decision to relocate they are also likely to pick this up. Using the time before departure to investigate and research your destination with your children could be a useful exercise for the whole family.

USING YOUR INITIATIVE

No matter how supportive a company might be, in the end the trailing partner role is unlikely to be an easy one. Investigating all the possibilities and opportunities before you go is vital: whether it be job opportunities, further education or building a network of contacts to develop a social life. The last of these might also provide openings that will not become apparent until you have arrived in your new location, such as voluntary work or job opportunities. The stresses and strains on relationships should also be expected and a positive approach to the experience might help ease them. As with your partner's career change, relocation could add to your own career or life expectations by giving you international work experience and/or new skills – such as a language – and by opening new horizons. Having decided to make the move, a flexible approach will be the best way of ensuring that you are open to the opportunities available to you.

Checklist: Partner issues

1. Can you find work in the new location and are your qualifications recognised?
2. Can you work as a dependant or will you have to apply for a work permit in your own right?
3. Is your new location sympathetic to unmarried partners, same-sex partners and women who want to work – all of these can affect your chances of being granted a work permit?
4. Can your company or your partner's company find work within their organisation for you in the new location?
5. What are the educational possibilities in your new location and can your partner's employer help you identify them and/or training opportunities? Consider qualifying as an EFL teacher.
6. Does the company have a network for expat partners either on the internet or through telephone communication?
7. If your company does not have a network for expats, are you in a position to start one yourself?
8. Talk to other expats about the host country's environment for children and give particular thought, if you have teenagers, as to what kind of social life they might be able to have.
9. Involve your children in finding out about the new destination through different media or by making contact with expat children already in situ.
10. Encourage your children to use communications technology to keep in touch with friends and family.

7 Your Children's Education

For those contemplating a job abroad, the issue of schooling cannot be taken lightly. Not only can an unsatisfactory educational solution prejudice a child's chance of achieving academic success, it can also create tensions that have an adverse effect on the home and working environment. In some cases it may lead to the premature termination of overseas contracts.

Educational options certainly demand careful thought and planning. Among the possibilities to be considered are:

1. A boarding school in the UK.
2. A day school in the UK (with guardianships/relatives).
3. An expatriate school abroad.
4. A company-sponsored school abroad.
5. A local national school abroad.
6. Home teaching abroad.

The ultimate choice will be determined by the age, ability and personality of your child, together with the quality of education available abroad and the expected duration of a contract. It will also be based on personal financial considerations and on the education support policy of the employer.

School fees (all, or a substantial part) may be paid by major international companies and organisations, and in some cases by governmental agencies. Whether such an allowance is used to contribute towards education at a UK boarding school or at a local fee-paying school will depend on local availability and the employer's policy. Some of these organisations employ trained staff to offer advice and support. They may also cover travelling expenses to and from the school in the UK, including air fares.

Smaller British companies may indicate that the salary they offer includes an unspecified sum towards the cost of schooling. Locally owned companies, particularly in developing countries, rarely provide an educational allowance.

MAINTAINING CONTINUITY

One factor that must be considered at the outset is that few organisations can be relied upon to give any help with school fees once the assignment abroad has been completed. On return to the UK many parents may find it difficult to finance boarding school fees from a lower, and often more heavily taxed, personal income. However, it can be disruptive to move your children from one school to another and particularly inadvisable at a sensitive stage in their schooling when they have begun a GCSE or A-level course. On the other hand, if you have chosen a school abroad with a curriculum that bears little or no resemblance to that followed in the UK, your child may find it hard to cover lost ground. When selecting a school it is crucial to look ahead and to make plans which will serve your child's best interest when your overseas contract comes to an end.

Most schools will go to considerable trouble to make arrangements to see prospective parents, often at short notice. Where possible take your child with you when you visit a school and listen to his or her comments. Whatever your personal feelings about education, it is essential that those of your child are fully respected. Many children have sensible views about what is best for their own development and, where necessary, they should be persuaded rather than instructed.

Your child may be eager to make the transition from state to private school and adapt well to a new environment. However, you should be aware that moving back to the state system can be difficult for ex-independent school pupils. These difficulties can also be encountered by children returning to a local school routine after the cultural diversity of an international educational environment.

The major problem for most children of expatriates is the lack of educational continuity, particularly when they are obliged to move from country to country, and school to school, every few years. If your child is to realise his or her potential you must try to provide educational stability. Much can be done to ease the process of transition by providing a new school with a detailed profile of your child. Reports, syllabus information, titles of books which he or she has been using and levels of attainment can enable a teacher to assist your child to settle happily into life in a new school with the minimum of disruption.

CONTINUED SCHOOLING IN THE UK

Many parents find it difficult to decide whether to send their child to a day or boarding school. For parents who are working overseas boarding is an obvious choice. Indeed, some parents may opt for a job abroad in order to finance their children's education at a boarding school.

How to find a boarding school

Selecting the most appropriate school for your child can be a time-consuming and confusing process, but there are several organisations to help you make your choice.

The Independent Schools Information Service (ISIS), Grosvenor Gardens House, 35–37 Grosvenor Gardens, London SW1W 0BS (tel: 020 7798 1560, website: www.isis.org.uk) produces a number of helpful publications including *Choosing Your Independent School* (£12.95 including postage and packing). They also offer a comprehensive placement service (£350 + VAT), with reductions for siblings, and a consultancy service, which consists of an interview at the London office (£100 + VAT) or a telephone interview (£40 + VAT). A clearing house service is available to provide a shortlist of suitable schools, at a charge of £30 + VAT.

Advice is also available free of charge from Gabbitas Educational Consultants Ltd, Carrington House, 126–130 Regent Street, London W1B 5EE (tel: 020 7734 0161, fax: 020 7437 1764, website: www.gabbitas.co.uk). Gabbitas invite parents to tell them as much as possible about their child, their circumstances and the type of school they are looking for. On the basis of this information they are able to recommend a selection of suitable schools from a wide range of independent boarding and day schools. Shortlisted schools are asked to send parents a prospectus. It is then up to the parents to visit the schools personally. There is no charge for this service. Gabbitas also offer detailed guidance on education at all levels (a fee of £135 + VAT per hour is charged for such consultations).

Experienced consultants deal with a range of educational issues, including options at 16+ and planning for higher education and career opportunities.

How to choose a boarding school

Having shortlisted several schools, either with or without the guidance of a professional organisation, parents are well advised to read the prospectus through carefully, and to prepare a checklist of questions in readiness for a visit to a school.

Many of the factors governing choice are self-evident and conclusions will be arrived at quickly. Access to an international airport, proximity to relatives, religious denomination, co-educational or single-sex, the academic aims of the school and the scale of fees are points which all parents will need to consider. Also important are:

- [ ] the academic record of the school;
- [ ] the qualifications and approach of the teaching staff;
- [ ] the staff/pupil ratio;
- [ ] the physical environment;
- [ ] the attitude to discipline;
- [ ] the quality of sports education;
- [ ] the range of information technology;
- [ ] the range of extra-curricular activities;
- [ ] the quality of pastoral care;
- [ ] costs;
- [ ] the numbers in the sixth form;
- [ ] the quality of careers counselling;
- [ ] contact with parents;
- [ ] the house system;
- [ ] school publications;
- [ ] references.

Entrance examination

To be admitted to an independent secondary school your child will normally be required to pass the school's entrance test or the Common Entrance examination, which is set for candidates of 11+, 12+ and 13+ (the appropriate examination is normally determined by the child's age on 1 September in the year of entry).

☐   At 11+ the subjects examined are English, mathematics, science and reasoning. Examinations take place in January and November.
☐   At 12+ candidates sit papers in English, mathematics, science and French (written and oral). Latin may be offered as an optional paper. Examinations take place in February/March and November.
☐   At 13+ the papers are English, mathematics, science, French (written and oral), history, geography and religious studies. English as an additional language, German, Spanish, Latin and Greek may be offered as optional papers. Examinations take place in February/March, June (for most candidates) and November. Candidates for boys' schools most commonly take the 13+ examination.

Each senior school sets its own entrance standards and is responsible for the assessment of papers. Some schools require candidates to sit their own independent examinations in addition, or as an alternative, to Common Entrance. The examinations are normally taken at the candidate's own school.

Children applying to boarding schools from abroad or from state schools will be in direct competition with those who have been tutored for the entrance examinations at UK prep schools. Many schools will take this fact into consideration when making their assessments. However, in some cases it may be necessary to arrange individual coaching in advance of the examination. Consultancy and assessment, as well as tuition, are available from members of the Association of Tutors, Sunnycroft, 63 King Edward Road, Northampton NN1 5LY; tel: 01604 624171. Supportive tuition or complete coverage can be provided for primary and secondary work, as well as some university-level work. Some services are available on a distance basis, and some as intensive, holiday-period schemes. Examination advice and preparation for particular exams, like the Common Entrance, is a particular expertise.

The syllabuses for each subject, and the examination papers, are set by the Independent Schools Examinations Board. Copies of syllabuses, past papers and information are available from: The Independent Schools Examinations Board, Jordan House, Christchurch Road, New Milton, Hants BH25 6QJ; tel: 01425 621111, fax: 01425 620044.

Scholarships

Many independent schools offer entrance scholarships to children of outstanding ability or potential. These may be based either on general academic standard or on particular strengths, notably musical, sporting or artistic. Individual schools will supply details on request.

A number of schools offer bursaries for means-tested families. Others make specific awards to the children of clergy and service families.

ISIS runs an advisory service on scholarships and bursaries for parents seeking general advice.

Insurance and financial planning

A growing number of financial service groups and independent financial advisers are able to offer school fee plans, with obvious benefits for those who are able to plan and save well in advance. For those with a more immediate requirement, loan schemes, both equity and non-equity based, are available. ISIS produce a useful leaflet called *School Fees*.

Many schools cooperate with insurance companies in schemes for the remission of school fees during unavoidable absence through illness. Other policies are available that guarantee the continued payment of fees in the event of a parent's death, disablement or redundancy before the completion of schooling.

Maintained boarding schools

Some local authorities run their own boarding schools or offer boarding facilities alongside day schools. Eighteen of these maintained schools have opted out and are now grant maintained (grant maintained schools have been given a new status under government plans but this should not affect the education provided). Although any child with a legal right to attend school in Britain may seek entry to any maintained school, some authorities give priority to local children, even for boarding places. As tuition is free at these schools and parents pay only for boarding, the overall costs are approximately a half to two-thirds of the cost of an independent school. Many pupils are from service families, or have parents who work for banks or government agencies abroad.

The Guide to Accredited Independent Boarding Schools in the UK is published by the Boarding Schools Association. Copies may be obtained from them at 35–37 Grosvenor Gardens, London SW1W 0BS, tel: 020 7798 1580, fax: 020 7798 1581, e-mail: bsa@iscis.uk.net, website: www.boarding.org.uk or from the DfEE Publications Centre, PO Box 5050, Sudbury, Suffolk CO10 6ZQ (tel: 084560 22260, fax: 0845 6033360, website: www.dfee.gov.uk).

Local authority grants

Some education authorities are prepared to give grants to assist with boarding school fees when both parents are abroad and there are no places available in a state boarding school. Application should be made to the director of education or chief education officer for the area in the UK in which the family is normally resident.

Arrangements for your child

A boarding school accepts responsibility for the day-to-day welfare of its pupils in term-time, but overseas parents will naturally want assurance that their child is being cared for at all times, including short holiday periods and occasions when they may be in transit between school and home. There are a number of organisations that care for children in these circumstances.

Child supervision

Some boarding schools are able to send a school bus or driver to collect children from, and deliver them to, the nearest airport. Where this service is not available parents may wish to use a commercial escort service.

☐ Universal Aunts Ltd, PO Box 304, London SW4 0NN (tel: 020 7738 8937) can arrange for children to be taken to and from school according to parents' instructions. They try to allot the same 'aunt' to a child so that a warm relationship is established. When required to do so they can also arrange for children to be accommodated for the night in the home of one of the aunts. Holiday accommodation is also available.

☐ Corona Worldwide, c/o The Commonwealth Institute, Kensington High Street, London W8 6NQ (tel/fax: 020 7610 4407) provide a dependants' (adults and children) escort service for members.

Finding a guardian

Most boarding schools require parents to appoint a local guardian for their child. Several organisations are able to offer a guardianship service for parents who do not wish to impose upon relations or family friends.

Guardianship schemes have developed in response to demands from parents and schools to cover welfare, education and finance. They are provided by, for example, the following organisations:

☐ Clarendon International Education, 41 Clarendon Square, Royal Leamington Spa, Warwickshire CV32 5QZ (tel: 01926 316793, fax: 01926 883278, www.clarendon.uk.com).

☐ Guardians and Tutors, 131 Pomphlett Road, Plymstock, Plymouth PL6 7BU (tel: 01752 401942).

☐ Gabbitas Educational Consultants Ltd (www.gabbitas.co.uk) run a comprehensive guardianship service which takes care of all aspects of education, welfare and finance.

☐ Joanella Slattery Associates (JSA), Gilpin, Station Road, Withyham, Hartfield, East Sussex TN7 4BT (tel: 01892 770585/ 0850 943106; fax: 01892 770120, e-mail: joanella@sol.com, website: www.cea.co.uk).

☐ GJW Education Services, Southcote, Coreway, Sidmouth EX10 9SD (tel: 01395 512300; fax: 01395 577271; e-mail: gjweaver@netcomuk.co.uk).

Day schools in the UK

If you feel that your child is unsuited to boarding school life, or that it would be too disruptive to move schools – for example, during the GCSE years – you may wish to consider a day place. Where relatives and friends are available to care for your child this arrangement can work smoothly, particularly when a child continues at his or her present school. Many older children are reluctant to leave their friends and interests behind, and are able to respond positively to a new degree of independence.

In some cases, where there are no relatives or friends to rely on and parents wish to avoid placing their child in lodgings, mothers stay behind with their children. Although this offers the child continuity it can cause strains in the marital relationship and may offset the financial benefits of the posting.

Few employers offer more than a token allowance for lodging if your child remains at a day school in the UK.

SCHOOLS ABROAD

Neill Ransom, Chelstoke International

Expatriate schools

Unlike other nations such as France, Germany, Japan, Switzerland or the United States, Britain provides no financial assistance for the creation and management of schools for British expatriates. This means that British parents moving abroad must expect to pay substantial school fees unless they choose to send their children to local national schools.

British schools

There is a large and increasing number of 'British' schools operating in many countries of the world, the majority based in the major cities, which attract large numbers of international companies and diplomatic services.

Most of these follow the British National Curriculum (beware – as there are many similarly termed 'National Curricula'). However, also beware – in many countries one can also find 'British school' used as a name for local private schools, which provide an 'old style' English school curriculum but are populated almost entirely by local national children.

While most British schools abroad are not 'government' approved or registered and as independent organisations are not subject to Ofsted inspection, the majority of the most successful and best performing British schools nevertheless undertake inspections or take part in recognised accreditation schemes.

There are various groups of British schools, either relating to membership of an association, such as the British Schools of the Middle East (BSME – see www.bsme.uk) or group ownership, such as the British Schools of America (currently comprising the British Schools of Washington, Boston, Chicago, Houston and Charlotte – see www.britishschools.org). The latter were set up as a direct response to British companies and staff relocating abroad and expressing concern that local schools (even where the language was similar) did not prepare their children for the British National Curriculum and any return home. Similarly, a number of British schools, for example in Eastern Europe, are currently operated by Nord Anglia, a listed UK company. In Hong Kong the well-established English Schools Foundation (www.esf.ed.hk) operates a number of high quality primary and secondary schools and is somewhat similar to an independent LEA (Local Education Authority).

One of the best established groups, comprising individual British International Schools, is COBISEC (The Council of British Independent Schools in the European Community), comprising 35 members and 28 affiliates, from 36 countries. This group is uniquely recognised by the DfES and their teachers can join the UK teachers superannuation scheme. COBISEC has recently agreed to act jointly with FOBISSEA (The Federation of British International Schools in South and East Asia). The respective websites are www.cobisec.org and www.fobissea.org.

A small number of British schools abroad are affiliated to UK professional associations including HMC (the Headmasters' and Headmistresses' Conference, GSA (the Girls' Schools Association) and NAHT (the National Association of Headteachers). These and other links allow headteachers and staff to keep abreast of UK educational developments.

The European Schools

Starting with the first European School established in Luxembourg in 1953, there are now 12 European Schools situated in Luxembourg, Belgium (Brussels I, Brussels II, Brussels III and MoI), Germany (Karlsruhe, Munich and Frankfurt), Italy (Varese), The Netherlands (Bergen), the UK (Culham, near Oxford) and Spain (Alicante).

Linked to and supported by the European Commission, this network of schools enjoys government and Community support. A particular feature of the education provided is the European Baccalaureate, specially established for this group of schools.

US schools

US schools offer a US curriculum, but may be an option for British children because the language of instruction is English. It is important to remember that the educational approach will be quite different and that pupils will be prepared for US examinations at college entry level, such as the Standard Achievement Tests (SATs). To graduate from a US school a certain number of credits are required. Credit courses in the final two years of schooling may include Honours and Advanced Placement Sections which provide able students with special challenges. British universities are familiar with the entrance requirements of leading US universities and set similar entry requirements for applicants from US-style schools.

International schools

International schools are established in most capital cities of the world. They may be distinguished by the fact that they are independent of any state system and aim to educate children from a variety of nationalities.

Many are outstanding, offering intellectual pluralism and exceptional cultural variety – typically 50 to 60 different nationalities are represented in the student body. Some are members of international associations such as the United World Colleges and the European Council of International Schools (ECIS), others have headteachers in membership of the (British-based) Headmasters' and Headmistresses' Conference or the Girls' Schools Association.

In many respects they are as varied as their locations – large or small, monolingual, bilingual (using a foreign language as a medium of instruction for some subjects) or even multilingual (using more than one foreign language as a medium of instruction), traditional or emphatically modern. Some are subsidised by local governments, others are among the most costly schools in the world. Almost all are co-educational, and in the majority the language of instruction is English.

Curriculum options

International schools may follow a standard US college preparatory programme or a standard GCSE or International GCSE (IGCSE) programme, or a combination of these. Although a number of schools also work towards national examinations such as the German Abitur or the Spanish Bachillerato, at sixth-form level many are now preparing for the diploma of the International Baccalaureate Organisation (IBO).

A few years ago, the choice of curriculum at international schools was between a US 'international' curriculum and a British 'international' curriculum. However, there is now a range of specially designed international curriculum options available, the majority of which are well established, well supported and recognised internationally. The curriculum offered can often be a determining factor in choice of school – at least where the luxury of choice exists.

The highly successful International Baccalaureate (IB) for post-16 students has led to the development of both the MYP (Middle Years Programme) and the PYP (Primary Years Programme) also administered and accredited by the International Baccalaureate Organisation (IBO) from its headquarters and offices in Geneva and Cardiff. The PYP followed by the MYP are thematic skills-based curricula, designed to lead students through to the IB and as such are gaining popularity in increasing numbers of International Schools – details on the IBO website at www.ibo.org.

The other well-established alternative at primary level is the IPC (International Primary Curriculum). This was originally developed by Fieldwork (www.fieldworkeducation.co.uk) for the worldwide Shell Group of International Schools and its success and credibility had led to its being taken up by many successful International Schools. The IPC is operated by Fieldwork Education Services (see www.internationalprimary curriculum.com), which is now a division of World Class Learning Schools & Systems Group (www.greatlearning.com).

The alternative – and somewhat less international – option at secondary level is those schools that follow a curriculum leading to the IGCSE (International General Certificate of Secondary Education), which is a derivative of the UK GCSE.

For post-16 students, the International Baccalaureate (IB) is based on a two-year curriculum that maintains a balance between the sciences, the arts and languages. The programme is broader than A-levels as all students must offer one subject from each of six groups:

- Language A (first language)
- Language B (second language)
- Individuals and societies
- Experimental sciences
- Mathematics
- Electives (including art, music, IT).

Of the six subjects studied, three are taken at Higher level, and three at Standard level. This represents a deliberate compromise between the European emphasis on breadth and the British tradition of rigorous specialisation. In effect students offer three subjects to A-level equivalent standard and three subjects to a standard somewhat above GCSE. To be eligible for the award of the Diploma candidates must score a minimum of points and meet three additional requirements: submission of an extended essay; satisfactory completion of a Theory of Knowledge Course; and compulsory participation in a CAS programme (Creativity, Action, Service).

Students holding the IB Diploma have entered more than 700 universities throughout the world. All UK universities accept the IB as satisfying their general requirement for entrance. For further information contact: The International Baccalaureate Organisation, Curriculum and Assessment Centre, Peterson House, Malthouse Avenue, Cardiff Gate, Cardiff CF23 8GL (tel: 02920 547 777, fax: 02920 547 778, website: www.ibo.org).

Another worldwide school-leaving certificate, which has been available to English-medium schools throughout the world since 1986, is the Advanced Intermediate Certificate of Education (AICE). AICE is a 'group' certificate which is awarded on the basis of a broad and balanced curriculum of five full-credit courses or their equivalent. All candidates must take at least one course from three subject groups: mathematics and sciences; languages; and arts and humanities. The AICE curriculum, which is designed to be of worldwide relevance, offers a high degree of flexibility. As there are no compulsory subjects, student programmes may range from the highly specialised to the general. Most UK universities now accept AICE as an alternative to A-levels. AICE is administered by the University of Cambridge Local Examinations Syndicate (UCLES), 1 Hills Road, Cambridge CB1 2EU (tel: 01223 553311, fax: 01223 460278, website: www.ucles.org.uk).

Special Educational Needs

If your child has Special Educational Needs (SEN), then it is very important to check in detail with likely schools as very many international schools are not able to provide relevant and sufficient support for such students. This is because the support facilities and back-up agencies we rely on in the UK often do not exist abroad. It is therefore important to discuss things in detail with any possible school, so there can be no misunderstanding.

How to find an overseas school

Finding out what schools are available abroad in specific countries and cities can be done via two main routes.

The first is via the internet, where a majority of schools – especially successful international schools of every type – maintain a website presence. Indeed many of the websites are extremely professional and give enormous insight into the life of the school. A search for schools and city/country or international schools, etc will invariably bring up some options.

However, a second and perhaps more inclusive start will be via those organisations that exist to support and advise on international schools and education abroad. The most comprehensive and best established is ECIS (European Council of International Schools), in itself a misleading name as it has now expanded to include membership schools in most countries of the world. The success of ECIS has led to the founding of a sister organisation – CIS (Council of International Schools) which, as a service organisation, deals with the regular accreditation of international schools and headteacher and staff recruitment, in parallel with ECIS which is the membership organisation for conferences and professional support and development. Websites (www.ecis.org and www.cois.org) give full details. The membership list of ECIS/CIS in their annual *International Schools Directory* is the most comprehensive list of international schools available, with the advantage of showing which are fully accredited, or in earlier stages of membership such as affiliate members. The directory is available from John Catt Educational at www.johncatt.com with an online version via the ECIS website.

Various other websites and groups give information and lists of schools, but very few are totally comprehensive and it is unclear what is being missed.

How to choose a school abroad

Depending on the city or country and its standing as a centre of international trade or diplomatic missions, there will be a degree of choice available. In smaller, developing countries, there may be only one or two appropriate schools. In the more established international cities there will be a range of schools catering for differing national and international curricula and providing healthy competition and choice. There will often also be a number of smaller private schools with names suggesting they are British or similar, when in fact they cater predominantly for local nationals. It is thus important to discover how established and successful a school is. The first step is to check whether it has

Accredited status – ideally from ECIS and associate organisations, or for example as an IBO accredited school.

Information from company HR departments and other colleagues may be useful, but the needs of your children and your aspirations for them may be very different. There is no substitute for actually seeing and visiting a school, to really gain a feel of its ethos and atmosphere and meet the headteacher and key staff.

For senior executives, many international companies provide the services of an educational relocation specialist as part of their HR relocation support – often using Education Relocation Associates (ERA) (www.erauk.demon.co.uk), whose contact in Egham, Surrey is via rowena@erauk.demon.co.uk. ERA can provide a similar service advising on school placements to individual families, suggesting schools available, advising on their standing and in certain cases arranging visits and providing a specialist consultant/adviser.

Preparation is important to get the most from any school visit, or seek answers to key questions. The list below may be a helpful starter:

1. Many employers pay for families to visit the country before their projected move. This gives them the opportunity to visit the available schools (it is useful to obtain prospectuses beforehand) in person, and to consider the alternatives with existing expatriate parents and organised parents' groups which are attached to the schools. However, it is important to remember that other people may have standards which do not correspond to your own.

    In many instances expatriate schools become both a community and a social centre for expatriate families. This can be a great help for incoming families.
2. It is advisable to link house-hunting with the choice of school so that transportation problems can be considered in advance.
3. By their nature, with families being moved by companies as their agreed contract period finishes, international schools experience a steady turnover of pupils – often with 25 to 30 per cent a year moving. Similarly there will be staff turnover, as two- and three-year contracts are often the norm. The best international schools will have strategies to minimise this potential disruption – so ask the question.
4. It is important to establish how schools overseas are controlled. Many schools are run by boards composed of leading figures

from the local community, including representatives from the parent body and the organisations which use the school. The latter may be relied upon to ensure that the facilities available to their employees are of a high standard.

5. Every effort should be made to meet the headteacher, who is responsible for the quality and organisation of the school. He or she will be able to tell you whether there is a waiting list for admission to the school and when you need to register your child. In some instances the waiting time for admission can be a full academic year. Other schools may be ready to accept pupils at almost any time.

6. Take time to consider the curriculum. How far does it correspond to the National Curriculum in the UK? How straightforward will it be for your child to transfer back to the UK? Try to establish how much support, both pastoral and academic, is provided for individual children, to enable them to cope with the process of transition.

7. It is important to consider the type of report and record-keeping system which is in operation in the school. How much information will be available as a record of your child's achievement at the school? Pupil profiles are particularly essential for children who move from school to school frequently.

8. The language of instruction will be of key importance to your child. Find out what kind of English is used – whether it is American, British or non-mother-tongue English. How many children and staff do not have English as a first language? Are they likely to hinder your child's progress?

9. Expatriate schools are geared to accept pupils at any stage during the school year. However, the process of transition is generally easier when pupils begin school at the start of a new term.

10. If your company does not offer an educational allowance, or pay school fees – which is increasingly the case – then your homework needs to include fee levels. School fees tend to vary with age, with secondary and post-16, where subject specialisms increase, attracting the highest fees. In London these can be up to £16,000 for the more expensive day school fees; across Europe the fee can be €16,000 or more. While the fee may be payable in local currency, many schools operate in the more stable currencies of pounds sterling or US dollars and so exchange rate fluctuation may be a consideration. In addition to the tuition fees, it is common practice to charge a

one-off registration fee and also an initial building or development fee – the latter put towards new development or buildings either planned or recently completed.

Company-sponsored schools

In more remote countries or areas where initial development is occurring, such as new oil or gas fields, there may be no schools available. In such cases some companies will sponsor and develop a school. The trend, however, is to bring in specialist operators to operate the school on their behalf. The original worldwide network of Shell Schools, for example, is now supported and, for many aspects managed, by Fieldwork Educational Services (www. fieldworkeducation.co.uk).

Local national schools

Within Europe there are significant advantages to be gained in sending your child to a local national school, not least an opportunity to acquire proficiency in another language and to absorb a new culture. Although the standard of educational provision may vary there is no doubt that in some countries, such as France and Germany, it is excellent. However, a complete immersion in another language and culture is demanding and it will depend very much on the age and ability of the children as to how successfully they can adapt.

Learning the full range of school subjects in a new language can be exacting, particularly where no provision is made for extra language tuition. Parents who do not speak the necessary language themselves must remember that they will be able to offer little advice and assistance to their child, who may feel isolated as a result.

For those on short-term contracts it is important to consider how well such a schooling will prepare children for the next stage in a UK education. Certainly, a child working towards GCSE examinations could expect to be disadvantaged. The experience may also pose difficulties for younger children returning to the UK.

Transfer into and out of school systems in other parts of the world can also pose problems. Traditional teaching methods which rely on rote learning are still applied in many developing countries, where schools are frequently ill-equipped and crowded. As education is so highly prized as a route out of poverty, expatriates will not be encouraged to supplant a local child. However, where no alternative exists, parents may need to compensate for a restricted curriculum by providing supplementary lessons at home.

Differences in attitudes to schooling are particularly marked in countries where religious and political beliefs have shaped the curriculum. Even in other parts of the English-speaking world there are fundamental differences in approach. For example, in Australia formal schooling starts at 6 and secondary education at 12.

This section has been edited and revised by Neill Ransom, Chelstoke International (tel: 07860 212109, e-mail: neill@chelstokeinternational.com).

Checklist: Your children's education

1. Consider the options in relation to your child's age, ability and personality, and in relation to the quality of education in your new location.
2. Consider whether your organisation will contribute towards your child's education.
3. Does your host country's education system bear any resemblance to your native country's?
4. If you are considering using the independent sector, what are the financial implications, particularly when you return from your assignment?
5. If your child is to go to boarding school, what arrangements can be made for a local guardian?
6. What are the local alternatives and can you speak to other expat parents to find out what educational facilities are like in your new location?
7. Are the qualifications offered by your local national or international schools compatible with your domestic ones?
8. Can you team up with other expat families to provide a home teaching group?
9. If not, will your company provide support in setting up a company school?
10. If your child has special needs, contact support agencies for advice.

8 Health, Security and Welfare

HEALTH RISKS

Whether you are relocating to a new country by yourself or with your family, one of the most important pre-trip considerations is what health hazards might be encountered in your host country. You might feel that developed countries might not represent too many risks to a visitor. However, it is always advisable to seek expert advice, regardless of your destination. This advice should include information not only about local health risks but also about the health service and access to medical care in your host country. While the emphasis is on developing countries, travellers should also be aware that risks in non-Third World countries are still prevalent, for example the hepatitis virus in areas of Turkey, and a recent outbreak of diphtheria in Russia.

A useful book that can be thoroughly recommended is *Travellers' Health* by Dr Richard Dawood (published by Oxford University Press). This provides detailed information and guidance on every conceivable medical area and is essential reading before departure.

The risks to children will also need to be identified. Some illnesses, such as gastroenteritis, present a far greater risk to children than to adults and it is essential that you arm yourself with information concerning symptoms and medical treatment, such as the administration of a fluid-replacement solution. You will also need to make sure that your child's immunisations are up to date and to identify any specific vaccines that may be required. Seek advice for babies under six months who are not able to have these immunisations.

Specialist organisations

Good general advice on health preparations before departure is available from the website of the Medical Advisory Service for Travellers Abroad (MASTA) at www.masta.org and is shown below:

☐ Make sure you are up to date with your immunisations such as tetanus and polio, and check which others you might need for your destination.

☐ Allow 6–8 weeks to undergo a full course of immunisation.

☐ Malaria tablets should be taken 1 week before entering a malaria area or 2–3 weeks before if taking Mefloquine.

☐ Find out what your blood group is to ensure prompt treatment in an emergency.

☐ Find out how you can contact emergency services in your new location.

☐ If you are taking medication, make sure that you have adequate supplies and make a note of the medicines you are taking and the dosage to inform a doctor in an emergency.

☐ Do not take any drugs to a Third World or developing country unless they are prescribed and labelled.

☐ Keep a record of your medical history and briefly note down the relevant details of treatment and medication.

☐ Note down any pills or medicine to which you are allergic.

MASTA also offers health briefs on 230 countries. Information can be obtained direct from MASTA on 0113 238 7575, and from their Traveller's Health Line on 0906 8224100 (charged at 60p per minute). A particular feature is a personalised health brief, combining a personal medical check-up with very up-to-date information on the country (or combination of countries) to be visited, from the MASTA database, which covers more than 250 countries and includes the latest data from the Foreign Office. Central billing for companies can be arranged to cover all their employees who travel abroad. One MASTA service particularly geared to the intending expatriate is a detailed health brief and an extensive individual health report on the country concerned.

Other organisations specialising in travel medicine are as follows:

☐ The Malaria Reference Laboratory at the London School of Hygiene and Tropical Medicine, which runs a helpline on 09065 508908 (charged at £1 per minute).

THE AXA
"What if I get back pain in Bahrain?" PLAN.

International Health Insurance from **AXA PPP healthcare.** Get the cover that's right for you. Call **+44(0)1892 508791** quoting reference WA2006

BUPA International –
The World Health Service

As part of the British owned BUPA Group which has been trading since 1947 and has operations in seven other countries, BUPA International who are based in Brighton, are the largest international expatriate health insurance provider in the world. It has nearly 650,000 members of 115 nationalities in over 190 countries from local communities, businesses and expatriates, who all put their trust in BUPA. They provide a wide range of flexible, high quality global health insurance options for groups and individuals living in their home country or living or working overseas for six months or more.

Depending on the member's requirements, BUPA International's schemes – Lifeline for individuals and Company schemes for 3 or more members, offer flexible benefits including primary care, maternity cover, home nursing, routine and emergency dentistry, as well as hospital treatment and accommodation, health checks, cover for chronic conditions, emergency road ambulance and cover for sports injuries.

It is essential to know that you are covered by the world's largest international expatriate health care provider as there is so much to think about when you're moving abroad that it's easy to feel overwhelmed. People who are looking to live overseas need support and guidance not only on practical arrangements such as learning the language and finding accommodation, but advice on local medical facilities and what to do if they have a medical emergency.

Safeguarding your health is one of the key decisions you must make when considering moving overseas. Getting ill abroad can be no joke. International health insurance can provide you and your family with the reassurance about your health and care. It is important you know that you are fully covered no matter where you are.

According to the Office of National Statistics around 200,000 Britons leave these shores every year to live abroad, and the growth in the expatriate population means that the international health insurance market is expanding.

Generally people are looking for a fast and efficient service, access to the healthcare facilities they need, when they need them, and at the right price.

Research at BUPA International has shown that peace of mind wins when choosing a provider. While price is a determining factor, quality of service, comprehensive coverage and the reputation and experience of the insurer is more important in terms of retaining customers.

But with so many policies available it can be difficult to know which is the most appropriate one for you. So – consider the experiences of those people who have already made the move to relocate to another country. Their advice can be invaluable.

If taking out international health insurance, make sure you choose a scheme that suits your needs, circumstances and budget and an insurer that can offer you advice and support on medical facilities and advice on referrals for treatment.

Being abroad can bring its health challenges. You should consider whether you would like to be covered for emergency evacuation and repatriation. If you travel a great deal, or live in some less developed parts of the world, it is vital that you have evacuation and repatriation cover so that you can get to the nearest centre of medical excellence to receive the treatment you need and find out what your rights are if you want to return home for treatment.

It is also important that an expatriate knows where to go for advice and information about local healthcare arrangements. Look for an insurer that offers a multi-lingual telephone advice line 24-hours a day, 365 days a year, which can answer questions about things like inoculation information, visa requirements, medical service referral and legal and embassy referral.

To safely move abroad getting appropriate medical arrangements in place must be a priority. Private medical insurance offers people peace of mind and the security and confidence to enjoy life overseas.

For more information about BUPA International's insurance policies go to
www.bupa-intl.com

☐ The Travel Clinic, Hospital for Tropical Diseases, 4 St Pancras Way, London NW1 0PE, which offers preventative advice and has an extensive range of health products and immunisations available. For information, call their Healthline on 0839 337733 to make an appointment, telephone 020 7388 9600.

☐ Only two British Airways Travel Clinics are to be found now, both in London. For details and to book appointments, call 0845 600 2236. Details are also available on the British Airways website: www.british-airways.com. The clinics offer a one-stop service, providing immunisation, health protection items such as mosquito nets and water purification tablets, and anti-malarial tablets. The British Airways Travel Clinics are affiliated to the Geneva-based international charity the Bloodcare Foundation, which can send screened and tested blood worldwide. Cover is available for individuals or families, or for a company, on a monthly or yearly basis.

There is, however, one major international health hazard that has come to the fore since earlier editions of this book: the problem of acquired immune deficiency syndrome (AIDS). It has reached epidemic proportions in some parts of Africa and other developing countries. It is no longer sufficient to warn expatriates against the dangers of promiscuity. People can become infected through transfusions of infected blood or treatment with instruments that have not been properly sterilised. Expatriates are now advised to contact the local British embassy or high commission, which keeps a register of reliable blood donors among the expatriate community. It is also inadvisable in many countries to attend local doctors' or dentists' clinics unless they are known to enforce the highest standards of hygiene. Medical kits should also be top of the packing list. Organisations such as MASTA can advise on the appropriate contents.

Those working in Saudi Arabia should note that they will have to produce a doctor's certificate to show that they are HIV negative. It has been pointed out that this can raise problems when applying for medical insurance. Even the answer 'yes' to the question 'Have you ever been HIV tested?' can raise the suspicion that your lifestyle exposes you to the risk of AIDS. Thus, if you have been HIV tested in connection with an assignment to Saudi Arabia, you should point this out if the question arises on a medical insurance form.

An extremely useful leaflet, *Travellers Guide to Health*, which covers prevention and planning, emergency care and international health care agreements, and contains a copy of form E111 for free or reduced-cost emergency medical treatment in most European countries, can be obtained from your GP, or through the Health Literature Line on 0800 555 777. A comprehensive guide is available in the form of *Health Information for Overseas Travel* (published by The Stationery Office, £7.95, tel: 0870 6005522, website: www.tsonline.co.uk). This detailed work is primarily intended for reference by GPs, but serious travellers will find it most useful, as it provides a thorough guide to disease risk, immunisation and other hazards, as well as child-specific information.

EXPATRIATE MEDICAL INSURANCE

Most of the countries that expatriates go to do not operate a national health service like that of the UK. It comes as something of a shock to find oneself paying £100 or more for a routine visit to a doctor or dentist and the costs of hospitalisation can be such as to wipe out the savings of months, or even years. In places like the EU, South Africa, Australia or other developed Commonwealth countries there are established local methods of medical insurance, and in many cases the cost of this is included in the remuneration package. If not, it is certainly a matter which should be clarified while you are negotiating the job offer.

Some OPEC and similar resource-rich countries do have state medical schemes, and as a matter of fact their hospitals are, in many cases, better equipped than our relatively rundown institutions. They are, however, established primarily for the benefit of local nationals, which means that the customs and culture of medical care are different from those which most westerners are used to. For this reason, most expatriates in those countries arrange for attention in private hospitals which, needless to say, tends to be very expensive indeed. Medical insurance for anyone going to these places is therefore essential, and a number of plans have now been developed specifically for expatriates by AXA PPP healthcare, BUPA International and others. The health insurance business is fiercely competitive; if you are paying your own insurance you should ask your broker for a complete list of all the plans that are available, so that you can compare them in detail. You will need to establish whether quoted premiums include or exclude insurance premium tax and how long companies take to settle claims. You will also want

When you are considering buying any insurance policy it is always important to bear in mind what you are covered for and if you have specific requirements or considerations.

Alongside it's International Health Plan, AXA PPP healthcare has relationships with partner companies in Europe and the Middle East.

If you are thinking of, or currently live or work in, Malta, Cyprus, Bahrain, UAE or Saudi Arabia you can benefit from unique, tailor-made, health plans which have been established with our partners in these countries to meet local healthcare needs.

Atlas Insurance agency is Malta's largest agency operation and its roots go back 100 years as one of the first agencies in Malta for a a major British insurance company. The company is a product of a merger between 3 major British general insurance agencies and more recently AXA Insurance. Atlas has now created a specialist agency for healthcare, Atlas Healthcare Insurance Agency Limited and has been selling a range of PMI products for AXA PPP healthcare since its appointment in May 2000.
Atlas Insurance Agency Ltd
Ms Claudine Gauci
Health Insurance Department
Abate Rigord Street
Ta'Xbiex, MSD 12, Malta
Telephone: (356) 21 322600

Universal Life has been in partnership with AXA PPP healthcare since 1995 having been established in 1970. t acts as AXA PPP healthcare's partner in Cyprus. It is one of the largest medical insurers on the island having entered the market in 1987.
Universal Life
Mr Stelios Sofroniou
Universal Tower
85 Dhigenis Akritas Avenue
PO Box 21270, 1505 Nicosia, Cyprus
Telephone: 00 357 22 882222

AXA Insurance and AXA PPP healthcare formed a new partnership in the United Arab Emirates in July 2002. Both companies are part of the same leading global group, AXA. With operations in more than 60 countries, the strength of AXA, with AXA PPP healthcare's 65 years of specialist customer care, offers customers both security and expertise.
AXA Insurance E.C.
The Healthcare Manager
PO Box 32505
Dubai, UAE
Telephone: 00971 4 3436161

Gulf Union's relationship dates back to 1998. Gulf Union operates in Saudi Arabia and Bahrain where it is a leading independent composite insurer since being incorporated in 1982.
Gulf Union Insurance and Risk Management Co. (EC)
Mr Roy Samuel
PO Box 5719
Dammam 31432, Saudi Arabia
Telephone: 00966 3 8812070

Gulf Union Insurance & Reinsurance
Mr Roy Samuel
PO Box 10949
Manama, Bahrain
Telephone: 00 973 17 257 018 or 00 973 17 255 292

to check that the plan you choose includes, as do AXA PPP healthcare's and BUPA International's, the typical health services that every expat has come to expect, such as medical evacuation, 24-hour helpline, translation services and arranging for direct payment in nearly every hospital throughout the world.

AXA PPP healthcare is one of the longest established and largest medical insurers in Britain and has nearly 2 million customers worldwide. Its International Health Plan has three different levels of cover, of which the benefits are detailed in Table 8.1:

☐ **Prestige.** A top of the range plan, providing all the benefits of AXA PPP healthcare's comprehensive and standard options but with the addition of routine pregnancy cover, adult health screen, disability compensation cover and annual travel insurance.

☐ **Comprehensive.** As the name suggests, the plan provides comprehensive cover, in-patient, day-patient and out-patient treatment and, in addition, covers non-routine dental treatment.

☐ **Standard.** A plan specifically designed for members who do not require out-patient cover but which offers similar in-patient and day-patient treatment cover to the comprehensive option.

As well as the private healthcare aspect of its plans, AXA PPP healthcare also gives members access to its overseas evacuation or repatriation service, which provides emergency medical advice and assistance worldwide, 24 hours a day, 365 days a year.

All the essential services are, of course, also provided by BUPA International, the largest specialist health insurers for expatriates, with a network of over 5,000 participating hospitals and clinics worldwide. BUPA has nearly 8 million members in 190 countries of 115 nationalities and can pay claims in up to 80 different currencies. BUPA International also offers its members its 'Membersworld' online service available across the range of territories covered.

The benefits available under each of BUPA International's three levels of Lifeline cover are summarised in Table 8.2. Current premium rates, which have changed recently, will be quoted on application.

It is important to be sure that the scheme covers medical attention irrespective of the circumstances that caused it to be necessary. A case has been reported where an expatriate was seriously injured by an assault while at home, only to discover that his medical insurance did not cover injuries sustained outside his workplace. Another point to watch, though it does not strictly

For more than 3 years Dr Charlie Easmon and his team at 1 Harley Street have looked after private individuals, charities and business travellers.

Dr Charlie Easmon, MBBS, MRCP, MSc, Public Health DTM&H, DOccMed, DFPH, trained at St George's. London. He did his elective in Ghana (his country of birth) and has since worked with, among others, Raleigh International and Save the Children in Rwanda, and ECHO in Armenia, Georgia and Azerbaijan.

With the Foreign Office he has visited Egypt, Israel, Tunisia, Japan, Korea, Taiwan and the Philippines.

His route into travel medicine and public health was through medical evacuations, working abroad and stints at the Hospital for Tropical Disease's travel clinic. He enjoyed several years on the board of the British Travel Health Association and is one of the few UK medical practitioners to have obtained the International Certificate in Travel Health from the International Society of Travel Health.

In October 2002 Dr Easmon set up a private service for out-going and in-coming travellers, Travel Screening Services, based at Number One Harley Street.

The business has now re-branded as the Number One Health Group **www.numberonehealth.co.uk**

The Number One Health Group a convenient and easy-to-reach 1 Harley Street location, operate a family of linked services:

Travel Health – safeguarding the health of the travellers, with pre-travel screening and innoculations through to after-travel care.

Health Screens – with at-your-office testing and comprehensive check-ups undertaken in our custom-designed clinic, along with complementary advisory services.

Sexual Health – providing peace of mind through discrete screening and prompt and convenient treatment of sexually transmitted diseases:

Visa Medicals – Full medicals for Australia, New Zealand, Canada, Saudi.

Dr Easmon lectures extensively, has appeared on BBC radio and television, and is widely regarded as one of the UK's leading authorities in travel health.

Our Clients include:
Amec
BSkyB
Rolls-Royce
Rolls-Royce Power Ventures
Barclays
AXA-PPP OHS
Centrica
BP
Heineken
The governments of Australia, New Zealand and Canada
Teknica
International SOS
Norwich Union

Number One
Health Group

Number One
for Travel Health

Number One
for Health Checks

Number One
for Sexual Health

Number One
Harley Street
London W1G 9QD

Number One for all your travel health needs
www.numberonehealth.co.uk

Tel: **0207 307 8756** or **0207 043 0524**
Email: **info@numberonehealth.co.uk**

Adult and child vaccinations

Malaria medication and Travel advice

Returned traveller health checks

Fast, reliable sexual health tests

(HIV, Chlamydia, Syphilis, Gonorrhoea and FULL Sexual Screening)

Standard, Gold and Platinum health checks

Nutrition advice

Fitness and posture counseling

Table 8.1   AXA PPP healthcare – summary benefits table

The three options you can choose from	Prestige	Comprehensive	Standard
Policy benefit limit	Up to £1,250,000 each year	Up to £1,000,000 each year	Up to £750,000 each year
Hospital and accommodation charges	No annual maximum	No annual maximum	No annual maximum
In-patient and day-patient treatment including surgeons', anaesthetists', physicians' and consultants' charges, diagnostic tests and physiotherapy	No annual maximum	No annual maximum	No annual maximum
Out-patient surgical procedures	No annual maximum	No annual maximum	No annual maximum
Radiotherapy, chemotherapy, computerised tomography, magnetic resonance imaging and positron emission tomography (brain and body scanning). Received as an in-patient, day-patient or out-patient	No annual maximum	No annual maximum	No annual maximum
Evacuation or repatriation service	Paid in full	Paid in full	Paid in full
Parent accommodation. Charges for one parent staying with a child member under 18	Paid in full	Paid in full	Paid in full
Outside area of cover. Emergency treatment, or treatment of a medical condition which arises suddenly while outside your area of cover. Limit for USA/Canada	Up to 10 weeks treatment in any year £20,000	Up to six weeks treatment in any year £15,000	Up to six weeks treatment in any year £10,000

Table 8.1 *continued*

The three options you can choose from	Prestige	Comprehensive	Standard
Dental care We will pay up to 50% of the costs incurred. The maximum we will pay in a year is:	Area 1 £600 Area 2 £500 Area 3 £400	Area 1 £400 Area 2 £320 Area 3 £240	Area 1 £400 Area 2 £320 Area 3 £240
Accidental damage to teeth	Up to £10,000 each year	Up to £10,000 each year	Up to £10,000 each year
Cash benefits for each night you receive free in-patient treatment	£100 a night	£100 a night	£100 a night
Ambulance transport for emergency transport to or between hospitals	Up to £500 each year	Up to £500 each year	Up to £500 each year
Health at Hand	Included	Included	Included
Doctor, Dental, Optical Helpline	Included	Included	Included
Interpretation service helpline	Included	Included	Included
The International Travel Plan	Included	Optional	Optional
Out-patient treatment i) Medical practitioner charges for consultations ii) Consultations and treatment for psychiatric illness iii) Complementary practitioner charges iv) Diagnostic tests and physiotherapy v) Travel and childhood vaccinations administered by a medical practitioner	Complementary practitioner charges limited to £300 each year	Complementary practitioner charges limited to £300 each year	
Combined overall limit	£5,000 per year	£3,000 per year	
Excess per visit (applying to i, ii and iii only)	Nil	£20	

Table 8.1 *continued*

The three options you can choose from	Prestige	Comprehensive
Hospital-at-home	Up to 28 days each year	Up to 14 days each year
Out-patient drugs and dressings prescribed by a medical practitioner	Up to £500 each year	Up to £200 each year
Optical cover	Up to £100 each year	Up to £100 each year
Eyesight test cover	Paid in full for one eyesight test each year	Paid in full for one eyesight test each year
Adult health screen	Up to £300 each year towards a health screen for each adult on the policy	These plans provide cover for a period of one year
Disability compensation cover	Up to £50,000	We will of course provide full details of the benefits and terms of membership upon enrolment, or they are available on request
Pregnancy and childbirth (after 10 months cover)	Up to £4,000	

Table 8.2 BUPA summary benefits

Overall annual maximum	Essential	Classic	Gold
£ Sterling	£500,000	£750,000	£1,000,000
$ US Dollar	$900,000	$1,200,000	$1,600,000
€ Euro	€750,000	€1,000,000	€1,500,000
Out-patient treatment			
Out-patient *surgical-operations*	Paid in full	Paid in full	Paid in full
Wellness – mammogram, PAP test, prostate cancer screening or colon cancer screening (after one year's membership)	Not covered	£500/US$900 / €750	£500/US$900 / €750
Consultants' fees for office visits	Not covered	£3,000/ US$4,800/ €4,500	£3,000/ US$4,800/ €4,500
Pathology, X-ray and *diagnostic tests*	Not covered		
Costs for *treatment* by *therapists* and *complementary medicine practitioners*	Not covered		
Consultants' fees and *psychologists'* fees for *psychiatric treatment* (after two years' membership)	Not covered		
Costs for *treatment* by a *family doctor*	Not covered	Not covered	
Prescribed drugs and dressings	Not covered	Not covered	£600/US$960 / €900
Accident-related dental *treatment*	Not covered	Not covered	£400/US$700 / €600
In-patient treatment			
Hospital accommodation	Paid in full	Paid in full	Paid in full
Surgical operations, including pre- and post-operative care			
Nursing care, drugs and surgical dressings			
Physicians' fees			

Table 8.2   *continued*

Overall annual maximum	Essential	Classic	Gold
Theatre charges and *intensive care*	Paid in full	Paid in full	Paid in full
Pathology, X-rays, *diagnostic tests* and physiotherapy			
Prostheses and *appliances*			
Parent accommodation			
Psychiatric treatment (after two years' membership)			
Further benefits			
Cancer *treatment*	Paid in full	Paid in full	Paid in full
Maternity cover (after 10 months membership)	Not covered	£3,000/ US$5,500/ €4,500	£5,000/ US$9,000/ €7,500
MRI, CT and PET scans	Paid in full	Paid in full	Paid in full
Transplant Services			
Local Road Ambulance			
Home nursing after *in-patient treatment*	£100/US$160 / €150 per day up to 10 days	£100/US$160 / €150 per day up to 20 days	£100/US$160 / €150 per day up to 30 days
In-patient cash benefit	£75/US$120/€110 per night up to 20 nights each *membership year*		
HIV/AIDS drug therapy including ART (after five years' membership)	Not covered	£10,000/ US$18,000/ €15,000	£10,000/ US$18,000/ €15,000
Hospice and palliative care	£20,000/US$36,000/€30,000 for the whole of your membership		
Healthline services	Included	Included	Included
Optional benefits (if purchased)			
USA cover	100% of costs in network, 80% out of network		
Assistance cover	Full refund	Full refund	Full refund

speaking come under medical insurance, is personal accident cover and consequential loss of earnings. It is worth checking whether your cover extends to that eventuality.

It is also necessary, when it comes to making claims – and particularly when requesting repatriation for urgent treatment – that the local practitioner should be credible from the point of view of the insurers. It is a good idea to make yourself known to him or her at an early stage after your arrival and to notify your insurers about his or her identity. You should also carry the name of your insurers with you or at least keep it in some convenient place. BUPA International and Integra Global each issues a card which provides a convenient *aide-mémoire*. These carry the policy number and also emergency contact numbers. Most international and other leading health care providers offer 24-hour customer service. An individual does not have to be in a medical emergency; one can call 24 hours a day, 365 days a year, to discuss a claim or membership entitlements or just to ask for advice. This is particularly useful for people moving farther afield, where the time zones may be very different.

Another firm which issues its clients with a card is International SOS Assistance, whose medical and security schemes enable the holder, or those looking after him or her, to call for medical assistance at six main centres throughout the world. They specialise in emergency medical evacuation to the nearest high-quality medical facility, repatriation and return of mortal remains. PPP, BUPA, Goodhealth Worldwide, Expacare, IPH, William Russell, Carecard International and other private insurers use these services. As they point out, it is only of limited use to have cover for repatriation unless it can be implemented easily. GESA Assistance provides a similar service to, among others, Falcon Healthcare.

Catering particularly for the retired expatriate, the Exeter Friendly Society does not automatically increase premium rates with advancing age, making their policies a good buy for the over-50s.

John Wason (Insurance Brokers) Ltd, founded by a former expatriate, offers a specialist 'Overseas Personal Insurance' scheme, which includes optional medical and personal accident/sickness cover worldwide. Levels of cover accord with 'units' purchased.

Finally, there is the possibility of free, or subsidised, local medical care courtesy of a reciprocal agreement with the UK health authorities. The EU and many other countries have such agreements, but the terms do vary. Form E111 is the required paperwork and can be obtained from your GP, or through the Health Literature Line on

0800 555 777. However, this scheme is no substitute for a good insurance policy.

Some of the questions you should ask about your medical cover are as follows:

1. Does the scheme cover all eventualities?
2. Are the scheme's benefits realistic in the light of local costs?
3. Can you make claims immediately or is there an initial indemnity period during which claims are disallowed? (Some insurers insist on this to protect themselves from claims caused by 'pre-existing medical conditions'.)
4. Is there a clause providing for emergency repatriation by air, or air ambulance, if suitable treatment is not available locally? If so, who decides what constitutes an emergency and/or adequate local treatment?
5. Is the insurer's nearest office accessible personally or by telephone?
6. What is the length of the insurer's settlement period for claims?
7. Is there a discount for members of professional or other associations?
8. Does the policy continue to apply, partly or fully, while you are back in the UK?
9. What is the insurer's attitude to AIDS and HIV tests?

PERSONAL SECURITY

There are overseas countries where crimes against persons, either for gain or to make political points, are a serious hazard. Countries where Islamic fundamentalism is rampant are a case in point. Other places, notably in Africa and Latin America, qualify as high-risk locations in terms of personal safety, eg Colombia, Zimbabwe, Brazilian cities and Johannesburg. There are also corporate or national connections that may be the target of terrorists:

☐ Anything to do with Israel. It is still advisable to carry a separate passport if you have a visa for Israel but also travel to the Middle East.
☐ Employees of companies associated with pollution, nuclear waste and animal experiments.
☐ Nationals of countries that have recently been, or are currently, in serious dispute with countries in which an expatriate is living – or even its allies.

Choose your health cover wisely

For people living abroad, quality healthcare isn't a luxury – it's a necessity. State healthcare isn't always available, or may only provide the minimum level of care, and private medical treatment without any insurance cover can be extremely costly. If you're looking for cover for you and your family it can be confusing. It's vital to understand what insurers offer, so here are some points you may wish to consider.

Will they settle my claims directly with the hospital?
Paying up front will leave you out-of-pocket after your medical treatment. To help relieve this inconvenience AXA PPP healthcare has arrangements with over 560 hospitals around the world to settle in-patient bills directly.

Speed of payment
Healthcare providers vary in the length of time they take to pay a claim, so make sure you choose a company that has a good reputation for the efficiency of its claims settlement.

The age factor?
If you're approaching retirement age check with the company that it will be able to cover you, some providers may not accept applicants over 65.

Where you live
If you take out an insurance policy that covers you for treatment whilst in a specific country or geographical area, will your medical bills be paid if you are taken ill elsewhere in the world?

How quickly can you contact your medical provider when you need them most?
Check the opening hours of customer service helplines and whether they are open at the weekends. Can you get in touch with them around the clock, 365 days a year, in case of emergency?

Customer Service Helplines
When you are living or working away from home, you need to know that any queries you have about your cover can be dealt with. Do you, for example,

have access to telephone based interpretation services and facilities to help you find English speaking doctors and dentists locally?

INCLUSIONS AND EXCLUSIONS

Make sure you appreciate the scope of your cover to avoid costly misunderstandings. No insurance policy is designed to cover all eventualities so, before you buy your medical insurance policy, have you thought about:

- Being able to pre-authorise your treatment before it commences so you can be assured of your cover and, in some cases, arrange for bills to be settled directly with the hospital.

- The level of cover provided under the in-patient benefits. For example will your benefit be sufficient to pay for treatment received in the USA?

- The level of cover for day-patient and out-patient treatment: this includes procedures which don't require an overnight stay, diagnostic tests and physiotherapy. Most insurance companies vary the level of out-patient cover depending on what plan you chose.

- Parent accommodation – can you stay with your child whilst they are receiving hospital treatment?

- Emergency dental cover for accidental injury.

- Nursing at home following treatment.

- Private ambulance transportation costs.

- Cash benefit – you will receive a cash sum for each night you stay in a hospital bed when you have received free in-patient hospital treatment.

- Options for cover of pre-existing conditions and chronic conditions.

- Travel – whilst your healthcare policy should take care of your medical costs, you will also want to ensure that you have the option to be insured for any holiday and business travel outside of your area of cover.

The final point to take into consideration is that you may not see a large difference in policy and price between two insurers although the services and levels of support they offer could differ immensely. It can make all the difference to be dealing with a company who is supportive of its members, regardless of whether you need to claim on your policy or not.

AXA PPP healthcare offers its members information about the countries they may travel or move to, helping to reduce the uncertainty you may feel before you arrive. General health advice and information on different illnesses or diseases you may encounter while abroad are an invaluable asset and can be available through 24-hour helplines such as Health at Hand, AXA PPP healthcare's health information line, which is staffed by healthcare professionals 365 days a year.

With over 35 years experience in the international health insurance market, AXA PPP healthcare is dedicated to looking after the healthcare insurance needs of people who are living, working or retired outside the UK for more than six months a year and in certain areas, residents residing in their home countries.

Our International Health Plan covers individuals as well as businesses of all sizes. We offer the choice of three levels of cover Standard, Comprehensive and Prestige. In addition to choosing their level of benefit, members also select an area of cover to suit their needs.

Alongside this, we have relationships with partner companies in Malta, Cyprus, Saudi Arabia, Bahrain and the United Arab Emirates, allowing us to distribute our medical insurance plans to a wide number of people worldwide.

We believe that what really makes AXA PPP healthcare different from other healthcare providers is our excellent support and service coupled with our personal touch. These are values that, alongside access to private healthcare, allow AXA PPP healthcare to give peace of mind to their members and intermediaries alike. Not only are our employees friendly, professional and efficient, they have also made it their business to help and look after you.

For further information on international health insurance from AXA PPP healthcare please contact:

+44 1892 508 791 for individuals

+44 1892 508 795 for corporate groups

or visit **www.axappphealthcare.com**

According to the international security consultants Merchants International Group (MIG), resident expatriates tend to be more at risk in these circumstances than visiting businessmen. However, the terrorist attacks on the World Trade Center in New York and the Pentagon in Washington of 11 September 2001 and the rigorous new entry checks and routines that the United States has introduced on all incoming airline passengers have brought to the forefront the constant risks from terrorism to which all business travellers are exposed, even in the most developed countries. The same is, of course, true for visitors to European cities, as the London bombing incidents in July 2005 demonstrated. MIG, which speculates in the 'grey areas' of risk often associated with developing countries, is available for advice on these matters. For more information, visit the MIG website at www.merchantinternational.com. Since 11 September 2001 it seems less likely that the chances of winning the lottery jackpot are higher than that of being anywhere near a terrorist attack.

ACCIDENTS

Finally, it is worth sounding a note of warning. In many countries getting involved in legal action can be disastrous – even when it is over a minor incident. It is certainly worth researching your host country's attitude to such events and what kind of ethical stance it takes on such matters – including that of bribery. Check if your company has an ethical policy on such matters.

In some parts of the world it might be wise to hire a driver rather than take the risk of getting involved in an accident yourself. It is important not to take any unnecessary risks, as many countries are unsympathetic to practices accepted as normal in other parts of the world, such as drinking alcohol or gambling.

THE AXA "what if I get peritonitis in Paris?" PLAN.

International Health Insurance from **AXA PPP healthcare.** Get the cover that's right for you. Call **+44(0)1892 508791** quoting reference WA2006

INSURANCE   INVESTMENTS   PENSIONS   **HEALTHCARE**

—— Be Life Confident ——

Checklist: Health, security and welfare

1. Avoid daily routines, like taking the same route to work every day at a fixed time.
2. Remove bushes and thick vegetation around the entrance to your house or place of work – they could make a hiding place for criminals and people tend to be least vigilant as they approach familiar places.
3. If you think you are being followed, head immediately for a place where there are as many other people around as possible. Criminals prefer not to strike when there are witnesses about.
4. Report suspicious incidents to the police and encourage your family to be alert for them; for instance, 'students' coming to your door to make unlikely-sounding surveys. If you get threatening telephone calls, report these to the police, and try to remember any peculiarities of voice or accent, or any background noise that might give a hint as to where the call was made from.
5. Watch out for abandoned cars in the vicinity. These are sometimes dumped by criminals to test police vigilance.
6. Avoid conspicuous displays of affluence.
7. Try to have a room in your house to which you and your family can retreat if serious danger threatens. It should have good doors with stout locks, and windows that can be secured from the inside but which do not bar escape routes. If possible, get professional advice on how to prepare what is called a 'keep' in your house.
8. Using firearms as a form of self-defence is fraught with danger. You will nearly always be faced with more than one assailant and you have to be prepared to shoot to kill. That in itself is much less easy than it is made to look in the movies; furthermore, in some countries foreigners are always in the wrong in such circumstances.
9. The best form of defence and survival is to rehearse a plan of action in your mind in case you are attacked or in danger – and to stick to it if you can. The thing to avoid above all is panic, because if you panic you lose control of the situation.

9 Adjusting to Living and Working Abroad

Living and working overseas can be extremely rewarding in personal, financial and career terms. It is also likely to herald a dramatic change of lifestyle. All expatriates, no matter to which country they are posted, have to make some adjustment to life overseas, and all members of an expatriate's family will be affected by the move, whether or not they venture abroad. If, as a married person, you go abroad 'on unaccompanied status', you and your family will have to make a number of adjustments to living separately. There is much to be gained in going abroad as a couple, but in so doing you may be asking your partner to give up a career and possible future chances of employment, and, if you have children disrupting their education, and removing your family from their normal sources of comfort and support (see Chapters 6 and 7).

For families who do decide to relocate together, a failure to adapt might mean having to terminate the contract early. Such unscheduled returns to the UK tend to cause considerable disturbance and hardship to all concerned. There is a high turnover rate among expatriates, so before you commit yourself and your family to working abroad it is important to discuss the likely consequences of the move with other members of your family.

CULTURE SHOCK

In contemplating a move overseas you have probably tried to imagine what it will be like. Most people think about the physical differences: the heat, the humidity, the dirt, etc, although they are rarely able to assess how these differences will affect their daily lives. How will working in 90 per cent humidity impair your effectiveness?

Could you negotiate an important contract in an atmosphere more suited to the tropical house of your nearest botanical gardens? It is difficult to appreciate how much of the background to daily life is taken for granted; for example, drinking water from a tap, flicking a switch for light, pushing a button for instant entertainment. In underdeveloped countries many of these basics of everyday life either do not exist or function irregularly. While it is easy to imagine that things will be different, it is hard to envisage how this affects the quality of daily life and your sense of well-being.

But the differences that prove the greatest barrier to adjustment are the ones that cannot be seen and that are not normally even thought about. Despite regional differences in the UK most people have grown up with common experiences and expectations of how the world works. In any given situation, most people have a fairly clear idea of what is expected of them and what they expect of others. However, different nationalities do not necessarily share the same assumptions and expectations about life, or about how other people should behave. In Britain we share a common culture and, on the whole, common beliefs about what is right and proper. Other cultures, though, have quite different underlying values and beliefs, different expectations and concepts of 'normal behaviour'. Britain is nominally a Christian country, yet although much legislation and ordinary behaviour have their origins in Christian teaching, a relatively small proportion of the population would see Christianity as the driving force of British society.

By contrast, in Saudi Arabia, Islam underlies everything. It regulates the legal and political system and the conduct of all aspects of everyday life and is so perceived by its own nationals. It can be difficult to understand how other people operate; it is easy to assume that the motivations of others are understood, while misunderstanding them utterly. In Britain the ground rules of human behaviour can be taken for granted, but overseas they must be questioned and come to terms with. For example, in Malaysia it is not uncommon for expatriates to feel that their local subordinates are disloyal when, instead of discussing some decision with which they disagree, they simply choose to ignore it. Yet to the Malaysian it would be unpardonable to cause a superior to lose face by questioning him in public; far more polite simply to ignore what is considered to be a poor suggestion.

Even unconscious behaviour is open to misinterpretation. For example, in the UK an individual who avoids eye contact would usually be categorised (unconsciously) as shifty or guilty. In Nigeria the same individual would be seen as respectful, because to avoid eye contact with an older person is a mark of respect. The classic example of how the smallest physical cues are subject to different interpretations is one of distance. The British tend to feel comfortable standing two to three feet apart when chatting; the Saudis prefer to stand closer together. A Saudi and a Briton talking to each other will each unconsciously try to establish the distance at which each feels comfortable. The Briton will feel threatened when the Saudi edges nearer and the Saudi will feel rebuffed as the Briton sidles backwards. Neither will appreciate the impact of his or her unconscious behaviour on the other. This kind of disorientation is experienced constantly by the fledgling expatriate, causing many expatriates to respond aggressively when no hostility was intended.

The expatriate experiences considerable anxiety when faced unknowingly with the loss of minor cues: the familiar signs and symbols that are taken for granted in the UK but are open to different interpretations in the host country. This constant disorientation is unnerving and can cause considerable stress. The syndrome is so common that it has been given a name – culture shock.

Doctors have long recognised that changes in normal lifestyle can result in stress, and ultimately physical and mental illness. Change of home, change of friends, change of job, change of lifestyle, loss of or separation from the marital partner may all be experienced by the expatriate, who may be deprived of his or her traditional means of support and solace. A new job is always stressful, but when the job is in a new (and seemingly hostile) environment, the tensions are even greater. Symptoms associated with culture shock include heightened anxiety and worry, feelings of isolation and helplessness, and a poor performance at work. Most expatriates eventually settle down, more or less successfully, but there is a predictable cycle to the adjustment and three main stereotyped responses to adaptation.

First, there is the chauvinistic expatriate, whose response to his or her predicament is to try to create a mini encapsulated UK or 'Little England'. This expatriate's attempts to understand the local way of doing things, or local colleagues, are minimal. Faced with the difficulties of this new environment he or she retreats from what is perceived as a hostile host country and people. The blame for misunderstandings is never anything to do with him or her, but is always the fault of the 'stupid' locals. This expatriate falls into a trap of denigrating everything local and idealising everything from home, ultimately provoking real hostility from local counterparts and making a reality of his or her view of him- or herself alone against the world. Local expatriate clubs are full of this kind of expatriate, who often indulges his or her aggression over more drinks than are healthy.

The chauvinistic expatriate is experiencing culture shock. He or she is disorientated by the environment and feels constantly at sea. The symptoms of this state are incessant complaining, glorification of the UK, alcoholic over-indulgence, marital difficulties and general aggression. At this stage the expatriate will find it hard to work with local colleagues or clients and will be permanently miserable. It is at this stage also that expatriates tend to terminate their contracts, prior to completion, with major repercussions for their families and their own careers. Fortunately for most expatriates, this is a passing stage and after their first home leave, when the realities of life in Britain are forced upon them, they manage to adapt successfully.

The second, much rarer, response is to 'go bush'. This expatriate eschews the company of his fellow expatriates, and tends to over-idealise all things local. He identifies totally with the host culture, which many of his local colleagues find both patronising and suspect.

The third and probably most appropriate response, but the most difficult to achieve, is that of the 'open-minded expatriate' who, without abandoning his or her own values, is able to accept the new culture and attempt to understand it. This involves understanding how the host society's values are reflected in everyday behaviour. Decisions are made without the necessity for qualitative judgement. While differences are acknowledged, they are not categorised as better or worse.

If, prior to arriving abroad, you can come to terms with the idea that there are real cultural differences which need to be understood, you will find it much easier to adjust. These cultural differences affect work and home life. Often at work the differences are hidden because on the surface the work to be done is the same as at home, but local colleagues may have different ways of doing business and different attitudes to time and concepts of loyalty. Management styles may differ and motivation and discipline have quite different connotations. For example, many other nationalities find Western haste in business negotiations unpalatable; it is good manners and a useful way of assessing a business associate to chat seemingly inconsequentially before getting down to real negotiations. The Westerner considers it a waste of time, even insulting. In many parts of the world ethnic loyalty is a salient feature of everyday life, and a member of one tribe may be under an obligation to find jobs not only for his extended family, ie sons and daughters of aunts, uncles, cousins, and children of his father's other wives, but also for members of his own ethnic group. Outside the West, age is still considered to bestow authority and seniority, even at work. Social adjustment can also be difficult. Business is often conducted at social events; business entertaining at home may be the norm. Social life can be restricted, as in many areas expatriates make little attempt to get to know local people and mix almost entirely in expatriate circles. This can cause considerable pressure, as any minor upset at work or at home is common knowledge and long remembered.

The married expatriate living alone abroad often has the most difficulty in adjusting, both when working and when on leave. Single people often feel excluded from much social activity which revolves around the family. Single women suffer especially, as other expatriate women may resent or even fear them, and friendship with local colleagues can be misinterpreted. However, it is often the partners who bear the brunt of culture shock and have the greatest difficulty in adapting, as discussed in a previous chapter.

PREPARING YOURSELF FOR THE CHANGE

So how can you, as a prospective expatriate, prepare yourself and your family to make the appropriate adjustments? First, you and your family should try to find out as much as possible about the country before you accept the assignment, and preferably before you go to the job interview. Once you have accepted a job offer, some employers will give you a briefing of some description. Relatively few employers seem to appreciate that the cost of staff turnover, in money, time, effort and damage to relationships with their clients, merits an outlay on briefing expatriates and their families before their departure.

You will need to know something about your employer, the nature and responsibilities of your job, the terms and conditions of your contract and whether the benefits offered match the prevailing conditions in the country. You will want to learn about the country, its history, geography, climate, politics, economics, form of government, people and religion, etc. Much of this basic or factual information will be available in standard publications from the national embassies and tourist offices (although most countries naturally like to present a favourable picture of themselves). There are a number of specialised directories available in public reference libraries containing this information and some banks, such as HSBC, produce factual booklets. The DTI produces a vast range of publications aimed at business abroad, many of which contain information of value to intending expatriates. A full list is provided in the Export Publications Catalogue, available FOC from DTI Export Publications, Admail 528, London SW1W 8YT; tel: 020 7510 0171, fax: 020 7510 0197, as well as details of other services. Your local Government Office or Business Link is another source of information linked to the DTI. Corona Worldwide produces its own *Notes for Newcomers* which contains background on each country with advice on setting up home.

The financial problems of expatriate life, such as personal taxation, insurance, etc, and other aspects of interest to expatriates are covered in several magazines catering specifically for their needs, available on subscription:

☐ *Nexus* (monthly), annual subscription rates £66 for the UK, £72 for Europe and £78 for the rest of the world, published by Expat Network, 1st Floor, 5 Brighton Road, Croydon CR2 6EA ; tel: 020 8760 5100, fax: 020 8760 0469, e-mail: expats@expat-network.com, website: www.expatnetwork.co.uk;

☐ *Resident Abroad*, published by FT Finance, and available via the Subscriptions Department, PO Box 387, Haywards Heath, West Sussex RH16 3GS; tel: 01444 445520, fax: 01444 445599 (Europe, £59 plus VAT at local rates; rest of the world, £69).

In addition, Expat Network offers a total support service for expatriates. It is a leading expatriate membership organisation which enjoys a firmly established reputation within the overseas recruitment sector. The expatriate community and the overseas employment market need a level of understanding which can only be achieved over time. Most things are different, from the way in which contracts are negotiated, the job search itself, the problems involved with tax, personal finances, currency, locations, social security, pensions, etc. Expat Network can offer advice for each and every eventuality. A number of services are offered. The monthly magazine *Nexus* deals with expatriate issues, offers in-depth industry features, contractual news and has a 12-page job supplement.

Some companies run their own; others use outside organisations. If your employer will not pay for you to attend a course, it would be worthwhile paying out of your own pocket. Ideally, both partners should attend, and children can also benefit.

Corona Worldwide runs one-day 'Living Overseas' briefings for men and women (price around £250) providing information and advice on living abroad and a one-to-one briefing, with a recent returner, on the country of your posting. Prices quoted are subject to revision. Emergency telephone and other briefings are also organised – fees for these can be obtained on request.

The Centre for International Briefing provides residential programmes and training for men and women taking up long-term appointments or short-term contracts abroad, and for home-based managers responsible for international personnel. Cultural and business briefings cover all major regions of the world, include all aspects of living and working, and allow a rapid transition to the destination country. Customised programmes provide training in international negotiation and communication skills, intercultural communication, international team-building and skill-transference in a foreign culture. Language tuition is also available, and the Centre's Language Plus programme combines intensive language and communication studies with business and cultural briefings. Details of programmes are available from the Customer Services Department, The Centre for International Briefing, Farnham Castle, Farnham GU9 0AG; tel: 01252 721194, fax: 01252 719277.

For expatriates going to Japan, China, Korea or other East Asian countries, individually prepared briefing and language sessions are available from East Asia Business Services at the University of Sheffield. Contact the EABS at 317 Glossop Road, Sheffield S10 2HP; tel: 0114 222 8060, fax: 0114 272 8028, e-mail: EABS@Sheffield.ac.uk. These briefings are tailor-made and can be residential or in-company, according to the client's requirements. Family participation is encouraged. Sister organisations in destinations can provide further services. Briefings are modular and designed to provide new skills and practical knowledge. Sessions are conducted by business people with specific experience of the region.

The External Services Division of the School of Oriental and African Studies within the University of London provides a wide range of briefing and language services for business/government and private individuals. Open briefings on Japan and China are offered on a regular basis, including the two-day Japan Business Orientation Programme and the China Business Orientation Programme. Briefings may be integrated with language tuition if required and are offered on a tailor-made basis for most of the countries or regions of Asia and Africa. Details are available from the Co-ordinator, Ms Dzidra Stipnieks, SOAS External Services Division, University of London, Thornhaugh Street, Russell Square, London WC1H 0XG; tel: 020 7898 4081.

Going Places Expatriate Briefing, 84 Coombe Road, New Malden, Surrey KT3 4QS; tel: 020 8949 8811, provide tailored briefings to individuals or groups, in-house or in the home. Briefings last from three hours to a full day and cover preparation, living in-country, working in-country, coming home. Expertise is available on over 50 countries for both the working and accompanying partner. Guideline costs indicate £950 plus VAT per day per individual or couple; £100 a head thereafter. Going Places will provide its own facilities if more convenient.

These courses, and some employers, arrange for you to meet recently returned expatriates, and this is particularly useful if you can work out in advance, preferably in the form of a checklist, what you and your family really need to know. Such a checklist can also be helpful if you are offered, as has become increasingly common for senior positions, the possibility of a 'look-see' visit to the location in question.

Some expatriates have reported that the British Council is often helpful in terms of overcoming entry shock and giving advice and information about local amenities and activities.

LEARNING A LANGUAGE

A further aspect of learning about the host country is to master a few basic greetings in the local language. Even when it is not strictly necessary, familiarity with the sound of a language makes everything seem less strange and it is appreciated locally.

The traditional picture of the Englishman who expects all foreigners to speak English or hopes to get by with schoolboy French has disappeared. In the modern world of fast-moving communications, language proficiency is an essential tool. It is true that English is the world's leading language for business and commerce and, in non-English speaking countries, is taught in most schools as the second language. But in many countries knowledge of the indigenous language is essential and often a prerequisite of employment. It is vital where a job involves contact with local people, particularly in administration or industry, where orders and instructions have to be given and understood. Even where a job is technical and does not involve direct communication, it is an advantage to be able to join in conversation and be more fully integrated with local society.

Anybody working in the EU should be proficient in French and/or German. In Spain and Latin America, Spanish is essential (except in Brazil, where Portuguese is spoken). In the Third World, and in the Middle East, knowledge of indigenous languages is not so essential but it is useful to speak Arabic or Swahili, particularly in more remote areas. So the best thing you can do if you are going to work overseas is to learn one or more languages or brush up on your existing knowledge.

The increasing demand for languages is being met in a number of ways. There is the 'do-it-yourself' approach which can include:

1. Learning at home, using Linguaphone courses or other self-study materials.
2. Hiring a private tutor. Try to find a native speaker, who is prepared to conduct most of the lessons in the foreign language rather than waste valuable time talking about the language in English.
3. Open learning courses at your local college of further education or university. Many have established 'drop in' centres where you have access to a language laboratory, and possibly also computer-assisted learning, with back-up from a tutor when you need it. This form of learning can be very effective for those whose time is limited and who need a flexible programme of study.

For those at the adult beginner level, *Oxford Beginner's Dictionaries*, published by Oxford University Press, offer all the words and phrases a beginner needs, as well as lots of extra help with learning including grammar, culture and travel information. *Beginner's Dictionaries* are available in French, German, Spanish, Italian, Russian, Chinese and Japanese and are exceptionally easy to use because they move away from the traditional dictionary layout. All main translations are preceded by an equals sign so that they are instantly identifiable, and all parts of the entry are spelt out in full, avoiding confusing jargon and abbreviations. Grammar and usage notes throughout the text warn of possible translation pitfalls, and thousands of example phrases show how language is used in the context. The centre section of the dictionary gives background information on lifestyle and culture, tips on etiquette and interaction in the language, as well as a phrase finder, which provides useful travellers' phrases.

You may prefer to attend a language class, and these are run by most local authority adult education institutes and colleges. However, learning on the basis of one or two sessions a week is not the most effective way of getting to grips with a foreign language – you will make a lot more progress on a more intensive course.

Private language schools generally offer intensive or 'crash' courses. Be careful to check the bona fides of a course before you enrol. An example of the type of tuition available is Berlitz (UK) Ltd (9–13 Grosvenor Street, London W1A 3BZ; tel: 020 7915 0909, fax: 020 7915 0222), which offers language programmes to suit the linguistic needs for all in both the business and non-business fields. Berlitz offers crash courses, private lessons and semi-private courses for two to three people in most languages. The full-time Total Immersion® course lasts from one to six weeks for those wishing to improve their existing ability quickly. In-house courses for companies are also available.

Conrad Executive Language Training (15 King Street, London WC2E 8HN; tel: 020 7240 0855, fax: 020 7240 0715), founded in 1974, is specifically geared towards meeting the linguistic needs of business people. Tuition is structured to suit both the schedule of each client and specific language requirements. Classes can be held at Conrad's Covent Garden centre, in-company or privately, after a thorough language evaluation and needs analysis. Conrad is registered to ISO 9000 by BSI. Courses available: the Crash Course (9 am–4 pm), suitable for all levels and held over five days (not necessarily consecutively); and the Extensive Course, also suitable for all levels, which be taken between 8 am and 8 pm – classes last at least one hour and are at times to suit the client. Conrad also offers cross-cultural training programmes for groups and individuals for all countries, and the Corporate Group Course (ideal for companies requiring language training for a small group of executives who have the same objectives and similar background knowledge).

The European Centre is a language consultancy helping individuals, companies and other organisations to communicate more effectively in international markets. Winner of two national awards in 1996, it specialises in the design, management and delivery of language training programmes for business and vocational purposes. All the programmes are designed to meet individual or corporate needs, based on a language assessment and training needs analysis. Further details from Jonathan Smith, The European Centre, Peter House, St Peter's Square, Manchester M1 5AN; tel: 0161 281 8844, fax: 0161 281 8822, e-mail: training@evcentre.co.uk.

Fees at language schools are high, but there is general agreement that they represent a worthwhile investment. Administrators of language schools sometimes complain that too few companies attach real importance to language proficiency and often leave it too late for effective action.

The Association of Language Excellence Centres (ALEC) is a professional body for providers of language training and related services for business. It aims to establish and maintain quality standards and help organisations and individuals to improve their performance in international markets, mergers and acquisitions with language training and consultancy geared to the needs of business, including: language training for business; translation and interpreting; country, cultural and trade briefings; needs analysis and language audits. For details of LX Centres in your area or application for membership contact Karen Wilkinson at ALEC, Cowley House, Little College Street, London SW1P 3XS; tel: 020 7222 0666, fax: 020 7233 0335, e-mail: kwilkinson@westminster.com.

Other options include foreign cultural institutes, such as the Alliance Française or the Goethe Institut, which run well-established courses, and organisations running courses abroad (nothing can beat learning a language in the country where it is spoken). Courses abroad are advertised in *The Times* and *The Guardian*.

Further information and advice are available from CILT (the Centre for Information on Language Teaching and Research), 20 Bedfordbury, London WC2N 4LB; tel: 020 7379 5101, fax: 020 7379 5082. Written enquiries are preferred. At the same address is NATBLIS, the National Business Language Information Service (tel: 020 7379 5131, fax: 020 7379 5082), which provides information on business language training and on providers of business language services – training, cultural briefing, interpreting and translation.

TAKE IT EASY

Once you arrive overseas you should take it easy, adjusting to climatic changes, as they will affect your physical and subsequently your mental state. Coping with so many new stimuli all at once is overpowering and you will need time to find your bearings. Tiredness and depression make it hard to react positively to your new situation. It is part of the adjustment cycle to feel frustrated and depressed, but if you can make the effort to understand the underlying cultural reasons for your frustration, you will be well on your way to adjusting successfully and enjoying your life abroad. After that you just have to cope with the culture shock of returning to the UK at the end of your tour.

Checklist: Adjusting to living and working abroad

1. Try to find out as much as possible about your host country – not just the physical conditions but its culture, values and beliefs.
2. Become familiar with the ground rules for behaviour towards colleagues and with attitudes to age and gender.
3. Be aware of the symptoms of stress and culture shock.
4. If you experience culture shock, find someone to talk to, perhaps an experienced expatriate, and seek professional help for prolonged symptoms.
5. Use the internet, public libraries and specialist services to find out as much information as possible about your new location.
6. Ask your employer to send you and your family on a briefing course before departure.
7. Try to learn the language of your host country – it will help you integrate into your local society.
8. Be aware that you might well experience culture shock on your return to your home country.

Part Four:

Making the Move

Letting your property?
Make sure you sleep easy at night

Nightmare! You're working abroad and the friends you asked to keep an eye on your privately rented house ring to say the tenants are causing 'a few problems.' Perhaps the rent isn't being paid. Is there a maintenance issue? The last thing you need to worry about when you're many miles from the UK is the well being of what is possibly your biggest asset.

Appointing a letting agent is the sensible answer. But how do you find a reputable one? There are no qualifications needed to become a letting agent and the unfortunate truth is that many landlords simply do not comprehend the risk they are taking when they sign the dotted line.

There is a better option. Over 7,000 landlords trust Leaders the Rental Agents to let their properties, many of them based overseas. Leaders is a member of ARLA (Association of Rental Letting Agents) which is your assurance of high standards of business practice and financial accountability.

Leaders specialises in letting and has done so for almost 25 years. A network of almost thirty branches markets and supports your property across Sussex, Hampshire, Surrey and Berkshire. In addition, such is Leaders strength in the market that each branch has lists of credit approved applicants looking to rent for all kinds of properties.

Once your property is let, Leaders can provide full support with an in-house Property Management team who will take care of day-to-day issues and make regular inspections. A range of specially negotiated insurances is also available to protect your property and even your rental income.

A significant investment in IT allows more effective marketing of your property, but is also invaluable in providing easy to read statements and reports to keep you fully informed.

Leaders' full letting and management service allows you to get on with your business abroad, sleep easy at night and it doesn't cost a fortune. To find your nearest Leaders branch please visit **www.leaders.co.uk** or phone Head Office on **0845 3454125**.

Let it!
Forget it!

Trust Leaders to look after your biggest asset while you're away. We've specialised in letting for almost 25 years and letting your property safely is our passion. 7,000 landlords can't be wrong! Please ring the number below to find your nearest branch or look us up on the internet at www.leaders.co.uk

We look forward to hearing from you.

- Extensive branch network throughout Sussex, Hampshire and Surrey.

- Waiting professional tenants.

- Exclusive contacts with reputable companies for longer term tenancies.

- In-house property management department and inspection teams for your peace of mind.

- Full ARLA and Investor in People accreditation.

bigger thinking

local service

Tel (Head Office)**: 0845 345 4125**
info@leaders.co.uk
www.leaders.co.uk

INVESTOR IN PEOPLE

ARLA
Association of Residential Letting Agents

10 | Moving Out

WHAT TO TAKE AND REMOVAL

Whatever agonising variables you feed into your mental computer about what and what not to take, you will certainly find that in the end you are left with two basic choices – either to take very little other than clothes, books, favourite possessions and whatever small items you and your family need to feel at home, or to take virtually everything.

It clearly depends on where you are going, how long you are going for, and who you are going to work for. If you are taking up an appointment in a sophisticated European capital or in North America, obviously you will not need the same kind of things as you would in a developing country, say in Africa or Asia, where everything tends to be scarce and expensive. If you are going to a tropical country, or the Middle East, clothes and equipment will be very different from what you will need in a temperate or northern area.

As a rule, travelling reasonably light is the best course of action. Even if you are going to be away for a long time, it seldom pays to take large items of household equipment, such as sofas, beds or wardrobes; the cost of shipping bulky items is very high. In any case, it can take quite a long time to clear them through customs when they arrive, so you will either have to send them ahead or find yourself arriving in a new place without any furniture.

Such situations are apt to be inconvenient and will probably result in your having to buy some things simply to tide you over. Clothes, bedlinen, crockery, kitchen equipment and so forth are cheap to transport – shipping companies usually convey some baggage free of charge – and usually expensive to replace at the other end. Furthermore, these items lend themselves to being sent ahead, and you can usually make do, or borrow, in the meantime.

Antiques are always worth taking, since they are vastly expensive in most places outside the UK, but remember that old furniture and pictures can be sensitive to climatic change. Such problems may also exist with electronic equipment, and your CD player or food mixer may have to go through costly adaptations to fit in with foreign voltages. Records, tapes and musical instruments deteriorate in hot climates. There can also be problems over import controls, though most authorities have special dispensations for personal possessions.

As far as household equipment is concerned, much depends on the terms of your contract. Most commercial firms in developing countries will provide a fully furnished house or apartment (possibly also a car). Fully furnished means that everything, down to the last lampshade, is provided and you only need your personal effects. National governments and public corporations usually supply 'hard furnished' accommodation. Hard furnished is what it implies. Only the bare necessities such as tables and chairs and a bed are provided, and you will need to supply curtains, cushions, linen, loose covers, cutlery, crockery and kitchen gear. Often you can buy these things from an outgoing tenant or returning expatriate, but you have to be on the spot for this.

It is strongly recommended that where a family is going out to a developing country the employee should travel out alone in advance, unless furnished accommodation is assured, and only send for the family when this has been fixed up. It may mean staying in a hotel or hostel for a time, but it is worth the inconvenience to be able to learn the ropes at first hand and decide what will be needed from home. Some companies arrange for both partners to go out in advance for a 'reconnaissance' visit.

In some cases, especially if the contract is a short-term one, in a difficult country, it is recommended that the employee should go out alone, leaving his or her family in the UK. This may sound heartless, but it does minimise the upheaval and avoids disrupting the children's education.

If you are going to a tropical country where conditions are difficult, you may not be able to buy such items as a deep freeze, food mixer, sewing machine, hairdryer and electric iron except in the main centres. A portable electric fan is useful if the house is not air conditioned. An electric kettle is a must and so is a torch. There may be power cuts, so stock up with candles.

If you have very young children with you, take pram, carrycot, pushchair and plenty of toys. Camping equipment, eg tents and sleeping bags, may be useful, and so may gardening tools, as many houses have quite large gardens. Take golf clubs, tennis rackets, photographic equipment, etc, since these leisure and luxury goods may be unobtainable or very expensive overseas, though this will again depend very much on where you go.

Stock up with cosmetics and toiletries, drugs and medicines since everything in this line is expensive and difficult to obtain. Find out the voltage and type of electric plug in use and, before you go if possible, check with the appliance manufacturer about any adaptations. A useful website address is www.kropla.com which is a comprehensive listing of worldwide electrical and telephone information and provides details of electric plugs and voltages used in different countries throughout the world.

Don't rely on somebody sending you something from home. Postage can be exorbitant, mails are slow and the contents liable to be pilfered. It may be possible to get your children, or your neighbour's children, to bring things out when they come on leave from school.

The best way to handle the question of actual removal is to consult one of the big removal firms. Overseas removal is not a job you should take on yourself, nor is it a good thing on which to try to save money. Moving abroad is a very different proposition from moving in this country and, in choosing your remover, it is better to ask for a good name than a good quote. The bigger removers are well informed about living conditions in overseas countries – check, though, that any printed literature they give you is fully up to date.

Removers are knowledgeable about what you can and should take with you, and most have agents at ports of entry who can help with the sometimes interminable business of clearing your belongings through customs. Another advantage of a 'name' remover is that they can generally get a better insurance deal than with a smaller firm. You should, incidentally, increase your insurance to cover replacement costs at the other end. If you cannot get any specific information about this, an increase of 50 to 80 per cent over UK values will serve as a rough guideline.

An alternative to using one of the 'big names' is to contact one of the specialist consortia of overseas removal companies. These are made up of hand-picked, privately owned companies specialising in overseas removals. As a team, members provide the strength and capacity of a large international concern; individually they are able to provide a local, personal service that many customers prefer.

All members conform to standards of service that are the same all over the world. So a remover operating out of the UK will provide the same level of service as his or her counterparts in Italy, for instance. Using the consortium method is rather like using a removal company with branch offices all over the world.

In the past there has been extensive publicity over the sudden demise of overseas removal companies, which – having received payment in advance – have left their customers' belongings either in the warehouse or, worse still, languishing in an overseas country. This usually resulted in families having to pay twice over for their household effects to be delivered, and many who could not afford to pay again had to abandon their belongings altogether.

Protection against this sort of disaster is now available through the Advance Payments Guarantee Scheme operated by the Overseas Group of the British Association of Removers. The Scheme provides that customers who have paid removal charges in advance to a firm participating in the Scheme are guaranteed that, in the event of the removal company ceasing to trade, their belongings will either be delivered at no further cost, or they will be refunded the cost of the removal charges.

It should not be assumed that all removers are in the Scheme. The safeguard provided by the Scheme is available only through members of the BAR Overseas Group. The guarantee is under-written by a mutual insurance company set up by the industry.

The British Association of Removers itself will be happy to supply readers with leaflets giving advice on moving abroad and brochures on the Advance Payments Guarantee Scheme. The Association also provides a list of companies participating in the Scheme. Readers should send a 9in × 4in sae to the British Association of Removers, 3 Churchill Court, 58 Station Road, North Harrow HA2 7SA (tel: 020 8861 3331, fax: 020 8861 3332).

Removal costs vary according to the distance to be covered, the method of transportation (land, sea or air), the terms of the arrangement (delivery to port or home, packed or unpacked) and a range of other factors. Customers should obtain *written* estimates from several companies. Beware of firms that quote on the basis of approximate measures. Be specific, understand exactly the terms of the arrangement and obtain a written agreement, so that you have what amounts to a contract with which to resist 'surcharges' imposed at the point of disembarkation.

Some people like to pack their own things. If so, it is best to use custom-made cardboard boxes, which are stout, light and can be banded to withstand rough handling and exposure. These generally come with movers' details, logo and grids in which details of the contents, origin and whether fragile or not, can be entered. It is essential to make a list of contents and advisable to see that your cases or boxes are readily identifiable for when you collect them at the other end. Smaller goods can be taken with you, up to the 20 kg allowable limit. Some things may be carried as hand luggage, depending on how full the plane is. But on all these points, be guided by the experts.

PETS

Pets often pose a problem. Some shipping companies and airlines require a bill of health from a veterinary surgeon. In all cases, before leaving the UK you should first obtain an export health certificate from the Ministry of Agriculture, Fisheries and Food. There are a number of specialist animal shipping services available. You will need to apply in good time beforehand to DEFRA for an information pack so that you can make the necessary arrangements. Quarantine has been replaced by a vaccination and electronic tagging procedure for animals being transported to and from rabies-free and EU countries. Details can be found on the DEFRA website www.defra.gov.uk.

Checklist: Choice of removers

1. The remover should provide a free estimate and a written quote.
2. Does the quote specify *professional* packing under your general supervision?
3. How will fragile items, furniture and articles be packed?
4. What insurance cover is offered? If there is any excess (ie a minimum figure below which you will not be reimbursed), what is it?
5. Can the removers immediately provide the name and address of the port agents at your destination?
6. Will they deliver to your residence at the other end, or will you have to arrange clearance yourself? Check that the quotation specifies whether the goods will be delivered to residence or to port only.
7. What proportion of their current business is in overseas removals?

VAT

You will almost certainly find that some of the things you want are cheaper to buy here, even allowing for shipping charges. You should make sure that you take full advantage of the various VAT export schemes under which a UK resident going abroad can escape having to pay UK VAT altogether. There are two schemes, one for motor vehicles and one for other goods.

Motor vehicles

If you will be living outside the EU

You have to purchase your new vehicle from a dealer who operates the Personal Export Scheme. He or she will give you VAT Form 410 to fill in, which will require you to fulfil certain conditions. The relevant notes are found in VAT Notice 705. Motor cycles and motor caravans are also covered by this scheme.

☐ You must personally take delivery of the vehicle, and it must be used only by you, or someone else who is also leaving the EU and has your permission to use it.

☐ You have to take the vehicle abroad within 6 months of delivery, or within 12 months if you have lived outside the EU for more than 365 days in the previous two years, or more than 1,095 days in the previous six years.

☐ You and the car must remain outside the EU for at least six consecutive months.

Alternatively, the supplier can deliver the car directly to your destination, free of VAT. See VAT Notice 703.

If you will be living within the EU

You must complete Form VAT 411, supplied by the motor dealer.

☐ The vehicle must be new, and you must take it to your destination within two months of delivery. Cars must not have been driven for more than 1,864 miles in this time.

☐ You must declare the vehicle to the member state's fiscal authority.

After you have had the vehicle abroad for at least 12 months you may re-import it without paying VAT, provided you are either a diplomat, a member of an officially recognised international organ-isation, a member of NATO or returning UK Forces personnel or you can prove that the duty and tax have been paid. Otherwise you will have to pay VAT on the value of the vehicle at the time of re-importation. If you return to the UK within six months of the date of export, the full amount of VAT on the sale must be paid. If the vehicle is found to be in the UK after the date for its export shown on the registration document (ie six months from purchase date if you are leaving the EU, or two months otherwise), you will have to pay VAT in full and it will also be liable to forfeiture. This applies even if failure to export the vehicle is due to circumstances beyond your control (eg theft or destruction). Therefore, while the car is still in the UK, before export, it is essential to insure it for its full value, including potential VAT. Obviously, it is important to license, register and insure the vehicle if you will be using it in the UK before departure.

Other goods

If you have been in the EU for more than 365 days in the previous two years and are going to a final destination outside the EU for at least 12 consecutive months, you may buy goods using the Retail Export Scheme. At participating retailers, you must ask to complete VAT Form 435 at the time of purchase. To receive a refund equal to the amount of VAT you must get this form certified by a customs authority when the goods are exported – the goods must be delivered to your shipper or freight forwarder at your final point of departure from the EU. You cannot take delivery of them in this country. The refund is then paid by the retailer, not HM Revenue and Customs (HMRC). See VAT Notices 704 and 704/1. As there is a lot of documentation involved, you may find this procedure is not worth your while unless you are making fairly large purchases and only in one or two shops.

TAKING A CAR ABROAD

British people tend to prefer right-hand drive and will therefore consider buying their car here and taking it with them. First check at the embassy of the country you propose to live in that private car imports are permitted.

Probably the best way to plan this is to make a list of what you will want your car to do. The road surfaces may be worse than those you are used to, so you may consider taking a good second-hand car rather than a brand new one. You will not then be so worried about driving through very narrow streets. In some places drivers actually park by shunting the cars ahead and behind!

If you buy a new car in the UK before going abroad, you can use it here for six months, run it in and have your first service before you take it overseas. Check the servicing facilities in the area where you plan to live. It would be unwise to take a car abroad if the nearest dealer service is 70 miles away. This factor may well limit your choice.

A big car will be expensive with petrol and difficult to park. If you will be living in an apartment and there is no garage, the car will usually be left in the street and possibly for long periods at that. Consider carefully the security of your car and what you may have in it. Choose a model with locking wheel nuts and high-quality locks so that it is hard to get into without smashing the windows. Radio thefts are prevalent in some countries; therefore you may wish to consider a demountable radio.

Should you decide to take a small car to a hot country, always buy one with a sun roof because the smaller cars tend not to carry air conditioning.

People moving to Spain will often choose diesel cars because the fuel is half the price of petrol and easily available. Lead-free petrol is now available in many countries and you should check whether your engine will take this quality. Some engines need minor adaptation.

The other possibility is to hire a car in the UK. First check whether the hire company is happy with your destination and route. Restrictions depend on insurance cover for more out-of-the-way locations. You should also have the hirer provide you with proof of ownership – in this case form VE103a. Hirers are more than happy to do business with expatriates because of the length of hire and the fact that most are credit- and trustworthy. With regard to this latter point, it will be essential to pay by credit card.

Taking your existing car abroad

If you take the car you own at present abroad for longer than 12 months, this is regarded as a permanent export and the procedure is described in leaflet V526, obtainable from your local Vehicle Registration Office.

The following procedure applies to exports from England, Scotland, Wales and the Isles of Scilly only, not to Northern Ireland, the Isle of Man or the Channel Islands, where cars are registered separately.

Complete section 2 on the back of the Vehicle Registration Document, entering the proposed date of export, and send the document to your local Vehicle Registration Office or to the Driver and Vehicle Licensing Centre. This should be done well in advance of your departure.

You will receive back a Certificate of Export (V561) which in effect confirms your vehicle registration and replaces the vehicle registration document (V5). Some countries, however, are failing to recognise this certificate as a registration document, which can cause problems when you wish to re-register your vehicle in another country.

A different procedure applies in Northern Ireland, the Isle of Man and the Channel Islands, where vehicles are registered locally; it is necessary to register and license a car taken *to* these places for over 12 months as soon as the current British tax disc expires, if not before. The Certificate of Export mentioned above will still be necessary, although these authorities may accept the vehicle registration document for re-registration purposes.

Motoring services in Europe

The Alliance Internationale de Tourisme (AIT) has its headquarters in Geneva, and motoring clubs throughout Europe are affiliated to it, including the Royal Automobile Club and the Automobile Association. There is also the Federation Internationale de l'Automobile, based in Paris, of which the RAC is a member. These clubs provide a wide range of services to each other's members travelling abroad, so membership of one is worthwhile.

CUSTOMS

Regulations and procedures vary. Most customs authorities allow you to take in used things for your personal use and often let people, eg newly married couples, bring in new things duty free. Wherever possible keep receipts to show to the customs officials.

In most places, you are allowed to take in 'household and used personal effects', including refrigerators, radios, TV receivers and minor electrical appliances, but duties on new items of this kind are usually fairly steep. There are bans everywhere on guns, plants and drugs. Many Middle East and North African countries operate a boycott list, so do not take anything without checking the situation. Duty free wines, spirits and tobacco up to a certain amount – check with the airline – are normally allowed, except in most Middle East countries.

ESSENTIALS BEFORE YOU GO

There are certain things you must see about before you actually leave. There are obvious chores, like cancelling milk and papers, etc. Have a thorough medical check for yourself and your family before you go, including teeth and eyes. Some jobs, of course, depend on physical fitness. Make sure you have the necessary vaccination certificates and check the requirements. Most tropical countries need certificates against smallpox and possibly cholera and yellow fever; other vaccinations may be advisable. If you are going to the tropics you should contact your GP about anti-malarial precautions. For the most up-to-date advice on malaria in the region where you are going, you should contact the Malaria Reference Laboratory at the London School of Hygiene and Tropical Medicine.

In many countries it is advisable to include a rabies injection in your schedule of jabs for yourself and members of your family. You should also warn children of the perils of cuddling strange animals which may harbour other diseases in addition to the rabies threat.

Check that you have all your documents to hand – up-to-date passport, visas, cheque book, permits, health certificates, letter of appointment. Take spare passport photos – it is probably best for partners to have separate passports – and all your diplomas and references, even birth and marriage certificates. The appetite for documents is well-nigh insatiable in some countries!

Melancholy though it may sound, you should also make some provision for the unthinkable: instructions in the case of death, disablement or catastrophe while you are abroad. Contact your financial adviser or insurance company for more information.

If you have a reliable solicitor, you might also consider the possibility of giving him or her power of attorney. This is a simple legal transaction that essentially means that the person having that power can act in your stead. If you need a large sum of money to be sent out to you in a hurry, it is very useful to have a responsible person in the UK whom you can fax and who can raise the money from your bank. Likewise, if you have left your house in the hands of managing agents who are not doing their stuff, you need someone on the spot who can sort things out. Giving someone power of attorney obviously implies a high degree of trust, but there are occasions when it could save you the cost of a return fare home.

KEEPING YOUR VOTE WHILE LIVING ABROAD

On moving abroad, you retain your right to vote in UK and European parliamentary elections; however, there are a number of conditions of which you should be aware. To be eligible you must be a British citizen and satisfy *either* of two sets of conditions:

Set 1

- ☐ you have previously been on the electoral register for an address in the UK;
- ☐ you were living there on the qualifying date;*
- ☐ there are no more than 20 years between the qualifying dates for that register and the one on which you now wish to appear.

Set 2

- ☐ you last lived in the UK less than 20 years before the qualifying date for the register on which you wish to appear;
- ☐ you were too young to be on the electoral register, which was based on the last qualifying date before you left;
- ☐ a parent or guardian was on the electoral register for the address where you were living on that date;
- ☐ you are at least 18 years old, or will become 18 when the register comes into force.

---

*The qualifying date in England, Scotland and Wales is 10 October each year and in Northern Ireland, 15 September. This is for the electoral register, which comes into force on 16 February of the following year and remains in force for 12 months from that date.

You have to register every year on or before the qualifying date and you may continue to register while overseas for 20 years from the qualifying date for the last electoral register on which you appeared as a UK resident.

How to register

To register you must fill in an Overseas Elector's Declaration form RPF 37, which you can get from the nearest British consular or diplomatic mission. The following information will be required: your full name and overseas address, the UK address where you were last registered and the date you left the UK. The first-time overseas elector will have to find someone to support the declaration who is aged 18 or over, has a British passport and is a British citizen, is not living in the UK and who knows you but is not a close relative. First-time overseas electors who left the UK before they were old enough to register will also have to provide a copy of their full birth certificate and information about the parent or guardian on whose registration they are relying.

How to vote and remain registered

You do not have a postal vote. Instead you must appoint a proxy who will vote on your behalf. He or she must be a citizen of Britain, the Commonwealth or the Republic of Ireland, a UK resident, and willing and legally able to vote on your behalf. The application form for appointing a proxy is attached to the Overseas Elector's Declaration form. Your declaration, proxy application and, if required, birth certificate should be returned to the electoral registration officer for the area where you were last registered. The electoral registration officer will write to tell you whether you qualify as an overseas elector and will be included on the register: if you do not, he or she will explain why. You will be sent a reminder each year, and another declaration form will be enclosed with this.

REMOVAL NOTIFICATIONS

Don't forget to tell the following organisations that you are moving abroad:

Your bank.

Income Tax Office. Notify HMRC giving the exact date of departure.

Contributions Agency, International Services (for information on National Insurance Contributions and related health cover), Longbenton, Newcastle upon Tyne, NE98 1YX, or *The Benefits Agency, Pensions and Overseas Benefits Directorate* (for advice on benefits and related health cover), at Tyneview Park, Newcastle upon Tyne NE98 1BA. Include your full name, date of birth and UK NI or pension number, together with details of the country to which you are moving and the duration of your stay.

Vehicle licence. If you are taking your vehicle abroad for longer than a year this is regarded as a 'permanent export'. In this case you should return your existing (new-style) registration document to the Driver and Vehicle Licensing Centre, Swansea SA99 1AB, filling in the 'permanent export' section. Alternatively, you can apply to your local Vehicle Registration Office for the necessary forms.

Driving licence. You will probably want to retain your British driving licence. Some countries recognise it as valid and a list of those that do not is available from the RAC and the AA.

International Driving Permit. An International Driving Permit is obtainable from the RAC or AA (even if you are not a member) and is valid for one year. The licence is not valid in the country where it is issued so you must obtain it before leaving the UK. Most countries require residents to hold a local driving licence so check whether this is the case on taking up your new residence. Contact RAC Travel Services, PO Box 1500, Bristol BS99 2LH (telephone 0800 550055 for information), or any Automobile Association shop.

Motor insurance. Notify your insurers of the date of your departure – your insurance should be cancelled from that date and you should obtain a refund for the rest of the insurance period. Ask your insurance company for a letter outlining your no-claims record to show to your new insurer.

Life and other insurances. Notify the companies concerned or your insurance broker if you use one.

Council tax. Notify the town hall.

Dentist and optician. Let them know you are moving, as a matter of courtesy. It will save posting useless check-up reminders.

Private health insurance. Notify subscriber records department.

Gas. If you use it, notify your local gas supplier giving at least 48 hours' notice. They will give you a standard form to fill in with details of the move and any current hire-purchase agreements. If appliances are to be removed they require as much notice as possible to arrange an appointment; there is a disconnection charge.

Electricity. Notify your local district office or showroom at least 48 hours before moving. Arrangements are much the same as for gas.

Water. The local water board should also be notified at least 48 hours before the move. Drain tanks and pipes if the house is to remain empty in winter.

Telephone. Notify your local telephone sales office as shown in the front of your directory at least *seven days* before the move.

Libraries. Return books and give in tickets to be cancelled.

Professional advisers such as solicitors, accountants, stockbrokers, insurance brokers, etc. Make sure they have a forwarding address.

Stocks and shares. Write to the company registrar at the address on the last annual report or share certificates.

Organisations and clubs – any business, civic, social, cultural, sports or automobile club of which you are a member. For the AA write to Membership Subscriptions and Records, PO Box 50, Basingstoke, Hampshire RG21 2ED and for the RAC write to Membership Enquiries, PO Box 1500, Bristol BS99 2LH.

Credit card companies. Advise them that you are leaving the country.

Hire purchase and rental companies. Notify the office where repayments are made. You will need to settle your account.

Local business accounts – department stores, newsagents, dairy, baker, chemist, dry cleaner, laundry, motor service station.

Publications. Cancel postal subscriptions to newspapers, magazines, professional and trade journals, book and record clubs, etc.

National Health Service. Return your NHS card to the Family Health Services Authority for your area, giving your date of departure, or hand it in to the immigration officer at your point of departure.

Pension schemes. If you have a 'frozen' or paid-up pension from a previous employer notify the pension trust of your new address.

TV. If you have a rented set, make arrangements to return it.

Post Office. Notify day of departure and UK contact address.

Personal Giro. The Post Office has a special sae for this.

Premium Bonds – anything rather than join the sad list of unclaimed prizes! Contact Premium Bonds, National Savings, Blackpool FY3 9XR to check the current position, because in a few countries, Premium Bond holdings may contravene lottery laws.

Save As You Earn and National Savings Certificates. It is important to notify any permanent change of address. Advise the Savings and Certificates and SAYE Office, Durham DH99 1NS, quoting the contract number(s).

National Savings Bank. Notify at Glasgow G58 1SB.

National Savings Income Bonds. Notify Income Bonds, Blackpool FY3 9YP.

Your landlord. If you are a tenant, give the appropriate notice to quit.

Your tenants. If you are a landlord, that UK address you've organised will be needed.

Your employer. Give new address details, or a contact address, in writing.

Schools. Try to give your children's schools a term's notice that they will be leaving. If you wish your children's education to be continued in Britain, contact your local education authority or the Department for Education and Employment, Sanctuary Buildings, Great Smith Street, London SW1P 3BT, for advice, and see Chapter 7.

Make sure your *removers* have any temporary contact address and phone numbers for you, both in the UK and abroad, so that they can get in touch with you when the need arises. It is also useful for them if you can tell them when you expect to arrive in your new country.

Checklist: Moving out

1. Be practical about what to take and try to travel light.
2. Check what will be available in your new accommodation and consider whether it might be better for the working partner to go out ahead of the rest of the family.
3. Consult with a reputable removal firm with experience in overseas removal.
4. Increase your insurance to cover replacement costs at the other end.
5. If you have a pet, think about what will be the best arrangement in the long term. If you are taking your dog with you, be sure to arrange for vaccination six months before you leave.
6. Think carefully about whether or not you should take your car with you, as it might not be suitable for the terrain of your new home.
7. If you decide to take your car, obtain leaflet V562 from your local Vehicle Registration Office.
8. Have a thorough medical check-up before you leave.
9. Check that you have all your documents available and take spare passport photos.
10. Fill in an Overseas Elector's Declaration form RPF37 to keep your right to vote.

11 | Settling In

You arrive, with or without your family, and may find you are not met at the airport. This is the first of many irritations which people going out to work for overseas governments may encounter. It does not usually happen with companies. You may have to stay in a hotel or hostel for a considerable time, so make sure in advance who is going to foot the bill. You will need money to meet such contingencies – and to pay for telephones and taxis to and from the airport.

Even if you are lucky enough to move into a house or apartment, you will find a bare larder. This is where any tins or packet foods you brought with you will come in useful. (In Jamaica, the Corona Worldwide branch will provide a loan of a 'basket' of essentials for people waiting for their baggage to be unloaded.)

One early need will be to fix up domestic help, if you want it. It is usually best to engage a house steward and/or any other servants on the personal recommendation of the previous occupant (you may inherit his or her staff) or a neighbour. Find out from the local labour office what the going rate is and negotiate accordingly, making it quite clear from the start what duties the staff will be expected to perform, eg in the kitchen, washing and housework. Living quarters are usually provided, but find out beforehand whether your steward plans to bring all his family and relatives to stay with him!

Both for insurance purposes and your own peace of mind, make proper security arrangements. Some people, either individually or in groups, employ nightwatchmen; others rely on dogs, or on special locks. The extent of pilfering and burglary in many African countries has grown alarmingly in recent years, so make sure your precautions are fully adequate. John Wason (Insurance Brokers)

Ltd, founded by a former expatriate, offers a specialist Overseas Personal Insurance scheme, which includes home contents, belongings, money and personal liability, as well as optional medical and accident/sickness cover. It is claimed to be the only such policy available on a stand-alone basis, and as such would be useful for those in rented or company property.

At an early stage it is a good idea to see to all your requirements for banking and for obtaining work and residence permits, income tax coding, and the driving licence and test requirements where necessary. Find out also about health products and medical facilities, contributions to provident funds and subscriptions to clubs. Many employers pay for these.

Finally, keep a close eye on the health of young children, particularly on persistent tummy upsets and fevers. It is advisable always to use water you have sterilised yourself, not bottled water of unknown provenance.

There is also the question of preparation, other than physical, for your move. Do you know what the country you are going to is like? What facilities are there for shopping, leisure and entertainment? What is the climate like and what clothes will you need? Are there any pitfalls you should know about or any special behavioural dos and don'ts? Nowadays, overseas countries are very sensitive about foreigners understanding that their new patterns of government and economic development are not just pale imitations of the West.

The importance of getting properly briefed beforehand cannot be overestimated. This will not only save you from possible embarrassing situations – for example, if you don't know the rules about drinking in the Middle East – but will help you to decide what you need to take with you and give you some idea of the atmosphere in which you will work and live. Companies specialising in country-specific briefings are described in Chapter 9. Details can also be found in the website directory at the back of this book.

GOING THROUGH DIPLOMATIC CHANNELS

Expatriates who work for British companies or those from other Western countries in the developing or newly industrialised world can usually expect their employers to come to their aid in case of a political upheaval, or even if they get into personal difficulties – deserved or otherwise. Furthermore, they can expect their contracts of employment to be clear-cut and to conform to Western norms. Neither of these things is necessarily true if you work for a local employer, as is increasingly the case. The money is often better, but the risk is greater.

Some guidance on points to watch out for in taking up an appointment with a local employer in a developing country is given in the Employment Conditions Checklist in Chapter 2. Ultimately, though, you have no protection other than your own vigilance and UK diplomatic channels in the country concerned. They are generally very much criticised by expatriates as being ineffectual or indifferent, but the Foreign and Commonwealth Office claim this is because their role is not understood. For a start, they cannot intervene in contractual disputes, *unless* a British subject is being discriminated against in comparison with other employees. They can, however, recommend you to a local lawyer who may be able to help you and they maintain carefully vetted lists of reliable legal firms. Best of all, they say, is to write to the British embassy or consulate nearest to your location before you leave the UK and ask them to put you in touch with someone who can give you a line on your prospective employer. Though UK diplomatic sources do keep track of known bad hats among employers, in the main they prefer such information to go through non-diplomatic channels, for obvious reasons.

The consular service of the Foreign Office is now very sensitive about the criticisms that have been made of it. If you fail to get an answer from the embassy or consulate you have contacted, or you are not satisfied with the service provided at a British embassy, high commission or consulate, you should write to: Director of Consular Services, Consular Directorate, Foreign & Commonwealth Office, Old Admiralty Building, Whitehall, London SW1A 2PA; tel: 020 7008 0223, fax: 020 7008 0152.

Primarily, of course, the role of British diplomats is to protect British subjects from the consequences of political upheavals. Any expatriate who goes to a notoriously high-risk place must take into account the circumstances there before deciding to accept an appointment. Diplomats are also not able to protect you from the consequences if you break the law of the land you are in. At most they can visit you in prison, arrange for you to be properly repre-sented legally and intercede discreetly for an amnesty for you. A

UK or multinational company would, in such cases, arrange for you to be flown out on the first available plane, usually with the connivance of the authorities.

Whatever your feelings about the efficacy or otherwise of British diplomatic protection, you should register with the embassy or consulate as soon as possible after you arrive to work in any developing country. This means they can contact you if a sudden emergency arises, whether personal or political. It cannot do any harm; and if you wake up one morning to the sound of gunfire, as has happened to many an expatriate, you may be very glad that you took that precaution.

Foreign & Commonwealth Travel Advice is designed to help British travellers avoid trouble by providing succinct and up-to-date information on threats to personal safety arising from political unrest, lawlessness, violence, natural disasters and epidemics. Some 650 notices are issued each year covering more than 130 countries. Notices are constantly renewed on the basis of information from posts overseas. The full range of notices is available on BBC2 Ceefax pages 470 onwards, and on the FCO's website, along with a range of Consular Division publicity material, www.fco.gov.uk. The public can contact the Travel Advice Unit direct between 9.30 am and 4.00 pm Monday to Friday on 0870 606 0290.

Other Consular Services information leaflets, including 'Checklist for Travellers', 'Backpackers and Independent Travellers' and 'British Consular Services Abroad' are widely distributed through travel agents, shipping companies and airlines, public libraries, Citizens Advice Bureaux and the UK Passport Agency, and can be obtained by faxing the Distribution Centre on 01444 246620.

READING MATTER

You may never have been much of a book buyer while living in the UK, but many expatriates report that not being able to get hold of books when they want them is an unexpected deprivation, especially in postings where other forms of entertainment, at any rate in English, are hard to come by.

Many places do, of course, have bookshops which stock some English titles, but the selection is often very limited (children's books are particularly hard to get) and prices are always much higher than the UK price shown tantalisingly on the jacket. You can, however, import your own books at standard London prices through the admirable Good Book Guide (23 Bedford Avenue, London WC1B 3AX; 24-hour tel: 020 7323 3636 (UK), +44 (0)20 7323 3838 (from outside UK), e-mail: enquiries@gbgdirect.com) or order books on the internet from Amazon.com. The Guide is a mail order book service with a substantial trade among expatriates all over the world. You can choose your books from the monthly guide, for which there is a modest annual subscription, but the service can also get any book in print for you, including paperbacks. There are also regular video and audio listings offering a wealth of entertainment: drama, documentary, comedy and children's programmes.

The choices in the guide are accompanied by brief, helpful notes written by outside experts (eg Chris Bonington on travel) and the selection of titles is broad, covering both high-brow literature and commercial best sellers, all chosen on merit alone. The subject areas are broad too, ranging through all kinds of interests. However, the Good Book Guide is not a book club – there is no obligation to buy. A free trial issue can be requested.

Payment is on a cash with order basis or by credit card and clear instructions are given with each issue of the guide on how to pay from anywhere in the world.

ENTERTAINMENT AND HOME COMFORTS

While your new home is likely to be a source of varied and new experiences, you might like to maintain some of the interests that you developed at home. The internet can provide an invaluable link for this. Football fans can follow their team's progress through the season by logging on to both official and unofficial websites. Chat forums can also keep you in contact with fellow fans. The internet might also be a way to find out if there are other expatriates or host-country fan clubs in your region, which could be a good way to meet people and set up a social network.

Using the internet to keep informed with both world and local news is also a new innovation. Many radio and TV companies now use it to broadcast. For example, CNN, Reuters and the BBC all have news information. Furthermore, you can listen to some radio programmes through the internet. The BBC has recently launched an audio online version of its news and entertainment programmes which can be found on the BBC site. National newspapers also use the internet and some, such as *The Daily Telegraph*, publish the whole day's paper on their website. Furthermore, local newspapers are also setting up websites, so it is quite possible to keep in touch with your local news – including football reports, and local issues such as education and government. A listing of websites can be found at the back of this book.

Sending for goods through mail order catalogues can make up for deficiencies in local shops when working abroad. Although many companies that provide goods by mail order confine their activities to the UK and will not send goods abroad (no doubt because of potential payment problems), there is nothing to stop you making arrangements to get catalogues through UK friends or relatives and ordering through them. Expatriates with young children are reported to find the Mothercare catalogue very useful. Harrods and Fortnum & Mason will send goods anywhere in the world and you can pay by credit card. Harrods also operate worldwide accounts, and franchise outlets in airports in some surprising places. However, e-commerce also means that receiving home comforts is no longer the complicated process it used to be and many large retail companies now have ordering facilities set up on their websites.

Checklist: Settling in

1. Try to organise domestic help as soon as possible and bring a few necessities with you.
2. Brief your domestic help as clearly as possible and identify duties from the start.
3. Make proper security arrangements and check that you have all your legal requirements for work, banking, medical help, etc.
4. Find out emergency numbers, including those of your consulate or embassy, and if you are relocating to a developing country, register with them as soon as possible.
5. Identify sources from where books and home comforts can be obtained, whether locally or internationally.
6. Seek out social networks through expatriate organisations, your employer or through the internet.
7. If you have not used the internet before, now is the time to become acquainted – it will be an invaluable source of information and support!

12 Coming Home

Having completed a foreign assignment you might feel that your return home will be an uncomplicated affair. However, increasingly both companies and individuals are paying attention to the practical and psychological issues involved in repatriation. Not only do domestic issues, such as finding accommodation or dealing with tenants, need to be tackled, but career considerations and family issues need to be addressed. Furthermore, although you might feel confident about fitting back into professional and social networks, surprisingly some expatriates do experience a reverse culture shock on their return.

PERSONAL POSSESSIONS

If you are to reap the full benefit of a spell as a non-UK resident, planning for your return requires forethought and preparation, particularly in the matter of bringing back personal possessions. Price differentials between countries are no longer as great as they used to be, but there are still quite a number of places where, even taking freight into account, it is worth buying things like electronic or audiovisual equipment, even cars, locally and shipping them back home. In countries that operate exchange controls this may also be a possible way of taking out assets in the form of goods. But beware of the catch: unless you can show that an article has been used and owned for six months, you are liable for import duty – and VAT on top of that. It is no use asking an obliging vendor to provide backdated invoices, because if you are unlucky enough to come under investigation, customs officials check serial numbers as well as documents. Another thing to be aware of is that once your personal possessions, including cars, are imported without payment of import duty and VAT, they cannot be sold or disposed of within 12 months, or they become liable for both these taxes.

Even with well-used goods, you can be in for unforeseen costs unless you get your timing right. The problem is that possessions shipped back to the UK will not be released until their owner arrives home. You can get a relative to clear them on your behalf, but that person would be liable for provisional duty on their value which is only repaid when you yourself get back. It takes about a fortnight to clear goods through customs anyway, so you will need expert advice at the other end if you are to steer the difficult course between paying warehouse charges in the UK because the goods have arrived too soon, and finding yourself without the basic necessities of life because you have sent them off too late.

The most important thing, though, is that they should actually arrive. The cheapest form of shipping may not be the best. The right course of action is to find a local firm that has a reputable agent in the UK, and to make sure you get door-to-door insurance cover.

ACCOMMODATION

Providing you have gone through the correct tenancy arrangements, reclaiming your property should not be too complicated. However, be aware that if you return earlier than planned, and your tenants have time left on their agreement, you might have to find alternative accommodation for the outstanding tenancy period. In particular, under an Assured Shorthold Tenancy – unless your tenant agrees to move earlier – you will have to wait until the contract runs its course with two months' notice given after that period.

You should try to give the letting agents who are looking after your UK property at least three months' notice of your return, so that they can give due notice to the tenants. However, should you be unfortunate enough to come across a tenant who is unwilling to move on, it is possible to insure against legal and hotel costs.

FINDING A NEW JOB

Unless you have been sent out by a UK employer, the biggest problem in returning home can be in finding another job. Well before that point you should be sending your CV round to head-hunters who are always on the lookout for those with specialist qualifications. If you feel that you might have difficulty placing yourself on the job market on grounds of age or lack of specific skills, it may be worth consulting a career counsellor. They cannot 'find' you a job – and you should be wary of those who imply otherwise – but their advice, though not cheap, has been found to be a good investment by many mid-career jobseekers.

Returning employees are also faced with career dilemmas. An Arthur Andersen Survey as long ago as 1999 reported that 21 per cent of companies expect their returning employee to initiate the search for their next position. The proportion of companies offering help is unlikely to have risen. Of those companies that do offer help, under 10 per cent begin to look for a position for the expatriate a year before return and approximately 40 per cent used to do so 6–12 months before the end of the assignment, but the latter percentage has probably fallen. Indeed, this is precisely what stops many employees taking on a foreign assignment in the first place: a lack of career opportunities on their return. Employees who are unable to return to their former job have a number of options available to them, which are shown in Table 12.1. The outlook today for returning expatriates is probably worse than in 1999.

Chapter 2 deals with this subject in some depth. However, it is worth repeating at this point that the issue of reintegration should be raised before taking on an assignment. An employer who values the skills that have been developed abroad will also be thinking about how best to utilise them on your return. Leaving this to chance, though, is not a good idea. At least a year before your return you should be entering into a dialogue with your employer about career opportunities for your return. If your company provides a mentor, he or she should also be able to help create a constructive dialogue and repatriation process.

Table 12.1 Post-assignment options

Redundancy	50%
Re-assignment to another expatriate position	31%
Extension of current assignment	32%
Appointed 'special projects' in the home country	57%
Other	8%

Source: Arthur Andersen Expatriate Survey 1999

If you are able to settle back into your former job or one of equivalent status, it is also worth bearing in mind that time will have passed since you were last part of your home office team. Different faces, work practices and projects should be expected and it might take some time to readjust to your altered office environment. Do not expect that you will necessarily be welcome, as you will probably be affecting other people's career prospects.

The same 1999 Arthur Andersen Survey found that a mere 11 per cent of respondents offered some form of post-repatriation support during the 12 months after return, and this tended to be with tax compliance rather than personal support. None of the respondents gave any form of help with readjustment to home-country living and working, which, as the report's author Barry Page commented, 'is interesting, since inability to re-adapt to home-country office culture is ranked as the most common reason given by returning expatriates for leaving their company following their repatriation'.

Of course, returning expatriates have the option of moving into self-employment and this may be particularly attractive to those who have the opportunity to take early retirement on favourable terms. In 2006, as final salary pension schemes are increasingly curtailed and changed to the 'money purchase' variety for the remainder of an employee's period of service, or where the employer requires increased contributions from pension scheme member to maintain benefits, it may make good sense to work for yourself and take your pension rights with you. As a returning expatriate, you may well have acquired skills and experience of foreign markets and industries that make you valuable as a consultant to companies that don't want to relocate their own staff – with the inevitable learning curve you went through when you took up your own assignment.

If you find that self-employment beckons, you should start researching the business opportunities and planning well before your return. In this day and age, there is no such thing as job security for life, and anyone over the age of 30 should have a 'Plan B' in the briefcase for self-employment or starting his or her own business. You might make a start by reading my book *Working for Yourself,* published by Kogan Page, and available at www.kogan-page.co.uk.

REVERSE CULTURE SHOCK

One of the most surprising aspects of returning home is the experience of reverse culture shock. Again, the passing of time needs to be taken into account. While you have been away things will have moved on in your home country and not only friends and family will have changed but your international experience will almost certainly have changed you as well. Your expectations might well have undergone a radical change abroad and coming home might mean that you, once again, have to re-adapt these to suit your circumstances. Much like any other major move, returning home requires a readjustment to new circumstances and time should be taken to absorb this process.

Fitting back into an office environment is one thing but it is also worth bearing in mind that partners and children might also experience difficulties settling back.

PREPARING THE FAMILY FOR RETURN

As with the move abroad, a trailing partner might well have to begin to search for another job on his or her return home. Beginning that search well in advance is well worth the time. Furthermore, enlightened companies are beginning to realise the need to provide information and support to enable partners to resettle. For example, Shell has 40 information centres worldwide providing information and support for partners. Children might also feel disorientated by returning home. Having to fit back into school and peer groups can be traumatic. Their experience of a different culture and returning to an unfamiliar environment might be disturbing for a period of time. Furthermore, they might not be able to return to their old school if places are scarce. Again, it is worth informing schools as early as possible about your return and to look for alternative arrangements should there be a lack of places. Children should be encouraged to keep in touch with home during a foreign assignment so that they are not completely out of step with changes on their return.

A foreign assignment is a fulfilling and life-enhancing experience. The re-adaption to home is part of that experience and its success or failure can affect the foreign experience in either a positive or negative way. Planning for your return is therefore a worthwhile process. Try to forewarn employers, tenants, schools and social contacts of your return well in advance. Keep your family in contact with friends and try to establish with your employer what job opportunities there are likely to be on your return. Most important of all, try to be patient with the new situation. It might be home, but home can also be a 'foreign' place if you have spent some years away.

Checklist: Coming home

1. Think about what goods might be worth buying to bring home and purchase six months before returning.
2. Plan the shipment of possessions carefully to coincide with your return or look into warehousing arrangements.
3. Inform your letting agents as soon as possible of the date you are to return in order to give your tenants as much notice as possible.
4. Look into short-term rental arrangements if you are unable to move back into your property straight away.
5. Discuss with your employer well in advance what plans there are for you on your return – this should ideally take place 12 months before return. If you are returning without a job, contact headhunters and agencies as early as possible.
6. Develop a 'Plan B' for self-employment in case you find that there is no acceptable job opportunity on your return.
7. Be prepared for reverse culture shock and give yourself time to become accustomed to changes in your home and work environment.
8. Contact schools in advance and make contact with your children's friends before returning home.
9. Contact partners' support centres run by your employer to identify career opportunities.

Part Five:

Country Profiles and Personal Taxation

Europe

WESTERN EUROPE AND THE EU

The following section gives information about 22 of the 25 member states of the European Union (EU) – Austria, Belgium, Cyprus, The Czech Republic, Denmark, Estonia, Finland, France, Germany, Greece, Hungary, Ireland, Italy, Lithuania, Luxembourg, Malta, The Netherlands, Poland, Portugal, Slovenia, Spain and Sweden. Similar information is included for Norway and Switzerland. It does not cover the UK, Latvia or Slovakia.

The European Union

The EU is the world's largest single trading group, and the largest market. It is heavily dependent on international trade – more so than either the United States or Japan. Increasingly, trade has extended from manufactured goods to services: the fastest growing sectors have been banking, insurance and telecommunications. However, after 2000 the EU suffered from the global economic downturn and the 12 member states of the Euro area have not yet shared in the general recovery.

In terms of GDP real growth, the Euro area registered 1.4 per cent for 2005 and only 1.9 per cent is forecast for 2006. Denmark, Sweden and the UK, the three remaining members of the old EU 15 outside the Euro area, have done rather better although the outlook for the UK may be fading. By contrast, the economies of almost all the 10 member states which joined the EU on 1 May 2004 are enjoying markedly higher growth rates. A more general cause for concern remains the growing EU trade deficit with China in contrast with its surplus with the rest of the world.

Consequently job opportunities, particularly in the Euro area, remain depressed.

The Single Market, in force since 1993, allows unrestricted trade and free movement of capital and currency within the EU. Union citizens are entitled to travel, reside, study and work wherever they wish within the EU. Anyone is entitled to apply for a job and sign a contract of employment in another member state, without losing pension or health insurance entitlements acquired elsewhere in the EU. Monetary union in January 1999 saw the introduction of a new currency, the Euro, which replaced 12 of the 15 local currencies.

The most important change so far this decade has been – in terms of employment – the right of any fully qualified professional from one EU or EEA state to be recognised as a member of the equivalent profession in another state without having to re-qualify (subject to a few safeguards). The rule applies to all professions to which access is in some way restricted by the state (or by Royal Charter in the UK) and which require at least three years' university-level education. This is creating many more opportunities for a whole range of professionals to work, set up businesses and offer services in other parts of the Union. Further details are given in the Department of Trade and Industry booklet, *Europe – Open for Professions*, available from DTI Business in Europe Hotline (0117 944 4888). These opportunities have been extended further from 1 May 2004 with EU enlargement from 15 to 25 member states. Of course, EU enlargement has also resulted in greater competition for job applicants throughout the Union, although some of the EU 15 states are exercising restrictions on immigrant labour from the EU 10, at least in the short term.

Other points that are worth noting are:

☐ *Passports and permits.* A British citizen can work in EU countries without a work permit; all he or she needs is a valid passport showing that the holder is a British citizen. In most EU countries, if the employment lasts longer than three months a residence permit must be acquired. The individual will need to present proof of employment, a valid passport and other supporting documentation.

☐ *Job opportunities.* In general, skilled or highly skilled workers and those with professional qualifications or particular technical expertise will be able to find employment, but priority will usually be given to qualified nationals. The best opportunities are with multinationals or with British firms operating in other European countries (lists can usually be obtained from the British embassy in that country, although embassies *cannot* help people to find jobs). Details of job opportunities can be obtained from your local Jobcentre, which keeps in touch with the employment centres of EU countries about vacancies. Before you accept a job, it is important to know exactly what to expect in the way of terms and conditions. A useful leaflet entitled 'Working Abroad', as well as others detailing specific countries, are available from Jobcentres or the Overseas Placing Unit of the Employment Service. The DTI Business in Europe Hotline can also provide a number of useful publications.

☐ *Unemployment benefit.* If you have been unemployed in the UK for four weeks, you can continue to draw unemployment benefit from the UK for up to three months while job hunting in the EU. You will need to sign on fortnightly at the local employment services office, and will receive the UK rate of benefit in the local currency. However, in view of the fact that this is nowhere near enough to live on while job hunting, people who decide to prospect should make sure they have enough money to keep themselves during this period, or to get home at the end. Furthermore, many EU countries have made this right very difficult to exercise.

☐ *Driving licences.* Newly qualified drivers are now issued with a pink EU driving licence. It is no longer necessary for drivers to exchange their old licence for a licence from their new country of residence within the EU.

AUSTRIA

The economy

Although Austria is self-sufficient in agricultural production, the economy is based on industry (steel, chemicals, and transport equipment) and tourism. More than 80 per cent of trade takes place with other European countries, predominantly Germany. Consequently, Austria's entry into the European Union has enhanced these trade links. Equally, the economy was affected by the downturn in Germany, although not to the same extent. GDP growth for 2006 is forecast at 2.1 per cent against 1.9 per cent for 2005. Unemployment in January 2006 was 5.1 per cent, well below the Euro area average of 8.8 per cent, while consumer price inflation at 2.3 per cent is in line with the average. Austria has enjoyed a foreign trade surplus on current account since 2003 and is estimated to have been in balance in 2005. The budget deficit at 2 per cent is comfortably within the EU Stability and Growth Pact parameter of 3 per cent.

Austria has also developed strong links with the emerging nations of Eastern Europe, particularly Hungary, where Austria is involved in a number of joint ventures, and also in Slovenia, Slovakia and the Czech Republic. Many businesses undertaking work in Eastern Europe have based themselves in Austria. As all these countries joined the EU in May 2004, the business flow between them and Austria has become seamless. Of the 15 prior EU members, Austria is considered to be one of the beneficiaries of enlargement.

Working conditions

The net wages of managers in Austria are similar to the wages in other Western European countries. Payroll taxes and social security contributions are higher in Austria (due to the extensive public welfare system) than in the UK, as well as the costs of living (except in the London area). Because of the variety of public services available, the general standard of living is higher in Austria, but not by much. In most other respects, working life in Austria is similar to that in the rest of Western Europe. It is normal for managers and professionals to be granted up to 30 days' paid vacation. A good knowledge of the German language is a basic requirement of any type of employment.

There are no restrictions for British citizens working in Austria. However, they must register with municipal district offices or the local registration office ('Meldeamt') within three days of arrival.

Useful information

Banking hours: 8.00 am to 12.30 pm and 1.30 to 3.00 pm weekdays, apart from Thursday 8.00 am to 12.30 pm and 1.30 to 5.30 pm. Closed Saturday and Sunday.

Shopping hours: 9.00 am to 6.00 pm Monday–Friday, 9.00 am to 5.00 pm Saturday. Closed Sunday.

Electricity: 220 V, 50 Hz ac.

Driving: Speed limits are 50 km/h in built-up areas, 100 km/h on overland roads, and 130 km/h on motorways. International driving licence, third-party insurance and wearing of seat belts are compulsory.

Education: Education is compulsory between the ages of 6 and 15. Public schools and universities are free of charge and normally offer a satisfactory level of education. There are good facilities for secondary, technical and professional education. There are 15 public universities, six colleges of art and seven colleges of higher education.

Media: There are four national radio and two national television channels as well as numerous private channels (mostly German). There are four national and various regional daily newspapers.

Useful contacts:
British Embassy, Jauresgasse 12, 1030 Vienna, tel: (43) (1) 716130, website: www.britishembassy.at
Austrian Embassy, 18 Belgrave Mews West, London SW1X 8HU, tel: 020 7235 3731, website: www.bmaa.gv.at/london
Austrian National Tourist Office, 9–11 Richmond Buildings, Off Dean Street, London W1D 3HF, tel: 020 7440 3830, websites: www.austria.info.at, www.salzburginfo.at, www.info.wien.at

PERSONAL TAXATION

Resident individuals whose established domicile or habitual place of abode (that is, with more than six months' physical presence per calendar year) in Austria are subject to unlimited tax liability on their worldwide income regardless of citizenship. Non-resident individuals are subject to tax only on certain Austrian-source income.

Income tax is a progressive tax assessed on a calendar-year basis, with each person being taxed individually by applying graduated tax rates to defined income bands ranging from 0 per cent through 38.33 per cent, 43.6 per cent to 50 per cent for taxable income exceeding €51,000 pa. Certain types of income are taxed at reduced rates. Income from one source generally may be offset by a loss from another source. In computing taxable income special expenses ('Sonderausgaben') and extraordinary charges ('aussergewöhnliche Belastung') subject to limitations may be deducted. Certain tax credits are granted according to the taxpayer's personal circumstances.

Income from employment such as wages, bonuses, benefits in kind (accommodation, cars, loans and so on; certain social facilities made available by the employer are explicitly tax-exempt), expense allowances received (except for travel expenses up to certain amounts) and any other remuneration deriving from employment, emoluments from statutory health insurance and pension plans are subject to salary tax withheld at source on a pay-as-you-earn basis after deduction of social security contributions. An employee's annual salary is usually paid in 14 parts, consisting of 12 monthly payments plus a Christmas and a holiday bonus, as these extra payments are taxed at a favourable flat income tax rate of 6 per cent. Expenses exclusively incurred to generate income are tax deductible by filing a personal income tax return. A special concession for expatriates provides for certain simplifications of tax assessment.

Other taxes

Investment income

After a change in legislation in 2003 domestic and foreign investment income is taxed at a flat rate of 25 per cent. Up to 31 March 2003, foreign investment income (dividends from foreign sources, interest on deposits with foreign banks and on bonds held in foreign depots) was taxed at progressive rates. For domestic investment income (as well as foreign investment income paid out in Austria) a 25 per cent withholding tax is deducted at source, which is considered as the final income tax payable for individuals with related expenses not being deductible. Foreign investment income not paid out in Austria has to be stated in a personal income tax return in order to profit from the reduced rate of 25 per cent.

Royalties and rental income net of related expenses are taxed at regular tax rates. Private capital gains are generally exempt from tax. Income from the sale of private property is subject to tax as speculative gain only if the retention period for real estate does not exceed 10 years (exceptions are granted for owner-occupied dwellings) and one year for other assets. Moreover, capital gains derived upon the sale of privately held shareholdings and unrealised capital gains in the case of giving up residence in Austria are taxed at half the average income tax rate if at any time during the last five years this shareholding amounted to at least 1 per cent. The provision leading to taxation of unrealised capital gains has been changed recently, so that on moving to another EU/EEA member state the tax liability is not assessed until the underlying shareholding is actually sold.

Tax treatment of capital

There are no taxes on capital in Austria.

Double taxation treaties

In the double tax treaties between Austria and the UK and the United States respectively, employment income is taxable in the residence state unless employment is only temporarily exercised in the other state. Dividends and interest are taxable in the residence state with the source state being entitled to levy a certain percentage of withholding tax on dividends for which a tax credit is granted.

For further information on tax and social security, contact:

Gudrun Wiedemann, BDO Auxilia Treuhand GmbH, tel: +43 (01) 5 37 37 339, e-mail: wiedemann@bdo.at, website: www.bdo.at

BELGIUM

The economy

During the latter part of the 1980s Belgium attracted wealth and investment out of all proportion to its size. At the crossroads of Europe, and host to the main EU institutions, Belgium has been well placed to attract investors.

Old industries have been restructured and small, hi-tech firms have been encouraged. The service sector now accounts for the majority of national income, with financial services making a major contribution. Nevertheless, Belgium is still very much a manufacturing country, and is one of the larger car exporters in the world.

The country is fairly wealthy with a strong current account trade balance and its budget deficit, formerly a weak point, now well under control. The current account surplus for 2005 is estimated to be 1.8 per cent of GDP and the 2005 budget is expected to balance. For 2006 the Federal Planning Bureau forecasts a 2.2 per cent GDP growth for Belgium following an estimated 1.4 per cent growth in 2005. As the administrative centre of the EU, Brussels is a major employment location for the nationals of member states but national unemployment is high and was reported at 12.9 per cent in December 2005 before seasonal adjustment. Consumer price inflation is estimated at 2.7 per cent for 2005 but a reduction to 2.2 per cent is forecast for 2006.

Working conditions

EU nationals with valid passports are free to come and go, but they must register at the local police or town hall within eight days of arrival. Children must also be registered. The period of their stay (more or less then three months) in Belgium and their capacity (employee, student, family member) will determine if a residence permit needs to be issued.

The level of managerial and executive salaries is higher than in the UK. An upper middle-ranked executive could expect to earn at least £55,000 gross a year. Increasingly, a company car could be provided in addition to the basic salary.

Useful information

Banking hours: 9.00 am to 3.30 or 4.00 pm Monday–Friday, 9.00 am to 12.00 pm on Saturday; banks close during the lunch hour.

Postal service: Post office hours 9.00 am to 12.00 pm and 2.00 pm to 4.00 pm or 5.00 pm Monday–Friday.

Shopping hours: 10.00 am to 6.00 pm Monday–Saturday.

Electricity: 220 V, 50 Hz ac.

Driving: Speed limits are 30 km/h in school areas, 50 km/h in built-up areas, 90 km/h on overland roads, and 120 km/h on motorways. Front and back seat belts compulsory. Maximum blood alcohol level 0.5 mg/l. Children (up to age 4 or 18 kilos) need to be placed in a child seat.

Transport: Distances are so short that most travel is done by train or car. Rail services are efficient and there is a good network of roads and autoroutes, with ring roads round the large towns. Urban transport in Brussels is adequate, but buses and trams get very crowded.

Health care: The health services are part of the general social security system, which is a very comprehensive one. Everyone has to belong to a 'mutualité/mutualiteit' (sickness insurance fund). You have to pay for a visit to a doctor and for prescriptions but about 75 per cent of the cost of medical treatment may be reimbursed by the 'mutualité'. Many hospitals and clinics are run by different denominational groups. People who are currently insured under the UK social security scheme should obtain the necessary forms for reciprocal treatment from the DSS before leaving the UK.

Education: Education, both primary and secondary, is free and compulsory for all Belgian children between 6 and 18. As well as the state schools there are many Catholic and independent schools in Brussels and elsewhere. There are a number of European and International Schools. The International School of Brussels takes in children from 3 to 19 (a 13th year is possible) in kindergarten, elementary and secondary schools and has over 1,000 boys and girls, the majority being from the United States. There is a smaller International School at Antwerp. The British School of Brussels, which is co-educational and follows the UK National Curriculum, has over 1,000 students aged 2 to 11. There is also a school in Antwerp offering a British curriculum. The small British Primary School in Brussels caters for children from 3 to 11. The St John's English-speaking school at Waterloo, near Brussels, caters for children between 3 and 19 (a 13th year is possible).

There are French- and Dutch-speaking 'free' universities at Leuven and Louvain-la-Neuve, state universities at Ghent, Brussels and Liège and university centres at Antwerp, Mons and Diepenbeek. Education is free and standards are high.

Useful contacts:
British Embassy, 85 Rue d'Arlon, 1040 Brussels, tel: 32 2 287 6211, website: www.britishembassy.gov.uk/belgium
Belgium Embassy, 103–104 Eaton Square, London SW1W 9AB, tel: 020 7470 3700, website: www.diplobel.org/uk
Belgium Tourist Offices (Brussels-Wallonia), 217 Marsh Wall, London E14 9FJ, tel: 0800 9545 245 (brochure line), website: www.belgiumtheplaceto.be
Tourism Flanders-Brussels, 1a Cavendish Square, London W1G 0LD, tel: 0800 954 5245 (brochure line), website: www.visit-flanders.co.uk
Websites: www.visitbelgium.com; www.belgique-tourisme.net

Expatriate information:
Expats in Brussels, www.expatsinbrussels.com
Expatriates Guide to Belgium, www.netcat.co.uk/rob/be/bel-idx-shtml, www.xpats.com, www.expatriate-online.com

PERSONAL TAXATION

Residence

Like many countries, Belgium taxes income on the basis of residence. In general individuals are considered to be resident in Belgium for income tax purposes if they establish their 'domicile' ('domicile/domicilie') or established place of residence or the centre of their wealth ('siège de fortune/zetel van fortuin') – the centre of their vital and economic interest, such as bank account, mail, household – in Belgium. Physical presence is not conclusive.

In order to determine whether someone is resident in Belgium, factual circumstances have to be taken into account. However, in absence of any rebuttal, an individual is deemed to be resident if he or she is registered at the Communal Population Register (refutable presumption). If a spouse (and children) is also living in Belgium, there is an irrefutable assumption of residence of the married couple in Belgium.

Taxation of personal income

Residents are subject to income tax on their worldwide income, divided into four categories:

1. (deemed) rental income from real (immovable) property;
2. income from movable property, including dividends, interest and royalties (investment income);
3. earned income, including business income, professional income, employment income and pension income;
4. miscellaneous income.

The net taxable income for each category amounts to the gross income less expenses incurred in acquiring or preserving the income and is computed according to each category's own rules. Certain additional deductions can be made from this total net income before applying the progressive tax rates.

As of 2004 (tax assessment year 2005), single taxpayers and married taxpayers are considered as equals in terms of the tax-free minimum income, which amounts to €5,780 (assessment year 2006) per person. Additional tax-free minima are available in respect of children and other dependants.

There is a possibility of benefiting from tax deductions.

The taxable period is the calendar year. Rates of income tax are progressive and range from 25 per cent to 50 per cent. Income is assessed on a previous-year basis, so that income for 2006 is assessed in 2007 at the 2006 tax rates.

Income from employment

Employment income (salary, benefits in kind, termination payments, and so forth) is fully taxable. However, employment income from a treaty country is exempt from tax for a Belgian resident, although it is added to the taxable income when determining the rate of income tax to be applied to the taxable income (this method is known as 'exemption with progression').

A tax credit of 50 per cent is available for employment income from a non-treaty country, provided that the income was taxed abroad, no matter at what rate. Foreign income is subject to income tax for its net amount (less expenses, including withholding and income taxes, regardless of the availability of any other relief).

Professional expenses are deductible, either on a lump-sum basis (the maximum deduction amounts to €3,110 for assessment year 2006), or on the actual amount incurred, provided this can be substantiated. Employees can also benefit from a number of tax-free 'social benefits' (such as meal tickets, hospitalisation insurance and sick-pay arrangements), provided that the related requirements are met.

Expatriates temporarily residing in Belgium can benefit from a privileged tax regime, provided that a number of conditions are satisfied, allowing them to be taxed as if they were non-resident. They are taxed on their remuneration, which is pro-rated on the basis of the number of working days spent in Belgium. Moreover, certain expenses borne by the employer (moving costs, housing allowance, costs of a yearly trip to the home country, tax equalisation, cost of living allowances, etc.) are considered as expenses proper to the employer and are, within certain limits – €29,750 (if working in control or coordination offices or scientific research centres) or €11,250 if working elsewhere – exempt from tax for the employee. The expat status must be specifically granted by the tax authorities.

A system of withholding tax operates on earnings.

Investment income
Dividends

Both domestic and foreign dividends received via an 'interme-diary' in Belgium are in principle subject to a final movable with-holding tax of 10, 15, 20 or 25 (general withholding tax percentage) per cent. As an alternative, taxpayers can elect for dividends to be included in their income tax return; these dividends are then taxable at progressive tax rates where this is beneficial. When divi-dends are reported in the income tax return, the aforementioned tax rates are increased by the communal taxes.

Interest

Domestic interest received via an 'intermediary' in Belgium is in principle subject to a final withholding tax of 15 per cent. As an alternative, Belgium residents can elect for interest to be included in their income tax return; the interest amount is then taxable at progressive tax rates where this is beneficial. When interest is reported in the income tax return, the aforementioned tax rates are increased by the communal taxes.

Foreign dividends not received in Belgium, and foreign-source interest, although exempt, still need to be reported in the Belgian income tax return.

Income from real property

Income from Belgian real property is taxable in Belgium. The amount of taxable income from real property in Belgium is normally an imputed income based on its cadastral value (deemed rental value).

As of assessment year 2006 the cadastral income of the owner-occupied property (only for one residence) is exempted from taxes. Property that is let to a business is taxable on the actual rental income, as reduced by qualifying expenses (standard deduction of 40 per cent for buildings, 10 per cent for land).

In the case of real property situated abroad, taxable income is the actual annual rent received, although a standard deduction of 40 per cent, on account of expenses, is allowed. However, where the property is unlet, its annual rental value is used as the base for tax. Where the real property is situated in a treaty country, however, income is exempt (with progression – see above) from taxation in Belgium.

An additional levy ('immovable withholding tax') on income from immovable property is imposed on deemed income from immovable property located in Belgium. This levy is computed as a percentage of the cadastral income. The rate varies according to the Region in which the property is located.

Taxes on capital

Capital gains

Capital gains on shares are generally exempt from taxation, as are all gains arising from the normal management of private property. However, some gains (considered to be of a speculative nature) are taxable as miscellaneous income.

Additional taxes

The income reported in the income tax return is subject to communal taxes, varying between 0 and 10 per cent of the federal income taxes due.

Wealth tax

There is no wealth tax in Belgium.

Double tax treaties

Belgium has concluded over 85 comprehensive treaties to avoid double taxation, among which are treaties with the UK and the United States.

For further information on individual tax and social security, contact: Jan Van Langendonck, Tax Manager, BDO Atrio G.IE, tel: (0032) 2778 0100, e-mail: jan.vanlangendonck@bdo.be

CYPRUS

The economy

As a full member of the European Union, Cyprus is successfully meeting the challenge of being part of the enlarged European family. Cyprus's economy is market-oriented, with the private sector playing the dominant role in the production sphere. The

government's role focuses on the creation of a favourable entrepreneurial climate, through the maintenance of conditions of macro-
economic stability, the upgrading of socio-economic and legal
infrastructure, and the pursuit of sustainable development.

The population of Cyprus is approximately 700,000 and the island
is the third largest in the Mediterranean covering 9,252 sq. km.

The GDP growth rate in real terms for the third quarter of 2005,
estimated at approximately 3.8 per cent over the corresponding
period of 2004, compares favourably with the EU average. This
was accomplished in an environment of almost full employment
conditions (unemployment was about 3.8 per cent in 2005), low
inflation (about 2.5 per cent in 2005) and a stable and strong
currency (CYP 1= €1.72). Consumer price inflation, protected at
2.6 per cent for 2005, is in line with the inflation level of 2004 and
forecast inflation in 2006. Cyprus's foreign trade deficit on current
account is running at just over 6 per cent of GDP and the public
sector budget deficit has fallen from 6.3 per cent in 2003 to 2.8 per
cent in 2005.

In 2005, Cyprus's per capita GDP reached approximately 81 per
cent of the EU 25 average amounting to about €18,000. In addition,
it should be pointed out that important structural reforms within
the context of the Lisbon Strategy are in progress to modernise and
liberalise its market-oriented economy further, with a view to
enhancing its international competitiveness and EU compatibility.
These structural reforms, together with macroeconomic stability,
provide a strong foundation for the successful entry of the island
into the Euro area, scheduled for 2008.

Working conditions

Any European citizen can enter the territory of the Republic of
Cyprus with an identity card or a valid passport. EU nationals and
citizens of the United States do not require a visa for stays of up to
90 days. Other nationals can check requirements on the Cyprus
Ministry of Foreign Affairs website: www.mfa.gov.cy.

A citizen of Europe who comes to Cyprus and wishes to work
must register with the Department of the Population and
Migration Archive or with the Office of the Aliens and Migration
Service of the police in order to obtain the appropriate permit.

European citizens who work and reside legally in Cyprus have the
same rights as citizens of Cyprus as regards remuneration, working

conditions, residence, social insurance and trade union membership, etc. Dependants of European citizens have the same rights.

Working hours vary according to sector and profession. In the private sector most offices and enterprises work from 8.00 am to 5.30 pm, with a break from 1.00 to 2.30 pm, and in the public sector from 7.30 am to 2.30 pm. The standard working week is about 38 hours for a five-day week. A minimum of 18 days annual holiday is given plus 13 days of public holidays.

The standard of living in Cyprus is fairly high. The annual per capita income is about €18,000 per annum. The overall cost of living averages about a half to two-thirds of most parts of Europe.

Useful information

Banking hours: 8.15 am to 1.00 pm weekdays and 3.15 pm to 4.45 pm Mondays only.

Currency: Greek Cypriot area: Cypriot pound (CYP); Turkish Cypriot area: Turkish New Lira (YTL). Cyprus is set to adopt the Euro in 2007.

Shopping hours: 9.00 am to 7.00 pm weekdays except Wednesdays and Saturdays until 2.00 pm, closed Sunday and public holidays. Hairdressers closed on Thursdays.

Driving: Speed limits are 50 km/h in built-up areas, 80 km/h on overland roads, and 100 km/h on motorways; cars with trailers 80 km/h. Driving is on the left. Breakdown emergency number 199.

Electricity: 240 volts, ac 50Hz, sockets 13 amp.

Transport: International air flights are based on Larnaca airport and there are also regular flights to and from Paphos airport. There are no railway services and no domestic air flights due to the short distances. Transport is mainly through the use of private cars. There is also an efficient network of taxi and bus services covering all urban and most rural areas. Cities are linked with motorways with all necessary facilities.

Health care: Medical treatment is of a high standard. Government general hospitals and private clinics mostly concentrate in urban areas while health centres, subcentres and dispensaries function in the rural areas. Medical costs are low with most to be covered by insurance companies through medical plans other than dentistry, medicine, drugs and medical aids. Refunds for medical treatment are possible for EU citizens who are holders of Form E111, issued by their country's health care authorities.

Education: Education is compulsory from 6 to 18. A monthly fee is charged for nursery education between the ages of three and six. The standard of education in Cyprus is very high. Elementary and higher education is free but many expatriate parents as well as many locals send their children to private English-speaking schools operating and administered based on the UK educational models. Fees vary between CYP 2,000 and CYP 3,000 per year.

Emergency services: Police/fire/ambulance 199, 112.

Useful contacts:

British High Commission, Alexander Pallis Street, PO Box 21978, 1587 Nicosia, tel: +357 22 861100

Cyprus Tourist Organisation, Leoforos Lemesou 19, PO Box 24535, 1390 Nicosia, tel: +357 22691100

Ministry of Foreign Affairs, Presidential Palace Avenue, 1447 Nicosia, tel: +357 22 401000

PERSONAL TAXATION

Basis of assessment

As in most EU states, Cyprus tax resident individuals are subject to taxation in Cyprus upon the income accruing or arising from sources within and outside Cyprus (worldwide), while non-Cyprus tax resident individuals are subject to Cyprus taxation upon their income accruing or arising from sources in Cyprus.

The residence status is determined solely by the numbers of days spent in Cyprus during a calendar year. An individual who stays for a period or periods exceeding in aggregate 183 days in any year of assessment in Cyprus is considered to be a tax resident of Cyprus. For the purpose of calculating the days of residence in Cyprus the day of departure is considered to be a day out of Cyprus, the day of arrival is considered to be a day in Cyprus, arrival and departure on the same day is considered to be a day in Cyprus, while departure and arrival on the same day is considered a day out of Cyprus.

Taxation of chargeable income of an individual

The total chargeable income of an individual is subject to taxation at progressive rates; the first CYP 10,000 is tax free, any amount between CYP 10,001 and CYP 15,000 is taxed at the rate of 20 per cent, any amount between CYP 15,001 and CYP 20,000 is further taxed at the rate of 25 per cent, and any amount in excess of CYP 20,001 is taxed at the rate of 30 per cent.

Income from employment

Income or any other benefit, whether monetary or not, derived from any office or employment exercised in Cyprus is subject to Cyprus income tax. Salaried services exercised abroad for an aggregate period exceeding 90 days in any year of assessment are exempt from taxation.

The employer is liable to calculate and deduct the correct income tax (PAYE) of every employee on a monthly basis and submit it to the Tax Authorities on a timely basis.

A tax deduction is granted in respect of social insurance contributions, provident fund contributions, medical fund contributions, pension fund contributions and life insurance premiums. The deduction is restricted to one-sixth of the gross chargeable earned income of an individual. Professional expenses are also tax exempt.

A tax deduction amounting to 20 per cent of the remuneration of an individual is also granted where an individual has been residing abroad immediately before taking up employment in Cyprus. The exemption is valid for a period of three years commencing in the year following the year of employment and the exemption is restricted to the maximum amount of CYP 5,000.

Income from employment is also subject to social insurance contributions. The employee's share amounts to 6.3 per cent of gross employments and the employer contributes a further 10 per cent.

Investment income
Dividend income

Dividend income received by Cyprus tax resident individuals is exempt from personal taxation in Cyprus. It is, however, subject to special taxation at the rate of 15 per cent on the gross dividend income received. The special tax is withheld when paid by a Cyprus tax resident company and it is imposed when paid by a foreign company. Any foreign tax withheld abroad, however, is always given as a tax credit against the Cyprus special tax imposed, provided a double taxation agreement exists.

Interest income

The same tax system applied for dividend income applies for interest income. The only difference concerns the rate of the special tax imposed and/or withheld which in this case is 10 per cent. A lower rate of special tax is also applied, 3 per cent, in cases in which the interest income derives from government development stocks and savings certificates.

Rental income

Rental income is subject to taxation at the personal income tax rates prevailing minus 20 per cent deduction on the gross rental income representing repairs and maintenance expenses on the rented property. A deduction is also granted for interest payable on any loan amount used to finance the acquisition cost of the property and a further deduction is granted amounting to 3 per cent on the cost of the property representing wear and tear allowance.

Rental income is also subject to special taxation at the rate of 3 per cent on the 75 per cent of the gross rental income.

No further taxes arise in Cyprus in respect of rental income derived from property situated abroad in which a double taxation agreement exists.

Royalty income

Royalty income is subject to taxation at the personal income tax rates prevailing whether received from Cyprus resident companies or foreign companies. Again, any foreign tax withheld abroad is always given as a tax credit against the Cyprus income tax imposed on that income, provided a double taxation agreement exists.

Capital gains tax

Capital gains tax is imposed at the rate of 20 per cent on the profits derived from the disposal of any immovable property situated in Cyprus or the disposal of shares of private companies holding immovable property in Cyprus. A relief is given for inflation through indexation of the acquisition cost.

Capital gains derived from the disposal of securities are completely exempt from Cyprus taxation.

Wealth tax

There is no wealth tax in Cyprus.

Double taxation agreements

Cyprus has an extensive network of double taxation agreements, currently covering 40 countries. These include West and East European countries (including EU countries), the United States and Canada, and in many cases they are extremely favourable for tax planning.

For further information, contact:

Yiannos Ioannou, BDO Philippides Ltd, JF Kennedy Avenue, Papabasiliou House, PO Box 27007, 1641 Nicosia Cyprus, tel +357 25735450, fax +357 22493000, e-mail Yiannos.Ioannou@bdo.com.cy

THE CZECH REPUBLIC

The economy

Czechoslovakia was the first of the Central and Eastern European states to shed the yoke of communism in the Velvet Revolution of 1989, and since 1990 foreign direct investment (FDI) has been a key element in the economic development of both the Czech Republic and the Slovak Republic, its companion state in the former Czechoslovakia (which was split in 1993).

Since 1998, when a package of favourable investment incentives was introduced, the Czech Republic has become a favourite foreign investors' target, and FDI has been the main driver of continuing growth. Much of the FDI has been channelled into the successful privatisation of major state-owned enterprises, of which the VW acquisition of Skoda, the Czech auto manufacturer, is the prime example. Indeed, with more than €1 billion being invested subsequently by Toyota and Peugeot, the Czech Republic has grabbed pole position in the race to become the prime location for automotive manufacturing among the EU accession states, bringing with it the establishment of a raft of foreign-funded component manufacturers. Other significant manufacturing sectors that have attracted foreign investment include food products and beverages, non-metallic mineral products, and electrical machinery and apparatus. Service sectors in which foreign investors are heavily engaged include finance and insurance (with the privatisation of the major banks), transport, communications, repairs and maintenance, real estate, business services and trade in general.

In 2004, the year of the Czech Republic's formal entry to the EU, GDP grew 4.4 per cent and much the same is estimated for 2005 with forecast growth for 2006 rising to 4.6 per cent. Industrial production rose by 7.1 per cent year on year in December 2005 and foreign reserves are at a healthy US$29.5 billion, with a trade surplus of US$1.8 billion for 2005. Consumer price inflation continues to run at less than 3 per cent and the currency has held all but 5 per cent of its 86 per cent gain against the US dollar during 2004. The public sector budget deficit is expected to have risen to 6.3 per cent of GDP in 2005 but is forecast to fall back to 4.2 per cent in 2006.

Language and currency

Czech is the official language, with Slovak the second official language. These two languages are used in dealings with the tax authorities, and all written records. If documents are in another language, they must be provided with an authorised translation. Ethnic minorities have the right to use their own language in dealings with the authorities in the presence of a state-employed interpreter. People of other nationalities must have their own interpreter.

The currency is the ceska koruna (the Czech Crown, Kc, CZK), which is divided into 100 haler. In December 2005, the rate was approximately 23.8 Kc to US$1 and 28.80 Kc to €1. The introduction of the Euro in the Czech Republic is proposed in 2009/10.

Laws concerning ownership

Although the modern history of the country as an independent state started at the beginning of the 20th century, private ownership was revived after the downfall of the socialist regime at the beginning of the 1990s. The Restitution Act was a very important law, which returned properties taken by the previous regime to their original owners. This Act played an important part in the development of business, as did the so-called 'voucher privatisation', through which the property of former state-owned enterprises was divided among the citizens in the form of shares. The privatisation of the banking system is currently under way.

Forms of ownership

There are two major forms of ownership in the country: state and private. Ownership in the form of cooperatives mostly exists in agriculture and housing. State property is often leased to a person who then has similar rights and obligations to a property owner.

Financial leasing is possible, followed by the purchase of the leased property, and is mostly used with movable property. It is less used with buildings due to the long lease time prescribed by the law (a minimum of eight years). Financial leasing of land is currently not allowed.

State regulation

To regulate development in certain areas, the state has the power of veto, especially in the field of building and construction. As a result, the construction of new buildings and major renovations of existing buildings require the permission of the competent state authority. If the owner does not have this permission, the competent authority has the power to order the construction to be demolished.

Any change in the use of a building, such as from housing to business, requires permission from the competent authority; without this, the business entity is liable to sanctions.

Real estate market

There are substantial differences in the prices of real estate from one area to another, depending on the attractions of each area.

Generally the highest prices are in Prague and some other more densely populated cities, such as Brno. The prices are lower in less inhabited areas, and factors such as the local unemployment rate are also reflected in the price. As a guide to prices in Prague, 1 square metre of floor space in an apartment costs between 25,000 and 100,000 CZK. The valuation of real estate is an independent profession performed by state-authorised experts. Their cooperation is, in some cases, required by the state authorities, such as when changes are being made to the ownership of real estate.

Previously, property situated on Czech territory could only be acquired by a Czech citizen or by a corporation established in the Czech Republic. After access to the EU on 1 May 2004 this changed: now foreigners can also acquire real estate, if they can prove residence permission as an EU country citizen.

Those persons can acquire farms only on the condition that they have been listed in the register of farm entrepreneurs of an appropriate local authority and that they have had permanent residence in the Czech Republic for a minimum of three years.

Working conditions

Employment

The average number of employees in the third quarter 2005 was about 4.8 million (excluding the self-employed). The number of unemployed was about 404,600 and the registered unemployment rate as of 30 September 2005 was 8.8 per cent.

Legislation

The basic conditions for employment, rights and duties of employers and employees are laid down by law. The most important provisions are as follows:

- [ ] A written contract, if employment is agreed.
- [ ] Contractual conditions for beginning and terminating employment.
- [ ] Extent of working time and holiday time.
- [ ] Disciplinary procedures in the case of an employee's breach of contract.
- [ ] Right to compensation if the employment is terminated under specific circumstances.

Equal opportunities

A law recently passed in the Czech Republic prohibits discrimination on racial, ethnic or religious grounds, and discriminating against women in favour of men when applying for a job. If such discrimination is discovered, the entity concerned is liable to a penalty.

Labour safety

Every employer is obliged to obey labour safety regulations, and is liable to a penalty imposed by the competent authority if these are breached. The employer must also pay legal insurance for its responsibility for possible injury incurred through a labour accident or disease. The amount of insurance depends on the type of job (2 to 12 per cent of the total income paid by the employer), and the insurance cover is used to provide compensation for the injury incurred by the employee.

Maternity rights

Every employed woman has the right to special benefits during pregnancy (prohibition of notice, prohibition of strenuous work) and is also guaranteed wages during maternity leave (28 weeks), and financial support until the child is four years old. The employer may not terminate her employment until the child is three years old.

Minimum wage

As of 1 January 2006, the minimum wage in the Czech Republic was set at 7.570 CZK per month, and the minimum hourly rate at 44.70 CZK.

Trade unions

The law guarantees that employees can join trade unions, and lays down the obligations of the employer to the trade unions' organisation.

Agreements between the trade unions and the government are not covered by any law. However, in some fields the trade unions have pressed heavily regarding wages.

Wages and salaries

The average monthly salary in the Czech Republic amounted, in 2005, to 18,421 CZK (approximately €640). This varies according to the type of activity (figures supplied by the CZSO, Czech Statistical Office).

Employment of foreigners

According to current law, foreign citizens who intend to work in the Czech Republic must acquire a work permit. It is issued on condition that the person has a residence permit and that no Czech citizen could be employed in the post. As of 1 May 2004 a simplified procedure was introduced for citizens of EU member states.

Visas

EU nationals do not require any visa for any type of visit or stay in the Czech Republic. Citizens of the United States, Canada and Mexico are not required to have a visa for a period up to 90 days. Visas are required for work and stays exceeding 90 days. Other nationals can check requirements on the Czech Ministry of Foreign Affairs website: www.mzw.cz

Useful information

Banking system: Ceska narodni banka (The Czech National Bank) is the central bank of the Czech Republic. It determines general banking and monetary policy. The Czech banking system is governed by the Banking Act. The Czech banking system consists of a wide range of commercial banks, including universal banks, special banks and loan banks. Depending on its major activities, each bank provides products, services and financial instruments that are commonly available worldwide, for domestic and foreign trade and financial transactions. Mortgage banking as a new area in the banking sector in the Czech Republic has been developed within the framework of the existing banks, as well as special mortgage banks. Besides domestic banks, the banking system in the Czech Republic also consists of branch offices and representative offices of foreign banking institutions.

Czech capital market: The Czech Republic, owing to voucher privatisation, is the country with the highest number of shareholders in ratio to the number of inhabitants. The majority of shares no longer exist in traditional paper form, but as book shares. Shares are registered in the Czech Republic by the 'Stredisko cennych papiru' (share centre), which also registers ownership changes as a result of share trading carried out on the two official stock markets. These are the BCP ('Burza cennych papiru', the stock exchange) and the RM-System.

Stock exchange ('Burza cennych papiru'): The activity of the BCP is trading through authorised individuals. The transactions are carried out only among the members of the BCP. A special position is occupied by the CNB (Czech National Bank) and the FNM (National Property Fund). The BCP also publishes the transactions, distributes further information from the stock exchange, and provides general public information relating to trading in securities. Trading on the stock exchange can only be done through authorised traders who are registered at the BCP. These are mostly large banks, and specialised commercial companies that are entitled to act as security trade intermediaries for other individuals. In connection with joining the EU in May 2004 the BCP has become an ordinary member of FECE.

Under the RM-System, a joint stock company organises the market but does no trade itself. It offers a variety of services on the market, both for small owners and for stockbrokers and funds. More than 100 of its sales points throughout the country are run within PVT service centres. The RM-System is used for trading on the non-BCP markets, where securities excluded from trading on the BCP can be traded.

Population: The total population of the Czech Republic is approximately 10.3 million, of which 10 per cent reside in the capital city Prague. Administratively, the country which extends to 78,866 sq. km was divided into 14 regions ('VUSCs'), effective 1 January 2000, which in turn are subdivided into 77 districts ('Okres'). The most active regions economically, beyond Prague itself, are Plzensky, Ostravsky, Ustecky, South Bohemia and South Moravia, of which Brno is the regional capital.

Media: The leading television channels, in terms of advertising spend, are TV NOVA, CT1 and TV PRIMA. The daily newspapers competing for first place in nationwide circulation are *Blesk* and *MF Dnes*, each with readership in excess of 1 million, and *Super*, a national tabloid newcomer.

Education: School attendance is compulsory until the age of 15. The curriculum includes one compulsory foreign language, and today

95 per cent of students learn English. Universities have started to teach modern know-how, and international scholarships make it possible for students to study abroad. There are more than 24 universities with a total of 117 faculties in the Czech Republic. The best known are Charles University (one of the oldest in Europe) and the University of Economics (VSE) in Prague. Recently, the MBA has gained in popularity. It is usually taken by young professionals with two or three years' work experience, or by older people who graduated before the revolution. About 10 per cent of the population is computer literate.

Electricity: 220 volts/50 Hz.

Useful contacts:
Embassy of the United Kingdom and Northern Ireland, Thunovska 14, 118 00, Prague 1, tel: + 420 2 5740 2111, e-mail: info@britain.cz
Embassy of the Czech Republic in the UK, 28 Kensington Palace Gardens, London W8 4QY, tel: (020) 7243 1115
Association of Real Estate Agencies, Na Chodovci 3, 141 00 Prague 4, tel: + 420 2 7276 2953, e-mail: sekretariat@ arkcr.cz

PERSONAL TAXATION

Residence

Individuals are resident for tax purposes in the Czech Republic if they either have a permanent place of abode in the Czech Republic or spend more than 183 days there in any calendar year. The possession of a Czech temporary residence permit ('green card') does not of itself make an individual tax resident in the Czech Republic.

Non-residents are only subject to taxation on their Czech-source income. Income is considered to arise in the Czech Republic if it is from one of the following sources:

☐ work carried out on the territory of the Czech Republic;
☐ activities carried out through a permanent establishment located in the country;
☐ business, technical or other consultancy services and similar activities provided in the territory of the Czech Republic.

Broadly, resident individuals are taxed on their worldwide income; non-residents are taxed on Czech-source income only.

Taxation of employment income

Taxable remuneration includes all remuneration, whether monetary or non-monetary, and benefits in kind given to or provided for an employee, except where noted below. Reimbursement of travel expenses in excess of statutory limits is taxable remuneration for the employee, irrespective of whether the individual is an employee of a Czech entity or is seconded by a foreign entity.

Non-monetary benefits received in the form of training courses, onsite catering, temporary onsite accommodation and social insurance contributions paid by the employer are exempt.

Benefits in kind are valued in principle at market value, the main exception being cars, for which the taxable benefit is 12 per cent per annum of the purchase price of the vehicle (minimum from 100,000 CZK). The cost of private fuel is a taxable benefit to the employee if it is not reimbursed to the employer. Interest-free loans, up to the amount of 100,000 CZK for housing purposes or 20,000 CZK to cover an employee's temporary financial difficulty, are tax-free.

State pensions, annuities, family benefits, sickness benefits and maternity benefits are exempt from tax. Income of this type from foreign sources is also exempt, but an exemption ceiling of 162,000 CZK applies to income from annuities. Pensions from non-state sources are included in taxable income. Home-country pension, social and health insurance contributions are deductible if payment is a statutory obligation.

Other taxes
Social security

Czech employers must pay monthly health and social security contributions at 35 per cent of salary cost on behalf of all employees on the local payroll. Contributions are deductible for corporate tax purposes if paid on time. The employee pays a further 12.5 per cent of gross salary. There is no ceiling on the amount of salary subject to these contributions. Social security insurance paid abroad is deductible from the income from employment. Since 2003 foreigners are also included in the social security system when they have a work contract with a Czech employer, because of the international social security treaties that the Czech Republic has concluded with about 20 countries. According to the EU rules, an employee who comes from an EU country and works in the Czech Republic could stay 12 months in the home country social security system, after which he or she enters into the Czech social security system (provided certain conditions are fulfilled, eg E 101).

Taxation of small businesses

Self-employed individuals (entrepreneurs), most general partners and limited partnerships are liable to personal income tax on their share of business profit. Entrepreneurs registered in the Trade and/or Commercial Register are liable to personal income tax on their business profits. Taxable profits are calculated in the same way as for corporate income tax. Similar rules apply to entrepreneurs not registered in the Commercial Register and using the tax evidence (previously called 'single-entry bookkeeping').

Taxes on capital

Capital gains

Capital gains are taxable as income. Exemptions are available for gains arising on the disposal of assets that have not been used for commercial purposes and have been held for certain minimum periods, as follows:

- [ ] shares and securities held for more than six months;
- [ ] cars and other movable assets if held for more than 12 months;
- [ ] real estate held for more than five years;
- [ ] participation in a limited liability company if held for more than five years.

A gain arising on the sale of an apartment or house (containing a maximum of two apartments) that has been the taxpayer's residence for at least a two-year period preceding the sale is also exempt. Gains on the sale of property by the first owner in restitution are exempt from tax.

Other income

Interest earned on Czech savings deposits and dividends received from Czech companies are subject to a final withholding tax of 15 per cent. Interest, dividends and other investment income received from foreign sources may be added to taxable income and taxed at a progressive rate. Alternatively, they may be included in a separate tax base and taxed at a flat rate of 15 per cent.

Double taxation treaties

For non-residents the domestic 15 per cent withholding tax may be reduced according to the terms of a double taxation treaty. The Czech Republic has concluded tax treaties with about 65 countries, including the UK and the United States. Both tax treaties are based on the credit principle.

Tax computation

Income from each source, net of allowable deductions, is aggregated for the tax year. Losses arising on one source of income are mostly offset against income from any source (certain types of income cannot be negative, eg employment income and income derived from capital).

Tax credits

Instead of personal allowances, in 2005 tax credits were introduced. The early tax credits are: 7,200 CZK/person; 4,200 CZK/spouse; 6,000/child (maximum 30.000 CZK); 2,400 CZK/student; 1,500–9,600 CZK/disabled people.

Tax rates for individuals for 2006 are 12 per cent on taxable income up to CZK 121,200; CZK 14,544 plus 19 per cent of the excess over CZK 121,200 for income between CZK 121,200 and CZK 218,400; CZK 33,012 plus 25 per cent of the excess over CZK 218,400 for income between CZK 218,400 and CZK 331,200; CZK 61,212 plus 32 per cent of the excess over CZK 331,200 for income over CZK 331,200.

For further information, contact:

Mr Vlastimil Hokr, BDO CS s.r.o., Olbrachtova 5, 140 00 Prague 4, tel: + 420 241046 111/fax: + 420 241046 221, e-mail: vlastimil.hokr@ bdo.cz, fax: + 41 212 310 23 24

DENMARK

The economy

Denmark is traditionally an agricultural country and nearly three-quarters of its land is still used for farming and horticulture although employing only 6 per cent of the workforce. Though reduced in area since the end of the war, agriculture is highly efficient and food and dairy produce account for about one-fifth of total exports. The UK is a long-established market: Danish bacon and butter are found on many British breakfast tables. There has been a marked shift of resources towards manufacturing, the most important industries being food processing, metal and electrical engineering, transport equipment, textiles and clothing, paper, furniture, glass, IT, biotech and brewing. Firms are small scale; about two out of three manufacturers employ fewer than 50 workers. Standards of design, styling and craftsmanship are high. However, by far the greatest proportion of the population works in the service sector. With GDP growth estimated to have been 3.3 per cent in 2005 and forecast at 2.8 per cent for 2006, Denmark's economy is performing significantly better than the Euro area average and at a comparable level to that of Sweden. Unemployment fell 1 percentage point to 5.1 per cent in December 2005 compared to a year earlier, and the growth rate for industrial production stood at 5.5 per cent. With consumer price inflation staying low at a recorded 2.1 per cent for January 2006 and both positive current account and budget balances at 3 per cent and 3.7 per cent of GDP respectively expected for 2005, the economy seems to be set fair for the medium term.

Working conditions

Work permits are required for non-EU nationals. Rented housing is scarce and people are advised to try to arrange accommodation beforehand. Enquiries about residence permits should be made in advance to the Danish Embassy in London, or in Copenhagen to the Directorate of Immigration, 53 Ryesgade, DK-2100 Copenhagen Ø (tel: +45 31 393100). Holders of the residence permit must also get a personal code number from Folkeregisteret, Dahlerupsgade 6, 1640 Copenhagen.

The level of management salaries is appreciably higher than in the UK but deductions for tax and social security are higher too.

Employers only contribute to social security by very small fixed amounts.

The Danes have a good record of stable labour relations and co-operation between employers and unions. They have one of the lowest strike records in Europe.

The system of social security provides full cover against sickness, accident, retirement and other contingencies.

Useful information

Banking hours: 9.30 am to 4.00 pm Monday–Wednesday and Friday, 9.30 am to 6.00 pm Thursday.

Shopping hours: 9.00 or 10.00 am to 6.00 or 7.00 pm Monday–Thursday, 9.00 or 10.00 am to 7.00 or 8.00 pm Friday, and 9.00 or 10.00 am to 1.00 or 2.00 pm Saturday. Alcohol not sold after 8.00 pm.

Driving: Driving is on the right, and the roads are good. As in other Nordic countries, there are strict regulations against drinking and driving.

Transport: Copenhagen has an international airport (Kastrup) with frequent flights to European cities and to internal centres. Rail transport is efficient and reasonably priced – there are numerous concessions for families travelling together although public transport is expensive. Copenhagen has an underground train (the Metro).

Health care: The standard of medical treatment in Denmark is high. Health services have recently been remodelled on British NHS lines, with the emphasis on group practice and preventive medicine. Hospital treatment is free. Charges for doctors' visits and prescriptions are refundable.

Education: Education is compulsory from the ages of 7 to 17. English is taught in all schools. In Copenhagen there is an International School for 4–19 year olds with an international/US curriculum; Rygaards International School at Hellerup offers a UK curriculum for the age range 5–16 (website: http://www.rygaards.com).

Directory enquiries: 118.

Emergency services: 112.

Useful contacts:
British Embassy, Kastelsvej 36–40, 2100 Copenhagen Ø, tel: 35 44 52 00, website: www.britishembassy.dk/

Danish Embassy, 55 Sloane Street, London SW1X, tel: +44 020 7333 0200

Danish Tourist Board: www.denmark.dt.dk, www.visitdenmark.com/

Expatriate information:

www.zitech.dk/userwebs/zn7ccc0846/briteuro.htm

America Women's Club in Aarhus, www.homes8.inet.tele.dk/bonnie/awcaa

PERSONAL TAXATION

Residence

An individual is resident in Denmark for tax purposes if either the individual has his or her principal residence (home) in Denmark, or he or she spends at least six consecutive months (ignoring short breaks away) in Denmark. An individual's citizenship or nationality has no direct bearing on residence status.

Individuals who are resident are liable to income tax on their worldwide income; non-residents are liable on their Danish-source income only.

Income from employment

Domestic-source earnings, whether in cash or in kind, are taxable in Denmark whether or not the employee is resident. Employment income from a foreign source is taxable in Denmark only if the employee is resident in Denmark.

Payments to an employee for expenses of travel, entertainment or any other service to be performed on behalf of the employer are taxable only to the extent that they are not actually expended in the performance of the service. Special rules apply for free housing, and free use of a car or telephone provided by the employer. Some work-related benefits-in-kind worth less than DKK 5,100 (2006) are exempt.

Employment income is taxed as personal income to a progressive scale with a marginal rate up to 59 per cent.

Denmark has a special expatriate tax regime according to which under certain conditions it is possible to opt for a flat 25 per cent tax on cash salary income for a period of three years.

Investment income/capital gains

The taxable gains and investment income are added to taxable income. For an individual subject to full tax liability such income includes interest, gains on certain securities, and gains on property other than owner-occupied property. Gains on owner-occupied property are normally exempt. Such income, if the net income is positive, is taxed as capital income with a rate up to 59 per cent. Negative net capital income has a tax value of approximately 33 per cent.

Dividends received from both domestic and foreign companies, and taxable gains on shares are taxed as share income. Dividends from domestic companies are paid under deduction of 28 per cent withholding tax. This tax is final provided that the total share income for the year does not exceed DKK44,300 (2006). Share income in excess of these amounts must be taxed at a rate of 43 per cent. Special rules may apply for dividends from foreign companies and gains on shares in such companies.

Other taxes

Social security taxes

The employee must pay 8 per cent of gross salary (2006). The contribution to social security is deductible from taxable income. The employer only pays a small fixed amount to social security. Contributions to a supplementary old-age pension of DKK2,690 per annum must be made. The employer must pay two-thirds and the employee must pay one-third of the amount.

Tax on owner-occupied property

The owner must pay a special tax on owner-occupied property, calculated as a percentage of the official valuation of the property.

Wealth tax

The wealth tax was abolished in Denmark in 1997.

Double taxation treaties

Denmark has concluded tax treaties with about 85 countries, and has a double taxation treaty with both the UK and the United States. Both tax treaties are based on the credit principle.

For further information on tax and social security, contact:

Hans-Henrik Nilausen, Tax Director, Int. Tax, BDO ScanRevision A/S, tel: +45 39 15 53 20, e-mail: HHN@bdo.dk

ESTONIA

The economy

The Estonian economy is diverse – industry and transport, as well as commerce and different branches of services are all equally important. Due to the available natural resources, the Estonian economy largely relies on forestry-related industries. The Estonian energy sector is based on oil shale, a resource quite rare elsewhere in the world. Finland and Sweden are the most important trade partners. The Estonian economy profits significantly from the business generated by more than 3 million tourists a year, most of whom come from Finland and an impressive total in relation to the population of approximately 1.4 million.

After the introduction of the Euro the Estonian kroon is tied to the Euro (€1 = 15.6466 kroons). The successful monetary reform also meant swift changes in banking and in the financial sector as a whole. The local financial sector is nevertheless very small. Estonian banking is characterised by the widespread use of IT technologies – an impressive number of people own payment cards, internet banking has advanced rapidly, and the latest development, mobile payments, is all the rage.

Although the average price level in Estonia is much lower than that of the developed countries, it is one of the highest in Central and Eastern Europe. The reasons include the fact that prices were freed from governmental regulation at an early stage, and the proximity to Finland and Sweden whose high price level inevitably has some influence on the prices in Estonia, especially on those in Tallinn. The existing price differences are not too drastic – in Estonia services are relatively cheap but the price level of quite a number of goods is comparable to the European average. This applies most to imported industrial and household goods.

GDP growth for 2005 is forecast to have exceeded 9 per cent, the average wage is around €512 and the unemployment rate in 2005 should average 9.3 per cent. According to research by the *Wall Street Journal,* Estonia is ranked seventh in the world for its economic freedom. Although Estonia maintains a small public sector surplus, the current account deficit ratio to GDP at the end of 2005 was approaching 11 per cent and foreign debt is uncomfortably high at nearly 85 per cent of GDP.

Working conditions

Generally EU nationals may work and stay in Estonia for three months without a residence permit. If the stay in Estonia will be longer than three months it is necessary to apply for a residence permit. Applications have to be submitted to the Citizenship and Migration Board (website: http://www.mig.ee/eng/).

EU nationals may stay in Estonia without a residence permit:

1. for up to three months as of the date of his or her arrival in Estonia, also if he or she is employed in Estonia or engaged in business in Estonia;
2. if he or she is employed in another member state of the European Union but resides in Estonia and returns to Estonia at least once a week;
3. if he or she is a seasonal worker in Estonia;
4. for up to six months for the purpose of seeking employment if he or she has registered for job-seeking pursuant to the procedure provided for in the Employment Service Act.

Useful information

Banking hours: Usually from 9.00 am to 6.00 pm during weekdays and on Saturdays from 9.00 am to 3.00 pm. On Sundays the bank offices are closed. Estonian banks provide their clients with internet banking services, which enable transfers 24/7.

Driving: Traffic drives on the right. Speed limit is 50 km/h in built-up areas, 90–110 km/h on motorways. Using seat belts is compulsory.

Transport: The best way to travel in Estonia is to use a car. The motorways are not at the best condition everywhere, but the motorways linking the major towns are rather good. There are no tolls on roads and bridges.

Health care: Medical facilities are widely available.

Education: State provided education is compulsory from 7–16 years (primary school) and optional thereafter. The most important and valued university is University of Tartu (established in 1632). Generally the education programme is in Estonian, but there are also a lot of opportunities to study in English.

Electricity: 230 volts/50Hz.

Directory enquires: 1181, 1188 and 1183.

Emergency services: Police 110, emergency call (fire and ambulance) 112.

Useful contacts:

Tax and Customs Board, Narva mnt 9j, 15176 Tallinn, Estonia, tel: + 372 683 5700, website: http://www.emta.ee/?lang=en

Citizenship and migration Board, Endla 13, 15179 Tallinn, Estonia, tel: + 372 612 69 79, website: http://www.mig.ee/eng/

British Embassy, Wismari 6, Tallinn 10136, Estonia, tel: + 372 66 747 00, website: http://www.britishembassy.gov.uk/servlet/Front? pagename= OpenMarket/Xcelerate/ShowPage&c=Page&cid= 1046181009276.

Ministry of Finance, Suur-Ameerika 1, Tallinn 15006, Estonia, tel: +372 611 3558, fax: +372 696 6810, e-mail: info@fin.ee, website: www. fin.ee/?lang=en; Summary of Estonian tax system: http://www. fin.ee/?id=3814

Airport of Tallinn, tel: + 372 6 058 888, website: www.tallinn-airport.ee/ index.php?intro_eng=true

Port of Tallinn, tel: + 372 6 318 550, website: http://www.ts.ee/

PERSONAL TAXATION

Residence

A person is considered to be an Estonian resident if his or her place of residence is in Estonia or if he or she stays in Estonia for at least 183 days over a period of 12 consecutive calendar months. A person is deemed to be a resident as of the date of his or her arrival in Estonia.

Residents are taxed on the worldwide basis. Non-residents have a limited tax liability in Estonia, where only the Estonian-source income is taxed.

Income of a resident person

Income tax is charged on income derived by a resident person from all sources of income in Estonia and outside Estonia, including income from employment, gains from transfer of property and investment income.

The list of taxable income of a resident person is not limited.

Income from employment

Income tax is charged on all emoluments paid to an employee or public servant, including wages and salaries, additional remuneration, additional payments and holiday payments. Any goods, services, remuneration in kind or monetarily appraisable benefits which are given to an employee in connection with an employment are taxed as fringe benefits.

Taxes from employment

Employers are obliged to pay social tax at the rate of 33 per cent and unemployment insurance contribution at the rate of 0.3 per cent on employee's salary, and to withhold income tax at the rate of 23 per cent, unemployment insurance contribution at the rate of 0.6 per cent, and mandatory funded pension contribution at the rate of 2 per cent, if needed from an employee's salary.

The basic exemption deductible from the income of a resident person in a calendar year is 24,000 kroons.

Investment income
Dividends

Dividends paid to a resident or non-resident person by an Estonian company are taxed at corporate level only. No withholding tax is applied. Corporate taxpayers are subject to distribution tax on distributed profits, including transactions that are considered as hidden profit distribution. The flat tax rate is 23 per cent in 2006, but it is important to note that the tax rate is applied to the gross amount of distribution. It means that the net amount of the distribution has to be divided by 0.77 before the tax rate is applied (for example, if the net dividend amount is €77, it is divided first by 0.77, and the tax rate of 23 per cent is applied to the result – €100 – which makes the tax amount €23).

The income tax rate is set to decrease in 2007 to 22 per cent, in 2008 to 21 per cent and for 2009 to 20 per cent.

Income tax at the rate of 23 per cent is applied on dividends paid to a resident person by a foreign company. However, if income tax has been paid or withheld in the source country, the dividends in question are tax-exempt in Estonia.

Interest

Income tax (23 per cent) is charged on all interest accrued from loans, securities, leases or other debt obligations, including the amounts calculated on the basis of the debt obligations by which the initial debt obligations are increased. The amounts payable in the event of delay of the payment or other non-performance of the obligation are not deemed to be interest.

Income tax is not charged on interest paid to a person by a resident credit institution, a branch of a non-resident credit institution entered in the Estonian commercial register, or the Compensation Fund.

Tax treatment of capital

Capital gains

There is no capital gains tax as such in Estonia. Income tax (23 per cent) is charged on gains from the sale or exchange of any transferable and monetarily appraisable objects, including real or movable property, securities, registered shares, contributions made to a general or limited partnership or an association, units of investment funds, rights of claim, rights of pre-emption, rights of superficies, usufructs, personal rights of use, rights of commercial lessees, redemption obligations, mortgages, commercial pledges, registered securities over movables, or other restricted real rights, or the ranking thereof, or other proprietary rights.

In the case of a reduction in the share capital of a public limited company, private limited company or association, or in the contributions of a general or limited partnership, and in the case of redemption or return of shares or contributions, income tax is charged on the amount by which the payments made to a person exceed the acquisition cost of the holding or the contribution made by the person upon acquisition of the holding.

Wealth tax

There is no wealth tax in Estonia.

Double taxation treaties

Estonia has concluded treaties to avoid double taxation with 33 countries, including the UK and the United States.

For further information on tax matters, contact:

Ms Iris Gutmann, Tax Adviser, BDO Eesti AS, Uus-Sadama 21, 10120 Tallinn, tel: +372 627 5506, e-mail: Iris.Gutmann@bdo.ee

FINLAND

The economy

Finland is a highly industrialised country. The metal, engineering and electronics industries account for 55 per cent of export revenues, the forest products industry for 25 per cent. The current emphasis is on high-value, technology-intensive exports. Finnish glass, ceramics and furniture enjoy high international reputations. Finland consistently ranks high in international competitiveness for its high-quality labour, as well as for its scientific and technological expertise.

GDP growth fell back from its 2004 peak of 3.5 per cent to an estimated 1.9 per cent in 2005 but is expected to recover to perhaps 3.3 per cent in 2006. Finland maintains positive current account and budget balances running at a satisfactory 3.4 per cent and 1.7 per cent respectively for 2005. Consumer price inflation was 1 per cent in 2005 and is forecast to increase modestly to 1.7 per cent in 2006, whereas the downward trend in unemployment is forecast to continue throughout 2006 to a more acceptable level of 7.8 per cent.

Working conditions

In general, wages are not higher in Finland than in the UK. However, taxes and social security payments are much higher, while living expenses are about the same. Working hours are roughly the same in Finland as in the UK. Holiday entitlement is higher. Although English is widely understood, in some branches it might be difficult to find employment without a good knowledge of both English and Finnish (or Swedish).

Having a valid British passport entitles the holder to work and reside in Finland without a residence or work permit for a period of three months, after which he or she must register his or her residence in Finland. The local police handle the registration.

Useful information

Banking hours: Usually 10.00 am to 4.30 pm Monday to Friday.

Driving: Speed limits are 50 km/h in built-up areas, 80 km/h on overland roads, 100–120 km/h on motorways. Seat belts are compulsory.

Transport: Finland has an efficient rail and road network. Traffic drives on the right. The state railway system is comprehensive, efficient and popular. Finland also has one of the densest and cheapest domestic airline networks in Europe. In addition, there is a comprehensive range of international and domestic ferry services operating on the Baltic and the numerous inland lakes.

Health care: Medical facilities are widely available. Services are provided within each municipality.

Education: State-provided education is co-educational, free and compulsory from 7–16 years. In addition, there are some private schools that charge tuition (like the English School in Helsinki). University-level education is mainly in Finnish or Swedish with the exception of English-language BBA and MBA programmes in certain universities and polytechnics.

Directory enquiries: 118.

Emergency services: 112.

Media: Four national television channels. Newspapers, books, plays and films appear in both Swedish and Finnish. More than half of newspapers have their own online versions.

Useful contacts:

British Embassy, Itäinen Puistotie 17, 00 140 Helsinki, tel: 358 9 2286 5100, website: www.ukembassy.fi/

Finnish Embassy, 38 Chesham Place, London SW1X 8HW, tel: 020 7838 6200

Finnish Tourist Board, PO Box 33213, London W6 8JX, tel: 020 7365 2512, website: www.mek.fi

PERSONAL TAXATION

Residence

An individual is regarded as a resident in Finland if he or she has his or her main abode in Finland or stays in Finland for a continuous period of more than six months. The stay in Finland may be regarded as continuous in spite of a temporary absence from the country.

Taxation of employment income

Residents

Employment income, as well as other earned income, is subject to state tax and municipal tax (and church tax where a person is a member of an Evangelical-Lutheran church or of an Orthodox church). The state tax is levied according to a progressive rate. The communal tax and the church tax are taxed at flat rates, set annually in advance for the following year in each community.

The highest marginal tax rate of state taxation in 2006 is 32.5 per cent. The communal tax rate varies between 16 and 20.25 per cent.

Non-residents

Non-residents are only taxed on income derived from Finnish sources. For a salary income the rate of withholding tax is 35 per cent.

Withholding tax for foreign experts

Under the Act on Withholding Tax for Foreign Employees a withholding tax of 35 per cent may be applied to the employment income if the following requirements are fulfilled:

1. The individual becomes resident in Finland at the beginning of the period of employment to which the Act applies.
2. The pecuniary salary for this employment is at least €5,800 a month during the total period of employment to which the Act applies.
3. The tasks require special expertise.
4. The employee is not a Finnish national and he or she has not been a resident in Finland in the five years preceding the year in which this employment began.

A taxpayer can be regarded as a foreign expert for a maximum period of 24 months.

Tax treatment of investment income

Residents

Investment income is taxed at a flat rate of 28 per cent.

Non-residents

According to the general rule, a withholding tax is levied on the investment income of non-residents. Unless a lower rate or an exemption is provided by the tax treaty, the tax rate is 28 per cent.

Tax treatment of capital

The Net Wealth Tax Act was repealed on 1 January 2006, hence no tax is now levied on net wealth.

Tax treaties

Finland has a comprehensive network of double tax agreements, covering the UK and the United States among others, for income and capital taxation. Finland has also concluded double taxation treaties on inheritances with some countries (for example, with the United States).

For further information on tax and social security, contact:

Mr Heikki Muikku, BDO International Tax Coordinator, BDO FinnPartners Oy, tel: +358 20 743 2928, e-mail: heikki.muikku@bdo.fi

FRANCE

The economy

The French economy remained sluggish in 2005, although the stubbornly high level of unemployment eased slightly to 9.5 per cent in December. GDP growth for the year is expected to be no more than 1.6 per cent but is forecast to improve to 2 per cent in 2006, marginally above the average forecast for the Euro area. Consumer price inflation estimated at 1.8 per cent for 2005 is rather lower than the Euro area average of 2.2 per cent. At 3.2 per cent of GDP the budget deficit at the end of 2005 remains above the level of the EU Stability and Growth Pact criterion. The foreign trade deficit for 2005 was $32billion; however, the current account trade deficit is not expected to exceed 1.3 per cent of GDP through to the end of 2006. Although France is one of the largest industrial powers in the world, it is the world's second largest agricultural exporter. Foreign companies now account for more than 27 per cent of manufacturing output and 30 per cent of exports.

France is well off for natural resources, with coal, natural gas, iron ore, potash, bauxite and fluorspar. However, despite a strong nuclear power industry, the steep rise in the price of oil threatens economic recovery. Trade is primarily with EU countries, headed by Germany, with the UK as its third largest export market. Principal exports are food, wine and dairy produce, petroleum products, metals, steels, chemicals, cars, non-ferrous metals, and a wide range of consumer goods. Fashion and luxury items, and tourism, are also important sources of revenue. In 2005, steel industry performance was weak with consumption declining by an estimated 8 per cent for long products and 10 per cent for flat steel. Conversely, business activity in the building industry rose 3 per cent, driven by record levels of new home starts. Mechanical equipment manufacturing suffered from a 1.6 per cent decline in demand as a result of weak industrial investment, the Euro appreciation and higher steel prices. Predictably, textiles and clothing production declined 7.7 per cent and 9.7 per cent respectively in 2005 reflecting the competition from low value-added products imported from Asia.

Industry is fairly evenly dispersed, though Greater Paris has the largest and most heterogeneous concentration and some areas, such as Brittany and the south-west, are under-industrialised. Textiles, coal and steel have declined but new technologically advanced and science-based industries, such as chemicals, electronics and nuclear engineering, have been developed particularly in the Lyon-Grenoble region, the second most prosperous in France, while in the south-west, based on Toulouse, the aeronautical industry flourishes alongside the new technology industries.

Agriculture, largely dominated by small family farms, is still of major importance and influence, even though the numbers working on the land have steadily fallen and there has been a drift to the towns and cities. Residential property values in rural areas are much lower than in the UK, and in recent years, with improved air travel facilities, have been a major incentive for UK families to relocate to France. The recent significant increases in property values in those areas served by airports, particularly in the south-west since 2004, are likely to continue.

Working conditions

European Union citizens do not require work permits. As at the end of 2003 a law has been passed by which residence permits are no longer required by EU citizens subject to certain conditions. These were not known at the time of going to press. The 35-hour week is standard but this is under review. French workers are entitled by law to five weeks annual leave. There are 11 public holidays. Many firms and offices are shut for much of August.

The level of managerial salaries is around 30 to 40 per cent higher than in the UK. Employers' contributions to social security are among the highest in Europe, but direct taxation is relatively low. Secretarial salaries are much the same as in the UK.

Most wages are fixed by collective bargaining at national level. Equal pay is theoretically obligatory – the gap between men's and women's pay is narrower than in most EU countries. There is also a minimum legal wage. Given the current economic problems, these areas are under a great deal of pressure for change.

Many fringe benefits are provided and most employers have to contribute to housing and welfare. The practice of a 13-month bonus is widespread and most manual workers are now paid monthly, instead of fortnightly, and enjoy staff status. French workers attach as much importance to social security and fringe benefits as to money wages.

Useful information

Banking hours: 9.00 am to 4.30 pm weekdays (closed in the afternoon before a public holiday), some closed on Saturdays. May be closed for lunch in the provinces.

Post office: 8.00 am to 7.00 pm weekdays, 8.00 am to 12.00 pm Saturdays.

Shopping hours: 10.00 am to 7.00 pm Monday to Saturday, closed 1.00–3.00 pm and all day Monday outside Paris.

Electricity: 220 V (may vary).

Driving: Driving is on the right. Paris is congested and parking difficult, but the traffic flows. If you take your own car, you are obliged to have it fitted with seat belts back and front; yellow head-lamps are no longer compulsory for motor vehicles.

Transport: The main centres are linked by internal airways and there are airports at Lyon, Marseille, Nice, Bordeaux, Strasbourg and Toulouse, as well as two in Paris: Charles de Gaulle and Orly. The railway network is highly efficient, with a number of express and TGV (260 km/h) trains. Fares are cheaper than in the UK. A direct rail link with the UK is via the Channel Tunnel. The roads are good and there is a network of motorways, on which tolls are payable. These can be expensive on a long journey.

Health care: There is a reciprocal health agreement with the UK. Medical attention is expensive but 75 per cent of the fees for doctors and dentists working within the French sickness insurance scheme can be reimbursed. A proportion of the cost of prescriptions can be refunded (40–70 per cent), as well as outpatient hospital treatment (80 per cent) although this system is under review, and may face cuts. Private treatment is costly. There is a British hospital in Paris, the Hertford, and a more expensive US one.

Education: Some expatriate parents send their children to local schools, which are of a high educational standard and where they can acquire a good knowledge of French. There is free compulsory education from 6 to 16 and for children below that age there are many crèches and nursery schools. Secondary education is in two cycles, from 11 to 15 and from 15 to 18. Those who complete the second cycle can take the Baccalaureate examination before proceeding to university or institutes of technology. US and British schools in Paris cater for children of diplomats and businessmen. The British School of Paris is geared to the UK system; it takes pupils from 4 to 18 and offers boarding facilities.

Directory enquiries: 12.

Emergency services: police 17, fire 18, ambulance 15.

Media: Most provincial regions have their own newspapers, but some Paris papers, such as *Le Figaro* and *Le Monde*, circulate nationally. There is a wide range of weeklies, the best known being *Paris Match* and *L'Express*. TV is state controlled with limited advertising, though cable and satellite facilities are expanding rapidly. There are one state, four commercial and a number of local private radio stations.

Useful contacts:

British Embassy, 35 Rue du Faubourg St Honoré, 75383 Paris, Cedex 08, tel: 44 51 31 00, website: www.amb-grandebretagne.fr

French Consulate General, 21 Cromwell Road, London SW7, tel: 020 7838 2000

French Tourist Office, www.franceguide.com, www.maison-de-la-france.fr

Country information: www.paris-anglo.com, www.parisfranceguide. com

Further information: Living and Working in France, by Genevieve Brame (published by Kogan Page, www.kogan-page.co.uk) provides in-depth information for expatriates living in France.

PERSONAL TAXATION

Unless otherwise stated, all figures relate to 2006 income.

Torritoriality and rosidonce

An individual is considered to be French resident if one of the following three criteria is met:

1. The individual's permanent home ('foyer') is in France or, if the permanent home cannot be determined, the individual's principal place of stay, regardless of permanency, is in France.
2. The individual carries out an occupation or employment in France, unless subsidiary to a main occupation carried out elsewhere.
3. The individual's place of economic interest (main investments and their management), or main source of income is in France.

A French resident is subject to French tax on his or her worldwide income, while a non-resident is only subject to French tax on French source income.

Taxation of personal income

Individuals are subject to income tax on their annual taxable income. Taxable income is determined by adding together the various categories of income and deducting losses, expenses and relief.

Categories of income include:

- [ ] industrial and commercial profits;
- [ ] non-commercial profits;
- [ ] rental income;
- [ ] employment income;
- [ ] financial income;
- [ ] agricultural income.

The tax year for income tax purposes is the calendar year, and the yearly taxable income is determined for the whole household, that is, husband, wife and dependent children. Income tax is computed by the French Tax Authorities on the income of the preceding year (eg in 2007 taxpayers must complete and lodge their tax return for income received during 2006). Income tax is levied at progressive rates. Since 1 January 2006, the maximum rate is 40 per cent (the previous maximum rate was 48.06 per cent for 2005 income), to which miscellaneous social taxes must be added (different from social security taxes), amounting to up to 11 per cent, applicable on certain income (investment income, rental income and so on) for residents. In return for the reduction in the tax rates, taxpayers are no longer entitled to benefit from the 20 per cent supplementary deduction which has been incorporated by the Finance Bill 2006 in the new progressive income tax rates.

Employment income

Employment income includes all benefits in cash or in kind received by an individual. Professional expenses are deductible, with taxpayers choosing between a standard deduction of 10 per cent or a deduction of actual professional expenses. Social security contributions are also deductible from gross income. Pensions are taxed in the same way as employment income. For 2005, the 10 per cent deductions were limited to €13,093 for salary and €3,385 for pensions.

Financial income

Share dividends and bond interest are subject to income tax at the progressive rates.

Dividends are subject to income tax rates after application of a 40 per cent deduction and an annual deduction equal to €3,050 for a married couple and €1,525 for unmarried individuals. Taxpayers may also benefit from a tax credit, which cannot exceed €230 for a married couple and €115 for unmarried individuals.

Interest is generally subject to income at the progressive rates. However, taxpayers may opt for a final levy at the flat rate of 16 per cent.

In addition to income tax, dividends and interest are subject to social contributions taxes at the rate of 11 per cent.

Capital gains

There are two main types of capital gains.

Real estate capital gains

The calculation of capital gains has been totally modified with effect from 1 January 2004. The net taxable gain is reduced by 10 per cent per year of holding after the first five years. The gain is consequently exempt after 15 years. The rate of capital gains tax for French residents is 16 per cent, and 11 per cent social taxes, making a total of 27 per cent. The rate for European Union residents who are not French residents is only 16 per cent (ie non-French residents are not subject to 11 per cent social taxes.)

Securities capital gains

Capital gains on securities are taxed at 27 per cent (including 11 per cent social surcharges) if total sales of securities exceed €15,000 per annum. The taxable gain is reduced by 1/3 per year of holding after six years of holding as from 1 January 2006. The gain is consequently totally exempt after more than eight years of holding.

Net wealth tax

A net wealth tax is levied on individuals whose patrimony exceeds €750,000 on 1 January 2006. Non-residents are also affected by the net wealth tax, but only on properties located in France. Their financial investments are specifically exempt.

Tax treaties

France has signed tax treaties with more than 100 countries, and this includes the entire developed world.

For further information, contact:

Roslyn Innocent, BDO MG Tax and Legal, 2 Esplanade Compans Caffarelli, 31000 Toulouse, tel: +33 (0) 5 61 11 05 60, fax: +33 (0) 5 61 11 05 67, e-mail: r.innocent@bdo-taxlegal.fr

Carine Duchemin-Goddard, International Tax Co-ordinator, BDO MG Tax and Legal, 25 Quai Carnot, 92210 Saint-Cloud, tel: + 33 (0) 1 41 12 13 15, fax: + 33 (0) 1 46 02 36 18, e-mail: c.duchemin@bdo-taxlegal.fr

Frederic Mege, BDP Stoy Hayward LLP, Private Client Group – French Tax Desk, 8 Baker Street, London W1U 3LL, tel: + 44 (0)20 7486 5888, fax: + 44 (0)20 7487 3686, e-mail: frederic.mege@bdo.co.uk5

GERMANY

The economy

Germany's wealth, originally based on coal, steel and heavy engineering, is today founded on a broad spread of modern industries, including petrochemicals, artificial fibres, electric and electronic equipment, machinery, machine tools, scientific instruments, motor cars and commercial vehicles. New industrial development has been particularly noticeable in the south.

In 2005, GDP grew by 1.1 per cent, driven mainly by industry, trade and exports. Germany's foreign trade balance exceeded €200 billion at the end of 2005 and the current account surplus ratio to GDP is estimated at 4 per cent. However, the domestic unemployment rate of 11.6 per cent remained high. For a fourth year, the German budget deficit at 3.9 per cent far exceeded the parameters of the EU Stability and Growth Pact. This situation has arisen particularly as a result of declining revenue (lower income tax rates in 2005) and high social costs expenditure. Measures to reduce the cost burden were introduced during 2005 but it is uncertain how far the new coalition Federal Government under Chancellor Angela Merkel will be able to pursue structural reforms.

Sixteen years after reunification, the East continues to adapt to a market economy. Further measures to promote the economy in Eastern Germany are planned. Overall GDP growth for Germany as a whole is forecast to increase in 2006 to perhaps 1.7 per cent. The Federal Government plans to increase VAT to 19 per cent from 1 January 2007.

Frankfurt International School e. V.

Established 1961

Provides an excellent international education for children from all sectors of the business and international communities of the Rhein Main region.

For further information please contact:

Frankfurt International School e. V.

Petra Rischke
An der Waldlust 15
61440 Oberursel Germany
Telephone: +49(0)6171 / 2024-0
Fax: +49(0)6171 / 2024384
e-mail: petra_rischke@fis.edu
www.fis.edu

International School Wiesbaden is a branch of Frankfurt International School e. V.
Accredited by the Council of International Schools and New England Association of Schools and Colleges

Working conditions

British and other EEA nationals with valid passports/identification cards are free to enter and move about the country. However, all residents must register in the local community at special registration offices ('Einwohnermeldeamt') in Germany. If an EU national intends to stay for more than three months, he or she will need to apply for a residence permit at the Foreign Nationals Authority ('Ausländeramt'), which is valid for five years. Free entrance to the German labour market is being applied in stages to nationals of the new EU member states during a transitional period of seven years.

At managerial level, the Germans do considerably better than the British. Secretarial and skilled worker salaries are slightly higher than in the UK. The cost of living is lower in Germany than in the UK. The British Chamber of Commerce publishes annual surveys of salaries and fringe benefits.

The standard working week is 36–40 hours for five days. There is a minimum of 25–30 days holiday, plus 10–13 public holidays (depending on the federal state).

Wages and salaries are determined by collective bargaining, which usually has the force of law. There are separate arrangements for senior executives ('leitende Angestellte'). Individual contracts are usually for an indefinite period and terminated by written notice, with compensation according to age and length of service.

Employers may provide, by law or by custom, additional benefits, eg 13-month bonus and group/performance bonuses, and help towards housing, meals, transport and recreation.

There is a long-established and comprehensive system of social security, with benefits related to earnings. The public social security system comprises the old-age pension, unemployment insurance, health and nursing insurance. The employee and the employer both pay 50 per cent of the respective contributions in principle. The employer withholds social security contributions from the salary. For 2006, contributions amount to 19.5 per cent for old-age pension, 6.5 per cent for unemployment insurance, 1.7 per cent for nursing insurance (1.95 per cent for childless individuals having reached the age of 23 years) and approximately 15 per cent for health insurance (depending on the chosen health care insurance company). There are certain ceilings beyond which no further contributions need to be paid. If the remuneration exceeds the obligatory health/nursing insurance ceiling, the employee is not obliged to choose one of the public health insurance companies; the employee can opt for private health insurance. In such a case, health and nursing insurance contributions will differ from the public rates depending on the chosen programme and insurance company, and the employer will be obliged to pay the employer's portion based on the average public insurance company's rate.

Under certain conditions, individuals who are seconded to Germany can apply to remain in their home country's social security system, and German social security contributions will not become due.

Useful information

Banking hours: 8.30 am to 1.00 pm, 2.30 to 4.00 pm weekdays.

Shopping hours: 9.00 am to 8.00 pm weekdays, 9.00 am to 7.00 or 8.00 pm Saturday; closed Sunday and public holidays. Hairdressers and restaurants closed Mondays.

Driving: Speed limits are 50 km/h in built-up areas, 100 km/h on overland roads, and 130 km/h on motorways; cars with trailers 80 km/h. Driving is on the right. Breakdown emergency number: 01 8022 22.

Transport: There is a highly sophisticated network of air, rail and road transport, serving all parts of the country. All major cities are linked by motorways ('Autobahnen').

Health care: Medical treatment is of a high standard and most costs are met through insurance funds. Charges are made for dentistry, medicine, drugs and medical aids. Refunds are possible if you exchange your Form E111 for a 'Krankenschein' certificate issued by the German health insurance companies through the Local Sickness Fund.

Education: Education is compulsory from 6 to 18 (including three years at a vocational school on a part-time basis). A monthly fee is charged for nursery education between the ages of 3 and 6. The standard is high and thorough, and many expatriate parents send their children to local schools. Others want their children to continue education in the UK. There are International Schools at Düsseldorf, Frankfurt, Hamburg and Munich. The British Embassy runs a preparatory school in Bonn for children from 4 to 13. Fees vary, so it is necessary to check. Schools for the children of British military personnel sometimes admit children of civilians.

Emergency services: Police 110, fire 112.

Useful contacts:

British Embassy, Wilhelmstr 70–71, 10117 Berlin, tel: + 49 302 0457 0, website: www.britischebotschaft.de/

German Embassy, 23 Belgrave Square, London SW1X 8PZ, tel: 020 7824 1300

German National Tourist Board, PO Box 2695, London W1A 3TN, tel: 020 7317 0908, website: www.germany-tourism.de/

Expatriate information: www.german-way.com/

PERSONAL TAXATION

Residence

An individual who resides in Germany is subject to taxation on his or her worldwide income (unlimited tax liability) unless a double taxation treaty (DTT) disallows the taxation of an income portion. Non-residents are subject to taxation on certain German-sourced income (limited tax liability) only. Germany has concluded DTTs with numerous countries, including the UK and the United States.

To be considered a resident of Germany for tax purposes, an individual needs to maintain a permanent home or his or her habitual abode in Germany. The domicile of origin concept and citizenship have no impact on a person's tax status in Germany. A permanent home exists where an individual has possession of a house or apartment under circumstances that indicate he or she intends to stay not just temporarily in Germany. The German tax rules assume an habitual abode if the individual stays more than six months continuously in Germany. Short interruptions, such as for holidays or business trips, are disregarded. The unlimited tax liability arises (respectively ceases) in Germany as soon as the individual meets (respectively breaks) these residence criteria. Generally, married couples who are subject to unlimited taxation can elect to file jointly.

Taxation of personal income

German residents are subject to income tax on seven categories of income which include, among others:

- [ ]   income from employment;
- [ ]   income from investment;
- [ ]   other income (such as capital gains).

For these income categories taxable income is computed by deducting income-related expenses from gross income. The cash receipts and disbursement method is used to calculate taxable income. There are no special rules for expatriates.

Income from employment

Income from employment includes all benefits in cash and in kind received by an individual, such as salaries, bonuses, reimbursements of taxes, private use of a company car, and cost of living allowances. In general, employees may deduct all expenses incurred in order to acquire and maintain income. Expenses related to income from employment include commuting expenses, expenses for working tools, moving expenses, deductions for maintaining a second home where the employment is away from the centre of vital interests, and so on. In some cases there are ceilings on income-related expenses. The German income tax code provides for a standard lump sum deduction of €920.00 when the itemised expenses do not exceed this amount.

Investment income

Worldwide income from investment, including dividends and interest, is subject to German taxation. Fifty per cent of dividend income is tax-exempt. Accordingly, only 50 per cent of the related expenses are deductible. The German income tax code provides for a standard deduction of €51.00/€102.00 (single/joint filing) when the itemised expenses do not exceed this amount. Additionally, a personal allowance of €1,370.00/€2,740.00 (single/joint filing) is available with respect to income from investment.

Taxes on capital gains

Capital gains belong to the category 'other income'. Gains realised through the sale of private assets are generally not taxable if the time between acquisition and sale is more than 10 years for real estate and more than 12 months in the case of other assets, mainly stocks and securities. Gains of less than €512 after the offset of realised losses are tax-free.

Tax rates

Income tax is levied at progressive rates, starting at 15 per cent in 2006 for annual taxable income of €7,665.00/€15,330.00 (single/joint filing). The maximum tax rate is 42 per cent for taxable income exceeding €52,151.00/€104,302.00 (single/joint filing) in 2006. Additionally, a solidarity surcharge of 5.5 per cent is levied on the income tax due. Members of a church entitled to impose church tax, eg for Catholics and Protestants, are liable to church tax levied on income tax liability, at a rate of 8 or 9 per cent, depending on the federal state in which the taxpayer resides.

Tax administration

The tax year for income tax purposes is the calendar year. In principle, income tax returns must be filed by 31 May following the tax year; however, extensions to 30 September will be granted automatically if the tax return is prepared by a professional tax adviser. A further extension may be available on application.

Domestic employers are obliged to operate the 'pay as you earn' system, ie the employer withholds wage tax on behalf of the employee and transfers it to the respective tax office. To meet this rule the employee needs to provide a wage tax card to the employer that indicates the necessary tax information. The tax withheld is credited against the income tax liability levied on the basis of the filed income tax return.

The income tax liability is levied through an income tax assessment notice issued by the tax authorities. Income tax payments are payable within one month of the assessment's receipt. Refunds are paid out immediately after the issuance of the assessment. A protest against the tax assessment can only be filed within one month after the assessment's receipt.

The tax authorities can levy a penalty for delayed filing at a rate of 10 per cent of the tax liability, up to a maximum of €25,000. Furthermore, a late payment penalty of 1 per cent of the tax liability per month arises automatically on late payment.

For further information on tax and social security, contact:

BDO Deutsche Warentreuhand Aktiengessellschaft, Gerlinde Seinsche, Partner, tel: +49 (69) 95 94 1–265, e-mail: Gerlinde. Seinsche@bdo.de or

Alexia Christodoulou, Manager, tel: +49 (69) 95 94 1–263, e-mail: Alexia.Christodoulou@bdo.de

GREECE

The economy

After the relatively fast growth of recent years, the Greek economy is slowing down. Despite the fact that many businesses, including a number of listed companies in the Athens Stock Exchange, are closing down, stock prices are rising mainly because of foreign investment. The government continues to support the economy by public spending.

The main sectors of the Greek economy are shipping and tourism in services, and food, drink and tobacco processing, cement and other building materials and metallurgy in the manufacturing sector. Agriculture remains important for the economy, with olive oil and fruit being the main exports. Nevertheless, for 2005 Greece's current account deficit is estimated at 7 per cent of GDP.

GDP growth for 2005 is estimated to have been 3.5 per cent and 3.3 per cent is forecast for 2006, placing the outlook for the Greek economy in the upper quartile of the EU 15. Inflation, which has been the main problem of the Greek economy in recent years, runs now at approximately 3.5 per cent. Unemployment, on the other hand, is rising at almost 10 per cent and together with tax evasion, is the main target of government economic policy. The budget deficit at 4 per cent remains above the EU Stability and Growth Pact criterion but is forecast to moderate in 2006.

Personal finance and taxation

The level of executive salaries is still lower than in most northern EU countries but the gap is gradually closing. Employees receive 14 monthly salaries in Greece (half a monthly salary as Easter bonus and vacation bonus and one monthly salary as Christmas bonus). Income tax rises progressively on taxable income and the top rate of income tax is 40 per cent. Most benefits in kind are not

taxed on the recipient but on the employer. On an average executive salary, tax and social security contributions would be around
30 per cent. Tax is deducted monthly, and the final balance is
adjusted annually.

Working conditions

The EU provisions about free mobility of labour apply in Greece.
You can freely take up employment, or enter the country to look for
work, but you will need to register with the police (or the Alien's
Department Office if you are in Athens) within eight days. You will
need a residence permit for a stay of longer than three months.
Although improving, Greek bureaucracy is still fairly intimidating,
and can appear chaotic.

With the prevailing high level of unemployment and obstacles
that aim to give priority to Greek nationals, job prospects for
foreigners are not encouraging. Advanced technology and
education offer the best opportunities.

Working hours in the private sector are from 9.00 am to 5.00 pm
and in the public sector from 7.30 am to 3.30 pm. There are 11
public holidays, including religious holidays. The minimum
annual leave is 20 working days.

Useful information

Banking hours: 8.00 am to 2.00 pm Monday to Thursday, and 8.00 am
to 1.30 pm on Fridays.

Electricity: 220 V, 50 Hz ac.

Driving: Speed limits are 50 km/h in residential areas and 100–120
km/h on motorways. An international driving licence is required.

Transport: Transport is on the whole efficient and reliable and you
can choose between air, rail, sea or bus. Most international air
flights are based on Athens, and there are also regular services to
and from Salonika. Olympic Airways and Aegean Airways operate
domestic airlines serving some 30 towns and islands from Athens.
Railways serve the main centres north and south of Athens but
they are not efficient. Long-distance coach services provide a
means of seeing the country and many shipping routes connect
the mainland with the islands. Taxis and cars can be hired and they
are moderately priced. ELPA, the equivalent of our AA, and other

private insurers run road assistance services. Like all European cities, Athens has its traffic problems. The main roads in Greece are improving, but conditions on local roads can be difficult, especially in the mountains. Car prices are comparable to other EU countries.

Health care: Doctor and hospital treatment within the Greek national health system is free, but you will have to pay 25 per cent of prescription charges. If you are in a remote area, you can reclaim a proportion of private medical expenses.

Education: Public education is provided free of charge from nursery to university level, and is compulsory between the ages of 6 and 15. Because of language difficulties, expatriate parents tend to send their children to schools in the UK or, if they can get in, to an International School. The British Embassy school, St Catherine's, in Athens is a preparatory school for British children aged 3 to 13 years. The American Community School caters for boys and girls from 4 to 18. The fees vary according to age. Another recommended English language school in Greece is St Lawrence College (website http://www.st-lawrence.gr), which has two establishments at Glyfada and Varkiza.

Emergency services: police 100, fire 199, hospitals 106.

Useful contacts:
British Embassy, 1 Ploutarchou Street, 106 75 Athens, tel: (+30) 210 7272600, website: www.british-embassy.gr
Greek Embassy, tel: 020 7221 6467
Greek Tourist Board, 4 Conduit Street, London W1R 0DJ, tel: 020 7734 5996, website: www.greece.org.hellas/
Expat information: Americans Abroad, Greece, www.geocities.com/ Athens/7243/
Business contacts: www. business.hol.gr/

PERSONAL TAXATION

These details are as of January 2005.

Residence

Individuals permanently resident in Greece are liable to tax on their worldwide income and gains, while those temporarily resident are only liable to tax on income and gains derived from sources within Greece. Permanent residence is a concept of general law that denotes the place where a person has his or her permanent home or has the intention of establishing a permanent home. If you are coming to Greece from abroad for a temporary purpose, and without any fixed intention of remaining there permanently, you will be regarded as temporarily resident. On the other hand, if you come to Greece with the intention to settle, you may become permanently resident immediately.

Income from employment

In general, any income derived from an employment with a Greek employer is fully liable to Greek tax if the duties of the employment are exercised in Greece. Income derived from an employment held with a 'foreign' (non-Greek) employer is also liable to Greek tax if the duties are carried out in Greece, unless the provisions of a double taxation agreement exempt the income. Insurance by the public sector insurance fund (IKA), which covers pension, health, unemployment, etc is compulsory for all employees. EU member state nationals temporarily resident in Greece may be exempted if they continue to be insured in their own country.

Investment income

Greek permanent residents are liable to tax on their worldwide income, including investment income.

Deposit interest paid by Greek banks and financial institutions is subject to deduction of tax at source, currently at the rate of 10 per cent. There is no further income tax liability on such income. Interest income and dividends from foreign sources received by Greek permanent residents is liable to tax under the general rules. Dividends paid by Greek companies are not subject to any with-holding tax as they are paid out of fully taxed profits. Withholding tax, currently at the rate of 20 per cent, applies on the encashment of foreign dividends by Greek financial institutions. This is allowed as a credit against the final income tax liability.

Taxes on capital

Capital gains tax has been introduced on the disposal of real property at rates ranging from 0 per cent for properties held for 20 years, and up to 20 per cent for properties sold within five years of their acquisition. The sale of shares, partnership shares and certain other business assets are subject to income tax at rates ranging from 5 to 20 per cent.

Wealth tax

The taxable value of real property (which is on average 40 to 60 per cent of actual market value) is subject to an annual Real Property Tax at rates ranging from 0 to 0.8 per cent. Personal allowances of €243,600 are available to both husband and wife. The first two minor children are allowed €61,650. For more than two children the allowance is €73,400.

Double taxation agreements

Greece has an extensive network of double taxation agreements, currently covering 42 countries including the UK and the United States.

For further information on tax and social security, contact:

John Tentes, Partner, BDO Hellenic Auditing Company AE, tel: + 30 210 6122366, e-mail: hac@internet.gr

HUNGARY

The economy

Hungary is situated in East-Central Europe, with a total land area of 93,000 sq km and a population of 10.1 million and became a full member of the EU in May 2004.

The GDP per capita/PPS (purchase power standard) amounted in 2003 to €13,400. According to the June 2005 Eurostat Report, Hungary is 40 per cent below the EU 25 PPS average based on estimates for 2004. With the exception of Portugal, the 10 new EU Member States occupy the last 10 places. Eurostat estimates the Hungarian PPS to increase in 2005 to €14,940. GDP real growth in 2005 is estimated to have been 3.7 per cent and a slightly higher level of growth is forecast for 2006.

Foreign Direct Investment (FDI) has played a crucial role in the restructuring of the Hungarian economy since 1990. It has facilitated productivity growth, technological modernisation, etc. The

FDI reached €3.323 billion in 2004 following the latest results. In 2005 €3.5–4 billion of FDI is expected in the form of equity capital and reinvested earnings. Germany has been the single biggest FDI contributor in Hungary in the past 15 years (€9.7 billion or 29 per cent). So far more than two-thirds of all FDI has flowed into the Central Hungary region, consisting of Budapest and the surrounding Pest county. Central and Western Transdanubia are the two other dynamic regions to have benefited from the establishment of foreign industrial plants. The concentration of start-ups has been particularly heavy in the Gyor-Moson-Sopron county of the latter, where multinationals such as Audi, General Motors, General Electric and Philips have established themselves.

By the beginning of 2006, consumer price inflation rate had decreased to 2.7 per cent from 3.7 per cent in July 2005. The unemployment rate in 2005 is estimated at 7.1 per cent and no significant change is forecast for 2006. The budget deficit for 2006 is forecast to decrease from 6.1 to 5.2 per cent, outside the EU Stability and Growth Pact parameter. The current account deficit at the end of 2005 is estimated at 8.7 per cent.

Useful information

Administratively, Hungary is divided into seven regions, which are each subdivided into two or three districts, referred to in English as counties. Nearly one-fifth of the 10 million population lives in Budapest, and there is a marked contrast between the dynamic growth of the western part of the country and the near stagnation in eastern Hungary. These differences have been exacerbated by the uneven flow of FDI since 1989. The regions with the highest per capita GDP (and lowest unemployment) are Central Hungary, and Western and Central Transdanubia. Northern Hungary is the centre of traditional heavy industry, and its unemployment rate is now the highest in Hungary. The Northern Great Plain is the least developed region and is heavily agricultural. However, it also has a food processing industry and a well-developed pharmaceutical industry.

Visas and residence permits: an employee is only allowed to work upon receipt of all necessary permits.

Extended stay visas: British citizens can visit Hungary for up to 180 days without requiring a visa. Citizens of the United States and

European countries do not require visas and can stay for a maximum period of 90 days from the date of first entry. Foreign persons who wish to enter Hungary to work should normally apply for an extended stay visa unless there is an agreement between Hungary and their country of citizenship. An extended stay visa is granted by any Hungarian embassy in the home country of the applicant and allows single or multiple entry and a stay in Hungary for a period in excess of 90 days and for a maximum period of one year.

Residence permits: A residence permit is required if the foreigner intends to work in Hungary (and the extended stay visa has expired). Residence permits requested for the purpose of employment or other gainful activity may be issued for a maximum of four years when issued for the first time. Applications for the issue or renewal of residence permits must be submitted no later than 15 days prior to the expiration of the authorised period of stay.

Work permits: An application must be submitted by the employer to the labour centre in the area of which it intends to employ non-residents. This should be done prior to applying for an extended stay visa or residence permit. The work permit is granted for a maximum period of one year but may be extended. Chief executives (including managing directors, general managers, board members, members of the supervisory board, head of a Hungarian representation office and a Hungarian branch office) appearing in the company's documents filed with the Registration Court are not subject to work permit requirements. EEA citizens may travel to Hungary with a valid passport or valid personal identity card. They may stay in Hungary for a period of no more than 90 days. Stays of longer than 90 days require a residence permit.

As a consequence, EEA citizens are still required to be in possession of a valid residence and work permit in order to be allowed to perform professional activities in Hungary. Hungarian law provides, however, an exception for UK, Irish and Swedish nationals, who are allowed to reside and work in the Hungarian territory as from the day of their arrival. Should the stay in Hungary exceed 90 days, starting from the day of their arrival, a residence permit will still be required.

Social contributions: foreign nationals who are diplomats or members/employees of foreign-based companies, or Hungarian companies with full or partial foreign ownership, are not covered by the Hungarian social system and must pay the health care tax to contract insurance for medical services for themselves and their families. The monthly contribution rate, which also applies to foreign students, is 75 per cent of the current official minimum monthly wage. Hungary has bilateral agreements on social security with several countries but applies the 1408/71 EC Regulation on the citizens of the EU or third countries when applicable.

Permanent accommodation: expatriates living in Budapest can choose from a large pool of villas and apartments in all price categories for permanent and temporary accommodation. Most foreigners tend to gravitate towards the II, III, V, VI and XII districts where there is a wide selection of modern or refurbished houses and flats. Word-of-mouth information from colleagues and acquaintances may produce the best results, but you can find listings for flats and houses in the English language *Budapest Sun* and *Budapest Business Journal*. There are also weekly journals in Hungarian devoted to housing such as *Expressz Kepes Ingatlan* and *Ingatlan Magazin*.

During the previous regime, many flats were divided into two or three separate living quarters to maximise space; as a result, many apartments are oddly-shaped or divided. Most apartments come furnished, and those that are unfurnished usually include major kitchen appliances. To rent a house or flat in Hungary you need to sign a lease with the owner. Leases are variable but typically last for one year; owners will generally ask for a two to three months deposit. It is also possible to own property in Hungary if you get a permit. When buying, make all the usual searches and take precautions. Local real estate law demands detailed consultation with a Hungarian lawyer.

Education: There is a good selection of English, French and German language schools in Budapest providing a decent choice for parents wishing to enrol their children in a comparative curriculum. Hungarian universities provide a wide range of programmes and degree courses given in English. Details of courses offered can be found by visiting the home pages of the individual universities. For those who can summon up the courage to tackle the Hungarian language, there are a number of recognised language schools in Budapest. Details of private schools, universities and language schools, and much more, may be found in *Doing Business with Hungary* (Kogan Page, www.kogan-page.co.uk).

Electricity: 230 volts/50 Hz.

Useful contacts:

Embassy of the United Kingdom and Northern Ireland, Harmincad utca 6, Budapest 1051, tel: +36 1 266 2888, website: www.britishembassy.hu

Embassy of the Republic of Hungary in the UK, 35 Eaton Place, London SW1X 8BY, tel: 020 7235 2664

British Council, 1068 Budapest, Benczur u. 26, tel: +36 1 478 4700, e-mail: information@britishcouncil.hu

Mercer Human Resource Consulting, Budapest, Rakoczi ut 70–72, H–1074, tel: +36 1 888 2100

DTZ Zadelhoff Tie Leung Central and Eastern Europe BV, Bajcsy-Zsilinszky ut 42–46, Budapest 1054, tel: +36 1 269 6966, website: www.dtz.com/www.dtzresearch.com

PERSONAL TAXATION

Residence

Hungary has only a federal level of income taxation. The determination of an individual's Hungarian tax obligations will depend on a number of factors, including residence, the province/territory in which an individual is taxed, and the nature of the income earned. Like many countries, Hungary taxes on the basis of residence. The personal income tax legislation specifically defines residence. Foreign citizens become tax resident if their habitual abode is in Hungary.

Taxation of personal income

Hungarian residents are subject to tax on their worldwide income, including employment compensation, capital gains, interest, dividends, rents, professional fees, pensions and annuities. Non-residents are only subject to tax on income earned from Hungarian sources. The maximum rate is 36 per cent over HUF 1.55 million per annum.

Income from employment

All remuneration including most benefits derived from employment is taxable. Taxable benefits include living allowances, housing allowances, vacations and personal use of employer-owned or employer-leased vehicles.

Investment income

Interest income is generally subject to 25 per cent income tax, except for interest paid by financial institutions, which is tax exempt. Dividends from companies are taxed at 25–35 per cent. Hungarian residents are also taxed on dividends from foreign companies at 25 per cent. These dividends are not subject to the gross-up and tax credit mechanism, and therefore they are taxed at full rates.

Capital gains

Resident individuals are entitled to an exemption on gains arising from the sale of shares listed at the Budapest Stock Exchange (BSE) and recognised (regulated) exchange market of another EU member state. In all other cases the income tax on capital gains is 25 per cent. There is no adjustment in calculating capital gains to remove the effect of any inflationary increase. Capital losses suffered on the BSE can only reduce the capital gains achieved at the BSE.

Double taxation treaties

Hungary has over 60 comprehensive treaties or conventions in force with other countries for the elimination of double taxation on income, including treaties with the UK and the United States.

For further information on tax and social security, contact:

Zoltan Gerendy, Tax Partner, BDO Forte, 126 Budapest, Nagy Jen u. 10, tel: (36 1) 235 3010, fax: (36 1) 266 6438, e-mail: zoltan.gerendy @bdo.hu

REPUBLIC OF IRELAND (EIRE)

The economy

Thirty-three years after Ireland's entry to the European Union (then the EEC), the principal components of the economy are technology, pharmaceuticals and the services sector, including financial services. According to the OECD, Ireland is the world's largest exporter of computer software, and provides over 60 per cent of all packaged software in use in Europe.

Although Irish agriculture has benefited from heavy EU farming subsidies, it has long since ceased to play a predominant part in the total economy, and now employs only 6.33 per cent of the workforce.

GDP growth for 2005 is estimated at 4.7 per cent and similar growth is forecast for 2006, well above the Euro area average.

The annualised inflation rate of 2.5 per cent in 2005 puts Ireland among the higher inflation economies in the EU, which means that the cost of living is higher. However, the unemployment rate of 4.3 per cent was the lowest in the Euro zone, and the public sector budget deficit ratio to GDP was 0.9 per cent, which is clearly well within the EU Stability and Growth Pact parameter of 3 per cent. The current account deficit at a modest 1.5 per cent of GDP also poses no problem.

Working conditions

British and EU citizens do not need work permits. The Irish work an average of 40.2 hours per week. Agencies and Jobcentres are more common ways to look for jobs than through the press. The Irish language is *not* a prerequisite for most jobs, although teaching and some civil service jobs are notable exceptions. The normal holiday allowance is four to six weeks per annum. The gap between men's and women's salaries is similar to the rest of Europe, but closing.

Useful information

Banking hours: 10.00 am to 4.00 pm Monday–Friday, except Thursday 10.00 am to 5.00 pm.

Shopping hours: 9.00 am to 6.00 pm; many supermarkets stay open until 8.30 pm, Monday–Saturday. Lunch break in business is usually 12.30–1.30 pm.

Electricity: 220 V, 50 Hz ac.

Transport: Public transport prices compare with those in the UK. Urban bus routes are extensive and are now much improved. Season tickets are good value. One overground urban railway line (DART) services Dublin and runs north–south along the coast. Two recently built tram lines (LUAS) have opened to service areas in south and south-west Dublin. There is an inexpensive, extensive and frequent coach service to all parts of the country. Trains are more expensive, but still cheaper than in the UK.

Ireland's roads have been vastly improved over the last decade with new motorways and road widening. There are international airports in Dublin, Cork, Shannon and Knock.

Health care: Medical care is provided free of charge (subject to an admission charge) in public hospitals to all persons who are resident, or are likely to be resident in Ireland for at least 12 months. Out-patient services (eg visits to a GP) are generally private, except for those on social welfare, but exemptions and relief are available. A high percentage of the populace has health insurance.

Education: At both primary and secondary levels most schools are run by church groups (Roman Catholic or other), although largely state funded. Admission is usually possible for members of other religions. Primary education is generally free, and also most secondary education, although many church-run schools (especially in Dublin) charge fees to supplement their state funding; from €1,000 to €5,500 for non-boarders. Two schools with experience in schooling for expatriate children are Blackrock College, Dublin (12–18) and Newman College, Dublin (15–18).

Media: There are four national newspapers; the *Irish Independent* and *The Irish Times* are the most popular. There are also evening and Sunday papers. Ireland has four national TV stations and national and local radio stations.

Emergency services: 999 (police, fire, ambulance).

Useful contacts:

British Embassy, 29 Merrion Road, Ballsbridge, Dublin 4, tel: +353 1 205 3700

Irish Embassy, 17 Grosvenor Place, London SW1, tel: +44 020 7235 2171

Irish Tourist Board, Info Service, PO Box 273, Dublin 8, tel: +353 1602 4000, website: www.ireland.travel.ie

PERSONAL TAXATION

These details are as of January 2006.

Residence

Subject to certain exceptions, Irish residents are liable to tax on their worldwide income and gains, while non-residents are only liable to tax on income and gains derived from sources within the Republic of Ireland (Ireland).

Residence status for Irish tax purposes is determined solely by the number of days a person is present in Ireland during a given tax year. The Irish tax year coincides with the calendar year. You will be regarded as resident in Ireland for a particular tax year if you spend 183 days or more in Ireland for any purpose in that tax year; or if you spend 280 days or more in aggregate in Ireland for any purpose over a period of two consecutive tax years, you will be regarded as a resident of Ireland for the second tax year. For example, if you spend 140 days in Ireland in year 1 and 150 days there in year 2, you will be resident in Ireland for year 2, as the aggregate number of days over the two years equals or exceeds 280. (However, if you spend 30 days or less in Ireland in the tax year, the aggregate rule does not apply.)

A 'day' for residence purposes is one in which you are present in Ireland at midnight. Therefore, days of arrival are included and days of departure are excluded.

A person who is Irish tax resident for three consecutive tax years is regarded as 'ordinarily resident' for Irish tax purposes from year 4 onwards. Conversely, a person will not cease to be regarded as 'ordinarily resident' until he or she has been non-resident for three consecutive tax years.

Income from employment

In general, any income derived from an employment with an Irish or UK employer is fully liable to Irish tax if the duties of the employment are exercised in Ireland. Income derived from an employment held with a 'foreign' (non-Irish/non-UK) employer is also liable to Irish tax if the duties are carried out in Ireland, unless the income is exempted by the provisions of a double taxation agreement. The remittance basis of taxation, which previously applied to individuals resident in Ireland who were either not domiciled or not ordinarily resident in the state, provided that such individuals were liable to Irish tax only on the portion of their income arising outside the state or the UK that was remitted here.

With effect from 1 January 2006 the remittance basis of taxation has been discontinued.

Investment income

Irish residents are liable to tax on their worldwide income, including investment income. However, persons who are resident, but not domiciled or not ordinarily resident in Ireland, are only taxable on foreign (that is, non-Irish and non-UK) investment income to the extent that such income is remitted to Ireland.

Deposit interest paid by Irish banks and financial institutions to Irish residents is subject to deduction of tax at source, currently at the rate of 20 per cent. There is no further income tax liability on such income, but social security contributions at rates up to 5 per cent may be due. Interest income from foreign sources received by Irish residents is liable to tax at the recipient's marginal (that is, top) tax rate.

Dividend income is liable to income tax at the individual's marginal tax rate. Dividends paid by Irish companies suffer with-holding tax at the standard rate of tax, currently 20 per cent. This is allowed as a credit against the ultimate tax liability.

Encashment tax, currently at the rate of 20 per cent, applies on the encashment of foreign dividends by Irish financial institutions. This is allowed as a credit against the final income tax liability.

Taxes on capital

Capital gains

Capital gains tax is charged on gains realised from the disposal of assets, currently at the rate of 20 per cent. The taxable amount is generally the difference between the acquisition and sale price. Relief is given for inflation up to 31 December 2002 through index-ation of the acquisition cost.

Individuals who are Irish domiciled and either resident or ordi-narily resident in Ireland are liable to capital gains tax on their worldwide gains. Individuals who are resident but non-domiciled are fully liable in respect of gains from Irish and UK assets, and on foreign gains to the extent that such gains are remitted to Ireland. Individuals who are neither resident nor ordinarily resident are liable to Irish capital gains tax on the disposal of Irish specified assets, for example on the sale of land or buildings in the state.

Wealth tax

There is no wealth tax in Ireland.

Double taxation agreements

Ireland has an extensive network of double taxation agreements, currently covering 44 countries including the UK and the United States.

For further information on tax and social security, contact:

Oonagh Casey, Senior Manager, BDO Simpson Xavier, tel: + 353 (1) 4700 217, e-mail: ocasey@bdosx.ie

ITALY

The economy

Italy's economy has slowed down since 1999, and in 2005 GDP growth was minimal at 0.1 per cent. A recovery of growth to 1.2 per cent is forecast for 2006, which would still be below the Euro area forecast of 1.9 per cent. Unemployment was running at 7.5 per cent in September 2005. However, inflation remains modest, around 2.1 per cent, and public investment has remained solid. At 4.3 per cent of GDP, the budget deficit is well above the Stability and Growth Pact criterion. However, the foreign trade current account deficit at around 1.5 per cent of GDP is relatively modest.

Italy has few mineral resources, apart from scattered deposits of sulphur, iron ore, zinc and lead, and is therefore dependent on overseas trade. There are, however, significant gas and oil fields that are being exploited, and Italy provides over a quarter of the world's mercury. Its main exports are machinery, cars, metal manufactures, iron and steel products, artificial fibres, knitwear and hosiery, and a wide range of luxury and semi-luxury items, including fashion clothing, leather, fur and shoes, and food and wine, of which Italy is now a bigger exporter than France. Tourism, of course, is a major revenue producer and is one of the country's largest sectors.

Industry is unevenly distributed. The northern triangle – Milan, Turin and Genoa – produces about one-fifth of the national output and incomes are well above the national average. There has been a steady migration of labour from the impoverished south, both to the more prosperous north and to other EU countries. Governments have aimed at developing the 'mezzogiorno' but, despite national and EU aid, the south has remained relatively poor.

Working conditions

Citizens of EU countries can enter Italy freely to look for and take up a job; they do not need work permits, but they will need a residence permit. It is also necessary to obtain a tax number, which will be required for any relevant contract, including all banking and financial operations.

The 40-hour, five-day week has become the general standard.

Salaries are paid in 13–15 instalments, depending on the applicable collective labour agreement. Most collective agreements provide for four weeks paid leave for wage and salary earners. There are also 10 public holidays, and there is a growing trend towards accumulating public holidays for summer vacations, so as to minimise disruption. Most towns also have a holiday on the feast day of their patron saint, and there are several half-day holidays.

Employers face many additional charges, including assistance towards housing, transport and canteens, children's nurseries and kindergartens. Most of these concessions, which are negotiated, are common among the larger enterprises and, in the case of smaller firms, often arranged through consortia. Some firms also have savings plans.

There are works' committees in those firms that employ more than 15 workers.

Useful information

Banking hours: 8.30 am to 1.30 pm and 2.30 or 3.00 to 4.00 pm, Monday to Friday.

Post office: 8.00 am to 2.00 pm Monday to Friday, 8.30 to 12.00 am Saturday.

Shopping hours: Vary from region to region, 9.00 am to 12.30 pm, 3.00 to 7.30 pm Monday to Saturday; usually closed Monday morning.

Driving: Speed limits are 50 km/h in urban areas, 90 km/h on secondary and local roads, 110 km/h on main roads outside urban areas, and 130 km/h on motorways. Front and back seat belts are compulsory.

Transport: Rail fares are lower than in Britain, but some mainline trains require supplementary payments. The main cities are served by a network of toll motorways ('autostrada') and other highways are in good condition.

Health care: The national health service covers the whole of the employed working population, including registered foreigners. Private treatment is expensive but most foreigners prefer it. Italy has the highest doctor/patient ratio in Europe. A number of hospitals are run by the Church.

Education: There are American and English schools in Rome and Milan. These schools, inspected by HM Inspectors of Schools, include St George's English School, Rome; The New School, Rome; Sir James Henderson British School, Milan; and the International School, Milan. State schooling is free (although parents buy books and stationery) and most private schools are Roman Catholic day schools.

Emergency services: 118, carabinieri 112, fire 115.

Useful contacts:
British Embassy, Via XX Settembre 80a, I-00187 Roma Rm, tel: 39 06 4220 0001, website: www.britain.it
Italian Embassy, 14 Three Kings Yard, London W1, tel: 020 7312 2200
Italian State Tourist Board, 1 Princes Street, London W1Y 8AY, tel: 020 7399 3562, website: www.enit.it
Italian Tourist Web Guide: www.itwg.com

PERSONAL TAXATION

These details are as of December 2005.

Residence

An individual is subject to income tax in Italy depending on his or her residence status. An individual is considered resident in Italy if for the greater part (183 days or more) of the year that individual:

☐   is registered in the local population register ('anagrafe'), or
☐   has his or her habitual abode ('dimora abituale') in Italy, or
☐   whether physically present or not, has the centre of his or her business and vital interests in Italy.

Residence status may commence at any point in the calendar year when one or more of the above criteria are met. There are no special rules applying to years of arrival and departure.

Taxation of personal income

A resident in Italy is taxed on worldwide income; a non-resident is taxed only on Italian-source income. The tax year is the calendar year.

Personal income tax ('imposta sul reddito delle persone fisiche': IRPEF) is imposed at progressive rates, set from 23 to 43 per cent, on the aggregate taxable income of an individual from five distinct sources:

1. income from registered land and property;
2. income from capital;
3. income from personal services (which includes income from employment and professional income);
4. income from a business;
5. other income (including certain capital gains).

In addition to personal income tax, individuals have to pay regional tax ('addizionale regionale') set from 0.90 to 1.40 per cent, and municipal tax ('addizionale comunale') set from 0.20 to 0.50 per cent, if stated by the Council of residence.

Several categories of investment income are subject, either by election or mandatory, to a final flat-rate withholding tax rather than progressive taxation.

Husbands and wives are separately assessed and taxed. They may opt to file a joint return (only for employees who request fiscal assistance from the employer, as provided by national law). If this applies, the liability is calculated separately for each spouse and then aggregated. This procedure results in no change either to the total tax liability or the relative burden.

A part of the taxable income could be exempted (the so-called 'no tax area'). This is represented by the identification of a 'base deduction', equal for all taxpayers, of €3,000, to which a further amount is to be added that varies depending on the type of income and on the whole amount. Such amount increases to €4,500 for employees, €4,000 for retired persons and €1,500 for the self-employed and holders of income from a small enterprise. This further deduction is related to the work period or to the retirement period during the year, except for holders of income from self-employment or a small enterprise (for whom it is to be applied regardless of the work period during the year). Such deductions are progressively reduced with the rise of income, up to setting them at zero.

There are several personal allowances available to taxpayers in respect of their personal circumstances (ie dependent spouse allowance, child allowance, dependent relative allowance).

All taxpayers must in principle file a return (form 'Unico Persone Fisiche') by 31 July of the year following the year of income, if a tax return is produced directly by the taxpayer to a bank or a postal office, or by 31 October if the tax return is produced by electronic transmission.

There are two principal exceptions from the requirement to file a return: a) for taxpayers whose income is entirely exempt from personal taxation, or entirely subject to final withholding taxes; and b) for taxpayers whose income derives from sources other than employment or self-employment when the net income tax due does not exceed €12.00.

Income from employment
Social security contributions

Social security contributions apply to wages and salaries and must be withheld by the employer. The compulsory social security contributions for health insurance and for old-age pension are deducted from the total gross salary by applying different contribution rates according to the type of business and the category of employee.

Both employers and employees pay contributions for these insurances. Only employers pay contributions for health at work insurance, accident insurance and unemployment insurance, calculated on the gross total salary. Because of the complexity of the system, it is impossible to quote rates with any meaningful general relevance.

Certain payments are exempt from the taxable base for social security contributions. These include:

☐ termination payments;
☐ daily travel and subsistence allowances;
☐ reimbursement of actual subsistence and travel expenses.

Taxable salary

The gross salary minus health insurance and pension fund contributions is the taxable salary. Taxes are withheld at source by the employer by applying progressive rates so as to approximate by the end of the year to the final tax liability of the employee on the remuneration.

All kinds of income – including wages, bonuses, benefits in kind and termination payments – are taxable.

Reimbursement of expenses incurred on the employer's behalf is generally tax-free, as are payments for the use of the employee's own car for business purposes, within certain limits.

Investment income

Dividends

Dividends from both Italian and foreign companies are generally treated as taxable income. Taxation differs if dividends come from a 'non-significant' or from a 'significant' shareholding.

A 'non-significant' shareholding is a holding of no more than 2 per cent of the voting rights or 5 per cent of the share capital of a listed company, or a holding of no more than 20 per cent of the voting rights or 25 per cent of the share capital of an unlisted company. A 'significant' shareholding is a holding that exceeds these limits.

Dividends from 'non-significant' shareholdings paid by an Italian or a foreign company are subject to a withholding tax of 12.5 per cent on the total amount received. Dividends from 'significant' shareholdings paid by an Italian or a foreign company (if not resident in 'black-list' – tax-haven – countries) are subject to a withholding tax of 12.5 per cent on the 40 per cent of the amount of dividend paid, and moreover they are taxed at progressive rates (set from 23 to 43 per cent), together with other personal income, for the 40 per cent of it. The withholding tax can be deducted from the total income tax due, in the annual income tax return as tax credit.

Where a dividend comes from foreign companies no tax credit is recognised for the tax paid abroad and the only option is to ask the foreign country for a reimbursement.

Where a dividend comes from foreign companies resident in 'black-list' countries, the whole amount received is taxed.

Interest

Interest is subject to one of two different rates of withholding tax: 1) subject to withholding tax at 27 per cent is interest from bank deposits and current accounts, short-term bonds of banks and listed companies, and unlisted company bonds with a high-interest coupon; 2) subject to withholding tax of 12.5 per cent is interest from certificates of deposit, state and local authority bonds, medium- and long-term bonds of banks and listed companies, unlisted company bonds (other than those with a high-interest coupon), and any other interest.

For resident private individuals and for all non-residents, the withholding tax (where it applies) is final in every case.

Starting from 1 July 2005, according to the EEC Directive 2003/48/CE and the Italian Law Decree No 84 dated 18/4/2005, in order to remain anonymous the name of the recipient, interests paid to individuals tax resident in Italy, originating from Belgium (as well as from Luxembourg and Austria), until 30 June 2008 will be subjected to a withholding tax at source of 15 per cent (the rate will increase up to 20 per cent until 30 June 2011 and up to 35 per cent from 1 July 2011 onwards). However, special rules provided by the double treaties can avoid the withholding tax.

Income from real property

Income derived from real property situated in Italy is included in taxable income. However, where the property is recorded in the Land Register ('catasto'), as it will be in the great majority of cases, actual income is ignored in the first instance. Instead, a notional annual rental value based on the cadastral value (the value recorded in the Register) is imputed to the owner. It is only where actual rental income exceeds this cadastral income that it becomes taxable income.

In the case of non-cadastral land and foreign land, actual rents receivable are treated as taxable income. Deductions up to 25 per cent of the taxable income may be available. The income from main residence (cadastral value) is tax exempted. There is no withholding tax on rents.

Taxation of capital

Capital gains

Capital gains that derive from the sale of real property are subject to taxation, but only if the period between purchase and sale does not exceed five years.

Taxation is excluded if the property is the main residence of the individual. Gains from the disposal of real property are subject to income tax at progressive rates.

Capital gains derived from the sale of an interest in a partnership or a shareholding in a company are taxed as follows: a) by applying a special substitute tax of 12.5 per cent of the entire capital gain; or b) at progressive rates, for the 40 per cent of it respectively if the interest is considered 'non-significant' or 'significant' (see the section 'Dividends', above).

Wealth tax

There is no wealth tax in Italy.

Double taxation treaties

Italy has concluded treaties to avoid double taxation with over 75 countries, including the UK and the United States. Residents with income from non-treaty countries include the foreign-source income in their taxable income and receive a credit for foreign taxes paid, up to the amount of tax imposed by Italy.

For further information, contact:

Giorgio Farina, BDO International Liaison Partner, BDO Sala Scelsi Farina Società di Revisione per Azioni, tel: + 39 02 29 062 098, fax: + 39 02 65 75 867, e-mail: giorgio.farina@bdo.it

LITHUANIA

The economy

Lithuania is highly regarded by foreign investors (from Scandinavia, the United States and Germany) especially in the heavy industry (metallurgy, chemistry) and light industry (textile, house wares) sectors. Significant foreign investments span industry, financial services, business and telecommunications services. The main reasons for these concurring investments are Lithuania's highly qualified labour force, the lowest production cost in Eastern Europe and the favourable geographical location. Lithuania is at the centre of the communications highway between Eastern and Western Europe, a crossroads between EU and the Union of independent states. In recent years, the Lithuanian government has taken appropriate actions to improve the business environment, by giving exceptional attention to administration functions and the organisation of the business environment. Lithuania has a steady currency and a strong fiscal policy. In 2005 Lithuania's economic growth was among the most rapid in Eastern Europe, with GDP at 6.5 per cent compared to 7 per cent in 2004 and an exceptional growth rate of 10.5 per cent in 2003. In the second quarter of 2005 the lowest unemployment rate that was reached during the last 10 years was recorded at 8.5 per cent. However, unemployment for the full year is estimated at 11.3 per cent against rates of 11.4 per cent for 2004 and around 12.4 per cent in 2003. In foreign trade, Lithuania's deficit on current account was approximately 7.9 per cent of GDP in 2005. Lithuania became a member of the EU in May 2004; the 2005 public sector budget deficit at 2.7 per cent satisfies that EU Stability and Growth Pact criterion for Euro area entry.

Useful information

Capital: Vilnius.

Banking hours: 8.00 am to 5.00 pm Monday–Wednesday, 8.00 am to 4.00 pm Friday.

Shopping hours: 10.00 am to 6.00 or 7.00 pm Monday–Friday, 10.00 am to 5.00 pm Saturday and Sunday. Food stores are open every day, 7.00 am to 10.00 pm or midnight.

Driving: Driving is on the right. Speed limits are 50 km/h in built-up areas, 90 km/h on overland roads, and 110–130 km/h on motorways. An international driving licence, third-party insurance and wearing of seat belts are compulsory.

Transport: Lithuania has international airports in Vilnius, Kaunas, Siauliai and Palanga. Rail transport is efficient and reasonably priced. Vilnius and Kaunas have trolleybuses; buses are popular in the main cities and in the smaller ones.

Education: Education is free and compulsory from the ages of 7 to 16. There is secondary, technical and professional education in Lithuania. English is taught in all schools. Lithuania has 15 public universities and academies and six private higher education schools.

Directory enquiries: 118.

Emergency services: 112.

Media: There are four national television channels, 49 radio channels, and nine daily newspapers.

Useful contacts:

British Embassy, Antakalnio str 2, LT-10308 Vilnius, tel: +370 5 246 2900, fax: +370 5 246 2901; 8.30 am to 5.00 pm Monday to Thursday, 8.30 am to 4.00pm Friday, website: http://www.britishembassy. gov.uk

Embassy of the Republic of Lithuania to the United Kingdom of Great Britain and Northern Ireland, 84 Gloucester Place, London W1U 6AU, tel.+44 20 7486 64 01, fax: +44 20 7486 64 03, website: http://amb.urm.lt/jk

Lithuanian State Department of Tourism, http://www.tourism.lt

Working conditions

According to the established laws of the Republic of Lithuania, foreigners intending to live in Lithuania either temporarily or permanently must obtain a permit to do so. A permit to live in Lithuania is issued to foreigners regardless of their age. For foreigners under the age of 18 wishing to live in Lithuania, their parents or other legal guardians can apply for them. The Migration Department will examine the application to issue EU citizens and their family with a temporary permit and will decide accordingly within one month. Temporary permits are issued for up to five years, except in the case of students, whose temporary permits are issued for one year of study.

Foreigners who are EU citizens will be issued with a permanent permit if they have lived in Lithuania legally for the last five years, they have a place of residence in Lithuania, or they have a legal source of income in Lithuania. The Lithuanian government sets a minimum monthly salary. As from 4 April 2005, the minimum monthly salary is 550 litas (£109 or €159) and the minimum hourly salary is 3,28 litas (£0.65 or €0.95). The average gross monthly wage in the fourth quarter of 2003 was 1,208 litas (£233 or €350). In Lithuania, working hours cannot exceed 40 hours per week or

8 hours per day. The minimum annual leave in Lithuania is 28 calendar days. Annual leave is not reduced for part-time workers.

There is a wide range of accommodation available in Lithuania, from rooms in private homes in the outer suburbs to expensive flats in the city centre. Rent for flats in the capital varies from 400 to 8,000 litas (£76 to 1,538 or €116 to 2,317) per month. Rent for a house costs from 8,000 to 14,000 litas (£1,538 to 2,693 or €2,317 to 4,055) per month.

Your social security rights in Lithuania are the same as those that apply elsewhere within the EEA (European Economic Area). When you start work in Lithuania, you will contribute to the Lithuanian social security system and consequently gain the right to benefits. In Lithuania social security policies are the responsibility of the Ministry of Social Security and Labour. The State Social Insurance Board (SoDra) is the state agency responsible for coordinating benefits and pensions. Benefits provided by state social insurance include pensions, sickness allowances, maternity and childbirth benefits, child care benefits and unemployment benefits.

Residence

An individual in Lithuania is liable for tax on his or her income as an employee and on income as a self-employed person. In the case of an individual who qualifies as a 'permanent resident' of Lithuania, tax will be calculated on income earned in Lithuania and overseas. A foreign resident pays tax only on his or her income in Lithuania. To be considered a Lithuanian resident, an individual must meet the requirement of residence in Lithuania for at least 183 consecutive days in a 12-month period. Occasionally, an individual will be considered a Lithuanian resident even if he or she is resident in Lithuania for less than 183 days if he or she owns a home in Lithuania that is his or her permanent residence.

Taxation on personal income

An employer is obliged to deduct, immediately, each month, the amount of tax and national insurance due from a salaried worker.

A salaried employee's income that is derived mainly from a Lithuanian company is taxable at 33 per cent. Other forms of income such as rent, provision of services as a self-employed person, etc, are liable to tax at the rate of 15 per cent.

According to the Law on Amendment and Supplementing of Articles 6, 20, 27, 37 of the Law on Income Tax of Individuals No

X-235 of 7 June 2005, effective from 1 July 2006, the current individual income tax rate of 33 per cent (applicable, inter alia to employment income) will be reduced to 27 per cent in the period from 1 July 2006 to 31 December 2007, and 24 per cent from 1 January 2008.

Employees also pay 3 per cent social security contributions from their employment income.

Immovable property tax

The new immovable property tax is regulated by the Law on Immovable Property Tax No X-233 of 7 June 2005, effective 1 January 2006. The main features of the law are that taxpayers are legal entities and individuals that own immovable property used in economic activities. (Previously, immovable property owned by individuals was not subject to tax at all. Immovable property of individuals that is not used in economic activities remains not taxable.) Also, the tax rate is 1 per cent of the taxable value of immovable property, which is the average market value or the replacement value in respect of some groups of immovable property. Taxpayers may request to apply their own valuation, if the value so determined otherwise differs by more than 20 per cent from the average market value or the replacement value.

Double taxation

Lithuania has a broad treaty system with other countries, which at the present time covers 38 countries including the UK and the United States.

For further information on tax and social security, contact:

Virginija Sireviciene, BDO Auditas ir Apskaita, tel: + 370 37 320 390, e-mail: Virginija.Sireviciene@bdo.lt

LUXEMBOURG

The economy

The central location of Luxembourg within the EU and a liberal fiscal climate have attracted a large service sector there, particularly in international banking and finance. To some extent this has compensated for the decline in manufacturing. Both inflation (3.2 per cent) and unemployment (4.6 per cent) are low. Over 39 per cent of the population are foreigners attracted by the employment prospects. GDP growth in 2005 is estimated to have been 3.5 per cent, significantly above the Euro area average, and is forecast to be much the same in 2006. As a ratio of GDP, the budget deficit in 2005 ran at 2.3 per cent, and Luxembourg maintained a surplus on current account of 5.9 per cent.

Working conditions

Gross pay is somewhat higher than in the UK at senior levels; many enjoy company fringe benefits (for instance a car or a house).

The procedure for stay and work permits is as throughout the EU. A good knowledge of French and German (official languages in Luxembourg) is valuable as both languages are widely used in business, although English is also widely spoken. Knowledge of the Luxembourg language may be required for some jobs. All salaries and wages are tied to the cost of living index, which is increased yearly by 2.5 per cent. A 40-hour week is standard.

Minimum holidays are 25 days per year for all workers (the collective working agreement for bank employees, for instance, specifies 33.5 days), plus 10 public holidays. Most workers receive an end-of-year bonus or 13th month's pay. Salaried staff may receive contractual or extra-contractual bonuses.

Useful information

Electricity: 220 V, 50 Hz ac.

Transport: The airport, which is only four miles from Luxembourg City, is served by regular British Airways and Luxair flights from Heathrow, Stansted and London City Airport.

Health care: Medical facilities are of a high standard but costly, although social security reimburses most bills. Some doctors have been trained in the UK; many speak English.

Education: Three schools in Luxembourg cater for non-national children and are English speaking. The Ecole Européenne is intended for children of EU and ECSC personnel, but is open to others.

Media: Two daily newspapers and a weekly English-language newspaper, the *Luxembourg News.*

Useful contacts:
British Embassy, 14 boulevard Roosevelt, L-2450 Luxembourg, tel: +352 22 98 64, website: www.britain.lu

Luxembourg Embassy, 27 Wilton Crescent, London SW1, tel:
+207235 6961
Luxembourg National Tourist Office, 122 Regent Street, London
W1R 5FE, tel: 020 7434 2800, websites: www.luxembourg.co.uk,
www.etat.lu/tourism

PERSONAL TAXATION

These details are as of January 2006.

Residence

An individual is a Luxembourg resident for tax purposes if either
his or her permanent place of residence ('domicile fiscal/Wohnsitz')
or his or her customary place of abode is in Luxembourg. A
permanent place of residence can be any form of living accommodation, provided that the individual has the use
of it for a prolonged period and intends to keep it. A habitual place
of abode ('séjour habituel/gewöhnlicher Aufenthalt') in
Luxembourg is deemed to exist if an individual is physically
present in Luxembourg for a continuous period of six months,
ignoring short absences on holiday.

Taxation of personal income

A resident is liable to Luxembourg income tax on his or her
worldwide income; a non-resident is liable solely on income
arising in Luxembourg. Income tax is imposed at progressive rates
on the aggregate taxable income of an individual from one or more
of eight distinct sources, including employment income. The tax
year is the calendar year.

The top marginal rate of income tax, inclusive of the 2.5 per cent
surcharge for the unemployment fund, is 38.95 per cent (chargeable
in 2006 on the balance of taxable income over €34,500). Joint
assessment of husband and wife, provided that they are both
resident and living together, is mandatory (a split rate applies).
There are personal allowances available for certain classes of individual (single parent, senior citizen and so forth) and relief for family
circumstances is largely given by classifying taxpayers into three
classes, depending on their marital/family status and existence of

dependants. The rates of income tax are applied differently to these three classes.

Taxpayers whose annual taxable income exceeds €58,000 must fill in a tax return.

Income from employment
Social security contributions

Social security contributions apply to wages and must be withheld by the employer. The compulsory social security contributions for health insurance and old-age pension are deducted from the total gross salary up to a monthly ceiling of €7,517.12. Both employers and employees pay contributions for these insurances. Only employers pay contributions for health at work insurance and accident insurance (both calculated on the gross total salary). The public sector funds family allowance contributions. Unemployment insurance is withheld from employees' salary as an additional income tax.

The total monthly contribution rate is 11.8 per cent for white-collar workers, and varies between 11.44 per cent and 16.91 per cent for the employer.

Taxable salary

The gross salary minus health insurance and pension fund contributions is the taxable salary. Taxes are withheld at source, according to tax classes and a progressive tax scale issued yearly by the tax administration. Salary tax in the form of deductions from earnings is withheld by employers and pension providers.

All forms of income, including wages, bonuses, benefits in kind, travel allowances, indemnities for dismissal and pensions paid before definite cessation of employment, are taxable.

Special payments for overtime, work on a public holiday and so on are tax free up to €1,800 per year. Certain compensation for contract termination received by employees is tax-free, as well as amounts paid by the employer on special occasions (for instance €2,250 for 25 years of service).

Reimbursement of expenses incurred on the employer's behalf is generally tax-free, as are payments for the use of the employee's own car for business purposes, within certain limits. A minimum standard deduction of €540 (double for jointly taxed spouses) is available for non-reimbursed employment-related expenses, regardless of the actual amount incurred. An additional deduction is granted for the cost of commuting between home and the place of work, computed according to set rules (minimum: €396). A minimum standard deduction of €480 (double for jointly taxed spouses if both are employed) is granted for special expenses. Higher actual expenses may be deducted. Tax credit is granted on request and under certain conditions for extraordinary expenses such as sickness costs and child care.

Where an employee uses his or her own car on business and does not receive an allowance from the employer for this purpose, he or she may claim a further deduction. Actual expenditure incurred in obtaining and maintaining employment income is fully deductible if substantiated.

Investment income

Dividends and interest

Dividends from both Luxembourg and foreign companies are generally treated as taxable income. However, 50 per cent of dividends received by an individual from fully taxable Luxembourg and EU companies resident in a treaty-partner country are exempt from income tax. The 20 per cent tax withheld at source on 100 per cent of the dividends is credited against the income tax due on the taxable 50 per cent of dividends. Where foreign dividends have been subject to withholding tax, the grossed-up dividend, inclusive of the withholding tax, is included in the taxable income, and the foreign withholding tax can be claimed as a tax credit.

As from 1 January 2006 certain interest income is taxed at a rate of 10 per cent, representing the final tax charge. This tax will be withheld at source by the Luxembourg bank paying such interest. Interest income which is not covered by this new rule is taxed as ordinary income at standard rates.

In addition to the 50 per cent exemption for Luxembourg dividends, a basic deduction of €1,500 (€3,000 for married couples) applies to investment income.

Income from real property

Rental income net of relevant expenses is taxable. Owner-occupiers are deemed to receive rental income, based on the unit value of their property, which is assessed by the tax administration. The amount of this imputed income is 4 per cent of the first €3,800 of the unit value, plus 6 per cent of the remainder. Mortgage interest on the loan to acquire the property or build an extension may be deducted from this imputed income within certain limits.

Taxation of capital

Capital gains

Gains on the sale of land and buildings are generally taxable as income. The gain is computed by comparing the proceeds with the indexed cost of acquisition, increased by the incurred expenses. Capital gains are taxed at the quarter average rate (maximum: 9.7375 per cent) on the taxpayer's total income. A €50,000 tax relief is granted for individuals (€100,000 for jointly assessed spouses). Gains from the sale of the taxpayer's main residence are exempt.

Gains from the sale of shareholdings are also taxable, as are the gains from all other assets disposed of within six months of acquisition. A maximum rate of 19.475 per cent applies to gains from assets held for more than six months. Tax relief is available for the first €50,000 of gains realised in any 10-year period (the tax relief doubles for jointly assessed spouses).

Wealth tax

Net wealth tax for individuals has been abolished as from 1 January 2006.

Double taxation treaties

Luxembourg has concluded treaties to avoid double taxation with over 40 countries, including the UK and the United States. Residents with income from non-treaty countries include the foreign-source income in their taxable income and receive a credit for foreign taxes paid, up to the amount of tax imposed by Luxembourg.

All treaties provide double tax relief through the exemption-with-progression method. Interest, dividend and royalty income, however, are subject to the tax credit rules.

For further information on tax and social security, contact:

Guy Hornick, BDO Compagnie Fiduciaire S.A., tel: +352 45 123–1, e-mail: bdo.compagnie.fiduciaire@bdo-cf.lu

MALTA

The economy

Malta is an example of a small open economy, built around the contribution made by the tourism, manufacturing and financial services industries. Traditionally, the Maltese economy was reliant on the strategic importance of a military base but in the mid-1950s the government embarked on a policy of industrialisation mainly by offering incentives to foreign manufacturers to locate in Malta, with the aim of increasing employment opportunities. This policy was successful in attracting labour-intensive industries, and in recent years it has been successful in attracting the more technically advanced industries.

The banking system remains highly concentrated with two of the local banks accounting for about 90 per cent of total loans and deposits.

The Maltese government has pursued a policy of gradual economic liberalisation, taking some steps to shift the emphasis in trade and financial policies from reliance on direct government intervention and control to policy regimes that allow a role for market mechanisms. Malta's accession into the EU has marked the total dismantling of protective import levies on industrial products, increasing the outward orientation of the economy. However, in 2005 the foreign trade current account deficit was estimated at 10.5 per cent of GDP.

The fiscal situation remains difficult despite some progress in consolidating public finances. The budget deficit was brought down from 10.7 per cent in 1998 to under 4 per cent in 2005, mainly through increases in tax rates and improved collection of taxes due. Substantial privatisation proceeds have limited the increase in public debt. GDP growth rates are in line with those of the Euro area. Consumer price inflation is running at about 2.4 per cent. Pending entry to the Euro exchange rate mechanism, the Maltese lira is pegged to a currency basket in which the Euro represents 70 per cent.

The Maltese government has announced reforms to the pension and welfare system.

Language and currency

The official languages are Maltese and English. The majority of Maltese speak English fluently and nearly all business is transacted in the English language.

The unit of currency in Malta is the Maltese Lira (MTL), which is divided into 100 cents. As of 1 May 2005, Malta has joined Euro II and the Euro/Maltese lira exchange rate has been fixed at €1 = MTL 0.4293.

Working conditions

Work permits

In principle, non-Maltese nationals require a work permit to be able to take on employment in Malta. This also applies to EU citizens seeking employment in Malta. In fact for a period of seven years from accession (until 2011) Malta may apply safeguards against the right of EU nationals to work in Malta.

During this seven-year period, Malta will retain the work permit system and will grant permits to EU nationals. However, Malta will be able to refuse work permits in the case of a threat of disruption to its labour market either as a whole or in specific sectors. Work permits for non-EU citizens will continue to be required.

Visas

Visas are not required for visits of up to three months by EU nationals and US citizens. Other nationals can check requirements on the Maltese Ministry of Foreign Affairs website: www.foreign.gov.mt.

Useful information

Banking hours: 8.30 am to 2.00 pm from Monday to Thursday, 8.30 am to 3.30 pm on Friday, and 8.30 am to 12.30 pm on Saturday. Closed on Sunday.

Shopping hours: 9.00 am to 1.00 pm and 4.00 pm to 7.00 pm Monday to Friday, and 9.00 am to 1.00 pm on Saturday.

Electricity: 240 volts/Hz.

Driving: Driving is on the left. Traffic is heavy and parking difficult throughout Malta. Front and rear seat belts are compulsory.

Transport: The public transport network is reasonably good. It is operated by buses and the bus fleet is in the processes of being completely modernised. There is no train or tram service.

Education: Education is free and compulsory up to secondary level. There are good facilities for education at all levels. There is one university which prides itself as being one of the oldest in Europe.

Health care: The health services are part of the general social security system. Hospital treatment is free if received in any one of the state hospitals. Reciprocal health agreements are in place with the UK and a number of other countries.

Useful contacts:

Employment & Training Corporation, Hal Far, tel: +356 2220 1100, fax + 356 2220 1811, website:www.etc.gov.mt

Inland Revenue Department, Office of Inland Revenue, Floriana, tel: +356 2296 2248, fax: +356 2296 2802, website http://www. ird.gov.mt

Malta Tourism Authority, Auberge D'Italie, Merchants Street, Valletta CMR 02, Valletta, tel: +356 2291 5000, fax : +356 2291 5893, website: www.mta.com.mt

Department of Social Security, 38 Ordinance Street, Valletta, tel +356 2590 3000, fax +356 3590 3001, website: ww.msp.gov.mt

PERSONAL TAXATION

Territoriality and residence

The liability of an individual to Malta tax depends on the individual's domicile and residence status, as well as on the source of the income. 'Domicile' and 'residence' are technical terms, described below, but in general, one of the following situations will apply.

Individuals resident and domiciled in Malta are subject to income tax and tax on capital gains on their worldwide income, although generally they are able to claim relief for foreign taxes.

Individuals resident but not ordinarily resident and domiciled in Malta are subject to tax on income and capital gains arising in Malta as well as on foreign income (but not capital gains) received in or remitted to Malta.

Non-residents are subject to income tax on income arising in Malta and tax on capital gains from assets situated in Malta subject to any relevant double taxation treaties.

Non-residents are exempt from income tax on interest, royalties and profits from the disposal of shares in a Maltese company (except for shares held in a company that holds immovable property).

Residence, ordinary residence and domicile

The term 'resident' and 'ordinarily' resident are technical terms, the interpretation of which depends largely on Inland Revenue practice and Case Law. The Inland Revenue normally decides on a person's status after taking into account his ore her expressed intentions and his or her movements over a period, but the general principles may be summarised as follows.

Residence: an individual is resident in Malta

For any tax year during which he ore she is physically present in Malta for a total of six months or more, or if he or she is present in Malta with the intention of establishing his or her residence there.

Ordinarily resident

A person is ordinarily resident in Malta if he or she is regularly resident over a number of years. An ordinary resident ceases to be resident in Malta if he or she is absent from Malta in circumstances that, in the opinion of the Commissioner of Inland Revenue, are incompatible with the status of resident. The indications that would be taken into account for this purpose are the duration of the absence and the connections that the individual may have retained with Malta.

Domicile

An individual usually acquires the domicile of his or her parents on birth but may acquire a domicile of choice in another country if he or she regards it as his or her permanent home.

Rates of taxation

Individuals are subject to income tax at progressive rates on their total income attributable to each year. The following table is applicable.

	Income (MTL)		Tax rate (%)
Married Rates	On the first 4,300	0–4,300	0
	On the next 1,700	4,301–6,000	15
	On the next 1,250	6,001–7,250	20
	On the next 1,250	7,251–8,500	25
	On the next 1,500	8,501–10,000	30
	On the remainder	10,001 and over	35
Single Rates	On the first 3,100	0–3,100	0
	On the next 1,000	3,101–4,100	15
	On the next 900	4,101–5,000	20
	On the next 1,000	5,001–6,000	25
	On the next 750	6,001–6,750	30
	On the remainder	6,751 and over	35

Accounting period

Individuals are taxed for every year of assessment on the income derived during the preceding calendar year.

Earnings liable to tax

All remuneration, including all benefits and facilities derived from employment, is taxable. The values of fringe benefits are determined in accordance with the Fringe Benefit Rules.

Taxable capital gains must be reported together with the taxable income and tax is levied on the total amount.

Foreign personnel

The liability to Malta tax on employment income is dependent upon a combination of the following factors:

☐ the employer's country of residence;
☐ the employee's domicile status;
☐ the employee's residence status;
☐ the place where the duties are performed.

The possible variations and combinations of these factors are numerous and complex. The main principle is that all earnings from an employment performed wholly in Malta for a Maltese employer are taxable irrespective of the domicile or residence status of the employee.

Foreign pensions

Foreign source pensions received by a person domiciled, resident and ordinarily resident in Malta are taxable in Malta. Double taxation relief in respect of such pensions is normally available.

Business profits

Individuals doing business in Malta have their business profits taxed by applying the progressive rates applicable to individuals.

Investment income

Individuals are not required to report dividends received from companies resident in Malta. If they opt to report dividends they will be taxed, as in the case of other taxpayers, on the dividend gross of company tax, and the company tax will be allowed as a credit against their personal tax liability, with a right to a refund for excess credit.

There is also a final withholding tax on certain investment income such as interest on local bank accounts and government securities. Under the withholding tax system the payer deducts tax at the rate of 15 per cent, which is remitted to the Commissioner of Inland Revenue without disclosing the recipient's identity.

Where tax has been deducted at source, taxpayers have no further liability on the income received and individuals are not required to disclose such sums on their tax returns unless they wish to do so, in which case they are taxed at normal rates with a credit for the tax deducted at source.

All taxpayers, however, have the right to elect to have interest paid to them gross, in which case they are to disclose such income on their tax return and pay income tax at the normal rates applicable.

There can be no election to receive dividend payments gross of tax. Interest and dividend income received from overseas remain taxable at normal rates.

Capital gains

Capital gains derived by a person from the transfer of a capital asset are chargeable to income tax. The law specifies particular instances where a chargeable capital gain is deemed to arise:

☐   Gains or profits arising from any transfer of the ownership or usufruct or any moveable property or the assignment or cession of any rights on such property. The transfer of property which has been the transferor's only and main residence for a period of at least three years (immediately preceding the date of transfer) and which is disposed of within one year of vacating the premises is exempt from tax. Included in this exemption is a garage which is underlying a block of flats or which is situated within 500m of the dwelling house and which is transferred on the same deed. However, any part of the property used for commercial purposes is excluded from this exemption.

☐ Gains or profits arising from the transfer of ownership or usufruct of or from the assignment or cession of any rights over securities, business, goodwill, copyright, patents, trademarks and trade names. Exemptions from tax include:

– transfers of Malta government bonds and stocks;
– transfers of shares in a company listed on the stock exchange not being securities in a collective investment scheme;
– transfers of units and similar instruments relating to linked long-term business of insurance where the benefits are wholly determined by reference to the value of, or income from, securities listed on the stock exchange;
– securities assigned consequent to a separation or partition of the community of acquits;
– gains or profits arising from the transfer of the beneficial interest in a trust.

Deductions

As an individual who is subject to Malta income tax, an employee can deduct from his or her taxable remuneration any expenses wholly, exclusively and necessarily incurred in the performance of his or her duties. This rule is very rigid and excludes many expenses from relief. Subscriptions to professional associations related to a particular employment may be allowable.

Individuals may also qualify for a deduction in respect of alimony paid to an estranged spouse and of private school fees.

Wealth tax

There is no wealth tax in Malta.

Social security

Social security system

There is a basic social security system operated by the State. Through a system of contributions, benefits are provided during periods of sickness, maternity, unemployment and invalidity. Retirement pensions based upon contributions are also provided. State medical care is free of charge.

Social Security Contributions paid by an EU citizen while employed in Malta are credited to the Social Security system in the home country of the employee. This means that no benefits are lost because of employment in Malta.

Contributions – employees and employers

All persons in employment pay contributions to the State Social Security scheme known as National Insurance.

Both employees and employers contribute to the Maltese system. National Insurance contributions are one-tenth of the gross salary up to a maximum of MTL 13.38 (€31.17) per week.

The pension benefits derived from the National Insurance scheme consist of a State pension equivalent to approximately two-thirds of one's salary on retirement, with a maximum of MTL 4,638 per annum.

Contributions – self-employed persons

The self-employed are also covered by the National Insurance scheme. They are entitled only to the State pension and have restricted rights to other benefits particularly in respect of sickness.

Contributions depend on the annual income and vary from MTL 8.39 (€19.54) per week to a maximum of MTL 20.07 (€46.75) per week.

Double tax treaties

Malta has concluded 46 treaties to avoid double taxation, among which are treaties with the UK and Germany. There are also treaties with the United States and Switzerland, but both these treaties are limited to profits derived from the operation of ships or aircraft in international traffic. All treaties are based on the OECD Model Tax Convention.

For further information, contact:

Lino Buttigieg (e-mail: lb@bdomlta.com.mt) or John A. Psaila (e-mail: jp@bdomalta.com.mt), BDO Attard Buttigieg Psaila & Co, 136 St Christopher Street, Valletta VLT 05, tel: +356 2123 0624, fax: +356 2124 3219

THE NETHERLANDS

The economy

The traditional image of The Netherlands as a land of bulbs, windmills and wooden shoes is perpetuated for the sake of tourists but, in fact, its modern industrial basis and economic growth have placed The Netherlands in the forefront of European Union economies. Industry accounts for nearly one-third of both the national income and the working population.

The Netherlands has no natural resources, apart from natural gas and salt in the east. It is thus highly dependent on foreign trade and experiences recurrent balance of trade problems. The Netherlands is also dependent on overseas suppliers for oil, but has stepped up its natural gas production to counteract this. Trading, banking and shipping businesses are of particular importance to the economy. In 2005, the positive current account balance represented 5 per cent of GDP, and a similar outcome is forecast for 2006.

Agriculture, though its percentage contribution to GNP has fallen relative to industry, is still important and very efficient. Production continues to rise, with cattle and dairy products, fruit, vegetables and flowers as its principal products.

The main industries include electrical and mechanical engineering, textiles and clothing, steel, shipbuilding, processed foods and chemicals, with diamonds and furs in the luxury range. Oil refining and the petrochemicals sector dominate the Rotterdam area. The electrical and electronics industries are highly sophisticated and produce computers, telecommunications equipment and precision instruments. Coal mining, after being progressively run down, has ceased completely.

That the Dutch are internationally minded is shown in their industrial structures. The multinationals include Philips, the electrical giant, Unilever, Shell and other major oil companies. Joint German/Dutch enterprises have been set up in some sectors. Foreign investment is welcomed, particularly in the development areas in the north-east and south. The UK heads the list of foreign investors, with the United States second. Many of the large British companies have Dutch subsidiaries. Traditionally a free trade/free enterprise economy, the state role is limited to setting a favourable climate for growth and investment.

Until 2003, the Dutch economy remained in rather better shape than the stagnating German economy. GDP growth in 2005 was a little below that of Germany at 0.9 per cent but an improvement to 1.9 per cent in line with the Euro area average is forecast for 2006. Growth in industrial production of 1.4 per cent was reported for December 2005. The budget deficit ratio for 2005 was a modest 1.6 per cent of GDP. Unemployment of 6.2 per cent was recorded for the quarter ended January 2006, while consumer price inflation is running at approximately 1.5 per cent.

Working conditions

Executive salaries are about 30 per cent higher than in the UK; secretarial salaries are roughly comparable.

A legal minimum wage is fixed for all workers aged 23 to 65 and is reviewed at least once a year in the light of movements in average earnings and the cost of living index. Apart from this, wages are determined by collective agreements – the practice of plant agreements has grown with the increase in the size of firms.

Collective agreements usually lay down procedures for dealing with disputes and provide for reference to arbitration boards in the event of failure to settle. The country has been relatively strike-free. Most contracts are written and provide for a two-month trial period. Dismissals and resignations come under government supervision; length of notice is governed by the terms of individual contracts and length of service – for managers the notice period is usually three months. In most industries the 40-hour week has become standard.

Workers are entitled to three weeks paid holiday and most get more through collective bargaining. Five weeks is normal for managerial staff.

Useful information

Banking hours: 9.00 am to 5.30 pm Monday–Saturday.

Shopping hours: 11.00 am or 12.00 pm to 5.00 pm Monday, 9.00 am to 5.30 or 6.00 pm Tuesday–Friday.

Electricity: 220 V, 50 Hz ac.

Transport: Internal and urban transport is very efficient. Frequent train services link the main centres and there are country-wide bus services. The roads are good and not over-congested. Nearly everybody in The Netherlands cycles and there are special cycle paths on the main roads.

Health care: The Dutch health service is based on a mixture of compulsory and voluntary schemes. The compulsory scheme covers about 70 per cent of the population. Private medical treatment is expensive. The Dutch are healthy, and have the longest life expectancy of any EU nationals. There is a reciprocal health agreement with the UK.

Education: Education is free (though some schools may request a voluntary contribution) and compulsory from 5 to 16, with part-time schooling for a further year.

The British School in The Netherlands is in the vicinity of The Hague and provides for children between 3 and 18 years. The fees compare favourably with other international schools in The Netherlands.

There is a British Primary School in Amsterdam and a number of other International and American Schools in the major cities – details of these can be obtained from ECIS and COBISEC.

Useful contacts:

British Embassy, Lange Voorhout 10, 2514 ED, The Hague, tel: 31 70 427 0427

Dutch Embassy, 38 Hyde Park Gate, London SW7, tel: 020 7590 3200

Netherlands Board of Tourism, PO Box 30783, London WC2, tel: 020 7539 7950, website: www.goholland.com

PERSONAL TAXATION

Residence

In The Netherlands residency is based on facts and circumstances. Court rulings indicate that the place where the spouse and children live is the main criterion for the determination of residency.

The Dutch tax system – highlights

Dutch residents are subject to Dutch income tax on their worldwide income. Declared income consists of the following categories:

☐ Box 1: taxable income from work and home ownership (progressive rate up to 52 per cent). Wage tax on employment income is credited against income tax.

☐ Box 2: taxable income from a substantial (business) interest (fixed rate of 25 per cent). In general a 'substantial interest' refers to a shareholding of at least 5 per cent in a capital divided into shares.

☐ Box 3: taxable income from savings and investments (a deemed income of 4 per cent of the savings and investments taxed at a fixed rate of 30 per cent; effective rate 1.2 per cent).

Non-resident individuals are subject to income tax on specific sources of remuneration, such as employment income (box 1). Tax is assessed on a calendar year basis.

Special features

Treated as resident taxpayer: qualifying non-residents may choose to be treated as resident taxpayers. In that case they enjoy the same deductions as resident taxpayers. However, their worldwide income is taxable in The Netherlands, taking into account the provisions of the tax treaty of The Netherlands with the country of actual residence.

Tax credit: after calculating the total income tax payable (boxes 1, 2 and 3) a tax credit is granted. Non-resident individuals are only granted the social security part of the tax credit provided they pay social security premiums in The Netherlands.

Foreign employees '30 per cent ruling': if certain requirements are met, Dutch employers may grant a special tax-exempt allowance of 30 per cent of the wage income. When the foreign employee lives in The Netherlands there is the possibility of electing for deemed non-residency for tax purposes. A deemed non-resident taxpayer is considered as a non-resident taxpayer with regard to his or her income in boxes 2 and 3. For those boxes, he or she is taxable in the Netherlands on Dutch sources of income only. However, any box 1 income remains subject to Dutch income tax, as for a regular resident taxpayer.

Wealth tax

As of 1 January 2001 the wealth tax was abolished.

Double taxation treaties

The Netherlands has an extensive tax treaty network, for example with the UK and the United States. If no treaty is available there is a unilateral rule to avoid double taxation.

The Dutch social security system – highlights

In The Netherlands there is an extensive and complicated system of social security. However, there are two main categories.

National insurance scheme

The premium for this insurance is levied in a combined tax and social security rate (maximum premium over €30,631 (2006).

Employee insurance scheme

The premium is deducted from the employee's income. The premium for this insurance is capped.

For additional information on tax and social security, contact:

Hans Noordermeer, Tax Partner (e-mail: hans.noordermeer@ bdo.nl), Armand Lahaije, Tax Manager (e-mail: armand.lahaije@ bdo.nl), BDO CampsObers International Tax Services, KP van der Mandelelaan 40, 3062 MB Rotterdam, tel: +31 10 24 24 600, fax: +31 10 24 29 216

NORWAY

The economy

The exploitation of oil deposits in the North Sea revolutionised Norway's economy and transformed its entire industrial and social structure. Thousands of workers left their traditional occupations in farms, fisheries and forests to find work in the rapidly developing oil sector, leading to severe pressure on housing and other social resources.

The government, anxious to avoid too much disruption and the development of a 'gold rush' mentality, proceeded cautiously, limiting rates of production and exploitation, and taking care of the pollution and preservation aspects. It participates in operations through its ownership of Statoil and heavy taxation of companies. Norway is now the biggest oil producer in Western Europe, accounting for 40 per cent of its exports.

Oil apart, Norway is rich in mineral resources and has taken advantage of its cheap and abundant water power (which meets virtually all electricity requirements) to develop modern electro-metallurgical and electro-chemical industries. As a result Norway maintains a strong current account balance running at 17 per cent of GDP.

Consumer and service industries have developed, eg food and fish processing, clothing and textiles, but half the nation's food still has to be imported. Two-thirds of the population are engaged in service industries – predominantly connected with oil, shipping and tourism.

The state plans and regulates economic development. The steel industry is dominated by the state-owned concern in the far north. In some cases, the state is the majority shareholder, but most manufacturing, eg shipbuilding, is in the hands of private enterprise. The government welcomes regulated foreign investment, offering special incentives for under-developed and under-populated areas. The Norwegian economy was recovering from the world economic slowdown in 2005 for which, GDP growth of 3.7 per cent has been estimated, but is forecast to slacken to 3 per cent for 2006. Inflation is expected to remain around 2 per cent. Unemployment is predicted to be reduced to 4 per cent in 2006. The government achieved a budget surplus ratio to GDP of about 13.5 per cent in 2005.

Norway also maintains a foreign trade surplus on current account presently running at 17 per cent. Sweden is Norway's major trading partner, but trade with other EU countries – particularly the UK, Germany and Denmark – makes an important contribution.

Working conditions

In general, salaries are higher than in the UK, but so are deductions, and this is combined with a high cost of living.

The normal working week is 37.5 hours and overtime is limited. All employees have four weeks' annual leave, and there are up to 10 public holidays. Industry contributes towards a jointly managed training fund.

EEA nationals

Residence permits are not required for Nordic citizens. The EEA (European Economic Area) Agreement secures other nationals of the EU and EFTA countries the freedom of movement and establishment throughout the area. Under the provisions of the Agreement you may stay in Norway for a period of six months to seek employment provided you are financially self-supporting. Should you succeed in finding work during this period, you must apply in person for a residence permit at the nearest police station, taking with you your national passport, two photographs and a 'Confirmation of Employment' from your employer. Residence permits are not required for EU nationals staying less than three months in Norway, or those who commute to their home country at least once a week.

Nationals of other countries

A general ban on immigration has been in force in Norway since 1975. An exemption is most unlikely to be granted unless you have special skills which local job applicants do not possess. If you have received an offer of employment in Norway due to the demand for your qualifications you must apply for a work and residence permit through the Embassy, which will transmit your application to the Norwegian immigration authorities. The time required to process the application is normally at least three months.

Useful information

Shopping hours: 9.00 am to 5.00 pm Monday–Friday, except Thursday 9.00 am to 7 pm, 10.00 am to 3.00 or 4.00 pm Saturday. Shopping malls normally have longer shopping hours.

Electricity: 220 V.

Driving: Foreigners must be particularly aware of Norway's very strict 'drink and drive' laws. Anyone caught driving with more than 0.5 per 1,000 ml alcohol in their blood must reckon with an almost automatic prison sentence plus suspension of his or her licence for at least a year. An alcohol concentration of between 0.2 and 0.5 might trigger a substantial penalty.

Transport: Scattered settlements, and the country's topography, used to make transport and communications difficult. Regular shipping services serve the coastal towns throughout the year.

There are regular sea/rail links within Norway and with Europe, and Norway cooperates with Sweden and Denmark in SAS, which operates regular air services internally and externally.

Emergency services: 112 police, 110 fire, 113 ambulance.

Media: TV entertainment includes Sky as well as several Norwegian TV channels, with Swedish TV in the east.

Useful contacts:

British Embassy, Thomas Heftyesgate 8, 0244 Oslo, tel: 47 2313 2700, website: www.britain.no

Norwegian Embassy, 25 Belgrave Square, London SW1X 8QD, tel: 020 7591 5500

Innovation Norway, Charles House, 5 Lower Regent Street, London SW1Y 4LR, tel: 020 7839 8800

websites: www.norway.no, www.norway.org.uk/travel/, www.visit-norway.com; www.udi.no

PERSONAL TAXATION

These details are as of December 2005.

Residence

A resident individual is subject to tax in Norway on worldwide income/capital. A non-resident is taxable on certain Norwegian-source income only, such as from employment carried out in Norway. An individual is deemed to be resident to Norway if he or she stays in Norway more than 183 days in any 12-month period (each day counts), or more than 270 days in any 36-month period. The individual will be regarded as resident from the calendar year when the aggregated stay exceeds 183/270 days.

When emigrating to a permanent home abroad, the individual will still be considered resident in Norway as long as he or she stays more than 61 days in Norway during the income tax year or as long as he or she or someone closely related has a home in Norway. An individual who has been resident for more than 10 years will still be deemed resident for a three-year period after emigration, but residence will not cease as long as he or she or someone closely related has a home in Norway or he or she stays more than 61 days in any of the three years.

Taxation of employment income (tax rates 2006)

An individual's income tax is levied on general income and personal income.

General income

General income is a net tax base that includes income from work, business and capital. Personal income is reduced by deductible allowances, such as interest payments, a standard deduction of 34 per cent on employment income (maximum NOK 61,100/minimum 4,000), certain travel expenses, expenses for child care, etc. A personal allowance reduces the tax base with NOK 35,400 for a single person and NOK 70,800 for a married couple. A 10 per cent deduction of gross employment income is available for expatriates who stay a maximum of two years provided that commuting expenses paid by the employer are treated as taxable income. Most allowances are reduced pro rata where liability to tax does not extend over 12 months. General income is taxed at a flat rate of 28 per cent.

Personal income

Personal income is a gross income tax base from which social security taxes and surtax are calculated. Personal income includes income from self-employment, wages, bonuses, pensions, director's remuneration, sick and maternity pay, termination payments, fringe benefits and so on.

Tax rates

Social security contribution: employee's contribution 7.8 per cent; self-employed/business contribution 10.7 per cent; pension 3 per cent.

Surtax: income between NOK 394,000 and 750,000: 9 per cent. Income exceeding NOK 750,000: 12 per cent. The maximum tax on employment income is 47.8 per cent in 2006.

Taxation of investment income

There is no separate capital gains tax. Dividends and capital gains (that exceed a tax-free base return) derived by individual owners in limited companies, etc and partnerships are taxed at 28 per cent. Non-resident personal shareholders are liable for a 25 per cent withholding tax on dividends from Norwegian companies, or at a lower rate according to a double taxation treaty. Limited companies are exempted from tax on dividends and on capital gains related to the investment of shares in Norwegian and foreign companies. Investments in low-taxation countries outside the EEA area and portfolio investments (less than 10 per cent and/or owned less than two years) outside the EEA area are not covered. To avoid tax-motivated emigration, a new exit tax on shares has been introduced with effect from 1 January 2006. Capital gains realised on the sale of immovable or movable property are in general taxable, subject to some special provisions.

Taxation of capital

Resident individuals are subject to net wealth tax on their worldwide wealth. Non-residents are subject to net wealth taxes with respect to interests in Norwegian businesses, and for immovable and tangible movable property located in Norway. The maximum tax rate is 1.1 per cent.

Double taxation treaties

Norway has a relatively wide treaty network with other countries including the United States (1972/1981) and the UK (2000).

Links to information about the Norwegian tax system: http://www.skatteetaten.no.

For further information on tax and social security, contact:

Hilde Stensby, BDO Revico Oslo DA, tel: +47 22 47 86 00, e-mail: hildes@bdo.no

POLAND

The economy

With a population of 38.6 million, Poland is by far the largest of the three leading EU accession entrants. GDP growth in the third quarter of 2005 was 3.7 per cent higher than in 2004. In the January–September period GDP growth amounted to 2.9 per cent. In 2004 GDP growth peaked at 5.3 per cent and is forecast to rise again in

2006 to as much as 4 per cent. The most worrying feature of the Polish economy is still persistent high unemployment. According to official findings, the unemployment rate as of November 2005 amounted to 17.3 per cent. However, an increase of 1.9 per cent in average employment was registered during January–September over the same nine-month period of 2004. Consumer price inflation is running at around 2.7 per cent.

According to the estimates of The Main Statistic Office (GUS), in 2004 Poland recorded a 4.5 per cent budget deficit. The dominant fund sources offsetting the deficit were debenture issues and earnings from privatisation. The most significant privatisation sale concerned the leading state-owned bank, PKO BP S.A.

Utilising its EU membership, Poland has relied on its imports from and exports to the European Community. As in previous years, Poland's main commercial partner is Germany. In the January–November 2005 period exports hit €58,176 million, while imports amounted to €65,462 million. The deficit on current account for 2005 is estimated at 7.9 per cent of GDP.

In view of the low level of domestic savings, investments have been funded by foreign savings, foreign direct investments and credits. Significant amounts of foreign savings have been injected in the form of direct investments. Foreign direct investments have not only been a replacement source of funds but have also been a major factor in improving the pace of the economy's modernisation. As much as 58 per cent of overall investment in 2004 were in greenfield projects, compared to 51 per cent in 2003. This type of investment stimulates employment and introduces new production technologies.

Useful information

From January 1999 Poland has been divided administratively into 16 regions ('voivodships'), subdivided into 308 'poviats' (counties) and 65 towns with county status.

Visas: Citizens of the United States, the UK and other EU member countries do not require a visa when visiting Poland for up to 90 days. Other nationals can check requirements on the Polish Ministry of Foreign Affairs website: www.msz.gov.pl.

Electricity: 230 volts/50 Hz.

Currency: Zloty (PLN) : 1 PLN= 100 groszy. There is no definite date on when Poland plans to adopt the Euro.

Useful contacts:

British Embassy, Warsaw Corporate Centre, Ul. Emilii Plater 28, 00–688 Warsaw, tel: +48 22 311 0000, website: www.british embassy.pl

Master Page, Poland, the leading English-language source of information about Poland published in Poland, website: www.masterpage.com.pl

Polish Press Review, a review of the most essential and highlighted articles published recently in the Polish Press, website: www.cefta.org

Poland Regional Directory, categorised information for each region in Poland, website: www.anicheengine.com/regional

PERSONAL TAXATION

Residence

Like many other countries, Poland taxes on the basis of residence. As a matter of principle, an individual is deemed to be a Polish resident if he or she is staying in Poland with the intention of remaining permanently. An individual's citizenship or nationality has no direct bearing on residence status.

Individuals who are residents of Poland, with the exception of diplomats and certain other limited categories, including people benefiting from international privileges, are liable to tax on their worldwide income ('unlimited tax liability'). Individuals earning income in Poland, whose stay is temporary and who do not have the status of Polish residents, are subject to taxation on income arising in Poland or because of their 'work performed' in Poland, irrespective of the place of salary payment ('limited tax liability').

The above rule of territoriality and residence for the purposes of personal taxation has been in force since 1 January 2003. Until 31 December 2002, the binding regulation was slightly different, and also involved the principle that foreigners staying in Poland for more than 183 days in a tax year could be liable to an unlimited tax liability in certain circumstances.

The relevant double taxation treaties need to be consulted to determine whether a foreigner is liable to pay taxes calculated on his or her worldwide income in Poland.

Income from employment

Income from employment, including benefits in kind, is taxed at standard progressive tax rates of 19, 30, 40 or 50 per cent depending on the taxable base. Taxable employment income includes, *inter alia*, basic remuneration, payment for overtime work, allowances of different types and awards. A limited number of employees' benefits are tax exempt, such as statutory *per diem* allowances.

Non-resident individuals who receive remuneration from Polish companies are subject to standard progressive tax rates. A final flat rate of 20 per cent may be applied to income gained by non-residents from membership in management or supervisory boards of Polish companies or from management contracts.

Investment income

Dividends paid by Polish companies to individuals are subject to a 19 per cent withholding tax. For non-resident individuals a relevant double tax treaty may decrease this tax rate. However, a certificate of residence (a document confirming an individual's tax residence, issued by a foreign tax authority) is required to adopt a treaty rate. As a matter of principle, Polish residents are also taxed on dividends from foreign companies in accordance with the 19 per cent tax rate.

Interest paid to individuals by Polish entities is subject to a final withholding tax of 19 per cent. For non-resident individuals a double tax treaty may decrease this rate, but to apply a treaty rate a certificate of residence is needed. Interest received by Polish residents from foreign sources is taxed in Poland in accordance with the 19 per cent tax rate.

Capital gains

There is no separate capital gains tax in Poland. Capital gains of individuals are taxed under the Personal Income Tax Act. The Act determines the rules of taxation for income derived from sharing in the profits of legal entities. Income obtained from sharing in such profits includes, *inter alia*, income from redemption of shares and the value of property received in connection with the liquidation of a company. The flat rate of tax is 19 per cent. For non-resident individuals a respective double tax treaty may decrease this tax rate, but a certificate of residence is required to adopt a treaty rate.

Social security

All employees, whether employed on a full- or part-time basis, must be covered by social security contributions. The social security system in Poland is composed of social insurance and health (medical) insurance. The employer and the employee share the costs of the employee's social security insurance. However, it is the employer who pays the entire required amount to a respective local ZUS office. Generally, the employee's gross income (remuneration) constitutes the base on which social security contributions are calculated. In 2005 the rates of social security contributions were as follows:

☐   Retirement insurance: 19.52 per cent of the base (9.76 per cent by each party).
☐   Disability insurance: 13.00 per cent of the base (6.50 per cent by each party).
☐   Sickness insurance: 2.45 per cent of the base (only by the employee).
☐   Accident insurance: 0.97–3.86 per cent of the base (only by the employer).
☐   Health insurance: 8.75 per cent of the base (only by the employer).

Effective 1 May 2004, Poland adopted EU legislation relating to social security.

Double taxation treaties

Poland has concluded approximately 60 tax treaties for elimination of double taxation on income and gains, including treaties with the UK and the United States.

For further information on tax and social security, contact:

Rafal Kowalski, Head of Tax Department, BDO Polska Sp. z o.o., ul Postepu 12, 02–676 Warsaw, tel: + 48 22 543 16 00, fax: + 48 22 543 17 77, e-mail: rafal.kowalski@bdo.pl

PORTUGAL

The economy

In 2005 Portugal stagnated, with GDP growth down to just 0.3 per cent, continuing the weak performance shown in the last few years.

However, minor improvements in economic growth are forecast at 0.8 per cent for 2006 and 1 per cent in 2007. Consumer price inflation in 2005 was running at 2.3 per cent, 0.2 per cent lower than in 2004. Employment has performed relatively well over the past 20 years. In 1986 Portugal had one of the highest unemployment rates in the EC (now the EU) but by 1997 it was among the lowest rates in the EU at 6.8 per cent. However, in recent years the employment situation has been deteriorating and in the third quarter of 2005 the unemployment rate stood at 7.7 per cent, where it is forecast to remain through 2006. Services now employ nearly 60 per cent of the active population and generate 64 per cent of Gross Added Value (GAV). Employing about 35 per cent a decade ago, the agricultural sector has declined in importance and today accounts for only 13 per cent of jobs and 3 per cent of GAV.

The budget deficit ratio is running far above the EU Stability and Growth Pact criterion at an estimated 6 per cent in 2005 but is forecast to improve to 4.5 per cent in 2006. Portugal runs a foreign trade current account deficit at an estimated 6.5 per cent of GDP for 2005 but forecast to improve to 5.8 per cent in 2006.

Language and currency

Portugal has a population of approximately 10 million people, of whom 9.5 million reside in Europe, 257.000 in Madeira and 241.000 in the Azores; 4.7 million constitutes the working population. Women make up 45 per cent of the labour force. Portugal's population is largely concentrated in its capital Lisbon and other coastal cities on the Atlantic, particularly Oporto. Around 10 million of its inhabitants are economically active. In land area, Portugal is more than twice as large as Switzerland and a quarter that of Germany. Life expectancy is 81 years for women and 74 for men.

Until 1 January 1999 the unit of currency in Portugal was the escudo (PTE), which was divided into 100 centavos. In 1998 Portugal qualified for the European Monetary Union (EMU) and, since January 1999, has been a member of the Euro area. The conversion rate was fixed from 1 January 1999 at €1 = 200.482 PTE.

Residence and work permits

Foreigners wishing to take up residence or employment in Portugal for more than six months are legally required to obtain a work permit and a residence permit. Certain foreign nationals wishing to stay for a shorter period must obtain a special visa, which is renewable every 60 days. For EU citizens it is only mandatory to have a residence permit.

Working conditions

A minimum monthly salary must be paid to all employees. Since 1 January 2006 the minimum national rate is €385.90. There are usually 14 salary payments per year, which include two extra months salary paid at the time of summer holidays and at Christmas. EU citizens and some nationals of countries who engaged in international agreements with Portugal may maintain liability to social security of the original country. The general rate of the contributions paid by employees and employers are 11 per cent and 23.75 per cent respectively.

Generally, the legal working week is 40 hours, and it cannot exceed eight hours per day. However, employees can work additional hours and receive an additional compensation up to the limits established in the legislation. All employees have the right to two days paid holiday for each month worked, up to a maximum of 22 working days. This can be increased by up to three additional days.

Useful information

Banking hours: 8.30 am to 3.00 pm Monday to Friday.

Post office: 8.30 am to 6.30 pm Monday to Friday.

Shopping hours: 9.00 am to 7.00 pm Monday to Friday, 9.00 am to 1.00 pm Saturday.

Electricity: 220 V.

Health care: Hospital treatment and essential medicine are free, but you will have to pay half the cost of non-essential prescribed medicines. There is a small charge for treatment by a doctor.

Education: There is a sizeable British community in Portugal, a couple of British schools and a British hospital in Lisbon. Portuguese is essential in most areas.

Emergency services: 112.

Directory enquiries: 118.

Useful contacts:

British Embassy, Rua de Sao Bernardo 33, 1249–082 Lisboa, tel: 351 21 392 4000

Portuguese Embassy, 11 Belgrave Square, London SW1, tel: 020 7235 5331

Tourist information: www.nervo.com/pt/.

PERSONAL TAXATION

Residence

According to the provisions of the Personal Income Tax Code a taxable person is considered to be a Portuguese resident if:

- [ ] the individual has a permanent home in Portugal, which presupposes that he or she has the intention to maintain and occupy a main abode;
- [ ] the individual spent more than 183 days therein, uninterrupted or interpolated;
- [ ] at 31 December, the individual is part of a ship or aircraft crew, liable to the service of entities with residence, head office or effective in that territory;
- [ ] the individual is abroad as a civil servant or in an official commission.

If any one of these four criteria is fulfilled an individual is considered as a resident and will be liable to Portuguese income tax on the whole of his or her income.

Individuals who are not considered to be residents of Portugal are only subject to Portuguese income tax for income deriving from sources located in Portugal.

Taxation of personal income

Taxation for personal income taxes is divided into several categories: income from employment, income from self-employment and independent work, capital investment income, real estate income, income rises and pensions; tax assessment for each category has specific rules regarding tax relief and deductions.

Taxation of capital

Capital gains

A sale of bonds and shares owned for a period of more than 12 months is not liable to taxation. However, capital gains arising from the sale of shares in a company, of which the assets are constituted over 50 per cent of real properties located in Portugal, are liable to taxation.

Taxation of dividends

Dividends obtained from resident companies or EU domiciled companies, both taxable for corporate income tax purposes, are only taxed on 50 per cent.

Taxation of companies

Taxable entities

This tax is payable by entities that have a statutory seat or management and control in Portugal. Residents are taxable over their worldwide income. Non-residents are only taxable over incomes received in Portuguese territory. The standard rate of taxation is 25 per cent.

Investment income

Dividends received from companies resident in Portugal (subject to Corporate Income Tax) are fully deductible. If the beneficiary company has a participation in the capital (of the company distributing dividends) of 10 per cent or more, and the acquisition value of this participation was more then €20 million and is being kept for at least a year without interruption, dividends are also fully relieved from the taxable basis. This benefit will also be extended to dividends received from EU resident companies falling under the umbrella of the Parents/Subsidiary Directive.

Double taxation agreements

Portugal has an extensive network of double taxation treaties regarding taxes on income (and in some cases on capital), currently covering 46 countries, including the UK and the United States.

SLOVENIA

The economy

The smallest by land area of the accession countries that joined the EU on 1 May 2004, Slovenia is one of the most prosperous. Growth in real GDP in 2005 is estimated to have been 3.9 per cent and similar growth is forecast for 2006. GDP per capita in 2004 was €12,979 and is expected to have risen to €13,896 in 2005. Annual average retail price inflation in 2004 was 3.6 per cent and is expected to have declined in 2005 to 2.5 per cent

The export of goods and services in 2005 is estimated to have increased to €17,608 million from €15,500 million in 2004. Imports of goods and services in 2004 were €15,700 million and are expected to have risen in 2005 to €17,741 million. There was a trade balance deficit of €168 million in 2004 and the expected outcome for 2005 is a deficit of €133 million. The current account deficit represents 0.3 per cent of GDP. Unemployment in 2004 was 6.4 per cent and is estimated to have fallen slightly to 6.2 per cent in 2005.

Slovenia is among the most successful of the countries that are in transition from socialism to a market economy. It boasts a stable growth in its GDP and it is viewed as a safe country, ranked among those with the lowest degree of risk. Since its independence, Slovenia has privatised its economy, stabilised inflation and wage growth, halted rising unemployment, strengthened its currency, relaxed the flow of capital and modernised its taxation system.

On the June 2004 Slovenia entered the ERM II Exchange Rate Mechanism.

In the economic sphere, Slovenia's level of development is rapidly catching up with that of the rest of the EU. Its major trade partners are Germany, Italy, Croatia, Austria and France. In 2005 the largest exports were in transport equipment, metals, medical and pharmaceutical products. The inflow of foreign direct investment is still increasing and the majority of the foreign investors in 2005 came from the EU (Austria, Germany, France and Italy), and from Switzerland.

Working conditions

Since Slovenia became a member state of the EU, all legislation from the EU regarding the free flow of labour is valid, though in most cases a transitional period has been imposed. On the principle of reciprocity, EU nationals with valid passports are free to come and go, as long as Slovenians can do the same in their country.

Slovenian labour legislation is largely harmonised with the international contracts of the ILO. Labour law specifics are: working by civil law contracts is limited; higher taxation of salaries; and increased freedom in the field of manager contracts (regarding working hours, salary, working overtime, etc).

The working conditions resemble those in other European countries and the normal working week is 40 hours. Most Slovenians are fluent in English and knowledge of it is becoming a basic requirement for employment. Slovenia is a small country with a low rate of criminality and the standard of living is increasing every year, as are salaries.

Useful information

Banking hours: Most banks are open from 9.00 am to midday and 2.00 to 5.00 pm. They are open until midday on Saturdays and closed on Sundays.

Currency. The Slovenian tolar (SIT) (As Slovenia entered the ERM II, the central parity has been set at SIT239.64 = €1).

Shopping hours: 8.00 am to 8.00 pm, Monday–Saturday and closed on Sundays.

Electricity: 220V, ac 50Hz.

Driving: Speed limits are 50km/h on roads in settled areas, 30km/h in speed limit zones, 10km/h in steady traffic zones and pedestrian zones, 130km/h on highways, 100km/h on roads reserved for motor vehicles and 90km/h on other roads.

Health care: Health care is a public service provided through the public health service network. This network also includes, on an equal basis, other institutions, private physicians and other private service providers on the basis of concessions. Taking into account the relatively limited public funds available for this purpose, the level of health care in Slovenia is entirely comparable with the level of health care in the advanced countries of Europe.

Education: The education system in Slovenia is almost entirely financed from the state budget, though a small share of the finance is also contributed from municipal budgets. Public expenditure for education includes expenditure on compulsory basic, secondary and tertiary institutions, as well as the running costs of pre-school education, postgraduate study and expenditure related to boarding at some secondary schools and university accommodation. Included are both state schools and private schools with concessions, and also other private schools, to an extent determined by law. The educational profile of Slovenia's population is improving. In the 25 to 64 age group, the average number of years spent in education is 9.6. The best educated are those employed in the area of education and public administration. In comparison with other countries with a medium or high level of development, in 1992 Slovenia followed Austria, Switzerland, Belgium, Denmark, Israel and Hungary with regard to years spent in education. Ninety-eight per cent of primary school leavers decide to continue their education and 84 per cent of secondary school leavers continue on to tertiary education. The number of graduates is increasing too: in 2000 the total exceeded 10,000 for the first time. Slovenia has three universities: the University of Ljubljana, the University of Maribor and the University of Primorska. The competent body for planning and implementing education is the Ministry of Education and Sport.

Emergency services: Ambulance: 112, fire: 112, police: 113.

Useful contacts:

The Embassy of the United Kingdom of Great Britain and Northern Ireland, Trg Republike 3/IV, Ljubljana, tel.: +386 1 200 39 10

The Embassy of the Republic of Slovenia, 10 Little college Street, London SW1P3SJ, tel.: ++44 20 7222 5400

The Slovenian Tourist Office, New Barn Farm, Tadlow Road, Royston, Herts SG8 0EP

Websites: www.slovenia-tourism.si, www.sloveniapartner.com, www.gzs.si/sloexport

PERSONAL TAXATION

In 2005 Slovenia introduced a tax liability on the worldwide income of Slovene tax residents. Residency is linked in most cases to the permanent place of residence, secondly to the usual place of living or centre of vital interest, and thirdly to the presence in Slovenia for over 183 days. Non-residents pay Slovene tax on income that has its source in Slovenia. The primary principle for residents is that all personal income is taxed, unless it is exempt.

Personal income tax is divided into several income categories that are used in connection with the payment of advance tax. These categories are: employment income, income from business activity (including sole proprietors), property income, capital income and other income. A standard yearly tax system is used, where advance income tax is calculated. This yearly tax liability is calculated upon a yearly tax rate, which is progressive. The highest scale begins with circa €43,000 per year and is 50 per cent. There are no limitations to the amount of taxation. Advance tax is paid along with the salary according to the monthly tax scale of the individual. Social contributions, also not limited, are paid at the same time, as well as a special tax on salaries (a progressive scale).

For comparison purposes we have calculated the net salary of the middle class workers in the capital city Ljubljana: a net salary of €1,042 per month, monthly advance tax of €323, social contributions of €669, and tax on salaries of €110. Together the total cost of the worker to the company (net salary + advance tax + social contributions + tax on salaries) is €2,145 per month. If the net salaries are higher, then the taxation is also higher according to a progressive scale, and the total cost to the employer can reach up to three times the net salary. Residents can make use of several tax allowances, such as for family members, and there are some other special allowances. Slovenia has special regulations for travel, lunch and other expenses, and they can be paid out without taxation up to certain amounts.

For capital income (excluding income from property, such as rent from real estate), Slovenia has introduced a 'cedular' (separate) tax in 2006 of 20 per cent on the profit made on capital (such as shares). This is final taxation and is not included in the yearly tax declaration.

The yearly tax declaration has to be filed by the end of March for the previous year and the tax year within a calendar year. In all, the taxation of personal income in Slovenia is still much higher than in other EU countries but is expected to be lowered through a forthcoming reform in one or two years.

Investment income

From 1 January 2006, the domestic and foreign investment income of individuals is taxed at a flat rate of 20 per cent (cedular taxation). Investment income represents dividends, capital gains and interest on deposits. For interest, there is special treatment in 2006 and 2007: it is taxed at the rate of 15 per cent. Up to 31 December 2005, investment income (dividends, interest and capital gains) was taxed at progressive rates. Taxation of domestic investment income is the same as that from foreign sources.

Royalties and rental income net of related expenses are taxed at regular tax rates (progressive taxation with a maximum tax rate of 50 per cent).

The tax treatment of capital

From 1 January 2006 capital gains are taxed at a flat rate of 20 per cent (before that a progressive taxation system applied). When an individual possesses capital for 5 to 10 years, a capital gain from such capital is taxed at the rate of 15 per cent. For possession of capital for 10 to 15 years, the tax rate is set at the rate of 10 per cent, for 15 to 20 years at a rate of 5 per cent, and more than 20 years at a zero rate.

Before 1 January 2006, capital gains were taxed at a progressive tax rate, but after three years of possession, capital gains became free of taxation.

Double taxation treaties

Slovenia has double taxation treaties with all EU members and with the United States. Under the tax treaties, employment income is taxable in the state of residence unless employment is not exercised more than temporarily in the other state. Dividends and interest are taxable in the state of residence with the source state being entitled to levy a certain percentage of the withheld tax on dividends for which a tax credit is granted.

For further information on tax and social security, contact:

Bostjan Petauer, Certified Tax Consultant, BDO EOS Svetovanje d.o.o., tel: + (386) 1 53 00 932, e-mail: bostjan.petauer@eos.si, tel: +41 21 310 23 23, fax: + 41 212 310 23 24

SPAIN

The economy

Spain's real GDP growth remains above the Euro area average. Having registered 3.1 per cent in 2004, growth of 3.4 per cent is estimated for 2005 but forecast to ease in 2006 closer to 3 per cent. Unemployment fell to 8.5 per cent in December 2005 from 10.3 per cent a year earlier. However, consumer price inflation at 4.2 per cent in January 2006 compares with 3.1 per cent a year earlier. Export markets are no longer buoyant, and the current account deficit was running at 6.7 per cent of GDP at the end of 2005 and is expected to increase slightly in 2006. Nevertheless, Spain has the resources to bounce back from its present difficulties. It has a large and successful agricultural sector and plentiful mineral resources. Tourism is a major industry. Important manufactures include cars, ships, steel and chemicals. In the meantime, the public spending budget remains in surplus at 0.3 per cent of GDP.

Working conditions

Working conditions in Spain increasingly resemble those in other European countries, with city offices abandoning the siesta. The normal working week is 40 hours, and overtime (paid at the rate of at least 175 per cent of normal rates) cannot be forced. Annual leave is 30 days, plus 12 public holidays.

Useful information

Banking hours: 9.00 am to 2.00 pm Monday–Friday, 9.00 am to 1.00 pm Saturday (except in the summer).

Shopping hours: 10.00 am to 8.00 pm, closed between 1.00 and 4.00 pm, Monday–Friday.

Electricity: 220 or 225 V ac.

Health care: Under the social security system, hospital and medical treatment is free, and 40 per cent of prescription charges are covered, but you will have to pay for dental work other than extractions. About 40 per cent of hospitals are private.

Education: State education, compulsory between ages 6 and 14, is free; private education (much of it run by the Catholic Church) is not as expensive as in other countries. There are estimated to be at least a quarter of a million British residents in Spain, and they have created a market for private English-speaking schools, which exist in most of the main cities – Madrid, Barcelona, along the east and south coasts and in the Balearic and Canary Islands. Up-to-date information on fees can be obtained from Mr A Muñoz, Legal Adviser, National Association of British Schools in Spain, Avenida Ciudad de Barcelona 110, Esc. 3a, 5oD, 28007 Madrid.

Emergency services: 112, police 91.

Useful contacts:

British Embassy, Callde de Fernando el Santo 16, 28010 Madrid, tel: 3491 700 8200

Spanish Embassy, 39 Chesham Place, London SW1, tel: 020 7235 5555

Instituto Cervantes, 102 Eaton Square, London SW1W 9AN, tel: 020 7205 0750

Labour Office of the Spanish Embassy, 20 Peel Street, London W8 7PD, tel: 020 7221 0098

Spanish Tourist Office, 22–23 Manchester Square, London W1M 5AP, tel: 020 7486 8077, website: www.uk.tourspain.es

PERSONAL TAXATION

The principal jobs available for expatriates in Spain relate to employment with a multinational firm. Here international salary standards apply and prospective expatriates at executive levels should earn at least as much as in the UK, plus removal and other disturbance costs.

Spain is no tax haven, and income tax rates go up as high as 45 per cent. Taxes are levied at two levels: national and local. National taxes include corporate income tax, personal income tax, VAT, wealth tax, inheritance and gift tax. Local taxes are: property taxes, municipal tax, and various licence fees. Taxes are payable yearly, on 31 December.

Liability for income tax depends on residence (irrespective of whether a person has a work permit or residence permit); an individual is regarded as a resident if he or she is physically present in Spain for at least 183 days in the year. Residents pay tax on their worldwide income. A typical expatriate employee with a dependent spouse would pay 30–40 per cent of gross salary in tax and social security contributions. VAT (IVA) ranges from 6 to 16 per cent.

SWEDEN

The economy

Sweden is one of the world's most prosperous and politically stable countries, rich in natural resources and with a highly diversified manufacturing sector, particularly strong in engineering. Its economy is mainly private. The standard of management is probably the highest in Europe, and the emphasis is on technologically advanced and science-based industry. Sweden has survived the European slowdown rather better than most northern European economies, and still managed to achieve GDP growth in 2005 of 2.6 per cent, with increased growth of 3.2 per cent forecast for 2006. Unemployment in 2005 was around 5 per cent but rose to 6.3 per cent in January 2006, while consumer price inflation was less than 1 per cent in 2005 although it is forecast to rise to perhaps 1.4 per cent in 2006. Both foreign trade and the fiscal budget remain in surplus at 7 per cent and 1.2 per cent of GDP respectively. During 2003, a national referendum rejected entry to the Euro zone in the near future.

The government encourages foreign investment and offers special incentives for its northern and western development areas. UK companies are second to those of the United States, both in number and in the total of employees. Immigrant workers represent about 5 per cent of the labour force, over 50 per cent coming from other Nordic countries, which form a common labour market.

Working conditions

Sweden became a member of the EU on 1 January 1995. Since then, residence and work permits have no longer been required for stays of less than three months.

Although Sweden has been, and still is, short of skilled workers, it adopts a cautious attitude towards the employment of foreigners. As in Norway, there are openings for people who possess exceptional technical qualifications. Most British people work in a managerial or specialist capacity in a subsidiary or branch of a UK company.

The 40-hour, five-day week is standard, though hours may be slightly shorter for salaried staff. Opportunities for overtime are limited. Swedish workers are entitled to five weeks annual holiday with up to 12 public holidays. (There is no substitute day if the holiday falls on a Saturday or Sunday.) Periods of notice according to age and length of service are laid down by law in agreements. Employer–employee relationships are highly egalitarian both in practice and in terms of legislation. Possibly for this reason, industrial disputes are rare.

Many employers provide subsidised canteens and contribute towards transport, holidays, health and leisure facilities. They are obliged in certain circumstances to provide language teaching, as well as housing, for immigrants. They bear a heavy proportion of contributions towards social security and pensions.

Useful information

Banking hours: 9.30 am to 3.30 pm Monday–Friday.

Shopping hours: Generally between 9 am and 6 pm on weekdays and between 1 pm and 4 pm on Saturdays. In larger towns, department stores remain open until 8 or 10 pm and some are also open on Sundays between noon and 4 pm. Shops generally close early on the day before a public holiday.

Post office: Postal services in Sweden are now provided by supermarkets and kiosks marked with the blue and yellow post sign.

Driving: The Swedes drive on the right. The roads are mainly good and there are motorways between the main cities in the south. UK and international driving licences are accepted; after two years you must obtain a Swedish licence. The main car manufacturers are Volvo and Saab. A Ford Focus would cost approximately Kr 163,900. If you import a car from the UK it must pass the very strict Swedish roadworthiness examination, which includes tough exhaust emission tests. It can be very expensive to bring a car up to the required standard if it fails. Seat belts are compulsory and the laws on drinking and driving are very strict.

Transport: Public transport is clean, efficient and universally available.

Health care: The level of health care is high, and charges are generally modest (free to the under-18s except for emergency hospital admission). There is a fee of Kr 140 for a visit to the doctor; house calls cost Kr 200. Specialist consultation costs up to Kr 260. Emergency hospital admission is Kr 260, but once you are admitted to hospital your treatment is free. Medication for hospital patients is free, but outpatients and those who are prescribed medicines by their GP must pay prescription charges. The dental service is subsidised, and is free for children and young adults up to 20.

Education: State education is free, and of a high standard. A third of pre-school children go to nursery schools run by the communities. Children of foreign residents have special courses in the Swedish language if they attend Swedish schools. There are international schools in many of the larger cities, eg Internationella Engelska Skolan with schools in the Stockholm area.

Emergency services: 112.

Directory enquiries: 118 118.

Useful contacts:

British Embassy, Skarpogatan 6–8, Box 27819, SE-115 93 Stockholm, tel: +46–468 671 3000, website: www.britishembassy.se. There is also a British General Consulate in Gothenburg, Sodra Hamngatan 23, SE-411 14 Goteborg, tel: +46–31- 339 33 00

Swedish Embassy, 11 Montagu Place, London W1, tel: 020 7917 6475

Swedish Travel and Tourism Council, 11 Montagu Place, London W1H 2AL, tel: 020 7870 5600, websites: www.cityguide.se/, www.visit-sweden.com

PERSONAL TAXATION

These details are as of January 2006.

Residence

A continuous stay of six months establishes a habitual place of abode in Sweden and makes the individual resident from the first day. If the stay stretches over two years, the individual is resident in both years. A real dwelling or home in Sweden will also result in residency.

As soon as an individual satisfies one of the above criteria, he or she is considered resident in Sweden from that date. The residence of an individual and liability to Swedish tax on current income is determined under the same basic rules in the year of departure as for any other, including the year of arrival. The individual will be taxed in Sweden on worldwide income until the day he or she departs from the country and ceases to be resident.

For further information on tax and social security, contact:

Emilio Margallo, BDO Audiberia Auditores, S.L., tel: + 34 93 200 3233, e-mail: emilio.margallo@bdo.es

Tax liability if the stay in Sweden is less than six months

If an individual stays in Sweden for less than six months, his or her tax liability is limited. This means that he or she only has to pay tax on certain income arising from sources in Sweden, and not on income arising from sources in his or her country of residence. Taxable earned income is subject to special withholding income tax on non-residents with a rate of 25 per cent (SINK).

If the stay in Sweden does not exceed 183 days in a 12-month period, the income from a foreign employer who does not have a permanent establishment in Sweden is not taxable.

Income from employment

Income tax in Sweden consists of municipal and state tax. Municipal tax varies by municipality, from approximately 26 per cent to approximately 35 per cent. Taxable income that exceeds SEK 298,600 (income year 2006) is subject to national income tax at a rate of 20 per cent. Taxable income that exceeds SEK 450,500 (income year 2006) is subject to a rate of 25 per cent.

All compensation that a wage earner receives from his or her own labour is regarded as wage income. Benefits that are not paid in cash are generally valued at market value. Some benefits – such as meals, a free car and loans with low or no interest – are valued according to a standard rate.

As a general rule, income from employment is taxed on a cash basis. Deferred remuneration would not normally be taxable until receipt. An executive about to become a resident of Sweden should consider whether it would be preferable to arrange to receive any previously deferred remuneration prior to entry into Sweden. There is no special treatment for termination or redundancy payments.

Non-employment income

Non-employment income such as capital gains on shares, dividends and interest is taxable for residents at a rate of 30 per cent. Dividends and capital gains from the disposal by active shareholders of shares in closely held companies might be deemed to be remuneration from employment.

Sweden has no exit tax on shares when an individual leaves the country and ceases to be resident.

Double taxation treaties

Sweden has signed double tax treaties with approximately 80 countries, including the United States and the UK.

For further information on tax and social security, contact:
Pether Rombo, Tax Partner, BDO Nordic AB, tel: +46 (0) 31 704 1318, e-mail: Pether.Rombo@BDO.se
Jessica Otterstal, Tax Manager, BDO Nordic AB, tel: +46 (0) 8 459 5783, e-mail: Jessica.Otterstal@bdo.se

SWITZERLAND

The economy

Switzerland is prosperous commercially. It is split into 26 cantons which have different expanding sectors. Zurich is one of the leading European banking and commercial centres; the HSG in St Gallen ranks among the world best educational institutions; and in Geneva the UN, the WTO and other important organisations are based. Lausanne, the Olympic capital, contains the headquarters of international sports federations, and the region around Lucerne is a favourite for a lot of tourists. There is an efficient agriculture sector in several regions such as the Valais or Grisons. The economic progress has been sufficient to attract large numbers of migrant workers, particularly from Italy, Germany, Austria, former Yugoslavia, Turkey and Sri Lanka. Apart from tourism and banking, Switzerland's main manufactured exports are machines and metal products, chemicals and pharmaceuticals, electrical goods, precision instruments, textiles, clothing and watches. The small and medium-sized companies, which are highly specialised and often very flexible, are typical for the technologically advanced industrial sector. Its main markets are the EU, mainly Germany, and the United States. Switzerland also exports know-how to different countries by educating immigrants.

Overall, the Swiss economy is in much the same condition as the EU member states, with GDP growth of 1.8 per cent estimated for 2005 and 2.2 per cent forecast for 2006. The unemployment rate stays at around 4 per cent. Consumer price inflation in 2005 was close to 1 per cent, well below the Euro area average of 2.2 per cent and forecast to remain at the same level in 2006.

Working conditions

Managerial salaries are among the world's highest. Consultants or technical staff of EU-based companies may work without a work permit in Switzerland for a maximum of 90 days per year, so it is compulsory to register. Consultants and technical staff who wish to work for a longer period will have to obtain a work permit regardless of their nationality. A work permit application must be made in the canton in which the individual intends to work.

The Swiss government is at present reluctant to grant visas to foreign workers, and has imposed numerical limits on long- and short-term labour permits. According to agreements between the EU and Switzerland, short-term labour permits for EU citizens no longer fall under the numeric limit. For long-term labour permits, EU citizens have a good chance of success. For US citizens, long-term permits are available only to people with special skills or qualifications who have been offered a position by a Swiss employer. Unsolicited applications are, therefore, not encouraged and have little or no chance of success.

It is clear that the best chance of long-term employment is with a British or US firm, or international agency with offices in Switzerland. Once you have obtained a position with a Swiss employer, or a UK company based in Switzerland, your prospective employer must obtain the labour and residence permits you need. On entering the country you will need to produce a valid passport.

Useful information

Banking hours: 8.00 am to 4.30 pm Monday–Friday (may vary).

Post office: 7.30 or 8.00 am to 12.00 pm and 1.30 or 2.00–6.00 pm Monday–Friday, 7.30 or 8.00–11.00 am Saturday (may vary).

Shopping hours: 8.15 am to 6.30 pm Monday–Friday, 8.15 am to 4.00 pm Saturday (may vary).

Electricity: 220 V, 50 Hz ac.

Health care: Switzerland is, in general, a healthy place to live. Expatriates are strongly advised, in their own interest, to join a health insurance scheme from the very beginning. You should seek information from your employer on this point. The insurance should comprise not only medical and hospital treatment but also adequate sickness benefit, since employees have only a limited claim to payment of wages in the event of illness. Everybody in Switzerland is insured against illness and accidents through the 'Krankenkassen', which tries to exert control over physicians' fees. Specialists, as a rule, charge significantly more than general practitioners. Employment accidents are covered by mandatory employer insurance.

Social insurance agreements between Switzerland and various other countries and the EU make it easier to join specific health insurance schemes and in certain circumstances shorten the waiting period. Under some agreements, moreover, the Swiss employer is required to make sure that an employee coming from the country concerned is insured for medical care (doctor and hospital) and, if not, to take out adequate insurance for him or her. In cases of doubt enquiries should be addressed to the appropriate consulate.

Driving: Speed limits are 50 km/h inside a community, 80 km/h on overland roads, and 120 km/h on motorways. Seat belts are compulsory. Driving is on the right.

Education: In Switzerland education begins with the pre-school level, primary level and secondary level, and goes on to the upper secondary level (intermediate diploma schools, Matura schools, etc) and tertiary level (universities of applied sciences, universities, etc). There is also special and continuing education. It is organised by cantonal laws. For further information, see www.educa.ch.

Media: There are two national television and three national radio channels. A wide range of international, local and regional television and radio channels is available. Additionally there are a number of daily or weekly newspapers.

Languages: In Switzerland four languages are written and spoken. The biggest parts of Switzerland are Swiss German and French. There is a smaller part, which is Italian and a tiny number of Swiss people are still Romantsch. English is taught in school but not in every canton at the same age or for the same duration.

Useful contacts:
British Embassy, Thunstrasse 50, 3005 Berne , tel: 41 31 359 7741
Swiss Embassy, 16–18 Montagu Place, London W1H 2BQ, tel: 020 7616 6000
Switzerland Tourism, Swiss Centre, 10 Wardour Street, London W1D 6QF, tel: 020 7292 1550, website: www.myswitzerland.com
Tourist information: www.uk.myswitzerland.com, www.swisstin. com; www.about.ch

PERSONAL TAXATION

In addition to the federation, each of the 26 cantons levies income and wealth taxes according to its own tax laws. Although the cantonal tax laws have been harmonised, the tax rates vary widely from canton to canton. Additional to the cantonal tax, each community levies income and wealth taxes with a multiple on the cantonal tax. The tax rate also includes a church tax (for the Protestant, the Roman Catholic and Christ Catholic churches), which is calculated as a percentage of the cantonal/communal rate. The tax burden depends therefore in large measure on the choice of place of residence.

Residence

The extent to which an individual is liable to Swiss federal, cantonal and communal income tax depends on the individual's residence status. Residence status generally begins with the date of arrival and ends on the day of departure. An individual is considered resident if he or she has a home in which he or she intends to dwell or has a place of abode. (A presence of 30 days, combined with gainful activity, or 90 days without gainful activity, is sufficient to establish a place of abode in Switzerland.)

A resident is liable to tax on worldwide income and net wealth, with the exception of foreign real estate and income there from.

Personal income tax

All tax rates (federal, cantonal and communal) are progressively rated. Married people are taxed jointly, not separately, on all types of income. There are different rates for single and married people. Some cantons have only one rate for single and married people, but divide the total income of married people by a factor of 1.9, for instance. Income tax is levied on all sources of income:

☐ work income (including base salary, bonus, stock options, etc);
☐ income from investments (dividends, interest, etc);
☐ income from real estate;
☐ income from pension payments.

Private capital gains on movable assets (shares, derivatives and so on) are in general not taxed.

A federal withholding tax of 35 per cent is levied at source on income from Swiss movable capital (such as interest and dividends from Swiss sources), Swiss lottery gains and Swiss insurance benefits. For a Swiss resident individual taxpayer, withholding tax is reimbursed by way of credit against income tax payable. For non-

Swiss residents, relief may be obtained depending on the residency of the taxpayer and the provisions of any relevant double tax treaty.

Net wealth tax

No net wealth tax is imposed on a federal level. All cantons and communities levy a net wealth tax on worldwide assets, with the exception of real estate, a fixed place of business, or a permanent establishment located abroad. Tax rates are reasonably low. The tax is based on the market value of the assets. All debts are deductible. The rates are progressive, and two different rates exist for single and married people. Some cantons have only one rate for single and married people, but divide the total income of married people by a factor of 1.9, for instance.

Double taxation treaty

Switzerland has a double tax treaty with many countries, including the UK and the United States, as well as the EU.

Contacts in Switzerland

Swiss German and Italian part of Switzerland:
Hans Peter Mark (hans-peter.mark@bdo.ch), Thomas Kaufman (thomas.kaufman@bdo.ch)
BDO Visura, Fabrikstrasse 50, 8031 Zürich, tel: + 41 44 444 35 55, fax: + 41 44 444 37 64

French part of Switzerland:
Richard Pochon (richard.pochon@bdo.ch), BDO Visura, Place Pépinet 1, 1002 Lausanne, tel: +41 21 310 23 23, fax: + 41 212 310 23 24

The Middle East

It is not practical to generalise about the political and security situation throughout the Middle East. Undoubtedly, there are some risks of terrorism, which are greater in some countries than others. The only way to keep abreast of these dangers is to obtain up-to-date advice from the British embassies in the countries to be visited. For instance, there are clearly serious daily risks in Iraq and less risk in Saudi Arabia, whereas for the time being the United Arab Emirates may be considered relatively safe. Indeed, there is probably as much risk of a terrorist attack in the UK or against British interests as there is in much of the Middle East at the time of writing (early 2006). The overall advice is to be cautious and avoid potential trouble spots. By far the majority of people throughout the Middle East want to lead secure and peaceful lives. They are as much against the limited number of extremists as anyone else. It needs to be borne in mind that acts of terrorism are totally contrary to the teachings of Islam, which is of course the predominant religion in the Middle East.

THE ARAB COUNTRIES: SOME NOTES ON ETIQUETTE

One of the things that worries expatriates about living and working in the Arab world is the idea of having to conform to a society whose customs and etiquette are very different from our own. All sorts of stories circulate about niceties of social behaviour, failure to observe which will mortally offend the Arabs, but most Arabs you are likely to meet will have travelled or studied in the West and be quite used to Western ways. Of course if, while talking to an Arab, you lounge in your chair in an arrogant or disrespectful fashion, it will not go down well. Nor will it be appreciated if you smoke, eat or drink in the presence of Muslims during the holy month of Ramadan, the time when their religion enjoins abstinence from such activities. But what one is really talking about then is simple good manners, and simple good manners will take you a long way in contacts with members of your host country.

This is not to say that there are not some points of etiquette that you should bear in mind on such occasions as you come into social contact with local people. If you are invited to dinner in an Arab country you will be expected to arrive on time (although Arab guests to your home will be much more casual about punctuality). You should be very careful about admiring any object in the house in which you are a guest because your host may press you to take it as a present, but he will, in due course, expect a present of at least similar value from you. When food comes, you will have more heaped on your plate than you can eat. It is not considered bad manners to leave most of it, rather the reverse, because to leave nothing on your plate suggests you think the host has not been sufficiently generous. If food is being eaten with the fingers (or indeed when you are offering anything to an Arab), use your right hand only; the left is considered impure, since it is associated with what one might politely call the exercise of intimate bodily functions.

If there are long periods of silence over dinner, do not consider yourself a social failure. Arabs do not regard constant talk as a social necessity. Nor should you be taken aback if they ask you rather personal questions – this goes for talk between women in particular. They are not restrained as we are about the things concerning other people that we are dying to know but are always too polite to ask – while hoping they will come back to us in the form of gossip. Nor should you feel the evening has gone badly if your Arab guests leave immediately after dinner. This is customary, and they expect you to do likewise. Incidentally, few Arabs, except the more Westernised and sophisticated, will bring their wives in response to an invitation, and neither will they expect the guest to do likewise.

There are other points of social etiquette as well, and if you are being asked into an Arab home or vice versa, you should certainly seek advice from someone who knows the local scene. It is worth acquainting yourself before your departure with the dos and don'ts of everyday behaviour. For instance, all Arab countries, even the more liberal ones, frown on what the Americans politely call 'public displays of affection' between the sexes. Women wearing revealing clothes are apt to attract attention which varies, according to the country, from what would be described in the UK as rude stares to being told by the police to go home and put on something more suitable. It is unwise to argue with the police in an Arab country since the processes of justice are, to say the least, different from those in the West. This does not mean, even in Saudi Arabia, that they will cut off some valued part of your anatomy if you are found guilty of a crime; but they will unceremoniously put you on the next plane out of the country if they do not like your behaviour. Public flogging incidents which receive so much publicity are extremely rare (as far as Westerners are concerned). This sort of punishment would only be put into practice in the face of the most open and provocative breaches of the law. However, in countries where Koranic law is strictly observed, particularly in Saudi Arabia, there is no right to representation in court and lengthy periods of arrest before trial can occur. On the positive side, Islamic law lays great emphasis on the fulfilment of contractual obligations – by both parties.

Drinking is severely punished in the various countries where alcohol is forbidden and it is criminal and foolish to try to smuggle it in. This does not mean to say that smuggling of alcohol does not go on. There are a few places where whisky is available, at prices of up to £80 a bottle. But it is best to leave smuggling to others; and if you are offered smuggled booze be very discreet about drinking it – no raucous parties, and avoid being seen under the influence in public.

The maxim about good manners getting you a long way also applies to business etiquette. There will be some things about business contacts that you will find frustrating or annoying but you will just have to accept them with good grace. For instance, Arabs are lax about keeping appointments; and when you do get to the person you may have waited hours or even days to see, all sorts of individuals will probably pop into his office while you are there and interrupt your conversation for minutes on end. Arab customs are also different concerning the acceptance of gifts. This is a tricky one for business people, but a lot of what we could castigate as bribery is the normal custom in an Arab country. This is not to say that you should go about trying to bribe people to get favours – this is generally considered to be a bad idea because, as a Westerner, you would not know who to bribe and how to go about it for a start – but if you are offered a present in a business context you should not refuse it, unless it patently is a bribe. To a Muslim, the return of a gift implies that it is unworthy of the recipient and can be a tremendous slap in the face for the giver. It is difficult to tread the narrow path between integrity and self-righteousness, but then few things about leaving home to go and work in another country are easy – though they are nearly always interesting.

One final question that tends to be asked now is whether and to what extent the backlash against Western ways and influence which marked the rise of Muslim fundamentalism has spread. Certainly, there is unlikely to be any loosening up of observances regarding alcohol consumption, dress, religious holidays and so on. More doubtful is the long term outcome of the robust reaction of the United States and its allies against global terrorism and the intervention in Iraq. The encouraging outcome of the Iraqi elections at the end of January 2005 has caused hopes to rise, but this is only the first step in a long and difficult process towards democratic self-government and internal security.

EGYPT

The economy

Economic growth has improved significantly following an IMF reform programme. Theoretically, with its large population, Egypt could become the manufacturing centre of the Middle East. In 2005, Egypt's economy enjoyed GDP growth of 5.2 per cent and a similar rate of growth is forecast for 2006. The foreign trade current account is roughly in balance showing a surplus ratio to GDP of about 0.9 per cent in 2005. Inflation at December 2005 was 3.1 per cent. Investment has been encouraged by recent regional reform programmes, such as reduction of tax rates and customs tariffs, in addition to a major restructuring in the banking industry. Egypt's budget deficit ratio stood at 9.7 per cent of GDP in 2005 but a reduction is forecast in 2006 to below 9 per cent.

Working conditions

A work permit is needed, which must be arranged by the local employer. It is advisable to take a plentiful supply of passport photos and duplicates of essential documents as bureaucracy in Egypt is an industry in its own right and there are many occasions when form filling, supported by documents, is called for.

Useful information

Government offices: 8.00 am to 3.00 pm Sunday to Thursday (some from Saturday to Wednesday).

Banking hours: 8.30 am to 2.00 pm Sunday to Thursday.

Post office: 8.30 am to 3.00 pm Saturday to Thursday. Allow six days for airmail post to Europe, 8–10 days to the United States.

Shopping hours: 10.00 am to 9.00 pm in winter, 9.00 am to 10.00 pm in summer. Most are closed on Sunday.

Climate: The two main cities are Cairo and Alexandria. Both have long, hot summers, where the temperature averages 32°C and can be higher, and short winters. These run from November to March and though mild by European standards they do require warmer clothing and a certain amount of indoor heating on colder days. In upper Egypt temperatures are much higher, though it is a dry heat. Alexandria, on the other hand, is inclined to be humid because of its position by the sea.

Electricity: 220 V, 50 Hz ac. Plugs are usually the two-pin, round variety.

Education: The local situation regarding schools is quite good but they are expensive.

Health care: Medical attention is also good in theory – Egyptian doctors are much sought after throughout the Middle East – but the standards of hygiene in hospitals can leave something to be desired. Private hospitals are much better in this respect. Egypt insists on HIV tests for anyone staying longer than a month.

Alcohol: There are no constraints on the consumption of alcohol and the practice of Islam, though universal, is not exercised with any degree of fanaticism.

Media: 13 television channels, European Radio Cairo 557AM and 95FM, BBC World Service Middle East Broadcast 639 kHz. *The Egyptian Gazette*, English-language newspaper.

Useful contacts:
British Embassy, Ahmed Ragheb Street, Garden City, Cairo, tel: 202 794 0850
Embassy of the Arab Republic of Egypt, 2 Lowndes Street, London W1, tel: 0207 235 9777
Egyptian State Tourist Office, Egyptian House, 170 Piccadilly, London W1 V 9DD, tel: 020 7493 5282

Country information: www.touregypt.net, www.arab.net.eg, www.horus.ics.org.eg (website for children)

Expatriate networks:

www.outpostexpat.nl; www.expatexchange. com; Community Services Association, Cairo, tel: 202 358 5284; British Community Association, Cairo, tel: 202 348 1358; British Egyptian Business Association, Cairo, tel: +202 349 1421; Egyptian British Chamber of Commerce, London, tel: 020 7499 3100

PERSONAL TAXATION

These details are as of January 2004.

Residence

Egypt taxes individuals on a hybrid source and residence basis. Generally speaking, an individual is considered resident in Egypt if he or she is physically present in Egypt for a period exceeding 183 days in the tax year.

Taxation of personal income

Individuals resident in Egypt are liable to salary tax on their income. Resident individuals working in Egypt have the same salary tax exemption as Egyptians.

Amounts paid to non-residents from any source and amounts paid to residents from other sources than their employers, are subject to 10 per cent taxes, without any deductions.

Income from employment

Taxes are imposed on all the amounts paid to taxpayers as a result of their work for others, in any role or for any reason, whether the work has been performed inside Egypt or aboard and payment received in Egypt, in addition to payments received from a foreign source against work performed in Egypt.

Salary tax exemptions are as follows:

☐ personal exemption of LE 4000;
☐ social insurance subscription and private insurance funds;

- [ ] life insurance instalments and medical insurance;
- [ ] fringe benefits: employees meals, medical care, employees' group transportation, employees' uniform, housing allowed by the employer to employees in relation to their work;
- [ ] employees' share in profit distribution.

Investment income

Dividends received by an Egyptian resident from Egyptian companies are exempt from tax. Dividends received from abroad are subject to corporate tax of 20 per cent. The same rules apply to interest.

Rental income from real property situated in Egypt is liable to unified income tax, net of related expenses.

Taxes on capital

Capital gains

There is generally no tax on the private capital gains realised by an individual outside the course of a trade or business. However, a 2.5 per cent tax is levied on the gross proceeds from the disposal of urban land and buildings, whether or not in the course of a trade or business. Other assets of business are subject to 20 per cent capital against tax upon disposal.

Wealth tax

There is no wealth tax in Egypt.

Double tax treaties

Egypt has concluded over 49 comprehensive double taxation agreements, including those with the UK and the United States. Both these treaties exempt earnings of a non-resident from Egyptian tax if he or she stays in Egypt for less than 183 days in the case of the UK, or 91 days in the case of the United States, and those earnings are not charged to an Egyptian-resident entity.

For further information on tax and social security, contact:

Taha M Khaled, BDO Partner, BDO Zarrouk, Khaled and Co, tel: + 202 303 9779, e-mail: tmkhaled@bdoegypt.com, website: www.bdoegypt.com

THE GULF STATES

Economies

Oil is the salient factor in the economies of all the Gulf States, although the level of reserves varies. Most of these countries are making efforts to diversify into other activities and to invest oil revenues in the creation of infrastructure. Bahrain is developing large-scale industrial enterprises, including aluminium smelting and shipbuilding; it has a longer established trading tradition and is an important offshore banking centre. It is emerging as a regional centre for technology and light industry. Oman, whose oil reserves are modest by Middle Eastern standards, is developing copper mining and smelting, cement production and fisheries; it also has a programme to expand health, education, communications and public services such as electricity and water. Qatar produces fertilisers and cement, and is also making rigorous efforts to develop its agricultural industry. Prospects for all the Gulf States depend on the fall-out from the second Iraq war and the strength of the rebound in US growth.

BAHRAIN

Oil was first commercially exploited in Bahrain in 1932 and now provides 75 per cent of export earnings. Owing to the gradual decline in crude oil production during the past few years and the fact that present reserves are forecast to run out in the near future, the government is actively encouraging foreign investment in diversified industrial development – with some success. Recent estimates put the population at about 550,000, increasing at a rate of 3.5 per cent a year, one-third of whom are expatriates.

GDP growth rose sharply from 5.4 per cent in 2004 to an estimated 9.2 per cent in 2005 and is expected to maintain a similar rate of growth through 2006. Inflation has been brought down from 5.3 per cent in 2004 to the current level of 3.1 per cent and is forecast to fall further. A public sector budget surplus at 2.9 per cent of GDP was recorded for 2005 but the surplus is expected to fall back to less than 1 per cent in 2006.

The foreign trade current account has been in surplus since 2003, rising from 3.7 per cent in 2004 to 9 per cent of GDP in 2005.

Useful information

Tax: There is no income tax.

Government offices: 7.00 am to 2.15 pm Saturday–Wednesday.

Commercial organisations: Vary, but 8.00 am to noon and 3.00–5.30 pm normal, Saturday–Thursday.

Banking hours: 7.30 am to noon and 3.30–5.30 pm Saturday to Wednesday, 7.30–11.00 am Thursday.

Shopping hours: 8.30 am to 12.30 pm and 3.30–7.30 pm six days a week, plus Friday morning.

Climate: November–April: 15–24°C, July–September: 36°C (average), high humidity.

Media: Bahrain Tribune and *Gulf Daily News* English-language newspapers, two Arabic newspapers, one television station.

Useful contacts:
British Embassy, 21 Government Avenue, Manama 306, PO Box 114, Bahrain, tel: 973 574100, website: www.ukembassy.gov.bh
Embassy of the State of Bahrain, 30 Belgrave Square, London SW1, tel: 020 7201 9170.

Country information:
Bahrain Tourism, www.bahraintourism.com/

KUWAIT

The rebuilding of Kuwait, liberated from Iraqi occupation in 1991, has generated renewed opportunities. The expense of rebuilding was a drain on the economy. GDP growth since 2003 has been strong but is forecast to be easing from 6.3 per cent in 2004/5 to 5.6 per cent in 2005/6. Inflation started to rise modestly after 2003/4 but was contained at 1.1 per cent in 2004/5, although it is forecast to exceed 3 per cent this year. Kuwait maintains a strong trade balance and the current account surplus as a percentage of GDP stands at 36.4 per cent and rising. The public sector budget was also held in surplus at an estimated 27.5 per cent of GDP for 2004/5.

More detailed up-to-date information about the economy remains difficult to come by. Certainly, Kuwait is not likely to attract any but the toughest, single-status, pioneering-minded expatriates – though for them the rewards may well be considerable. Salaries in

Kuwait are still high, and there is a high standard of living, including free education and health care.

Useful information

Commercial organisations: Thursday and Friday official days off, but banks and international companies take Friday and Saturday off.

Electricity: 240 V, 50 Hz ac.

Driving: Apply to the Traffic Department for a Kuwaiti driving licence.

Health care: Medical insurance advised; Expacare and BUPA can be bought in Kuwait. Local medical schemes available but with exclusions. Medical required for residence, with entrance barred to those suffering from serious infectious diseases.

Useful contacts:
British Embassy, Arabian Gulf Street, Dasman, PO Box 2, Safat 13001, Kuwait, tel: 965 240 3334
Embassy of the State of Kuwait, 2 Albert Gate, London SW1, tel: 020 7590 3400

Country information:
www.kuwaitview.com

Expatriate contact:
American Women's League of Kuwait, Kuwait PO Box 77, 13001 Safat.

PERSONAL TAXATION

Taxation of personal income

Kuwait does not impose income tax on individuals (as at April 2005).

Taxes on capital
Capital gains

There is no tax on private capital gains.

Wealth tax

There is no wealth tax.

Double tax treaties

There are comprehensive double taxation agreements between Kuwait and 32 other countries including the UK but not currently the United States, although negotiations have started.

For further information on tax and social security, contact:

Hilmi Mukhaimer, Tax Partner, BDO Burgan, tel: + 965 242 6862, e-mail: bdoburgn@qualitynet.net

OMAN

Economic growth fell back from a high of 7.5 per cent in 2001 but has recovered steadily since 2003, and a GDP growth rate of 4.6 per cent is expected for 2005 with 6.9 per cent forecast for 2006. Consumer price inflation rose in 2005 to 2.1 per cent but is forecast to fall back below 2 per cent in 2006. The trade surplus is consistently strong and the current account surplus as a ratio of GDP returned to the 2001 level in 2005 at 9.9 per cent. Oman also maintains a budget surplus which peaked in 2005 at 11.9 per cent of GDP.

Visas

Anyone going to Oman, even on a non-business visit, must obtain in advance a 'No Objection Certificate' (NOC) issued by the Sultanate immigration authorities and obtainable in the country by the employer or a local sponsor. The NOC is necessary in order to obtain a visa even for family visitors. This proviso does not apply, though, to visitors born in the UK, who can obtain visas in London for visits of less than 14 days' duration.

Useful information

Government offices: 7.30 or 8.00 am to 1.00 pm Saturday to Wednesday, 7.30 or 8.00 am to 11.00 am, Thursday.

Business hours: 8.00 am to 1.00 pm and 4.00–7.00 or 7.30 pm, except Friday evening. Businesses closed Thursday afternoon.

Banking hours: 8.00 am to 12.00 pm Saturday to Wednesday, 8.00–11.00 am Thursday.

Electricity: 220/240 V 50 Hz, ac.

Climate: Summer 31–48°C and humid, winter 20–25°C.

Media: English-language newspapers *The Times of Oman* and *The Oman Daily Observer.*

Useful contacts:

British Embassy, PO Box 185, Mina Al Fahal, Postal Code 116, Sultanate of Oman, tel: 968 609000

Embassy of the Sultanate of Oman, 167 Queens Gate, London SW7, tel: 020 7225 0001

Expatriate contacts:

Muscat Information Network Centre, tel: 986 677197, e-mail: minco@openmail.minco.pdomus.simis.com; Historical Society of Oman, PO Box 3941 Ruwi, Post Code 112

Country information:

www.oman.org (excellent links from Oman Studies Centre); www.omanet.om, www.omania.net

QATAR

Situated on the east coast of Qatar is the capital city and chief commercial centre, Doha, a fast-developing, modern metropolis from which 1,080 km of excellent roads radiate to the rest of the peninsula. Other important urban centres are Umm Said, also on the east coast, which is the centre for industrial development, and on the west coast, Dukham, which is a major oil producing centre.

GDP growth for 2005 is forecast at 12 per cent but is considered likely to slacken to 2002/3 levels in 2006 at around 7.2 per cent. Inflation is believed to have fallen from 6.8 per cent (2004) to 4.5 per cent (2005) and is forecast to fall as low as 3 per cent in 2006. Qatar runs a healthy budget surplus which stood at 8.6 per cent of GDP in 2005 and the current account surplus in 2005 represented 36.2 per cent of GDP, with imports running at little more than 25 per cent of exports.

Useful information

Business hours: 8.00 am to 12.00 pm and 5.00–7.00 pm.

Alcohol: Expatriates can obtain a liquor permit from the British Embassy in Doha.

Emergency services: 999.

Airport arrival/departure: 351550.

Directory enquiries: 180.

Useful contacts:
British Embassy, PO Box 3, Doha, tel: 974 442 1991
Qatar Embassy, 1 South Audley Street, London W1, tel: 020 7493 2200

Country information:
www.qatar-info.com; www.arabnet.com

SAUDI ARABIA

The economy

The backbone of the economy is, of course, oil. The country is rich in other minerals and much is being done to exploit them. Gold, silver and copper are now being produced. The income from oil has been largely devoted to improving the country's infrastructure, developments such as petrol refining, gas liquefaction plant and other petroleum-based activities, and the expansion of a wide range of manufacturing industries. There has also been a good deal of investment in agriculture to increase self-sufficiency. Another major form of investment has been in various measures of water conservation and deployment and there are now 33 desalination plants.

Economic growth has risen sharply since 2002 and GDP growth for 2005 is estimated at 6.5 per cent. Inflation was contained below 1 per cent until recently: 1.1 per cent was registered in November 2005. Not unexpectedly, there are surpluses on the Kingdom's public sector budget and the foreign trade current account, estimated at 18.7 per cent and 33 per cent of GDP respectively for 2005. Exports are running slightly under four times the level of imports.

Working conditions

A work permit must be applied for by your Saudi agent, employer or contact in the country. When this is forthcoming you must supply its details to the Saudi Embassy which will issue a visa. This is apt to be a lengthy procedure and plenty of time must be allowed for the documentation to come through. It is a good idea to have smallpox and cholera vaccinations, and polio, TB and anti-tetanus are also advisable.

A particular point to bear in mind is that, if you arrive in the time of Haji (pilgrimage to Mecca), special precautions against cholera have to be taken and certified. Check details before leaving as conditions are sometimes changed without notice. The Saudi Arabian Embassy in London requires all expatriate residents in the Kingdom to undergo an AIDS test before they are issued with visas.

The working week runs from Saturday to Thursday. Work often starts early in the morning, at 7.00 or 8.00 am, with a long break in the afternoon, but working hours are variable, depending on region and prayer times.

Foreigners should carry their ID, driver's licence and residence permit at all times. It should also be borne in mind that exit visas are required to leave the country, and these sometimes entail bureaucratic delays before you get them. You also need a letter of release if you are changing employers within Saudi Arabia. The conditions under which you can terminate your employment should therefore be clearly set out in your contract.

Many jobs, particularly at more junior levels, are single status. Where accompanying partners are allowed, you are advised to bring several copies of your marriage certificate.

Useful information

Government offices: 7.30 am to 2.30 pm Saturday–Wednesday.

Banking hours: Vary from province to province but generally 8.00–11.30 am and 4.00–6.00 pm Saturday–Wednesday, 8.00–11.30 am Thursday.

Commercial hours: 7.30 or 9.00–11.00 am or noon, and 2.30 or 4.30–10.00 pm

Saturday–Wednesday. During the month of Ramadan official business hours are 10.00 am to 3.00 pm.

Electricity: 110 or 220 V, 60 Hz ac.

Climate: For most of the year the places where expatriates are likely to find themselves in Saudi Arabia are extremely hot and summer temperatures of 42–50°C are usual. Almost all buildings are air-conditioned. Around Jeddah and the eastern province oilfields, humidity is high and even during the winter season (December to March), it is never really cool. The interior is dry and, though equally hot in summer, can get very cold in winter. Thus warm clothing is necessary in winter in places like Riyadh. There is little rainfall anywhere, although irregular heavy showers do occur in the winter months. Prevailing winds come from the north and sometimes produce uncomfortable dust storms.

Driving: Women are not allowed to drive, which means that they must either walk or take a taxi, unless they are lucky enough to have a chauffeur. In fact, although cars are essential and petrol is comparatively cheap, owning one is not without its hazards. Driving standards are poor but improving; there is no legal insurance requirement, but the compensation that has to be paid for an accident involving loss of life is high. Maximum comprehensive cover and third-party liability are most strongly advised, although expensive. However, the consequences of being involved in a traffic accident are always serious and the Saudi police tend to deal more strictly with offenders than is common in the West.

A car usually goes with the job, in any case with executive or supervisory posts. You will need a Saudi licence, which may be obtained, with a three-month delay, on production of a UK one. Eyesight and blood tests are also required.

Health care: Expatriate jobs generally include free medical attention, and hospitals in the main centres are extremely good. Private treatment, of course, is very expensive – even an ambulance journey to hospital costs around SR600. Oculist services are improving but if you need glasses you should bring spare pairs with you. Sunglasses are also a good idea, because of the strong glare.

Education: There are several international and US schools for children up to the age of 15. There are British private primary schools in Jeddah, Riyadh and Al Khobar. Below this level there are playschools run by expatriate wives. On the whole, taking children of school age to Saudi is not a good idea and in any case school places are very hard to get.

Alcohol: It must be remembered that the import of alcohol is forbidden and visitors should not try to take alcohol with them, even in small quantities. The penalties are severe.

Banned products/substances: The import of pork, pig meat products, salacious literature, narcotics, firearms, games of chance and non-Islamic religious symbols/books is also forbidden. No formal religious practices other than Islam are allowed and discretion should be exercised when informal religious practices are engaged in.

Clothing etiquette: Men should not wear shorts in public and there are very severe restrictions on what is considered proper for women in public. Thus, no 'revealing' dresses (décolleté or see-through), no hems above the knee, sleeves at least to the elbow, trousers only if worn with a top that goes below the thighs and, on the beach, one-piece bathing costumes only.

Photography: It is forbidden to take photographs of airports, military installations, or other sensitive buildings such as government offices or institutions and foreign embassies. Photography is better tolerated in rural areas than in the city, but care should be taken not to photograph individuals (without their consent) and particularly not veiled women.

Media: Saudi television has an English-language channel. It is generally possible, also, to pick up English TV channels from Bahrain and other countries in the Gulf, as well as Sky News.

Useful contacts:
British Embassy, PO Box 94351, Riyadh 11693, tel: 966 1 488 0077
Royal Embassy of Saudi Arabia, 30 Charles Street, London W1, tel: 020 7917 3000
Saudi Arabia Information Centre, Cavendish House, 18 Cavendish Square, London W1, tel: 020 7629 8803
Country information:
www.us-saudi-business.org; www.saudinf.com

PERSONAL TAXATION

Salary differentials between Saudi Arabia and the UK are not as high as they were, but you could still expect to increase your UK gross salary by up to 25 per cent, on average. Salaries are highest in the more arduous, inland posts. These high salaries are accompanied by generous fringe benefits, which include furnished accommodation, ample home leave with air fares paid, a car, medical attention, and free or subsidised education for children in the case of more senior jobs. The level of remuneration reflects the rather arduous social and climatic conditions in the country, which women in particular find hard to take.

There is no personal income tax in Saudi Arabia, and no restriction on the amount of currency that may be taken into or out of the country.

UNITED ARAB EMIRATES

The economy

The United Arab Emirates (UAE) is a Federal sovereign state that consists of seven Emirates: Abu Dhabi, Dubai, Sharjah, Ajman, Umm Al Qaiwain, Fujairah and Ras Al Khaimah. This Federation was established on 2 December 1971 with six Emirates. The Emirate of Ras Al Khaimah joined the Federation on 10 February 1972. Abu Dhabi, which is the capital of the UAE, has invested in building up its infrastructure – roads, schools, housing, hospitals, hotels – and developing the harbour. Dubai is an important banking, business and tourism centre, and its harbour is one of the largest in the Middle East. The UAE's economy has grown considerably since the country was created and is one of the richest nations in the world. The country's massive oil wealth has been used to finance development projects, and the government is continuing its ongoing economic diversification drive to guard the economy against unpredictable oil exports earnings, attain substantial growth and ensure jobs for its citizens.

GDP growth held steady at 7.3 per cent in 2005 but is forecast to slide below 7 per cent in 2006. Inflation rose slowly from 2001 to 2005, where it stands at 5 per cent. The forecast for 2006 is that unemployment will improve to around 3.8 per cent. Like other Gulf states, the UAE maintains a strong budget surplus and current account balance, forecast at 28.6 per cent and 24.1 per cent respectively for 2005. Exports and imports are predicted to continue their steady progress in 2006, but the current account surplus ratio may be slightly reduced.

Working conditions

Work and residence permits are required by every expatriate in the UAE. The application must be accompanied by a medical certificate. Dubai will only issue permits if skills are not available locally.

Throughout the Gulf, you would be well advised to take a supply of passport photos with you, to help speed up the process of obtaining official documents. You should also check for last-minute changes to visa requirements, which are apt to be brought in with minimal notice. At present, passports bearing evidence of a visit or a proposed visit to Israel will still cause some problems, though this restriction may be lifted; you are advised to consult your nearest Regional Passport Office.

Useful information

Population and language: In addition to its native population, the UAE is inhabited by a fairly large expatriate community including Arab nationals as well as Asians, Iranians and Europeans. The official language of the UAE is Arabic according to the constitution of the country, while English is widely spoken, especially in business and trade.

Banking hours: 8.00 am to 1.00 pm Saturday–Wednesday, 8.00 am to 12.00 pm Thursday.

Business hours: 8.00 am to 1.00 pm, 3.00 or 4.00 pm to 6.00 or 7.00 pm Saturday–Wednesday.

Shopping hours: As business hours but open until 9.00 or 10.00 pm.

Electricity: 220 V, 50 Hz ac in Abu Dhabi, and 240 V, 50 Hz ac elsewhere.

Climate: The region is characterised by hot and humid summers, with temperatures over 100°F, the hottest months being July, August and September. Air conditioning and lightweight clothing are essential.

Driving: Check with the local police about driving licence regulations, you will be able to obtain a UAE licence on payment of a fee, presentation of a valid British licence and passing an eye test.

Health care: This is best funded privately, although the purchase of a health card means you gain admission to government hospitals.

Education: There are a number of British and international schools with three months' summer holiday, although many parents prefer to send their children to boarding school in the UK.

Alcohol: Except for the Emirate of Sharjah, available in hotel and club restaurants and bars, but non-hotel restaurants are not permitted to serve alcohol. Non-Muslims are usually able to buy alcohol for private consumption (except in Sharjah), but in the UAE it is necessary to obtain a liquor permit from the police.

Media: Daily English newspapers – *Gulf News*, *Khaleej Times*, *Emirates News* and *The Gulf Today*. Four TV channels. English language UAE Radio Dubai on 92 MHz FM. There are also various digital satellite channels providing a wide variety of news and entertainment, and several cinemas showing English films.

Useful contacts:
British Embassy, PO Box 248, Abu Dhabi, tel: 971 2610 1100; website: www.britain- uae.org/

Embassy of United Arab Emirates, 30 Princes Gate, London SW7, tel: 020 7581 1281

Expatriate contacts: Abu Dhabi Information Network Centre (Shell employees), tel: 971 2 263016, e-mail: nouland@emirates.et.ae. For children: pincokm@emirates.net.ae

Country information:
www.uae.org.ae; www.uaeinteract.com

PERSONAL FINANCE

Generally, salary levels in the UAE are similar to those in the UK, but there is no taxation (however, check UK tax regulations if employed by a UK-domiciled company), which boosts earning power. Also, there are many financial benefits, such as housing, schooling, car, trips home and health insurance, although these are not on such a grand scale as before. Four weeks leave per year is the norm, although people of bachelor status, especially if working in the offshore oil industry, can enjoy more frequent trips home. There are no currency transfer restrictions.

Property ownership

In certain areas of Dubai, Ras Al Khaimah and Ajman, expatriates and foreign nationals are now allowed to own freehold properties, with a facility of obtaining a residence visa, renewable every three years.

ABU DHABI

Abu Dhabi is the largest and richest of the seven Emirates that make up the UAE. The main population centre is Abu Dhabi city, which is on an island 10 miles (16 kilometres) long and which until relatively recently was little more than a fishing port. Abu Dhabi city and Emirate have developed very fast since the 1950s, when there was little more than a fort and barasti huts in Abu Dhabi town and small settlements dotted throughout the Emirate.

In 2005, Abu Dhabi city is thriving, with tall buildings, six-lane highways and very comfortable hotels, shopping centres and cinemas. Infrastructure is excellent and all amenities that can be found in the UK are available. Housemaids and houseboys are readily available, women are welcome in the workplace and schooling is good. There are many schools teaching in English and the school that most closely follows British standards, Al Khubairat, now provides secondary education.

Christian churches are also present in Abu Dhabi city, and services are conducted in the second city, Al Ain. Outdoor activities are readily available; there are a number of clubs, catering for all kinds of sports, together with beaches, and there are two grass golf courses and one sand course. Camping in the desert or mountains is a favourite activity for expatriates. Abu Dhabi is an ideal place to raise a family, as the weather is pleasant, except for the summer months.

As for the rest of the Emirate, towns and farms are being built at an alarming rate. In some places there are 'forests', so that it is difficult to recall that this used to be mainly a desert country. Al Ain is justifiably called the 'garden city'.

DUBAI

Standing at the crossroads of the world's busiest trading routes, the Emirate of Dubai has created a city that ranks as the commercial and tourist heart of the Gulf region. From its origin as a small trading and fishing community, Dubai is now a modem city with strong infrastructure, sophisticated telecommunications and highly developed transport facilities, and has established itself as a regional centre for trade, commerce and services. Dubai has all the amenities that Abu Dhabi offers but on a grander scale: more shopping centres and golf courses. Dubai is more of a commercial city than Abu Dhabi and relies on these activities as a source of income since, unlike Abu Dhabi, its oil reserves are minimal. Dubai's economy enjoys a competitive combination of cost, market and environmental advantages that create an ideal and attractive investment climate for local and expatriate businesses alike. In fact, these advantages not only rank Dubai as the Arabian Gulf's leading multi-purpose business centre and regional hub city, but they place it at the forefront of the globe's dynamic and emerging market economies. Given the right attitude, Dubai is an ideal expatriate posting. The Dubai authorities are very pro-business and, to this end, have established many 'free zones', where expatriates may set up businesses without needing the participation (and cost) of a UAE national shareholder or sponsor.

SHARJAH AND OTHER 'NORTHERN EMIRATES'

Living conditions in the other five Emirates are comfortable but without quite the sophistication of Abu Dhabi and Dubai. Nevertheless, British expatriates, especially those who enjoy quieter and more relaxed conditions, live very contentedly in these Emirates.

For further information, contact:

Russi Patel, Managing Partner, BDO Patel & Al Saleh, tel: + 9714 222 2869, fax: + 9714 227 0151, e-mail: bdopatel@emirates.net.ae, website: www.bdo.ae

Africa

The continent of Africa is the second largest in the world, after Asia. It has 54 independent countries and has a population of approximately 700 million. Africa offers to the enterprising individuals exciting ventures, including joining multinational companies in the emerging markets. Some of these are oil and gas, mining, government privatisation ventures, international trade, infrastructure and stock exchange opportunities, as well as work with the international aid agencies.

ALGERIA

The economy and political climate

The Democratic People's Republic of Algeria has been an independent state since July 1962; it was formerly a French colony. The head of state since 1979 has been a president. The President is elected for a period of five years by universal suffrage. Although there are a Prime Minister and Vice-Presidents, executive power is virtually exclusively in the hands of the President; he shares legislative power with the People's National Assembly that is likewise elected for five years by universal suffrage.

Economic prospects have improved as a result of increases in oil production, high dollar oil prices, and growing natural gas exports. Algeria is the world's second largest exporter of natural gas, and has the world's 5th largest natural gas reserve and 14th largest oil reserve. Algeria is running a substantial trade surplus and is building up large foreign exchange reserves. In 2005 the foreign trade surplus on current account is estimated at 21.6 per cent of GDP. The government is trying to diversify the economy by attracting foreign and domestic investment. Foreign investors can benefit from certain tax incentives. Algeria lacks a modern financial services sector, which could pose a problem for future investors, but currently there are some encouraging moves by the government to address this problem. High unemployment and the associated living standards are making improving poverty difficult.

GFP growth for 2005 is estimated at 6 per cent with a budget surplus equivalent to 11.3 per cent of GDP. The inflation rate for 2005 was about 3.7 per cent; similar rates are expected for 2006 in both macro-economic indices. Foreign debt represents just over 20 per cent of GDP, which is a comfortable level for a developing economy.

Working conditions

Visa regulations for Algeria change regularly, so always check with the Algerian Embassy in your home country. Single entry visas for one month can be obtained throughout the world, and further extensions can be obtained from the Department des Etrangers in Algiers. Visa applications must be typed; handwritten visa applications will not be accepted. Business visas require an invitation from the company being visited and a company letter stating the trip's purpose. Work visas require an employment authorisation hand-delivered by the Algerian Ministry of Labour.

Housing and medicine continue to be pressing problems in Algeria. Failing infrastructure and the continued influx of people from rural to urban areas have overtaxed both systems. According to the United Nations Development Programme, Algeria has one of the world's highest per housing unit occupancy rates, and government officials have publicly stated that the country has an immediate shortfall of 1.5 million housing units.

The government has established a minimum wage.

Useful information

Money: Local currency Algerian Dinar (DZD) = 100 centimes. The only bank to change travellers' cheques is the Banque Nationale d'Algerie. There is also the Banque Centrale d'Algérie. Full banking services are available in most major towns. Banking hours: 9:00 am to 3:00 pm Mondays to Thursdays. Some are closed for lunch. During Ramadan hours are shorter.

Language: The official language is Arabic, but French and Berber dialects are also used extensively.

Capital: Algiers.

Local time: One hour ahead of GMT.

Climate: Arid to semi-arid with mild and wet winters. Hot and dry summers along the coast. Drier with cold winters and hot summers on the high plateau. The sirocco is a hot, dusty and sand-laden wind which is especially common in summer.

Transport: There are good connections between Algiers and major European cities. Flights also connect to the Middle East as well as North African cities, but there are no direct flights to Australasia or the United States. There are also various ferry services between Algeria and France. There are long-distance buses which are normally comfortable. There are train services between Oran, Algiers, Constantine and Anaba, also to the south to Bécher and from Constantine to Touggourt. Roads are mostly in good condition and sufficient fuel should be carried when travelling in the Sahara.

Electricity: Electric power is 230 V running at 50 Hz.

Communications. The telephone system in the country is outdated and in desperate need of repair. It is possible to gain access to international phone lines through a number of satellite links. Internet access is available but limited, with only a few private service providers.

Health and health care: Hospitals and clinics in Algeria are available, but are not up to Western standards. Doctors and hospitals often expect immediate cash payment for services. Most medical practitioners speak French; English is not widely used.

Prescription medicines are not always readily available. Some pharmacies may at times be out of stock. In addition, the medicine may be presented under a different brand name and may contain a different dosage than in the United Kingdom. Please be aware that some newer medications may not yet be available in Algeria. It is usually easy to obtain over-the-counter products.

Emergency services are satisfactory, but response time is often unpredictable. One of the major public health concerns in Algeria is traffic-related accidents. Cases of tuberculosis are regularly reported, but do not reach endemic levels. Every summer, public health authorities report limited occurrences of water-borne diseases, such as typhoid. In addition, HIV/AIDS is a concern in the remote southern part of the country, especially in border towns.

Medical insurance is not always valid in Algeria and a medical insurance supplement with specific overseas coverage is recommended.

Useful contacts:

London Algerian Consulate, 6 Hyde Park Gate, London SW7 5EW, website: www.algerianconsulate.org.uk

British Embassy, 7th Floor, Hotel Hilton International, Palais des Expositions, Pins Maritimes, Palais des Expositions, El Mohammadia, Algiers, tel: (213) 21 23 00 68

PERSONAL TAXATION

Individuals with their fiscal domicile in Algeria are subject to tax on all their income from both domestic and foreign sources. The following are regarded as being domiciled in Algeria for tax purposes: people who own or have the right of enjoyment of a residence and tenants under tenancy agreements made for a minimum period of one year; people with their principal place of residence or centre of vital interest in Algeria; people carrying on professional activities in Algeria, whether as employees or not; state officials on secondment abroad who are not subject to taxation in the country of secondment.

Individuals who are fiscal domiciled outside Algeria are subject to tax on Algerian source income in the same way as individuals domiciled in Algeria.

Individuals who are both of Algerian and foreign nationality, irrespective of whether they are domiciled for tax purposes in Algerian or not, will be subject to tax on income or profits received in Algeria, where the taxation of such income is attributed to Algeria under a double tax agreement.

The tax rate varies from 0 per cent on income under DZD 60,000 to 40 per cent on income above DZD 3,240,000.

A final withholding tax of 24 per cent is withheld on income paid to people outside Algeria in respect of services provided in Algeria.

Capital gains realised from the disposal of real property (improved property at a rate of 10 per cent, or unimproved at a rate of 15 per cent) or rights in real property outside the framework of a professional activity, are subject to the individual total income tax.

People subject to the total income tax must file a return of total income on a specially provided form before 1 April of each year with the inspector of taxes.

Algeria has double tax agreements with Belgium, Canada, France, Indonesia, Italy, Romania, South Africa, Syria and Turkey.

ANGOLA

The economy and political climate

Angola became fully independent from Portugal on 11 November 1975, having been an overseas province since 1951. Executive power is vested in the President, who is assisted by an appointed Council of Ministers.

Angola has a fast-growing economy largely due to a major oil boom, but it ranks in the bottom 10 of almost every socio-economic indicator. Aside from the oil sector and diamonds, it is recovering from 27 years of nearly continuous warfare, corruption and economic mismanagement. Despite abundant natural resources and rising per capita GDP, Angola was ranked 166 out of 177 countries on the UNDP's Human Development Index. Subsistence agriculture sustains two-thirds of the population. Diamonds make up most of Angola's remaining exports. The oil and fishing industries are the only sectors that are attractive to foreign investors. Poverty remains widespread and was indicated at 65 per cent and even higher in the rural areas. The government has started to introduce measures to attract more foreign investment after the end of decades of civil war. There are huge tax savings for foreign investors.

In 2005 Angola is estimated to have achieved real GDP growth of 14.1 per cent after 11.2 per cent in 2004. However, growth is forecast for 2006 at about 9 per cent. The growth performance is the more impressive against the background of hyper-inflation which raged up to 2004 and the government deserves credit for having brought consumer price inflation down from 153 per cent in 2001 to 45.3 per cent in 2004 and now to 30 per cent at the end of 2005 where it is forecast to remain through 2006. The foreign trade surplus on current account fell back to 4.7 per cent in 2005 where it is expected to stabilise for 2006. After some years of budget deficits, the government also achieved a budget surplus in 2005 at 3.7 per cent of GDP on which further improvement is forecast for 2006.

Working conditions

Visas are required by all nationalities and an International Certificate of Vaccination is required, showing inoculations against yellow fever and cholera. Failure to do so may result in involuntary vaccinations and/or fines. Visa applications made at embassies abroad have to be referred to Luanda and enough time for processing should be allowed. An HIV test is required for all foreigners applying for work visas and resident permits.

The capital Luanda is a large and over-populated city. A variety of houses and apartments can be rented within the city itself. Luanda is a family post. Educational facilities are good, in English, French and Portuguese. Security in Luanda is improving, although extra precautions should be taken if out past midnight. Major incidences are harassment by teenage boys (begging, purse snatching) and being stopped by traffic police to verify documents. Security in the provinces varies.

The government continues to set, control, or manipulate wage rates and prices in almost all sectors of the economy.

Useful information

Money: The legal tender of Angola is the kwanza (AOK), which is divided into 100 leweis. Full banking services are available in most major towns. Banking hours: 8.30 am to 12.30 pm and 2.00–6.00 pm (Monday to Friday). Some banks are open from 8:30 am to 12:30 pm on a Saturday. The banks are the Banco Nacional de Angola, BNA (central bank), Banco de Poupança e Crédito, BPC (commercial bank), Banco de Comércio e Indústria, BCI (development bank), Banco de Fomento e Exterior, Banco Espírito Santo (Portuguese), Banco Português do Atlantico and Banco Totta e Açores, SA (Portuguese).

Local time: One hour ahead of GMT.

Language: Portuguese is the official language of Angola, but African indigenous dialects are also in common use.

Capital: Luanda.

Climate: The country's climate is tropical, locally tempered by altitude. Semi-arid in the south and along the coast to Luanda, the north has a cool and dry season in May to October and a hot and rainy season in November to April.

Transport: There are flights from South Africa (Johannesburg) to Angola. The major international harbours are at Lobito, Luanda and Namibe. There is an international airport (Aeroporto Internacional 4 de Fevreiro) at Luanda City. The government-owned rail network consists of more than 3,000 km of track and is under repair, since the damage caused by the civil war. Of more than 8,000 km of main roads, 2,000 are paved. The major roads are generally in good condition and there are numerous checkpoints. Taxis are difficult to find and are expensive. There are bus services throughout the country, but the services are poor and are normally very crowded.

Electricity: 220 V running at 50 Hz.

Communications: The telephone network is mainly limited to government and business use. There is only one internet service provider. There are a number of licensed mobile phone operators.

Health and health care: Adequate medical facilities are rare except in Luanda, where there are some good private clinics that usually have a 24-hour service provided by a general practice physician and with specialists on call. The US Embassy in Luanda can provide a list of such facilities. Routine operations such as appendectomies can be performed. However, many types of medicine are not readily available, travellers are urged to carry with them properly labelled supplies of any medicines they routinely require.

There is currently an outbreak of Marburg haemorrhagic fever, a severe and often fatal disease, in Uige province, Angola.

Useful contacts:

Embassy of the Republic of Angola, 98 Park Lane, London, W1Y 3TA, tel: + (44) 207 495 1752

British Embassy, Rua Diogo Cao 4, Caixa Postal 1244, Luanda, tel: (244) (222) 334582

PERSONAL TAXATION

Individuals in Angola are subject only to state taxes. Four direct taxes are levied at state level: a business income tax ('imposto industrial') on income from business activities of both companies and individuals; an earned income tax ('imposto sobre os rendimentos do trabalho') on Angolan-source income from dependent and independent personal services; an investment income tax ('imposto sobre a aplicação de capitais') on dividend, interest and royalty payments; and an urban real estate (income) tax ('imposto predial urbano') on actual or deemed income from urban immovable property.

The term 'Angolan-source income' comprises salaries and wages paid by or on behalf of an Angolan-based employer and professional fees paid by or on behalf of an Angolan-based entity. The term 'listed professional services' includes only independent scientific, artistic or technical activities.

A non-resident individual is liable for income tax on Angolan-source income if he or she renders dependent or independent personal services that are paid directly or indirectly by an Angolan-based entity (ie if the payer is a resident or a permanent establishment in Angola of a non-resident).

Employment income derived by non-residents is subject to tax at a rate between 0 and 15 per cent. This is deducted on a monthly basis and is a final tax and therefore no tax returns have to be submitted.

Fees derived by non-resident professionals are generally subject to a final withholding tax of 15 per cent.

An Angolan-based contractor must withhold tax at a final rate of 15 per cent of any remuneration paid to a resident or non-resident individual entertainer, sportsman, lecturer, scientist or technician for activities carried out in Angola.

BOTSWANA

The economy and political climate

The Republic of Botswana has been independent since 1966. The political structure consists of a uni-cameral legislature (National Assembly) elected every five years by universal adult suffrage. A House of Chiefs forms part of the system and its approval is needed for some measures. However, they cannot veto legislation. The National Assembly elects a President who holds executive power and appoints a Cabinet responsible to the Assembly.

Botswana's economy is one of the healthiest in Africa and the country has one of the world's highest growth rates, largely attributed to abundant diamond resources. Botswana is the world's biggest diamond producer. Diamond mining accounts for one-third of GDP, which grew about 3.7 per cent in 2005, and 70 per cent of export earnings. It is a peaceful nation and has high fiscal disciplines as well as sound management. The government recognises that HIV/AIDS will continue to affect the economy and is providing leadership and programmes to combat the epidemic, including free anti-retroviral treatment and a nationwide Prevention of Mother-to-Child Transmission programme.

The country's main exports are diamonds, vehicles, nickel, copper and meat. For 2005, the foreign trade surplus on current account is estimated to be 9.1 per cent of GDP.

With its proven record of good economic governance, Botswana was ranked as Africa's least corrupt country by Transparency International in 2004, ahead of many European and Asian countries. The World Economic Forum rates Botswana as one of the two most economically competitive nations in Africa. In November 2005, Standard & Poor's once again assigned Botswana an 'A' grade credit rating. This ranks Botswana as by far the best credit risk in Africa and puts it on a par with or above many countries in central Europe, East Asia and Latin America. Inflation rose to about 8.4 per cent in 2005 but is expected to decline to perhaps 7 per cent in 2006, close to the 2004 level. The government maintains a tight hold on public sector spending and a deficit at 2.2 per cent is forecast for 2005, falling to 1.5 per cent in 2006.

Working conditions

All nationals except those from the Commonwealth countries require visas. Stay permits issued at the border are valid for 30 days, but US citizens are able to stay for 90 days without a visa. Anyone wishing to stay for more than 90 days should contact the Immigration and Passport Control Officer, PO Box 942, Gaborone.

Useful information

Money: Local currency 1 Pula = 100 Thebe. Full banking services are available in most major towns. Banking hours: Monday, Tuesday, Thursday and Friday: 9.00 am to 2.30 pm, Wednesday from 8.15 am to 12.00 pm. The banks are the Bank of Botswana, Standard Bank of Botswana Ltd and Bank of Credit and Commerce (Botswana) Limited.

Local time: Botswana is two hours ahead of GMT.

Language: The official and commercial language is English. The other main language used is Setswana.

Capital: Gaborone.

Climate: Most of the country has a subtropical climate, with cooler temperatures prevailing in the higher regions. Extreme temperatures can be experienced in the desert regions of the Kalahari.

Transport: Internal flights are available between Gaborone, Francistown and Maun, and international flights from South Africa. Botswana has an extensive and fairly good railway service between Francistown, Gaborone and Lobatse. Bus and minibus services operate mainly in the eastern part of the country, but the service is not so good. Luxury Inter City Transport covering Southern Africa operates from Intercape Mainliner. Travelling by car in Botswana is safe and all major international car rental companies are represented. Roads are unpaved in the rural areas, where the government is trying to protect indigenous wildlife. Four-wheel drive vehicles are recommended when travelling off road.

Electricity: Electric power is 230V at 50 Hz.

Communications: The telephone system has been characterised by some officials as 'sparse'. There is a small system of open-wire lines as well as a few radiotelephone communication stations. There are two international exchanges. Several internet cafes are also available.

Health and health care: Medical facilities in Gaborone are adequate, but in other areas they are limited. Well-equipped emergency rooms and trained physicians are available in the capital, but services are rudimentary elsewhere. Professional private emergency rescue services operate air and ground ambulances throughout the country, but care is rendered only after a patient's ability to pay is established. Response times are often slow in less populated areas. Malaria is prevalent only in the north of the country, particularly around the Chobe and Okavango National Parks. Malaria prophylaxis is not required in Gaborone but is suggested for travel to the north. For advanced care Americans often choose to travel to South Africa. Most prescription drugs are available in Gaborone. The problem of HIV/AIDS in Botswana is as serious as that experienced by its neighbours. The infection rate is one of the world's highest.

Useful contacts:

British High Commission, Plot 1079–1084, Main Mall, Gaborone, Postal address: Private Bag 0023, Gaborone, tel: (267) 395 2841, e-mail: bhc@botsnet.bw

Botswana High Commission, 6 Stratford Place, London W1C 1AY, tel: +(44) 207 499 0031, website: www.botswana.embassy-homepage.com

Botswana Tourist Board, Southern Skies Marketing, Index House, St George's Lane, Ascot, Berkshire SL5 7EU, tel: (44) 1344 636430, e-mail: southskies@aol.com, website: www.southern-skies.co.uk

PERSONAL TAXATION

Individuals resident in Botswana are liable for taxation on their earnings generated from a source or deemed source within Botswana. Non-resident individuals in receipt of income arising in Botswana are generally taxed on the same basis as residents. Withholding taxes apply to certain payments made to non-residents. An individual is classed as a resident of Botswana when his or her permanent place of abode is in Botswana; he or she is physically present in Botswana for not less than 183 days in any tax year, whether or not he or she maintains a place of abode in Botswana; he or she maintains a place of abode and is physically present in Botswana for not less than 183 days in any tax year. In this connection, a taxpayer will be deemed to be physically present in any part of that period notwithstanding that he or she is temporarily absent for business, recreation or similar purposes; or he or she is physically present in Botswana for any period of time in any tax year and such period is continuous with a period of physical presence in the immediately preceding or immediately succeeding tax year, provided he or she is treated as resident for such preceding or succeeding tax year.

Foreign employment income is normally not taxable in Botswana.

The tax year is from 1 July to 30 June. There are different tax rates for residents and non-residents, but the maximum tax rate is 25 per cent in both cases. Capital transfer tax is payable upon disposal by way of inheritance, donations or other gratuitous disposal of property; the sliding scale of taxation varies from 2 to 5 per cent.

Botswana has signed double tax agreements with Barbados, Namibia, Russia, Seychelles, Zimbabwe, the UK, France, Sweden, Mauritius and South Africa. Lower withholding tax rates apply in respect of interest, dividends, royalties and technical fees, in terms of the various DTAs signed.

CAPE VERDE

The economy and political climate

The Islands of Cape Verde obtained their independence in 1975 and one of Cape Verde's strengths lies in its political and social stability. There have never been any political or religious conflicts. The expatriate population of Cape Verde is greater than its domestic one. Cape Verde has few natural resources and suffers from poor rainfall and limited fresh water. The economy is service-oriented, with commerce, transport, tourism and public services accounting for more than 70 per cent of GDP. Economic reform by the government is aiming to develop the private sector. Cape Verde's strategic location at the crossroads of mid-Atlantic air and sea-lanes has been enhanced by significant improvements at Mindelo's harbour (Porto Grande) and at Sal's international airport. Ship repair facilities at Mindelo were opened in 1983, and the harbours at Mindelo and Praia were recently renovated.

The economy has grown steadily for the past five years with GDP real growth ranging from 6.2 per cent (2003) to 4.5 per cent (2004) and is predicted to have risen to 6 per cent in 2005. Annual inflation is low and has been below 2 per cent since 2001. The public sector budget deficit has remained below 10 per cent of GDP since 2002 and is estimated to be at 9.4 per cent for 2005. Cap Verde's foreign trade deficit is rising steadily each year in absolute terms but at a slower rate than the economy. As a result, the current account deficit ratio to GDP was brought down from 14.6 per cent in 2001 to 7.9 per cent in 2004. However, the deficit ratio is predicted to have risen to 9.4 per cent in 2005.

Working conditions

All visitors to Cape Verde require a visa. Visa approval can take several days and Cape Verde issues two types of tourist visas: a single-entry visa valid for up to 90 days or a multiple-entry visa valid for one year. There is no private-sector minimum wage, but most private wages are linked to those of equivalent civil servants.

Useful information

Money: The local currency is the Cape Verde escudo (CVE) = 100 centavos. Banking hours: Monday to Friday, 8.00 am to 2.00 pm.

The banks are the Banco de Cabo Verde (Central Bank), Banco Comercial do Atlântico (BCA), Caixa Económica de Cabo Verde, Banco Interatlântico and Banco Totta & Açores.

Local time: One hour behind GMT.

Language: Portuguese and Crioulo.

Capital: Praia.

Climate: Temperate with warm, dry summers and cool winters.

Communications: Effective telephone system with one internet service provider.

Transport: Flying is the best option for getting to and from Cape Verde, with regular flights that connect Sal island with Atlanta, Boston, Lisbon, Paris, Amsterdam, Munich, Zurich, Bergamo, Johannesburg, Las Palmas and Madrid. There is a network of expensive domestic flights between the islands. Taxis are very expensive and it is best to travel around the islands by bus or truck.

Electricity: Electric power is 220V at 50 Hz.

Health and health care: Medical facilities in Cape Verde are limited, and some medicines are in short supply or unavailable. There are hospitals in Praia and Mindelo, with smaller medical facilities in other places. The islands of Brava and Santo Antao no longer have functioning airports so air evacuation in the event of a medical emergency is nearly impossible from these two islands. Brava has a limited inter-island ferry service. Malaria is extremely rare in Cape Verde; however, there have been a small number of malaria fatalities in 2005, all on the island of Santiago. In 2004 there was a cholera scare, but public health campaigns and other preventive factors averted an outbreak.

Useful contacts:

Cape Verde Honorary Consul, 18–20 Stanley Street, Liverpool L1 6AF, tel: 0151 236 0206

British Honorary Consul, Shell Cabo Verde Sarl, Av Amilcar Cabral CP4, Sao Vincente, tel: (238) 232 2830

KENYA

The economy and political climate

Kenya is a republic, the country having become independent on 12 December 1963, after some 60 years of British rule. The government is headed by the President, who is elected by universal suffrage for a five-year term of office.

Kenya is best known for its tea and coffee, which form the backbone of the economy; it is the world's third largest tea exporter. Other crops include wheat, sugar, sisal, cotton, fruit and vegetables. Tourism is the most important source of foreign exchange, having overtaken coffee in 1988 as the main foreign exchange earner.

Eighty per cent of the population derive their livelihood from agriculture, which accounts for 52 per cent of exports. Major export commodities include cut flowers, fluorspar, gemstones, gold, petroleum, pyrethrum, salt, soda ash, sodium carbonate, sugar, tea and coffee.

There are few mineral resources, but the government is encouraging exploration. The manufacturing sector is being expanded – it includes food processing, canning, chemicals, drink, tobacco, car assembly, paper and printing, metal products, textiles, clothing, footwear and cement. An oil pipeline links the Mombasa refinery with Nairobi. Kenya also has an active chemicals industry, as well as being one of the larger lubricants markets in the East Africa region.

The government welcomes foreign investment, but it is anxious to see that as much commerce as possible is handled by indigenous Kenyans. As part of the ongoing economic reforms, the government has divested itself of many enterprises, some of which have been sold to foreign investors, who consider the Kenyan atmosphere a favourable one.

Economic development is based on national planning, with emphasis on agriculture and manufacturing and on encouraging export and labour-intensive industries.

Britain and Germany are the principal trading partners and the UK a major provider of external aid, particularly in sending experts, teachers and technical advisers.

There are serious balance of payments problems and the foreign trade deficit, estimated to be in excess of US$1 billion for 2005, is increasing rapidly and faster than economic growth, which measured about 5 per cent in 2005 and is forecast to continue at the same level in 2006. Therefore, the former surplus on current account has moved into deficit with a negative ratio to GDP estimated at 6.5 per cent for 2005. Annual inflation was in single digits up to 2004 but was running at 10.5 per cent in 2005, although it is expected to fall back in 2006. Kenya's foreign debt is high at 41.8 per cent of GDP but, fortunately, a large proportion is concessional debt. However, interest payments on domestic debt are a serious drain on government revenue, although the public sector budget deficit ratio was contained at some 3.4 per cent in 2005. Unemployment and under-employment have remained serious problems, particularly among the young. These are exacerbated by Kenya's rapid population growth.

The government has prioritised combating corruption by way of legislation and has taken steps towards strengthening the judiciary.

Nairobi continues to be the primary communication and financial hub of East Africa. It enjoys the region's best transport linkages, communications infrastructure and trained personnel, although these advantages are less prominent than in past years. A wide range of foreign firms maintain regional branch or representative offices in the city.

Working conditions

A valid passport is needed, but most Commonwealth citizens do not need a visa. Exceptions are Australian, New Zealand, Sri Lankan, Indian, Afghani, Somali, Iranian, Lebanese, Iraqi, Syrian, Libyan, Malian, Sudanese, Yemeni, Cameroon, Pakistani, North Korean, Armenian, Georgian, Tajikistani, Azerbaijani, Senegalese and Nigerian citizens and British passport holders subject to control under the Immigration Act of 1971. Stateless people do not need a visa. Many other nationalities qualify for a visa-free three-month stay. Entry permits vary according to the type of employment. Applicants must show that they have adequate financial resources and that their activities will benefit the country. It is advisable to check immigration regulations with the authorities, as these are liable to change. Evidence of yellow fever immunisation may be requested.

The employer must obtain a work permit from the Principal Immigration Officer (PIO) before the employee leaves Britain. The PIO's permission is needed for dependants to work. Work permits for partners, unless they are professionally qualified, are hard to obtain. Certain limitations exist on the number of expatriate professionals working in Kenya, ie lawyers and doctors. The local labour force is split into the formal and the informal sectors. Bonuses and certain allowances are normally included in salary packages.

The working week is normally 40 working hours, but does not exceed 120 hours in a two-weekly period. Employees are entitled to a minimum of 21 working days leave each year. There are 11 public holidays, both religious and official.

Social security contributions to the National Social Security Fund are payable by both employer and employee at the rate of 5 per cent of salary.

The French, Germans and Swedes offer community venture education with their own schools in Nairobi. There are three good schools running US curricula and several offering the British curriculum and 'common entrance' curricula for the UK public (private) schools.

Useful information

Banking hours: 9.00 am to 2.00 pm (4.30 pm in major cities) Monday–Friday, 9.00 am to 1.00 pm on certain Saturdays. The airport banks are open until midnight. The banks are the Kenya Commercial Bank, National Bank of Kenya, Barclays Bank of Kenya, Commercial Bank of Africa, Cooperative Bank of Kenya and Standard Chartered Bank Kenya.

Shopping hours: Main stores 8.00 am to 5.00 or 6.00 pm, but many have late shopping some nights of the week and some are open on Sunday.

Electricity: 240 V, 50 Hz ac in most centres and the supply is reliable. Lamps are mainly bayonet fitting; plugs are two-pin round and three-pin flat types. Adaptors are useful when travelling.

Local time: Kenya is three hours ahead of GMT.

Language: English and Kiswahili are the official languages of Kenya. Many different tribal languages are also widely spoken.

Capital: Nairobi.

Climate: Coastal areas tropical, lowlands hot and dry, highlands cooler with four seasons. Mount Kenya is perpetually snow-capped.

Local currency: 1 Kenyan pound = 20 Kenyan shillings; 1 Kenyan shilling = 100 cents.

Driving: Roads in the cities are of a fairly high standard. Driving is on the left. There is an AA of Kenya with headquarters in Nairobi. The AA and RAC have reciprocal arrangements with the Kenyan AA. Distances are given in kilometres, and petrol sold in litres. A valid British or international licence, which should be endorsed at a police station on arrival, is accepted for up to 90 days, thereafter exchanged for a Kenyan one – no test is imposed.

Outside the cities, roads are poor. It may be necessary to have a 4 × 4 type vehicle there. Many expatriates have two cars, though cars are very expensive. If you have to buy your own it is best to go for a cheaper model; otherwise they are difficult to re-sell when you leave the country.

Transport: International and national air services operate from Nairobi and Moi (Mombasa) International Airports. The main railway line runs from Mombasa to Nairobi, Kisumu and Malaba, the overnight Nairobi–Mombasa service offers first- and second-class options and includes sleeping compartments. Local rail and bus travel are usually avoided. State-controlled taxis and international car hire companies are found at both airports. Most reputable car hire firms are members of the AA. A private car is essential for people staying any length of time and should be tough enough to withstand difficult conditions. Servicing facilities are adequate in Nairobi, but if you are taking your own car it is advisable to contact the manufacturer beforehand about spare parts, etc.

Health: Kenya is, in general, a healthy place in which to live, apart from the risk of AIDS, which is now prevalent in many parts of Africa and is affecting both the male and female population. It is preferable to seek medical treatment only after consultation with the British High Commission. There are the usual tropical hazards, particularly along the coast. Local diseases include cholera, hepatitis A, malaria, Rift Valley Fever, schistosomiasis, tuberculosis, typhoid fever and yellow fever (regional). Risk assessments are advised. Effective personal protection, such as the use of N,N-diethylmeta-toluamide (DEET) insect repellents against mosquitoes is strongly recommended. The anti-malaria drug, chloroquine, has been banned in Kenya and travellers should use mefliam or doxycycline.

Health care: Medical standards are high, particularly for private facilities in Nairobi. The National Hospital in Nairobi is managed, administered and staffed at senior levels by British staff. Doctors' fees are expensive, however, as are medicines, so bring out what you need. Hospital fees can be reduced through the National Insurance fund but, where insurance is not provided in their contract, many expatriates subscribe to a locally available scheme. If you need medical care, be aware that medical providers may not accept payment through your insurance company and you will have to pay up front.

There is a network of district hospitals, clinics and dispensaries, and also mission hospitals. Very remote areas are served by a flying doctor service, which requires a small annual subscription. There are frequent outbreaks of cholera, and malaria is endemic in Kenya outside Nairobi. Travellers who become ill with a fever or flu-like illness while travelling in a malaria-risk area and up to one year after returning home should seek prompt medical attention and tell the physician their travel history and what anti-malarials they have been taking.

Education: Most expatriate parents send their children to private primary schools, but many of these have long waiting lists. There is generally no problem about placing children in nursery schools and kindergartens. The Nairobi International School takes in children for both primary and secondary schooling, though fees are high. It follows the US curriculum but most private schools are geared to that of Britain. Hillcrest Secondary School, Nairobi, is highly regarded (website: http://www.hillcrest.ac.ke). There are schools in Mombasa and most other centres; some schools take boarders. There are a number of convent schools. Nairobi University, the Strathmore College of Arts and the Kenya Polytechnic admit students of all nationalities.

Media: The main English-language newspapers are the *Standard*, *Daily Nation* and *Kenya Times*; there are several weeklies and monthlies and most UK papers can be bought in Nairobi and Mombasa. There is one national radio station in Nairobi with provincial sub-stations in Mombasa, Kisumu and Mount Kenya. There are three TV stations and one cable station.

Useful contacts:
British High Commission, Upper Hill Road, Nairobi, PO Box 30465, tel: 254 020 2844 000, e-mail: bhcinfo@iconnect.co.ke
Kenyan High Commission, 45 Portland Place, London W1, tel: 020 7636 2371
Ministry of Tourism, Utalii House, off Uhuru Highway, PO Box 30027, Nairobi, or the Kenya Tourist Office, 25 Brook's Mews, London W1Y 1LF
Surekha Kukadia, Immigration Adviser, BDO Stoy Hayward, 8 Baker Street, London W1U 3LL, tel: 020 7893 2430, e-mail: sue.kukadia@bdo.co.uk

PERSONAL TAXATION

A resident is liable to tax on worldwide employment income. A non-resident is taxable on income that is deemed to have accrued in or is derived from Kenya. The individual tax year runs from 1 January to 31 December. Income tax is charged on total income (including benefits in kind) and ranges from 10 to 30 per cent.

A person will be classified as a resident if he or she is present in Kenya for a period or periods amounting in aggregate to 183 days or more in that year of income; or is present in Kenya in that year and the preceding two years for periods averaging more than 122 days in each year of income; or has a permanent home in Kenya and is present for any period. Most types of income remitted to non-residents are subject to special withholding tax rates charged on the gross amount received. There are special provisions when working at the regional office of a non-resident employer. If certain conditions are met, then only two-thirds of their employment income is liable to Kenyan tax.

Most employers provide housing and make allowances for children's education, cars, etc; these are fully taxable.

Personal allowances are given for single and married people, but there are no allowances for children.

International staff are required to make payments of their quarterly instalments by 20 April, 20 June, 20 September and 20 December. The instalments are based on the current or prior year's tax.

The non-resident withholding tax rate on dividends is 10 per cent, and 15 per cent in respect of interest. Capital gains tax has been suspended and there are no death duties.

Kenya has double tax treaties in force with Canada, Denmark, Germany, India, Norway, Sweden, the UK and Zambia.

MOROCCO

The economy and political climate

The Kingdom of Morocco has a constitution approved by the referendum of 10 March 1972. It provides for a constitutional monarchy with the King (at present Mohammed VI) as head of state.

Morocco's oil industry is an important sub-sector in the economy. It has an active chemicals industry and one of the largest lubricants industries. The agriculture, fishing and forestry sectors employ over a third of the working population. The government continues to implement its privatisation programme. The main exports are citrus fruit, energy, finished products, phosphates, phosphoric acid and raw materials. The main imports are beverages, energy, intermediate goods, raw materials and tobacco.

In June 2004, the United States and Morocco signed a bilateral Free Trade Agreement (FTA), ratified by the US Congress in July 2004 and signed by President Bush in August 2004. The Moroccan government ratified the FTA in January 2005, and King Mohammed signed the agreement in June 2005. The FTA provides new trade and investment opportunities for both countries and will encourage economic reforms and liberalisation already under way.

Economic growth stagnated in 2005 but is forecast to return to the 2003 level of 5.3 per cent in 2006. As a result the public sector budget deficit as a ratio of GDP rose to 5.9 per cent in 2005. However, inflation was held at 2 per cent in 2005, although it is forecast to rise slightly in 2006. The deficit on the foreign trade current account rose to 8.3 per cent in 2005 and is forecast to rise a little faster in 2006.

Working conditions

Nationals from Belgium, The Netherlands, Luxembourg and South Africa require visas; most other nationalities do not and are issued on arrival with a permit valid for a 90-day stay. The working week was reduced from 48 to 44 hours in June 2004. Morocco has one minimum wage for the industrial, trade and liberal professions sectors and another for the agricultural sector. Foreign workers in Morocco have to obtain permission from the Ministry of Employment and the police will issue a residence permit.

Useful information

Money: The local currency is the Dirham (DH) = 100 centimes. Major credit cards are widely accepted, as are travellers' cheques. Banking hours: Monday to Friday, 9.00 am to 1.00 pm. The banks are the Bank of Morocco, Algemene Bank Marokko, Banque Marocaine du Commerce Extérieur, Banque Nationale pour le

Développement Economique and Société Marocaine de Dépôt et de Crédit.

Local time: The same as GMT.

Language: The official language is Arabic but a large proportion of the population speaks Berber. Spanish is spoken extensively in the north of the country and French throughout the remainder of the country.

Capital: Rabat.

Communications: The telephone system in the country can be classified as modern and internet cafes can be found.

Climate: Mediterranean, becoming more extreme in the interior.

Transport: There are a number of international flights between Morocco and Europe. Domestic air travel provides regular, inexpensive flights to all major towns. The railway system is mostly concentrated in the north, linking major towns. The service is modern, fast and comfortable. The bus service also runs through the country, linking major towns. The ferry service runs daily between Algeciras/Tarifa to Ceuta/Tangier. All main roads in the north and north-west are in good condition, but deteriorate when crossing the Atlas Mountains into the interior.

Electricity. Electric power is 127V/220V (conversion to 220V underway) at 50 Hz.

Health and health care: Adequate medical care is available in Morocco's largest cities, particularly in Rabat and Casablanca, although not all facilities meet high-quality standards. Specialised care or treatment may not be available. Medical facilities are adequate for non-emergency matters, particularly in the urban areas, but most medical staff will have limited or no English. Most ordinary prescription and over-the-counter medicines are widely available. However, specialised prescriptions may be difficult to fill and the availability of all medicines in rural areas is unreliable. Emergency and specialised care outside the major cities is far below UK standards, and in many instances may not be available at all. Travellers planning to drive in the mountains and other remote areas may wish to carry a medical kit and a Moroccan phone card for emergencies. In the event of car accidents involving injuries, immediate ambulance service is usually not available. The police emergency services telephone number is 190.

Useful contacts:

Morrocan High Commission, 49 Queen's Gate Gardens, London SW7 5NE, tel: +(44) 171 581 5001

British Embassy, 17 Boulevard de la Tour Hassan, (BP 45), Rabat, tel: +212 (37) 238600

PERSONAL TAXATION

Individuals will be subject in Morocco to a general income tax on their total income, ie income from both Moroccan and foreign sources.

The general income tax applies to the following categories of income: business income, wages and salaries, agricultural income, income from rent (called land rent income in the new law) and income from movable capital.

Non-resident individuals will be subject in Morocco to the general income tax on total income which they derive from Moroccan sources. Finance Law 2005, however, also allows the taxation of income in respect of which the taxation right has been granted to Morocco under a tax treaty. This measure extends the scope of the tax (in treaty situations) to income that is normally outside of the scope of the tax provided that Morocco may tax such income under a tax treaty.

Individuals habitually resident in Morocco will be subject to the general income tax on total income from Moroccan and foreign sources.

The law defines habitual residence as follows: individuals will be regarded as having their habitual residence in Morocco when they have their permanent home there, their centre of economic interests is located there, or they reside in Morocco for any period or periods exceeding 183 days in any period of 365 days.

Non-residents will generally be subject to tax on their total income from Moroccan sources, irrespective of the length of their temporary stay in Morocco.

The tax is charged at progressive rates from 0 to 44 per cent on total income. The amount of foreign tax paid abroad on foreign income may be offset against the general income tax due in Morocco.

Special provisions relating to royalties, commission fees derived by non-residents of Morocco paid in consideration of work carried out or services rendered for individuals or legal entities domiciled or carrying on activities in Morocco, where such work is or services are not connected to an establishment in Morocco belonging to the non-resident individual in question, will be regarded as business income and as such subject to the general income tax. Ten per cent of such income will be withheld at source as a final tax.

MOZAMBIQUE

The economy and political climate

Mozambique became fully independent on 25 June 1975, having been an overseas province of Portugal since 1951. Executive power is vested in the President assisted by an appointed Cabinet headed by the Prime Minister.

Mozambique is one of Africa's success stories and is making economic progress, but is still dependent on foreign aid. In 2004 real GDP grew by 7.2 per cent and similar growth rates are estimated for 2005 and forecast for 2006. A major privatisation programme involving the banking and state manufacturing sectors are under way. The country has an agriculture-based economy and the inflation rate is continuing to decline from a peak of 16.8 per cent in 2002 to 8 per cent for 2005. The ratio of public sector budget deficits to GDP has declined steadily from 21.4 per cent in 2001 to 15 per cent in 2005.

Traditional Mozambican exports include cashews, shrimp, fish, copra, sugar, cotton, tea and citrus and exotic fruit. Most of these industries are being rehabilitated. In addition, Mozambique is less dependent upon imports for basic food and manufactured goods, as the result of steady increases in local production. Despite the rate of economic growth, 50 per cent of the population still lives in absolute poverty. Nevertheless, as a ratio of GDP the foreign trade deficit on current account declined from 26.1 per cent to an estimated 14 per cent at the end of 2005.

During their summit in Scotland in July 2005, the G8 nations agreed to significant multilateral debt relief for the world's least developed nations. On 21 December 2005 the IMF formalised the complete cancellation of all Mozambican IMF debt contracted prior to 1 January 2005.

Working conditions

Visas are required by all nationals and are valid for one month, but can be extended in Maputo. As from December 2004 all visas must be obtained prior to departure to Mozambique, as no visas will be issued on arrival. South Africans are exempt from obtaining a visa.

Social security contributions are payable monthly by employers and employees to the National Social Security Institute. Social security contributions are calculated on monthly earnings of employees (excluding subsidies) with no upper limit. The rates of contribution are 4 per cent for employers and 3 per cent for employees. Employers must withhold the contribution due by their employees.

Useful information

Money: The local currency is the Metical (MZM) = 100 centqavos. Major credit cards are accepted, as are travellers' cheques. Banking hours: Monday to Friday, 7.30–11.15 am and 3.00–4.30 pm. The banks are the Banco de Moçambique (the central bank), Grupo BIM (Mozambique's international and commercial banking group), Banco Comercial de Investimentos, SARL (commercial investment bank), Banco de Desenvolvimento e Comércio (development and trade bank), Banco Standard Totta de Moçambique, SARL, African Bank Corporation (BNP Nedbank), Banco Mundial (Branch of the World Bank) and Equator Bank Ltd.

Local time: Namibia is two hours ahead of GMT.

Language: Portuguese is the official language of Mozambique, but several indigenous dialects are widely spoken.

Capital: Maputo.

Climate: Tropical to subtropical with a wet season (November to March) and a dry season (April to October).

Communications: The telephone system in the country has been characterised as fair but not generally available. There are a number of internet service providers.

Transport: There are international flights to Europe and South Africa. A national airline supplies domestic flights connecting the major towns. There is a rail link between Beira and Tete and from Mozambique and Macala, via Monapo to Numpula and Lichinga. A train service also operates to Zimbabwe but can be overcrowded. There are regular bus services covering most major towns. Main roads are tarred but gravel roads may require a four-wheel drive vehicle. There are a few car hire companies in Maputo.

Electricity: Electric power is 220 V at 50 Hz.

Health and health care: Medical facilities are rudimentary, and most medical providers do not speak English. Medicines are not always available. There are both public and private medical facilities in the city of Maputo. All health care institutions and providers require payment at the time of service, and may even require payment before service is given. While some private clinics accept credit cards, many medical facilities do not. Doctors and hospitals outside Maputo generally expect immediate cash payment for health services. Outside of Maputo, available medical care ranges from very basic to non-existent.

Malaria is prevalent in Mozambique. Travellers to Mozambique should take malaria prophylaxis. P falciparum malaria, the serious and sometimes fatal strain in Mozambique, is resistant to the anti-malarial drug chloroquine. Because travellers to Mozambique are at high risk of contracting malaria, the Centres for Disease Control and Prevention (CDC) advises that travellers should take one of the following anti-malarial drugs: mefloquine (Lariam™), doxycycline, or atovaquone/proguanil (Malarone™). The CDC has determined that a traveller who is on an appropriate anti-malarial drug has a greatly reduced chance of contracting the disease. In addition, other personal protective measures, such as the use of insect repellent, help reduce malaria risk. Travellers who become ill with a fever or flu-like illness while travelling in a malaria-risk area, and up to one year after returning home, should seek prompt medical attention and tell the physician their travel history and what anti-malarials they have been taking.

Useful contacts:
Mozambique Embassy, 21 Fitzroy Square, London, tel: +(44) 171 383 3800
British High Commission, Av Vladimir I Lenine, 310, Maputo PO Box 55, Maputo, tel: 258 (21) 356 000

PERSONAL TAXATION

A single direct tax is levied at state level: a comprehensive individual income tax ('imposto sobre o rendimento das pessoas singulares').

Resident individuals are subject to individual income tax on worldwide income. Non-residents are liable to tax on any category of Mozambican-source income.

Individuals are considered to be a resident of Mozambique if: they are present in Mozambique for more than 180 days in any calendar year (ie anyone entering Mozambique prior to 30 June of a calendar year); they are present in Mozambique for a shorter period in a year, but on 31 December of that year have an abode in Mozambique in circumstances which imply their intention to keep and occupy the abode as their permanent residence; they are abroad providing services as a public employee of the Mozambican government; or they are a crew member of a ship or aircraft operated by a Mozambican resident entity. If the head of a household is a resident of Mozambique, all other members of the household are regarded as residents.

Resident individuals are liable to individual income tax on worldwide aggregate net income at progressive rates from 10 to 32 per cent. A flat-rate rebate is deducted from the tax payable.

The Individual Income Tax Code establishes an obligation for a non-resident individual to appoint a local representative for individual income tax purposes. However, this formality seems to be unnecessary for those non-resident individuals deriving directly (ie not through a local permanent establishment or fixed base) only Mozambican-source employment/pension income (first category), investment income (third category), lottery prizes and other gambling winnings (fifth category), because any local payer with organised accounts is obliged to withhold individual income tax on the gross amount paid.

Accordingly, it could be said that only non-resident individuals deriving Mozambican-source business/professional income (second category), capital gains (within third category) and/or income from immovable property (fourth category) must appoint a local representative for tax purposes. The representative is required to fulfil all the non-resident's tax obligations, including filing the final tax return and the payment of the tax.

Non-resident taxpayers deriving directly any Mozambican-source business income, capital gains or rent from immovable property which are not subject to a final withholding tax (thus excluding royalty and know-how-related payments to the original creator, professional fees, agency commissions and fees for services rendered or used in Mozambique) are subject first to an advance payment of individual income tax at a rate of 20 per cent. The final tax is assessed on the basis of a return filed by the non-resident's local representative at the progressive rates indicated above.

NAMIBIA

The economy and political climate

Namibia was for many years a protectorate of the Republic of South Africa, known as South West Africa. International sanctions were imposed on the territory after the adoption of United Nations Resolution 435 of 1978. The protectorate became legally independent after general elections by universal suffrage on 21 March 1990.

The major economic sectors include the extraction and processing of diamonds and the country is the world's fifth largest producer of uranium. Agriculture contributes 10 per cent of the country's GDP and consists mainly of cattle and sheep farming. The fishing grounds are some of the world's richest and fish processing is one of the main industrial activities.

Namibia is seeking to diversify its trading relationships away from its heavy dependence on South African goods and services. Europe has become a leading market for Namibian fish and meat, while mining concerns in Namibia have purchased heavy equipment and machinery from Germany, the UK, the United States and Canada. The main export commodities include copper, cut diamonds, gemstones, granite, lead products, marble, uranium and zinc. There was a negative trade balance in 2005, estimated at US$310 million; however, the foreign trade surplus on current account rose to 9.7 per cent of GDP and is forecast to reach almost 15 per cent in 2006 when there will be a positive trade balance.

The current foreign exchange control regulations are mostly identical to South Africa's.

The economy is one of moderate performance and growth in line with regional trends. Real GDP growth has been maintained at 4.2 per cent over the two-year period 2004/5 but is forecast to rise to 5 per cent in 2006. Inflation is running at a modest 2.7 per cent but may rise to 4.3 per cent in 2006. Mozambique runs a small public sector deficit estimated at 2.9 per cent.

Working conditions

Nationals of Angola, Australia, Botswana, Brazil, Canada, Cuba, Iceland, Japan, Kenya, Lesotho, Liechtenstein, Malawi, Malaysia, Mozambique, New Zealand, Norway, Russian Federation, Singapore,

South Africa, Swaziland, Switzerland, Tanzania, Zambia, Zimbabwe and the United States do not require visas for stays of up to three months. Passports must be valid for a minimum period of six months after the expected date of departure. Travellers coming for work, whether paid or voluntary, must obtain their visas prior to entering Namibia.

All employers are required to register themselves, and all employees under the age of 65 who work more than two days per week, with the Social Security Commissioner. Employers and employees are required to contribute an amount equal to 0.9 per cent of the monthly basic salary of the employee, limited to a maximum of NAD 27 per month per employee, to the Social Security Commissioner on a monthly basis.

Namibia's largest labour federation, the National Union of Namibian Workers (NUNW) represents workers organised into seven affiliated trade unions. The NUNW maintains a close affiliation with the ruling SWAPO party.

In late 2004, Namibia passed a new Labour Act to replace legislation dating back to 1992. The new law will be stricter with respect to discrimination in the workplace and will establish new protections for pregnant workers as well as employees infected with HIV/AIDS.

Useful information

Money: The local currency is the Namibian Dollar (NAD) = 100 cents and is linked to the South African Rand (the Rand is legal tender in Namibia). Major credit cards are accepted, as are travellers' cheques. Banking hours: Monday to Friday, 9.00 am to 3.30 pm and Saturday, 8.30–11.00 am. The banks are the Bank Windhoek Limited, Commercial Bank of Namibia Limited, City Savings and Investment Bank Limited, First National Bank of Namibia Limited and Standard Bank Namibia Limited.

Local time: Namibia is two hours ahead of GMT.

Language: English is the official language. A number of African languages are spoken as well as Afrikaans and German.

Capital: Windhoek.

Climate: Everywhere in Namibia enjoys a minimum of 300 days of sunshine a year. Extreme heat can be experienced from December to March in the desert areas. Rainfall is sparse and erratic.

Communications: Indicated as a good service, both international and domestic. There are currently a couple of internet providers.

Transport: Namibia caters for international and domestic flights through its airport in Windhoek and South Africa. The train service is good and operates between the major centres. Local minibus taxis also run between these centres and there are five luxury bus services available. Travelling by road is safe and the roads, tarred or untarred, are normally in good condition. Most international car rental companies are represented.

Electricity: Electric power is 220V at 50 Hz.

Health and health care: Medical services may require advance payments and can be expensive. Vaccinations may also be required prior to arrival and medical insurance should be arranged. The state of health, current immunisation status, location and local disease situation create the risk of positive contraction of hepatitis A, malaria and typhoid fever.

Useful contacts:

British High Commission, 116 Robert Mugabe Avenue, Windhoek, PO Box 22202, Windhoek, tel: (264) (61) 274800, e-mail: windhoek. general@fco.gov.uk, website: www.britishhighcommission.gov.uk/namibia

Namibian High Commission, 6 Chandos Street, London W1M 0LQ, tel: +(44) 207 636 6244.

The Namibian Tourism Board, 6 Chandos Street, London W1G 9LU, tel: +44 207 636 2924, e-mail: info@namibiatourism.co.uk, websites: www.namibiatourism.co.uk/index-1.htm

PERSONAL TAXATION

The Namibian tax system is based on the source principle and as a rule residency does not influence the taxability of income. Income will be subject to tax in Namibia to the extent that income was derived from a source within (or deemed to be within) Namibia. Foreign-earned employment income, while abroad, is generally not taxed in Namibia. Remuneration from a Namibian source is taxable regardless of where the employer is domiciled or where payment is made. Double tax agreements signed with various countries may affect this principle. The tax year is 1 March to 28 February and the maximum tax rate is 35 per cent. The tax rate for residents and non-residents is the same. Generally, the income of a non-resident which derives from Namibia is taxed in the same manner as that of a resident.

Double tax agreements have been signed with France, Germany, India, Mauritius, Romania, Russia, South Africa, Sweden and the UK.

There are certain withholding taxes on dividends (10 per cent) and royalties (10.5 per cent) paid to non-residents.

NIGERIA

The economy

Nigeria is a major oil producer in its own right and the leading economic centre of West Africa. During the 1980s and into the 1990s much of its oil wealth was squandered and a huge external debt built up. Since 1995, under the guidance of the IMF, which was first involved during the 1986 crisis, Nigeria has introduced further economic reforms and austerity measures, but the economic prospects remain disquieting. Corruption is endemic, reforms difficult to implement, the infrastructure is deteriorating and unemployment remains high. Political activists kidnapped international oil company employees in the second half of 2005 in an attempt to gain additional investment in the infrastructure and financial support for improved social conditions. The risks for Western expatriate employees in Nigeria have been correspondingly raised.

Successive governments have been aiming to diversify the economy away from oil, to encourage the development of agriculture and industry, and to overhaul the infrastructure – particularly transport, power supplies and water.

The country is a member of OPEC and is the largest oil producer in Africa. The main export products are petroleum and related products as well as cocoa and rubber. The main trading partners include India, France, Spain, Brazil and the United States. The Dutch auction system for foreign currency was introduced in June 2002 and has helped to slow reserve loss while allowing the exchange rate to be more market-determined. Thanks to its oil exports, Nigeria has maintained a current account surplus since 2003 and the 2005 surplus is estimated at 5.8 per cent of GDP.

Real GDP growth in 2005 is estimated at 4 per cent and forecast to rise in 2006 to 5 per cent. However, inflation at 18.8 per cent at the end of 2005 is unsustainable and is forecast to be reduced to about 12 per cent in 2006. More encouragingly, Nigeria has maintained a budget surplus since 2003, estimated at 9.9 per cent for 2005.

Nigeria is Africa's most populous country and, in spite of the difficult commercial environment, is therefore one of the most promising markets for international companies. About 66 per cent of the population falls below the poverty line and the country has a literacy rate of 66.8 per cent.

Working conditions

All visitors except nationals of certain neighbouring countries require a visa (easily obtainable for nationals of Commonwealth countries). A visitor's permit will last for a maximum of three months. Any non-Nigerian citizen wishing to live and work in the country either as a local hire or on a secondment requires a resident's permit and this is obtained by the employer within the quota allowed to the company.

Upon entry, the individual will be issued with a visitor's pass with a limited validation. The individual will then need to proceed to register with the relevant government office in order to convert to resident's status. The individual may commence working in Nigeria only when in possession of a resident's work permit.

Nigeria acknowledges both Christian and Muslim holidays as well as May Day, Democracy Day (29 May) and Independence Day (1 October). Because of the conditions of working in Nigeria, leave tends to be generous, particularly with companies that operate in other overseas markets. Three tours of three months a year with one month's leave after each tour is not uncommon, although a tour of six months is more normal.

Useful information

Money: Credit cards are not generally used in Nigeria and are accepted in only one or two hotels in Lagos. Credit is not usually given. All retail purchases are made in cash. A cheque from one state to another can now be cleared within 10 working days. Only 'certified' cheques, or bank drafts, are accepted as currency. Cheques tend to be used only to draw cash from one's own local branch. Cash is best taken in US dollars or Sterling. The official currency is 1 Naira = 100 kobo.

Banking hours: 8.00 am to 4.00 pm Monday–Friday. Some banks now offer Saturday banking from 10.00 am to 3.00 pm.

Electricity: The main voltage in Nigeria is 240 V at 50 Hz; however, most hotels/flats have outlets for 110 V electric showers. You need a standby generator because of the supply situation. Plug types are round pins with earth and rectangular blade plugs.

Climate: Temperature in the south is generally about 29°C with humidity almost as high. The rainy season begins in April/May and continues until September/October with a short break during August. Temperatures in the north are sometimes above 32°C and rain is restricted to the midsummer months. The 'harmattan', a dust wind from the Sahara, can be a nuisance to air traffic and is prevalent from November to February.

Local time: Nigeria is one hour ahead of GMT.

Driving: Driving is on the right and an international driver's licence is required. Trunk roads linking the various state capitals have improved considerably in recent years. A motorway runs from Lagos to Ibadan, and from Lagos to Benin. However, within Lagos itself traffic conditions are horrendous. For instance, you have to allow about four hours to get to the airport. Poor road maintenance can cause some hazards, and road accidents in Nigeria are very frequent. It is not safe to drive after dusk because of the risk of accidents and highway robbery; be cautious about unsolicited assistance with transport or other facilities, and unmarked road blocks.

Transport: Travel by rail is slow and not recommended. Most state capitals now have airports, the most recent addition being Makurdi, Benue State. Regular services are frequent, but delays can occur because of poor weather conditions. Bribery, known as 'dash', may be necessary to clear customs and immigration. In the north, a private airline links the state capitals, in competition with Nigeria Airways, and has a good reputation.

Where airports are some distance from the town only taxis operate. Care should be taken to ensure that the taxi is properly marked and that a reasonable fare has been agreed upon before the journey begins. Ideally, visitors should always be met at the airports.

Health: Anti-malarial pills should be taken regularly. It is also advisable to obtain immunisation against yellow fever, tuberculosis, typhoid, tetanus, polio, cholera and hepatitis A and B. There were epidemics of spinal meningitis, gastroenteritis, cholera and measles in the north of the country in early 1996. Water should always be boiled and fruit and salads carefully cleaned. Swimming pools can be a health hazard and advice should be sought from residents. Exposure to the sun can be a danger, particularly in the north. If there is a need to be hospitalised, it is best to return home if possible. AIDS is now prevalent in many parts of Africa, and is affecting both the male and female population.

Health care: It is advisable to seek such treatment only after consultation with the British High Commission. State hospitals have difficulty in maintaining international standards of hygiene, while private hospitals tend to be expensive and commercially oriented. Be aware that not all medical providers will accept payment through your insurance company and will expect payment up front.

Education: Most expatriates send their children to UK boarding schools at an early age and certainly for secondary education. There are private International Schools, often staffed by Europeans, which cater well for ages five to nine and provide a congenial atmosphere, in Lagos, Ibadan, Kano and Kaduna. Fees tend to be somewhat higher than in equivalent schools in the UK.

Communications: There has been a significant improvement in telephone services, especially with the introduction of Global System of Mobile (GSM) telecommunication in addition to services provided by Private Telephone Operators (PTOs). The privatisation of the telecommunication sector has brought about keen competition. There is a noticeable decrease in set-up costs and call rates. International direct dialling services can be made direct to the UK and other parts of the world from phones, including those operated by NITEL (Nigerian Telecommunications).

International post takes a minimum of six days (airmail) and four to six weeks by surface mail. Documents despatched by courier are usually faster than those handled by inland mail. Internal post takes about two to five days with the introduction of post codes for major towns.

There are some fax machines in Nigeria, but faxing has ceased to be a common means of communication as use of the internet has grown.

Special note: The newcomer to Nigeria should understand that while, with care, he or she will probably have a trouble-free tour, there is a crime problem in Nigeria. While appropriate precautions will vary from time to time, it is generally not considered safe to travel out of town at night.

Useful contacts:

British Deputy High Commission, 11 Walter Carrington Crescent, Victoria Island, tel: 234 1 2619531

British High Commission, Dangote House, Aguyi Ironsi Street, Maitama District, Abuja, tel: 234 9 413 4559

Nigerian High Commission, Nigeria House, 9 Northumberland Avenue, London WC2, tel: 020 7353 3776

Surekha Kukadia, Immigration Adviser, BDO Stoy Hayward, 8 Baker Street, London W1U 3LL, tel: 020 7893 2430, e-mail: sue.kukadia@bdo.co.uk

PERSONAL TAXATION

Details are as of April 2003.

Residence

Nigeria taxes individuals on the basis of residence. A person is deemed to be resident in Nigeria if he or she has stayed in the country for a period of 183 days or more within a 12-month period commencing in a calendar year and ending either within the calendar year or the following year. This implies that if the total period of stay exceeds 183 days within 12 months spanning parts of two consecutive calendar years, such an individual would be liable to pay income tax in Nigeria for the two relevant years of assessment.

The issue of residence is determined by the state in which an individual is deemed to be resident at the beginning of any particular year of assessment. The tax due on the individual's income is therefore payable to that state and not to the federal government.

Taxation of personal income

Personal income tax is levied under the Personal Income Tax Act No 104 of 1993. The Act regulates personal income tax throughout the federation and establishes the procedure for determining the total income of a taxpayer for tax purposes. There is thus one uniform law throughout the federation, but income tax accrues to each state and not to the federation. The provisions of the Act apply to foreigners working in Nigeria for as long as they are resident.

An individual is liable to income tax on his or her total income, which consists of earned income (such as income from employment) and unearned income (such as income from investments).

Certain allowances are available to taxpayers depending on their personal circumstances, in addition to reliefs specific to certain sources of income. The tax year is the calendar year. Income tax is charged at progressive rates of between 5 and 25 per cent. The rate will change as soon as the Taxation Bill before the National Assembly is passed and signed into law. An individual is liable to minimum tax at the rate of 0.5 per cent of total income if the reliefs and allowances exceed the total income or the regular tax computed is less than this minimum tax.

Income from employment

Employment income means income derived from working in Nigeria irrespective of whether the employer is in Nigeria or not, and no matter where the income is disbursed.

Taxable income from employment includes all kinds of remuneration, whether in cash or in kind, such as salaries, bonuses, cost-of-living allowances, gains from share options, employer-provided cars and so forth. Only specific expenses, such as professional subscriptions necessary for the individual's employment, are deductible from employment income. There is no standard deduction.

A pay as you earn system of deduction from earnings operates, and is designed to deduct the correct amount of tax from the employee by the end of the tax year.

Investment income
Dividends and interest

Investment income is income earned outside paid employment such as dividends, rental income, interest income and so forth, and it is subject to withholding tax in Nigeria at the rate of 10 per cent. For personal income tax purposes, the income is grossed up and forms part of the individual's unearned income. However, the 10 per cent tax withheld from Nigerian dividends is a final tax, and dividends are consequently not aggregated with other income.

However, withholding taxes suffered by deduction at source from other investment income may be offset against the total tax payable.

Income from real property

Rental income from real property is taxable as unearned income, less relevant expenses. As with other investment income, rents are subject to withholding tax of 10 per cent.

Taxes on capital

Capital gains

Individuals resident in Nigeria are liable to capital gains tax on gains arising from the disposal of their assets worldwide. However, gains from shares and securities and motor vehicles commonly used for carrying passengers are exempt. The rate of capital gains tax is 10 per cent of the chargeable gain and it is payable to the state where the individual resides, and not to the federal government.

Wealth tax

There is no wealth tax either at the federal or at the state level.

Double tax treaties

Nigeria has a limited number of comprehensive tax treaties in effect. There are treaties with the UK, Belgium, Canada, France, The Netherlands, Pakistan and Romania, but not currently with the United States.

For further information on tax and social security, contact:

E O Olabisi, Partner, BDO Oyediren Faleye Oke and Co, tel: +234 1–7942927/2713739/471069, e-mail: eo.olabisi@ yahoo.com, bdoofo@mwebafrica.com

SOUTH AFRICA

The economy and political climate

South Africa celebrated 10 years of democracy in 2004 and is the most advanced economy on the African continent. The most important contributors are the mining, manufacturing and agriculture sectors. The greater part of economic activity occurs in Gauteng province where most of the mining is located. South Africa has a sophisticated financial structure with a large and active stock exchange that ranks 17th in the world in terms of total market capitalisation. The South African Reserve Bank (SARB) performs all central banking functions. The SARB is independent and operates in much the same way as Western central banks, influencing interest rates and controlling liquidity through its interest rates on funds provided to private sector banks. The 2005 Moody's raised South Africa's sovereign rating to Baa1 as a result of the improved foreign exchange reserves and fast economic growth. South Africa has signed a regional trade protocol agreement with its SADC partners. The agreement was ratified in December 1999, and implementation began in September 2000. It intends to provide duty-free treatment for 85 per cent of trade by 2008 and 100 per cent by 2012.

Among emerging markets, South Africa increasingly stands out as a success story. Ranked against other economies, South Africa's global competitiveness has consistently improved over the last few years, whether measured in terms of business efficiency, government efficiency, infrastructure or economic performance. The real GDP growth rate increased from 3.7 per cent in 2004 to an estimated 4.1 per cent in 2005, and is forecast to rise further in 2006. The public sector budget deficit is estimated at only 1 per cent for 2005 and year-on-year inflation of 4 per cent was recorded for January 2006.

South Africa has been the leading exporter of minerals and mineral products to as many as 87 countries. The clothing and textiles industries have shown significant growth. There was a small trade deficit in 2005 with the estimated current account deficit running at 3.5 per cent of GDP. However, foreign debt is held at a modest 19.7 per cent of GDP.

The critical challenge of strengthening the link between economic growth and export success with employment creation, poverty alleviation, and a marked reduction in inequalities, remains. South Africa is one of the countries most affected by HIV, with 5 million HIV, infected individuals. A 2003 national operational plan provides the structure for a comprehensive response to HIV and AIDS, including a national rollout of antiretroviral therapy.

Working conditions

Fringe benefits are not a significant part of remuneration, although managerial jobs generally provide a car and holidays tend to be generous, six weeks a year being frequently quoted. Free or subsidised medical aid schemes are frequently offered to more senior people. If these are not available such costs, and they are considerable, should be borne in mind in assessing the true value of the remuneration package.

There are a wide variety of indirect sales duties, the most significant of which is on cars. The remission of duty on personal effects is marginal and it is not worth bringing a car into South Africa. If you are an approved immigrant you may, however, import one motor vehicle per family under full rebate of customs duty (but subject to VAT), provided that the motor vehicle has been owned and used by you and registered in your name, in your country of residence, for at least 12 months before your departure and before the date on which it was shipped to South Africa.

There are no restrictions on the amount of foreign currency you can bring in, but strict exchange control regulations are in force on taking money out of South Africa. For this reason, it is advisable to transfer no more of your assets than you need to South Africa unless you are absolutely sure you want to stay there.

At executive and professional level, working conditions (ie hours and leave) are very similar to those in the UK. There has been little industrial unrest in South Africa, though it has increased recently. Wages are fixed by industrial councils and vary according to occupation and region. Welfare benefits are minimal compared with the UK, although health care is now free, and there are numerous private schemes for medical care, pensions and disability.

Visitors to South Africa are required to have a visa upon arrival and valid international health certificates. Enquiries can be directed to South African diplomatic missions or to the Department of Home Affairs in Pretoria. Visas specifically for business purposes are available, although nationals from Canada, the EU and the United States are not required to have them. An application for a business visa must include the application form, a valid passport and a letter on the parent company's letterhead that undertakes financial responsibility for the applicant during his or her stay in South Africa. It is also necessary to provide flight details and addresses of businesses to be visited. Current legislation makes provision for no less than 13 types of temporary residence permits, and a foreigner has the option of no less than four types of work permit.

The main consideration in dealing with work permits is whether a South African citizen/permanent resident cannot perform the employment task to be undertaken. Work permits are therefore only issued to foreigners where South African citizens with the relevant skills are not available for appointment. Having said that, however, in some instances international concerns with branches/affiliated companies in the Republic may from time to time decide to transfer existing personnel from a foreign branch to a branch in the Republic. As these employees will be key employees they must apply for intra-company transfer work permits, in which instance no proof of steps taken to obtain the services of a South African citizen/permanent resident will be required.

A foreigner may only change his or her status while inside South Africa. This implies that a foreigner may only change from a temporary residence permit to a permanent residence permit within the country, as status has been defined as temporary or permanent residence. Any foreigner who therefore wishes to enter the RSA must apply for the appropriate temporary residence permit at the South African diplomatic representative in his or her country of origin. Travellers entering South Africa from countries where yellow fever is endemic are often required to present their yellow World Health Organisation (WHO) vaccination record or other proof of inoculation. If they are unable to do so, they must be inoculated at the airport in order to be permitted entry.

Most UK professional qualifications are recognised in South Africa.

Useful information

Climate: South Africa's climate is excellent, though by no means uniform. There is quite a difference at all times of the year between semi-tropical Kwazulu-Natal, the Mediterranean climate of the Western Cape and the dry, cold winters and hot, thunderstormy summers of Johannesburg. Most of South Africa has elevations of over 914m (3,000 ft) and Johannesburg is 1829m (6,000 ft) above sea level.

Education: According to the Bill of Rights contained in the Constitution of the Republic of South Africa, 1996 (Act 108 of 1996), everyone has the right to a basic education, including adult basic education and further education, which the State, through reasonable measures, must make progressively available and accessible. Education in state schools is free, but schools are allowed to charge a small fee to cover miscellaneous expenses. There are, of course, plenty of private fee-paying schools as well. Children who will not have reached the age of 6 before 1 July of the year of admission will not be allowed to attend school, even if they have done so previously. The school year begins after the Christmas holiday. It should be noted that the syllabus and atmosphere of South African schools is markedly more traditional and restrictive than is the case in most other countries. University education is not free. The British International College at Bryanston is well regarded (e-mail: bic@global.co.za).

Money: The local currency is 1 SA Rand (ZAR) = 100 cents. Travellers' cheques, credit and charge cards are widely accepted, including American Express, Bank of America, Diners, MasterCard, Standard Bank Card and Visa. Most banks are open Monday to Friday, 9.00 am to 3.30 pm and Saturdays 9.00–11.00 am. ATMs are found in most towns and operate 24 hours.

Local time: South Africa is two hours ahead of GMT.

Language: Afrikaans, English, Ndebele, Pedi, Sotho, Swazi, Tsonga, Tswana, Venda, Xhosa, Zulu.

Capital: Pretoria.

Transport: South Africa has international airports at Johannesburg, Durban and Cape Town. All major cities are connected by domestic flights. The railway system is well established and mostly privately run. All major towns are connected. The 'Blue Train' is famous for its sheer luxury and you can also experience a steam train tour on the 'Apple Express', 'Outeniqua Choo-Tjoe' and 'Banana Express'. A number of bus coach operators run an inter-city service. All major international car rental companies are represented in South Africa and the road network is of a high quality throughout the country.

Electricity: Electric power is 220/230 V at 50 Hz and the plug type used is 'South African' plug.

Communications: South Africa's communication system is well developed with 5.5 million installed telephones and 4.3 million installed exchange lines. The network is almost entirely digital with

Leana Nel International Relocations has been relocating families to South Africa for the past 11 years. Based in Sandton and Cape Town, our highly motivated team of experts will advise you on every aspect of your immigration/relocation. Whether you would like to start a business or retire and enjoy what South Africa has to offer, the choice is yours. There are various options available to individuals who wish to reside in the Republic whether temporarily or permanently.

The following categories of temporary residence permits are available:

- Visitors
- Business
- Work: 5 categories – Intra-company transfer; Quota; General; Exceptional skills and Visitor's permit endorsed for work
- Retired persons
- Exchange
- Asylum
- Study: no work
- Study: allow work
- Treaty
- Relatives
- Medical treatment
- Crew

Contrary to popular belief, it is not impossible or even difficult to obtain a permit to reside in South Africa. The changes implemented to, and requirements contained in the immigration legislation have been passed to ensure that only legitimate immigrants who wish to enter South Africa are able to do so. Provided that the necessary documents are obtained timously and submitted, there is no reason why any potential immigrant will be denied an appropriate permit to reside in South Africa. With adequate planning before arriving in South Africa most of your worries will be taken care of and you will be free to start your new life.

Through the years we have established good relationships with many partners and in the process have forged a credible association with blue chip companies worldwide. We are currently the leading Relocation Team for The Homecoming Revolution and have always believed in meeting with all our clients needs with utmost passion and attention to detail in the relocation process.

Our vision is to guide you seamlessly through the relocation process, finding the best employment opportunity, property or business, to make your investment into the South African market and lifestyle, as pleasurable, and easy as possible. Start living!

digital microwave and fibre optics serving as the main transmission media. Internet access is widely available. State-controlled Telkom is responsible for the installation and maintenance of these facilities. South Africa is the world's fourth fastest growing GSM market with a growth rate of 50 per cent per annum. There are three operators in the country: MTN, Cell C and Vodacom. Vodacom and MTN report more than 7 million and 5 million subscribers respectively. There are a large number of internet providers in the country.

Health and health care: The Department of Health is the government body responsible for the country's health facilities, which include well-equipped hospitals and primary health care clinics. The government has placed much emphasis on the primary health care sector specifically in rural and poorer areas. Treatment for TB is available free of charge at all clinics. Malaria is endemic in the low-altitude areas of the Northern Province, Mpumalanga and north-eastern KwaZulu-Natal, and the highest risk area is a strip of about 100 km along the Zimbabwe, Mozambique and Swaziland border.

Costs for admission to private and provincial hospitals vary and private hospitals usually require proof of membership of a medical scheme/aid.

The Department of Health has initiated the Extended Expanded Programme on Immunisation that aims to make immunisation facilities available to all children and women of childbearing age. Immunisation against TB, whooping cough, tetanus, diphtheria, poliomyelitis, hepatitis B and measles is available free of charge to all children up to the age of five years.

Useful contacts:
British High Commission, 256 Glyn Street, Hatfield, Pretoria 0083, tel: 012 421 7802, website: www.britain.org.za/
South African High Commission, South Africa House, Trafalgar Square, London WC2, tel: +(44) 207 589 6655
South Africa Tourist Board, 5–6 Alt Grove, Wimbledon, London SW19 4DZ, tel: +(44) 0870 155 0044, websites: www.satour.co.za/; www.satour.org
Worldwide Medical Consultants, Dr Albie De Frey, tel: +27 11 888–7488, website: http://www.traveldoctor.co.za, e-mail: wtmc@global.co.za
Elliots Relocation Services, Paolo Longa, tel: +2711 256 3097, website: http://www.elliott.co.za/relocations.htm, e-mail: paolol@elliott.co.za

Worldchoice Travel Airscape, Ken Brown, tel: 27 11 475 2902, e-mail: kenb.travelair@galileosa.co.za, websites: www.acitravel.co.za; www.africanleisure.co.za

PERSONAL TAXATION

These details are as of March 2005.

Residence

The worldwide basis of taxation of residents of South Africa came into effect on 1 January 2001 and applies to years of assessment commencing on or after that date. Critical to the application of the new tax system is a definition of residence, because the residential status of a person will determine his or her tax liability in the future. The tax year in South Africa runs from 1 March to 28 February.

A natural person will be resident if he or she is 'ordinarily resident' in South Africa, which means that it is the country he or she regards as home and to which he or she naturally and eventually returns from any travelling. If the person is not ordinarily resident, a time-based rule (physical presence test) applies: if a person is physically present for more than 91 days in the current tax year and more than 549 days in the preceding three tax years, then such a person is classified as a South African resident (shortly to be changed to 915 days in aggregate in the preceding five years).

Important considerations for the time-based rule are: if a person is present for less than 91 days in the current year, there is no South African residency. In previous years, the person had to be present for more than 91 days on aggregate in each of those years. If a person is resident under the physical presence test and is physically outside South Africa for a continuous period of 330 full days starting the day after leaving South Africa, he or she will not be deemed as resident from the date of departure.

A new addition to the definition refers to any arrangement regulated by a double tax agreement entered into by South Africa with any other country.

Non-residence

Non-residents are taxed on their South African income on source-based rules. Withholding amounts from payments to non-resident sellers of immovable property are equal to 5 per cent of the amount so payable in the case where the seller is a natural person, or in the case where the seller is a company, 7.5 per cent of the amount so payable, and at 10 per cent in the case where the seller is a trust. This amount must be paid over to the South African Revenue Service within a prescribed time limit. No withholding tax is levied on interest and dividends. Visiting entertainers and sportspeople are liable for a final withholding tax of 15 per cent. Royalty payments are subject to a withholding tax of 12 per cent, but can be reduced depending on the DTA signed.

Income from employment

Employment income earned by non-residents in South African is subject to tax in South Africa in terms of a source-based rule on a progressive scale, with a maximum rate being 40 per cent on income over R300,000 per year. Certain deductions are allowed against employment income, such as medical expenditure, travelling costs, donations to public benefit organisations, and contributions to pensions, retirement annuities and provident funds. All of the above are subject to certain limits, which might be deducted.

If employers grant various benefits to employees, such benefits are taxed in terms of fringe benefit legislation, which is contained in the Seventh Schedule. Such benefits include travelling allowances, company vehicles, low-interest loans, subsistence allowances, residential accommodation and entertainment.

South African resident employees who render services for any employer outside South Africa for a period which in aggregate exceeds 183 full days commencing on or ending during a period of assessment and for a continuous period exceeding 60 full days during such a 183 day period, will not be liable for income tax on their remuneration for the period that they are outside South Africa.

Investment income

Interest earned by a resident is fully taxable, except the first R15,000 which is exempt (R22,000 if the person is over 65 years of age). Interest earned by a non-resident from a South African source is exempt from normal South African income tax.

For a South African resident, dividends from a South African source (local dividends) are exempt from tax, while foreign dividends received are fully taxable in the resident's hands.

Dividends accruing to a non-resident are exempt from tax, as well as foreign dividends, which are not deemed to accrue to a non-resident.

Capital gains

Capital gains tax was introduced to South Africa with effect from 1 October 2001. Non-residents are not subject to capital gains tax except on gains made on immovable property situated in South Africa and gains made on assets of a permanent establishment of such a non-resident. The rates currently applicable are: individuals 10 per cent, companies 15 per cent, and trusts 20 per cent.

Double taxation agreements

Double taxation agreements are in place with 55 countries including the United States and the UK.

For further information on tax and social security, contact:

Kemp Munnik, Partner, BDO Spencer (Steward) (Johannesburg) Inc, tel: +27 (011) 643 7271, e-mail: Kmunnik@ bdo.co.za

TUNISIA

The economy and political climate

Tunisia, an independent republic since 20 March 1956, was formerly a French protectorate. The country is governed by the President who holds executive power and nominates the members of the Council of Ministers.

Tunisia has a diverse economy, with important agricultural, mining, energy, tourism and manufacturing sectors. Tourism is one sector of Tunisia's economic sector that suffered the most in the aftermath of terrorist attacks. The government has introduced certain measures to deepen the financial markets. In 1996 Tunisia entered into an Association Agreement with the European Union (EU), which will remove tariff and other trade barriers on most goods by 2008. In conjunction with the Association Agreement, the

EU is assisting the Tunisian government's 'Mise A Niveau' (upgrading) programme to enhance the productivity of Tunisian businesses and prepare for competition in the global marketplace.

The economy grew by 6 per cent in 2004 and real GDP growth is estimated at 4.8 per cent for 2005 and forecast to rise to 5.4 per cent in 2006. Inflation is running at between 2 and 3 per cent and the public sector budget deficit is measured at about 3.4 per cent of GDP. The foreign trade current account is almost in balance with a deficit running at only 1.4 per cent of GDP.

Working conditions

Visas are required by all except nationals from Algeria, Antigua & Barbuda, Bahrain, Barbados, Belize, Brunei, Bulgaria, Canada, Chile, Croatia, Dominica, Fiji, EU countries, Gambia, Ghana, Guinea, Hungary, Iceland, Ivory Coast, Japan, Kiribati, Niger, Norway, Oman, Qatar, Romania, St Kitts & Nevis, St Lucia, St Vincent and Grenadines, San Marino, Saudi Arabia, Senegal, Serbia, Seychelles, Slovenia, Solomon Islands, Switzerland, Turkey, UAE, the UK and the United States. A residence permit has to be obtained for a stay longer than four months, from the central police station of the district of residence.

Useful information

Money: The local currency is the Tunisian Dinar (TSD) = 100 millimes. Banking hours: Monday to Friday, 7.30–11.00 am and 2.00–4.15 pm (summer), 8.00–11.00 am and 1.00– 3.15 pm (winter).

Local time: one hour ahead of GMT.

Language: Arabic (official and one of the languages of commerce), French (commerce).

Capital: Tunis.

Climate: Temperate in the north with mild, rainy winters and hot, dry summers. Desert conditions are found in the south.

Communications: The telephone system has been assessed as above the standard of most African countries and internet access is also available.

Transport: There are international flights between Tunisia and Europe. There are regular domestic flights between Tunis and Djerba,

Sfax and Tozeur. Regular train services connect all major cities in the north. There is also a ferry service and an excellent bus service network. The road network is in a good condition.

Electricity: Electric power is 230V at 50 Hz.

Health and health care: Medical care in Tunisia is adequate with a number of new, private 'polyclinics' available, which function as simple hospitals and can provide a variety of procedures. Specialised care or treatment may not be available. Facilities that can handle complex trauma cases are virtually non-existent. While most private clinics have a few physicians who are fluent in English, the medical establishment uses French and all of the ancillary staff in every clinic communicate in Arabic and/or French. Public hospitals are overcrowded, under-equipped and under-staffed. In general, nursing care does not conform to UK standards.

  Immediate ambulance service may not be available outside of urban areas. Even in urban areas, emergency response times can be much longer than normal. Doctors and hospitals expect immediate cash payment for health care services, although some hospitals may accept credit cards. Over-the-counter medications are available; however, travellers should bring with them a full supply of medicines that are needed on a regular basis.

Useful contacts:

Tunisian Embassy, 29 Prince's Gate, London SW7 1QG, tel: +(44) 207 584 8117

Tunisian National Tourist Office, 77-A Wigmore Street, London W1H 9LJ, tel: +(44) 207 224 5598

British Embassy, Rue du Lac Windermere, Les Berges du Lac, Tunis 1053, tel: (216) 71 108 700

PERSONAL TAXATION

Income tax is due by all individuals with a habitual residence in Tunisia in respect of all profits or income realised in the preceding year. The following will be deemed to have an habitual residence in Tunisia: people whose main residence is in Tunisia; people who are present in Tunisia for a period of at least 183 days (whether this is a continuous period or not) in the calendar year concerned even when their main residence is outside Tunisia; civil servants and state employees carrying out their duties in a foreign country, in so far as they are not subject in that foreign country to a personal tax on total income.

Individuals who are not deemed to have their residence in Tunisia are subject to income tax therein only with respect to income and capital gains arising in Tunisia. Some listed items are, however, exempt from tax.

Tax is withheld at source, at 20 per cent in the case of interest and 15 per cent of gross proceeds in other cases (except for salaries), in full satisfaction of tax liability. Foreign individuals working for exporting enterprises or for enterprises operating in economic activity parks may be subject to a 20 per cent withholding tax on their gross remuneration. Note that a 25 per cent withholding tax is payable on the total amount paid under contract to foreign artistes providing entertainment of a commercial nature in Tunisia.

Tunisia has concluded a number of double taxation conventions. It may, therefore, be useful to point out here that these various conventions provide that remuneration which a resident of one contracting state receives in respect of a salaried employment exercised in the other contracting state will be taxable in that other state. However, such income will remain taxable in the country of origin if the following three conditions are fulfilled: the recipient is present in the country where the activities are carried on for a period or periods not exceeding a total of 183 days in the fiscal year in question; the remuneration is paid by an employer or on behalf of an employer who is not resident in the country in which the activities are carried out; and the cost of the remuneration is not borne by a permanent establishment or a fixed base which the employer has in the country in which the activities are carried out. It will suffice for only one of these conditions not to be satisfied for an individual who is not habitually resident in Tunisia but who carries out employment activities there to be subject to income tax on income from Tunisian sources in Tunisia and not in his or her country of origin.

The following types of income are exempt from tax: wages, salaries and other payments made by foreign states to personnel seconded to work for the Tunisian government under a programme of technical cooperation; expatriate allowances and other benefits received by employees working abroad where the employer is domiciled in Tunisia and where the activity is related to: technical, economic, social or environmental studies or to technical assistance; construction or assembly works and maintenance activities.

A graduated scale of rates applies, ranging from 0 to 35 per cent. Generally speaking, the taxes paid on capital gains will be final taxes on income.

ZAMBIA

The economy and political climate

Northern Rhodesia became an independent state as Zambia on 24 October 1964. A one-party system existed from 1972 until 1990. A constitutional change in 1990 allowed presidential and general elections to take place in October 1991 and the Movement for Multi-party Democracy (MMD) defeated the former ruling party, the United National Independence Party.

The economy is based on copper, which accounts for about 95 per cent of foreign exchange earnings, and is highly sensitive to fluctuations in world copper prices. As a result of falling world copper prices and increased oil prices, Zambia has faced serious economic difficulties and a huge balance of payments deficit. The main exports include cobalt, compressor lubricants, copper, cotton, cut flowers, electrical appliances and parts, hardwood, lead products, mineral products and lime. The Exchange Control Act has been abolished. The Zambian government is pursuing an economic diversification programme to reduce the economy's reliance on the copper industry. This initiative seeks to exploit other components of Zambia's rich resource base by promoting agriculture, tourism, gemstone mining and hydropower.

About 50 per cent of the people are engaged in agriculture, the main crops being tobacco, sugar and maize. Farming is on a subsistence basis. Like other developing countries, Zambia has adopted national plans to develop and improve its farming, encourage diversification and reduce its dependence on imports. The scale of manufacture is still small, but a wide range of industries has been, or is being, established, such as food and tobacco processing, grain milling, production of steel sheets, cotton, furniture, clothing, plastics, cement, beer, soap and detergents, fertilisers and copper products, and vehicle assembly.

There is still a shortage of technical and qualified manpower. Many white mining technicians have left the country to work in the Middle East or South Africa. Government policy aims to entice back qualified Zambians who have left for other countries offering better wages and conditions.

Outside the copper belt and the main towns there is little paid employment and considerable poverty.

Despite progress in privatisation and budgetary reform, Zambia's economic growth remains in the 5 to 6 per cent range with a high rate of inflation at 19 per cent, and the need to reduce poverty significantly continues. Although the trade balance was positive in 2005, a current account deficit remains estimated at 10.2 per cent of GDP for 2005. HIV/AIDS is the nation's greatest challenge, with 16 per cent prevalence among the adult population. HIV/AIDS will continue to ravage Zambian economic, political, cultural and social development for the foreseeable future.

Working conditions

Visas are not required by holders of valid UK passports. Expatriates need a work permit, obtainable by the prospective employer from the Chief Immigration Officer (PO Box 31984, Lusaka). Dependants are not allowed to work without his permission. There are limited opportunities for women to work as doctors, nurses and teachers, but the authorities can be reluctant to issue work permits to expatriate wives. Voluntary work, however, is possible. Business visas also require a company letter. Zambian immigration officials insist visitors carry the original or a certified copy of their passport and their immigration permit at all times. Certified copies must be obtained from the immigration office that issued the permit.

Working hours are as in other parts of tropical Africa, ie 8.00 am to 4.00 or 5.00 pm. There are 12 official public holidays. Leave arrangements for expatriates are negotiated individually.

Expatriates are usually expected to train Zambians working under them to acquire higher skills. This may not be explicitly stated, but it is assumed that sooner or later a job will be 'Zambianised'.

Visa requirements change fairly regularly, so it is advisable to check with your Consulate or Embassy.

Useful information

Money: Official currency: Kwacha (ZMK) = 100 ngwee. Major credit cards are widely accepted. Travellers' cheques are best taken in pounds sterling or US dollars; many businesses prefer payment in hard currency or travellers' cheques.

Banking hours: Monday to Fridays, 8.15 am to 3.30 pm. The banks are the Bank of Zambia (Central Bank), African Commercial Bank, Finance Bank, Meridian BIAO, Standard Chartered Bank and Zambia National Commercial Bank.

Language: English (official), Bemba, Kaonda, Lozi, Lunda, Luval, Nyanja, Tonga, 70 other indigenous languages.

Capital: Lusaka.

Climate: Because of its altitude, the climate is temperate, with extremes of heat and cold in summer and winter. The rainy season is December to March.

Electricity: 230V, 50 Hz ac, available in towns; many people in country areas use bottled gas or paraffin.

Local time: Zambia is two hours ahead of GMT.

Driving: The Zambians are exuberant drivers and have one of the world's highest accident rates. New arrivals in the country would be well advised to hire a car with a driver. Indeed, some companies employ drivers for their staff and these drivers' services may be available, for an additional payment, out of office hours.

Transport: There are internal air services serving five major centres. Zambia Airways operates flights to the UK and leading African countries. There is a single-track railway system from Livingstone to the copper belt, and the Tazara railway, covering nearly 1,600 miles (2,600 kilometres), serves 147 stations between central Zambia and Dar es Salaam, in Tanzania. Cross-country rail or bus travel is not recommended.

Most main roads are tarred, though secondary roads have potholed gravel or earth surfaces. Express buses link Lusaka with Livingstone and the copper belt, but urban transport is not much used by Europeans. Taxis and self-drive cars can be hired in Lusaka and other towns. Most car-hire firms do not permit self-drive.

Health: Health standards have declined in recent years with cholera becoming endemic, particularly during the rainy season, and an increase in strains of choloroquine-resistant and cerebral malaria. AIDS is prevalent, with an estimated 25 per cent of the adult population being HIV infected. However, Zambia is generally a healthy place, in part because of its elevation. Other possible contractible diseases are TB, hepatitis A, typhoid fever, yellow fever (regional) and schistomiasis (bilharzia).

Health care: Hospital and medical treatment carry only nominal fees, but there is a severe shortage of doctors, nurses, medical equipment and drugs. Dentists are few and far between. Most expatriate employers subscribe to private medical practices. The mining companies have their own hospitals and provide medical services for their personnel and families. Advance payments for medical services may be required and prescription medicines should be carried in their original containers together with the prescription. Vaccinations should be obtained before entering Zambia.

Education: Zambian state schools are geared towards Zambian needs and classes are often overcrowded and facilities poor to non-existent. For expatriates in Lusaka there are four private schools, all of which have long waiting lists. There are also privately run Italian, French and Scandinavian schools and a limited choice of nursery schools for which there are also long waiting lists. Elsewhere throughout Zambia there are a few other private schools and in the copper belt there are also trust schools and two private schools, Simba and Lechwe in Ndola and Kitwe respectively. Most expatriates send their children to be educated in the UK, Zimbabwe or South Africa from the age of 10, although some use home-teaching methods.

Media: Broadcasting on TV and radio stations is in English. There are two daily newspapers, the *Times of Zambia* and the *Zambia Daily Mail,* and four weeklies, the *Weekly Post*, the *Standard*, the *Financial Mail* and the *National Mirror.*

Useful contacts:
British High Commission, Independence Avenue, PO Box 50050, 15101 Lusaka, tel: 260 1 251133.
Zambian High Commission, 2 Palace Gate, Kensington, London W8 5NG, tel: +(44) 207 589 6655
Zambian National Tourist Board, 2 Palace Gate, Kensington, London W8 5NG, tel: +(44) 207 589 6343, website: www.zambia-tourism.com

PERSONAL TAXATION

Expatriate employees of overseas companies usually receive benefits such as a car, a house, travel and education allowances, which vary from company to company.

Expatriate inducement allowances are subject to taxation and the government intends to abolish inducement allowances altogether except for professions such as medicine where there is a shortage of qualified Zambians.

All individuals whether they are resident or non-resident and are in receipt of income, which has a source or deemed source in Zambia, are liable to tax. The Income Tax Act does not define residence or ordinary residence. What it does is to set out rules under which it will be decided that an individual is not resident for a tax year. Where an individual is in Zambia for a temporary purpose, and not with the intention of establishing a residence there, for not more than 183 days in the tax year (excluding days of arrival and departure) he or she will not be resident.

In practice, individuals who normally live in Zambia or go there with the intention of remaining for a period that will exceed 12 months, are regarded as resident and ordinarily resident from the date of arrival even when, due to unforeseen circumstances, they later leave Zambia before the 12 months have elapsed. An individual may also be resident and/or ordinarily resident in Zambia if he or she maintains a residence there available for his or her use and visits the country, or if his or her visits to the country over the years are substantial, for example, an average of three months per year over a period of three years. Generally, non-residents are not entitled to tax credits; where an individual is not resident for part of a tax year, his or her tax credits are reduced proportionately. A non-resident may, however, elect that the tax chargeable in Zambia be reduced to the extent that it does not exceed the amount of tax that bears the same proportion to the tax which would be chargeable if the taxpayer's worldwide income were chargeable under the Act. In this case tax credits will be allowed. The Income Tax Act requires all people or partnerships making payments to non-resident contractors that are engaged in construction or haulage operations to deduct withholding tax at the rate of 15 per cent. The deductions are made from the gross payments before any other deductions whatsoever. The tax year is from 1 April to 31 March. Personal income tax ranges from 0 to 37.5 per cent.

ZIMBABWE

The economy and political climate

Zimbabwe was the British colony of Southern Rhodesia. After the 1965 Unilateral Declaration of Independence, international sanctions were imposed on the country until 1980. On 18 April 1980, after the drawing-up of a new constitution and general elections by universal suffrage, the former colony became legally independent.

Under the restrictive regime of Robert Mugabe, who has been in power since 1987, the economy continues to disintegrate, and democratic government has been sabotaged. Inflation is now over 400 per cent, and exports are more than 40 per cent down on 1999. Shortages of basic goods such as fuel and bread are often reported. These problems are exacerbated by the negative effects of HIV/AIDS. Zimbabwe's main export items include tobacco, gold and cotton as well as wheat and other cereals, which are exported to South Africa, Malawi, Botswana and Japan. For the time being Zimbabwe must be considered a hostile environment for European and US expatriates, and you should think carefully before accepting any offer of employment there. The EU has recently renewed its personal sanctions against Mr Mugabe and his associates in government.

The sustained programme of commercial farm seizures has put a tremendous strain on the agricultural and tobacco sectors. The government has introduced numerous draconian laws to control the media and freedom of expression of the population. In May 2005, the government began Operation Restore Order and Murambatsvina, ostensibly to rid urban areas of illegal structures, illegal business enterprises, and criminal activities. The International Organisation of Migration estimated that at least 300,000 people were displaced nationwide, as the operation moved from urban areas into rural areas.

Macro-economic indicators underline the disastrous state of what was a prosperous economy. The economy continues to decline each year, with negative annual growth at 7.1 per cent in 2005. The trade deficit rose to an estimated US$359 million in 2005, with a current account deficit at 6.8 per cent of GDP. Foreign debt as a ratio of GDP has now climbed to 78.6 per cent and is expected to increase again in 2006.

Working conditions

Visitors are required to have a passport, return ticket and adequate funds. Visas can be obtained upon entering the country or in advance from the Zimbabwe Embassy. It is necessary for people wishing to work as journalists in the country to apply to the Zimbabwe government for accreditation. There is a compulsory departure tax of US$20 for all US citizens.

Useful information

Shopping hours: 8.00 am to 5.00 pm, though some stores stay open longer.

Duty: You need receipts of purchase on items you bring in that are less than six months old, because duty is charged. Personal effects can be imported duty free but be prepared for a long wait to clear customs. The authorities will want serial numbers of luxury and electrical items to check that, when you leave, you take out what you brought in. Come armed with a list of numbers. If any goods are impounded pending customs clearance, ensure that you obtain an official receipt and try to determine where they have been put, to facilitate claiming at a later date.

Language: English (official), Shona, Sindebele, numerous but minor tribal dialects.

Capital: Harare.

Climate: Because of Zimbabwe's elevation the climate is healthy and pleasant, with a daily maximum temperature of 27–32°C for most of the year. The rainy season is from November to March; it is warm and dry from August to October and cool and dry from May to August. There is no need for air conditioning.

Money: Local currency is Zimbabwe dollar = 100 cents. It is advisable to take small amounts of cash to settle smaller bills, because change will be given to you in local currency. Banking: Wednesday: 8.00 am to 1.00 pm, rest of the week: 8.00 am to 3.00 pm; Saturdays: 8:00–11:30 am.

Driving: A private car is essential. Many models can be bought locally and there is a wide choice of French, German and Japanese cars. Taxis are reliable. It is advisable to take a valid international driving permit. Strictly speaking, an international permit is valid for nine months; thereafter you require a Zimbabwe licence, for which you will have to take a test. A UK licence without the bearer's photograph is not valid.

Transport: There is an excellent system of main and feeder roads, with traffic control in cities and suburbs. The road network is fairly good, but some roads are in poor condition. Rail connections link the country with South Africa, Mozambique, Botswana and Zambia, and there are international flights connecting with the UK and South Africa, as well as domestic services from Harare to Bulawayo, Kariba, Hwange and Masvingo.

Health and health care: Medical facilities, particularly outside of Harare and Bulawayo, are limited. Travellers are urged to carry an ample supply of prescription and other medication, as they are unlikely to be available in Zimbabwe. Provincial hospitals in rural areas have rudimentary staffing, equipment and supplies, and are not equipped to provide medical care in case of a serious accident. The fuel shortage further diminishes emergency response capabilities. Emergency patients have sometimes had to arrange their own transport to the hospital. Doctors, hospitals and air ambulance medical evacuation services often expect immediate cash payment for health services.

The water supply is not always drinkable so it is recommended that bottled or distilled water is used for drinking.

Malaria is prevalent throughout Zimbabwe, except in Harare. It is strongly recommended that malaria prophylaxis and preventative measures are taken when travelling outside of Harare.

Electricity: Electric power is 220v at 50 Hz.

Education: There are both nursery schools and private schools, fees for which vary considerably, with waiting lists for all good schools, both government and private. You would be well advised to see what strings your employer can pull.

Communications: The telephone system is grossly overloaded and is one of the biggest frustrations. Private individuals often put up with party lines. An internal call can take a long time. Sometimes even a call booked with the operator can involve a wait of two hours. International calls are relatively easy provided you dial outside working hours. The postal service is generally good, if a little slow sometimes. There are a number of internet providers in Zimbabwe.

Media: There are two English-language daily papers: the *Chronicle* and the *Herald.*

Useful contacts:
British Embassy, Corner House, Samora Machel Avenue/Leopold Takawira Street, PO Box 4490, Harare, tel: 263 4 772990
Zimbabwe Embassy, 429 Strand, London WC2R, tel: +(44) 171 836 7755
Zimbabwe Tourist Office, Zimbabwe House, 429 Strand, London WC2R 0QE, tel: +(44) 171 6169

PERSONAL TAXATION

Taxpayers not ordinarily resident in Zimbabwe are subject to income tax only on their taxable income from sources within the country. Non-residents are subject to withholding taxes on interest, dividends, fees and royalties at a rate of between 10 and 20 per cent. The tax year is 1 January to 31 December. A 3 per cent social security tax is charged. The maximum personal tax rate is 40 per cent on income above ZD 108,000,001. A surcharge of 30 per cent applies in addition to the income tax payable. The surcharge is calculated on the income tax payable on the excess over ZD 108 million. A 3 per cent AIDS levy is charged.

Capital gains tax is imposed on immovable property and marketable securities at a rate of 20 per cent, but a lower rate of 10 per cent applies to the sale of listed shares.

Double tax agreements are in place with Bulgaria, Canada, France, Germany, Malaysia, Mauritius, Netherlands, Norway, Poland, South Africa, Sweden and the UK.

The North American Continent

CANADA

The economy

Canada is basically a very rich country, but its economy tends to follow relatively closely that of its neighbour, the United States.

Canada is one of the largest producers of valuable minerals and is also a major exporter of automotive, timber and paper products. Most trade is with the United States, particularly following the North American Free Trade Agreement in 1993. In 2005, real GDP growth was almost 3 per cent and is forecast to reach about 3.2 per cent for 2006. Growth in 2006 may be impacted negatively by the strength of the Canadian dollar relative to the US dollar and by upward surges in the cost of energy, which may affect consumer confidence and spending. Unemployment in January 2006 was 6.6 per cent, down from 7 per cent a year earlier. Consumer price inflation is expected to hold steady at the level of 2.3 per cent through 2006. Canada maintains both a budget surplus, currently at 1.3 per cent of GDP, and a foreign trade current account balance of 1.8 per cent.

Working conditions

The general working atmosphere and corporate style in Canada closely resemble those of the United States, but Canadian society is more stable, with lower crime figures. If you go to Canada intending to stay more than three months, you have to register this fact on arrival. You cannot change your status from visitor while in-country. Applications for visas or permanent residency must be made abroad.

An average executive job, requiring graduate or professional-level qualifications and some five years or so of experience, would command an annual salary of between C$75,000 and C$100,000. A senior managerial job would be worth C$125,000 to C$175,000, plus 10 to 30 per cent bonus. By and large, executive salaries are higher than in the UK, becoming more equal going down the scale.

Professional groups that are in demand include mathematicians, sales and advertising personnel, chemists and physicists. It is also possible to immigrate if you have capital available or intend to run a business in Canada under the business immigration programme. Other schemes include Temporary Employment Authorisation and Live-in Caregiver Programme, as well as work opportunities for foreign students.

In the public services, preference is given to Canadian citizens and here, as well as in many private sector jobs, a knowledge of French is essential. It should not be assumed that the status of French in Canada is merely a nationalistic gesture. It is the mother language of many Canadian citizens. However, people who do not speak it may still enter public service, as provision will be made for them to learn the language subsequently.

People who want to exercise professional skills will have to apply to the appropriate professional bodies and institutes to make sure that their qualifications are recognised and that they possess the appropriate licence. In some cases where training to achieve the qualifications in question is substantially different in Canada, further examinations may have to be taken to achieve recognition. In all instances, though, documentary proof of degrees, etc, should be taken with you, as well as such personal documents as birth and marriage certificates.

Anyone who is not a Canadian citizen or a permanent resident who wishes to work in Canada requires authorisation. In certain cases an individual is authorised by virtue of the Regulations, but in most cases the individual must obtain a work permit from Citizenship and Immigration Canada. A work permit can only be issued for a temporary position. In order to reside and work permanently in Canada, the applicant must qualify as a skilled worker.

For detailed information, visit the website at www.canada.org.uk/visa-info// or contact Surekha Kukadia, Immigration Adviser, BDO Stoy Hayward, 8 Baker Street, London W1U 3LL, tel: 020 7893 2430, e-mail: sue.kukadia@bdo.co.uk.

Useful information

Climate: Canadian winters are much colder than anything one is accustomed to in temperate zones, although similar to those of Scandinavia. This is true even in the population centres in the southern part of the country. If you are to arrive in Canada any time between October and March make sure you have plenty of warm clothes. On the other hand, the summer (June to September) can be very warm, with temperatures averaging around 32°C in midsummer in southern places like Toronto.

Electricity: 120 V, 60 Hz; conversion from other voltages is not really possible.

Health care: Canada operates a national health insurance programme, which is administered by the provinces, for both hospital and ordinary medical (though not dental) care. In all provinces except Quebec and British Columbia, which impose a brief residence qualification (though in the case of Quebec only for hospital insurance), these are available to immigrants immediately on arrival and you should be sure to obtain details of registration and premium payments as soon as possible. Many employers pay the employee's contribution as part of the remuneration package and this is a point worth checking in any job offer.

Education: Education is compulsory from 6 or 7 to 16 (15 in some provinces) and is free to the end of secondary schooling. Educational methods are progressive and similar to those in primary and comprehensive schools in the UK. There are also a small number of private schools. For registration you will need a birth certificate, visa, vaccination certificate and previous school records. In Quebec and French-speaking Canada the medium of instruction in many schools is French, and the teaching of French is an important part of the curriculum.

Post-secondary education is not free, but repayable loans are available from the province, and there are various other forms of monetary assistance including scholarships for able students. University fees vary but are mainly low.

Useful contacts:
British High Commission, 80 Elgin Street, Ottawa, K1P 5K7, tel: 1 613 237 1530, website: www.britainincanada.org
Canadian High Commission, Macdonald House, 38 Grosvenor Street, London W1K 4AA, tel: 020 7258 6600, website: www.canada.org.uk

Canadian Tourism Commission, 62–65 Trafalgar Square, London WC2N 5DV, tel: 020 7389 9988

Surekha Kukadia, Immigration Adviser, BDO Stoy Hayward, 8 Baker Street, London W1U 3LL, tel: 020 7893 2430, e-mail: sue.kukadia@bdo.co.uk

PERSONAL TAXATION

Canada has three levels of government that levy taxes: the federal government, the provincial/territorial governments (10 provinces and 3 territories) and the municipal governments. Only the federal and provincial governments (including the territories) levy income taxes.

The determination of an individual's Canadian tax obligations will depend on a number of factors, including residence, the province/territory in which an individual is taxed and the nature of the income earned.

Residence

Like many countries, Canada taxes on the basis of residence. Tax legislation does not specifically define residence, although it does include several rules under which an individual may be 'deemed' to be resident. Generally, residence is determined by common law principles. Under these rules, an individual is generally considered to be resident if he or she has a 'continuing state of relationship' with Canada, as evidenced by a dwelling held for year-round use, the presence of a spouse or other family members in Canada, or the maintenance of personal property or other social ties in Canada, such as bank accounts, furniture and club memberships.

Taxation of personal income

Canadian residents are subject to tax on their worldwide income, including employment compensation, capital gains, interest, dividends, rents, professional fees, pensions, annuities and alimony. Non-residents are subject to tax on income earned from Canadian sources.

Income from employment

All remuneration, including most benefits derived from employment, is taxable. Taxable benefits include living allowances, housing allowances, vacations and personal use of employer-owned or employer-leased vehicles. A limited number of benefits are excluded from employment income, such as employer contributions to a registered pension or private health services plan.

Investment income

Interest income is generally subject to tax on an accrual basis. Dividends from Canadian companies are effectively taxed at a lower rate through a dividend gross-up and tax credit mechanism. Canadian residents are also taxed on dividends from foreign companies. These dividends are not subject to the gross-up and tax credit mechanism and therefore they are taxed at full rates. However, where foreign taxes are withheld on the foreign source dividends, the individual will generally be allowed a tax credit not exceeding 15 per cent of the dividend. A deduction is generally allowed for the excess.

Capital gains

One-half of capital gains realised are included in taxable income. Resident individuals are entitled to claim an exemption to reduce gains arising from the sale of qualified farm property or qualified small business corporation shares. In addition, an exemption is available that effectively exempts capital gains arising from one principal residence. There is no adjustment in calculating capital gains to remove the effect of any inflationary increase. Capital losses can generally only be applied to reduce capital gains, and any unused portion can be carried back three years and forward indefinitely during the individual's lifetime. Capital losses carried over to the year of death can be claimed against all forms of income, subject to certain restrictions.

Double taxation treaties

Canada has over 80 comprehensive treaties or conventions in force with other countries for the elimination of double taxation on income, including treaties with both the UK and the United States.

Shadi Norman is the founder and president of Jobsearch-in-Canada.com. a division of Tri- Continental Global Services.

She is a registered member of the Canadian Society of Immigration Consultants (CSIC) and the Canadian Association of Professional Immigration Consultants (CAPIC) She provides immigration, Provincial Nominee Program Assistance, Employment Counselling and Job Search assistance to clients who are thinking of emigrating to Canada, jobsearch in Canada provides Clients assistance with Job search prior to their arrival, Shadi started working in the employment counselling field in 1992 as an employment counsellor in London, UK, in the Restart program funded by the UK Government Employment Services

She emigrated to Canada with her husband and 5 year old son in 1995. Since then she has provided career counselling to Foreign-trained Professionals from all over the world. She worked as an employment counsellor for Skills for Change a leading non profit agency in Toronto with Foreign trained engineers, health care workers and Accountants and gained extensive experience in guiding them through the complex maze of licensing, career, and education options in Canada.

Tri-Continental Global Services have helped many families emigrate from Europe to Canada and always on hand to offer readers advise and answer questions relating to Immigration, Job Search, Licensing requirements and general advice on moving to Canada . You can contact her at:

Shadi Norman

Telephone (Canada): 001-604-320-0962

Fax: 001-604-436-0962

Email: ansnorman@shaw.ca

Website: www.jobsearch-in-canada.com

For further information on tax and social security, contact:

John G Wonfor, CA, CFP, TEP, National Tax Partner, BDO Dunwoody LLP, 200 Bay Street, 30th Floor, Royal Bank Plaza, Toronto, Ontario M5J 2J8, tel: 1 800 805 9544, fax: (416) 367 3912, e-mail: jwonfor@bdo.ca

MEXICO

The economy

Mexico is an important oil producer whose policy has been directed to maintain oil production at the same level and to diversify its external trade. Agriculture, mining, steel and motor vehicles are other principal industries. The United States, Canada and the European Union are Mexico's most important trading partners.

As a result of membership of NAFTA (North-American Free-Trade Agreement) which opens trade between Mexico, the United States and Canada, the economy has benefited in some aspects. During 2005, the Mexican economy continued growing. GDP reached 2.7 per cent in the fourth quarter; consumer price inflation in January 2006 was contained at 3.9 per cent. The peso revaluation against the US dollar was 4.73 per cent. There is an estimated negative trade balance for the year ended in December 2005 of US$ 8.9 billions and foreign reserves stood at US$74.2 billion in December. The deficit on current account represents 1.5 per cent of GDP.

Although the Mexican economy has been stable since the late 1990s, it remains dependent on the United States. Mexico runs a public sector budget deficit which, at 2.2 per cent for 2005, is in line with 2004 and the forecast for 2006.

Working conditions

An expatriate requires a work permit and it is acquired by the local employer; it is rather difficult for foreigners to apply for a job position as it will be primarily offered to a Mexican national.

It is advised to have all legal documentation (eg birth and marriage certificates) certified by a Mexican Consul before arrival. The expatriate salary should be expressed in a strong foreign currency. Tax rates start at 3 per cent and rise to 29 per cent (fiscal year 2006). Tax brackets may be adjusted depending on inflationary effects.

The working week is usually 48 hours. Effective 18 January 2006, compulsory holidays are 1 January, the first Monday of February (Constitution Day on the 5th), the third Monday of March (Benito Juarez's birth anniversary on the 21st, effective until 2007), 1 May (Labour Day), 16 September (Independence Day), the third Monday of November (Mexican Revolution Day on the 20th) and 25 December.

Work permits and visas

Under Mexican immigrant legislation, a foreigner may enter the country to work either as immigrant or non-immigrant. Non-immigrants are issued a permit by the Ministry of the Interior under one of the following categories: non-immigrant board member, and non-immigrant technical visitor.

The non-immigrant board member is a foreigner who enters the country to attend meetings or sessions at a company's board of shareholders and general managers or directors. This immigration status is conferred for up to one year and is renewable yearly for five years. Non-immigrant board members may enter and leave the country as many times as they wish.

The requirements for entering the country as a non-immigrant technical visitor are the same as for a non-immigrant board member, but proof of speciality must be provided.

Foreigners are considered immigrants after the fourth consecutive renewal of their immigration permit.

Useful information

Electricity: There are fluctuations in the electricity supply (100–127 V, 60 Hz). Check if your equipment is adapted to this voltage. If not, you should also bring a 1kW voltage transformer.

International dialling code: 52.

Climate: Mainly hot and dry, though Mexico City is cooler because of its high altitude. However, air pollution is considerable. High altitude may produce breathlessness and insomnia, and those suffering from anaemia or excess weight may encounter some difficulties. The rainy season is from June to October.

Driving: Roads are in good condition and gas is cheap, compared to European standards. British or international driving licences are valid when driving cars that are registered abroad, but a Mexican drivers' licence is needed to drive cars registered in Mexico. Standards of driving are not so good, and third-party insurance is advisable.

Transport: A major improvement programme for the road network was launched some years ago. Public transport in Mexico City is rather cheap, although it is also one of the busiest transport systems in the world.

Education: For people who take children to Mexico there are some good English schools in Mexico City and in other main cities, which go up to A-level, but fees are high.

Useful sites:

British Embassy, Río Lerma 71, Col. Cuauhtémoc 06500, México, D.F., tel: 55 5207 2089, website: www.embajadabritanica.com.mx

Mexican Embassy, 42 Hertford Street, London W1, tel: 020 7499 8586

Mexican Tourism Board, 41 Trinity Square, London EC3N 4DJ, tel: 020 7488 9392, website: www.mexico-travel.com

The Bank of Mexico, website: www.banxico.com.mx

Mexican National Institute of Migration, website: www.inm.gob.mx

PERSONAL TAXATION

Residence and taxation of personal income

Individuals are considered Mexican tax residents when they have established a permanent home in Mexico, regardless of their country of citizenship or nationality. When an individual also has a permanent home in another country, he or she would be regarded as a resident of the country in which he or she maintains his or her centre of vital interests. Otherwise, Mexican nationals are assumed to be Mexican tax residents.

Mexican residents are subject to taxation on their worldwide income regardless of where that income is earned (eg salaries, professional fees, rents, income from commercial activities, employee benefits, interest and other remuneration, among others). Such residents are subject to income tax on their annual taxable income and may deduct tax losses and authorised expenses.

Among authorised deductions, individuals can include medical and dental expenses, hospital and funeral expenses of their spouse, children and other direct dependants (with no taxable income); medical insurance, donations to duly authorised public services, welfare or charities in benefit of social programmes run by the public sector.

For non-resident aliens, a tax liability arises only on Mexican sources of income.

Income from employment

All remuneration including most benefits derived from employment are taxable. Taxable benefits include living allowances, housing allowances, bonuses and any kind of compensation. Some benefits are exempt from assessment as taxable income by a limit of paid-days for vacations, compensation, pensions and other benefits.

Double taxation treaties

Mexico has a wide network of 30 tax treaties with other countries for the elimination of double taxation on income, such as the UK, Germany, France, Spain, Italy, Canada and the United States.

For further information on the Mexican tax system, contact:

Eduardo Díaz Guzmán, Tax Partner Director, tel: + 52 55 5901 3954, e-mail: e.diaz@bdo-mexico.com

THE UNITED STATES OF AMERICA

The economy

The United States has maintained its recovery from the period of weakness and near recession that lasted from the first quarter of 2000 through to the end of 2002. In 2005, GDP growth was rather lower at 3.6 per than the 4.2 per cent recorded for 2004. The forecast outlook for 2006 is a further erosion of growth to perhaps 3.3 per cent, which still compares favourably with the Euro area economies. There are certainly longer-term economic problems embedded in the United States' big fiscal and current account deficits now running at 3.7 per cent and 6.5 per cent of GDP respectively. The sheer size of the US market and the natural wealth of the country used to make it seem almost independent of the world economy; however, the growing impact of China is now a critical issue. At the same time, there are shifts within the US economy that have affected expatriates – principally the growing importance of the 'sunbelt' states in the south with their 'sunrise' high-technology industries and the relative decline of the old industrial north. Although business in the United States spans every imaginable type, the largest sectors are services, finance and manufacturing. Notable industries include high technology which, together with the telecoms industry, suffered when the investment bubble burst in 2001, although the sector is now reviving. The automotive, oil, mineral extraction, defence, steel, chemicals and agriculture industries provide a more stable base to the economy, although foreign imports and foreign invested automotive manufacturing plants in the United States have threatened the financial viability of the 'big three' US car manufacturers.

Working conditions

US salaries are around 40 per cent higher than in the UK, but there is nothing like the range of benefits and degree of employment protection that you get in Europe. The Medicare health scheme is limited to the elderly and medical treatment is very expensive. If insurance is not included in the remuneration package, this could make quite a hole in an imposing salary. US executive salaries are less perk-laden than those in some other countries; for example, very few US executives get cars unless their job necessitates it.

Job advertisements in the United States, certainly at executive level, tend to demand a lot from the applicant but to be rather coy about what he or she is going to receive. Salaries, for instance, are rarely stated. It is as well to get advice from someone who has worked in the United States before accepting any offer, unless it is from a multinational, where conditions are usually fairly standard.

According to one survey, a typical middle management salary would be around US$75,000, with more senior posts in the US$120,000–$175,000 range plus bonus; bear in mind that the cost of living in the United States is now around 20 per cent lower than in the UK. However, pay rates vary according to position, type of industry and area of the country – New York, for example, is very expensive, as is Chicago. In practice, an expatriate is unlikely to find a job in the United States with a multinational unless he or she has special skills in engineering, computing, R&D or electronics, a reputation in an academic discipline, or is a qualified doctor (salaries offered to GPs range from £80,000 to £120,000).

Although the 35-hour week prevails, working conditions are a great deal more strenuous and exacting than in some firms here. US employers expect results and are fairly ruthless about removing people who do not deliver them. Senior executives come and go and it is not unusual for a shake-up at the top to work its way right down the ladder. In some firms considerable conformity with the image of the company in relation to dress, lifestyle, etc, is expected, even in the private lives of their employees. Holiday entitlement is low.

There is no VAT in the United States but there are sales taxes, which vary from town to town – rates are generally between 2 and 10 per cent. Since they are not shown as part of the price of the goods, as VAT usually is, this can mean a nasty shock when you get your bill for an expensive item.

Work permits and visas

An essential part of moving abroad is to ensure that the individual travelling holds the requisite visa or work permit. Nowhere are immigration practices and procedures more complicated and arduous than in the United States.

There are almost 60 types of temporary visas for the United States, in addition to several routes to permanent residency, or 'the green card' as it is more commonly called. The greatest difficulty faced by individuals wanting to transfer to the United States is which visa they should apply for. US immigration law is very complex and can sometimes be very confusing. We have provided below a brief guide to visas specifically related to employment.

Visa waiver

Most visitors to the United States enter the country as tourists. With the introduction of visa-free travel to the citizens of 28 countries, it is now possible for many travellers, including British citizens, to enter the United States without a visa under the Visa Waiver Program (VWP). Visa-free travel is also available to qualified travellers who enter the United States on business or in transit.

Citizens of the following countries may travel visa-free under the Visa Waiver Program if they meet the relevant criteria:

Andorra	Ireland	San Marino
Australia	Italy	Singapore
Austria	Japan	Slovenia
Belgium	Liechtenstein	Spain
Brunei	Luxembourg	Sweden
Denmark	Monaco	Switzerland
Finland	Netherlands	United Kingdom
France	New Zealand	
Germany	Norway	
Iceland	Portugal	

Visa Waiver Program criteria

The candidate must meet *all* of the following requirements:

☐ The candidate is a citizen of one of the countries named above, travelling on a valid national or EU passport. (A passport indicating that the bearer is a British Subject, British Dependent Territories Citizen, British Overseas Citizen, British National (Overseas) Citizen, or British Protected Person does not qualify its owner for travel without a visa.) Note that a passport that states the holder has Right of Abode or indefinite leave to remain in the UK does not qualify for visa-free travel.

☐ The candidate should be travelling for the purpose of a single business trip, pleasure or transit only.

☐ The candidate should be staying in the United States for a period of 90 days or less.

From 15 May 2003, citizens of Andorra, Brunei, Liechtenstein and Slovenia must be in possession of individual machine-readable passports in order to travel visa-free. From 26 October 2004, citizens of the other 23 visa-free countries named above, including the UK, must be in possession of a machine-readable passport in order to travel visa-free.

Visa-free travel does not include those who plan to study, work or remain in the United States for more than 90 days; such individuals need to obtain a visa. If an immigration officer believes that a visa-free traveller is going to study, work or stay longer than 90 days, the individual can be refused entry.

B-1 and B-2 visas

In general, individuals seeking admission into the United States to conduct business require valid B-1 visas, unless they are eligible to travel visa-free under the Visa Waiver Program, or they are nationals of countries that have an agreement with the United States allowing their citizens to travel to the United States without B-1 visas.

The definition of 'business' in this instance is limited, and does not generally allow for gainful employment or productive activity, such as operating a business or consultancy work.

While in the United States as a business visitor, an individual may:

- ☐ conduct negotiations;
- ☐ solicit sales or investment;
- ☐ make investments or purchases;
- ☐ attend meetings, and participate in them fully;
- ☐ interview and hire staff;
- ☐ conduct research.

The following activities require a working visa, and may not be carried out by business visitors:

- ☐ running a business;
- ☐ 'gainful employment';
- ☐ payment by an organisation within the United States;
- ☐ participating as a professional in entertainment or sporting events.

There is an obvious 'grey area' between what is and is not permitted on the B-1 visa. It is advisable to err on the side of caution when bringing overseas individuals into the United States on business visitor visas. However, in certain strictly limited cases, paid employment may be possible using a 'B-1 in lieu of H1B'.

Further information relating to this can be found by contacting the United States Embassy or BDO direct (details below).

Those individuals entering the United States on visitor visas will generally be granted between 30 and 180 days leave to remain (the maximum allowable is one year) on entry at the discretion of the Immigration Officer. It may be possible to obtain a six-month extension to the visitor visa as long as the candidate will be maintaining visitor status, and there are good reasons to do so. It is sometimes possible to change status to another longer-term visa while in the United States as a visitor, as long as the candidate has advised the relevant US embassy or consulate of this possibility beforehand, or there was no preconceived intent to do so.

Note that a B-1/B-2 visa should generally be applied for in the country of which the individual is a citizen or permanent resident. Applications made in other countries often run a high risk of being turned down. The most common reason for refusal of B-1/B-2 visas is where the applicant has shown insufficient ties to his or her country of residence, to show that he or she has an intention to return home after the temporary visit.

If the individual is not eligible to travel visa-free, or is not a national of a country where B-1 visa requirements are waived, he or she will be required to apply for a visa before travelling.

Note that it is the responsibility of the individual to ensure that he or she has the correct documents for travel. If the individual is not eligible to travel visa-free under the Visa Waiver Program, or is not a national of a country where B-1 visa requirements are waived, a visa will be required. Failure to obtain a visa before travelling may result in the individual being denied entry to the United States.

In general, holidaymakers travelling to the United States require valid B-2 visas, unless they are eligible to travel visa-free under the Visa Waiver Program, or they are nationals of a country that has an agreement with the United States allowing their citizens to travel to the United States without B-2 visas. If individuals are not eligible to travel visa-free, or are not nationals of a country where B-2 visa requirements are waived, they will be required to apply for a visa before travelling. In practice the B-1 and B-2 visas are issued simultaneously.

Anyone going to the United States with the intention of working there temporarily must obtain a non-immigrant work visa. In general, non-immigrant work visas are based on a specific offer of employment from an employer in the United States.

If an individual is going to the United States with the intention of working there temporarily in specific prearranged employment, he or she requires a classification H visa. The employment must be approved in advance by the office of the United States Citizenship and Immigration and Naturalization Services (USCIS) in the United States, on the basis of a petition, form I-129, filed by the US employer.

A brief explanation of the various H visa categories

An H-1B visa (speciality occupation) is required by an employee who is coming to the United States to perform services in a prearranged professional job. To qualify, the individual requires a bachelor's or higher degree (or equivalent) in the specific speciality for which employment authorisation is being sought. The USCIS will determine whether the employment constitutes a speciality occupation, and whether the candidate is qualified to perform the services. The H-1B visa is subject to an annual quota. It is worth seeking advice before lodging an application under this category to ensure that the yearly quota has not been reached.

An H-2B visa (skilled and unskilled worker) is required by an employee who is coming to the United States to perform a job that is temporary or seasonal in nature, and for which there is a shortage of resident (US) workers.

An H-3 (trainee) visa is required by a trainee who is coming to the United States to receive training from an employer in any field, other than graduate education or training. The training cannot be used to provide productive employment and must not be available in the individual's home country.

Spouses and children under the age of 21 who wish to accompany or join the principal visa holder in the United States for the duration of his or her stay, require derivative H-4 visas. Spouses and children who intend not to reside in the United States with the principal visa holder, but to visit for vacations only, may be eligible to apply for visitor (B-2) visas, or if qualified, travel visa-free under the Visa Waiver Program.

Note that the holder of an H-4 visa *may not work* on a derivative visa. If he or she is seeking employment, the appropriate work visa will be required.

Intracompany transfer

Employees of an international company who are being temporarily transferred to a parent branch, affiliate or subsidiary of the same company in the United States require Intracompany transfer (L-1) visas. To qualify, the employee must be at a managerial or executive level, or have specialised knowledge, and be transferred to a position that is either the same or similar to his or her existing position. In addition, the employee must have been employed outside the United States with the international company continuously for one year within the three years preceding the application for admission into the United States.

An L-1 visa is also the appropriate visa classification for a qualified employee of an international company who is coming to the United States to establish a parent, branch, affiliate or subsidiary in the United States: that is, to commence business. When filing the petition, the international company will be required to show that sufficient physical premises to house the new office have been secured, and that within one year of the approval of the petition, the intended operation in the United States will support an executive or managerial position. Where the individual being transferred is a person with specialised knowledge, the employer will be required to show that it has the financial ability to remunerate the employee. A petition for a qualified employee of a new office will be approved for a period not to exceed one year, after which the petitioner must demonstrate that it is carrying on business activities as described above in order for the petition and employees to be granted an extension beyond one year.

Spouses and children under the age of 21 who wish to accompany or join the principal L-1 visa holder in the United States for the duration of his or her stay require derivative L-2 visas. Spouses of a principal holder may seek employment authorisation on derivative L-2 visas.

Permanent residency: the 'green card'

An immigrant visa is required for anyone who wishes to enter the United States to reside there permanently, regardless of whether that person plans to seek employment in the United States. US immigration law provides for the issuance of immigrant visas in four general categories:

1. Employment-based.
2. Family-based.
3. Immediate relatives.
4. Diversity Immigrant Visa Program, known as the 'green card' lottery.

As this guide deals with working abroad we will give a brief overview of the employment-based category.

In general, a specific offer of employment from an employer based in the United States is required to qualify for immigration in the employment-based preference categories, which are:

☐ *Priority workers:* people of extraordinary ability in the sciences, education, arts, business or athletics; outstanding professors and researchers; and certain multinational executives and managers.

☐ *Members of the professions:* people with exceptional ability in the sciences, arts and business, defined as a member of the professions holding an advanced degree or equivalent, or Baccalaureate degree plus at least five years of progressive experience in the speciality, and people of exceptional ability in the sciences, arts and business.

☐ *Professionals: a person who holds a Baccalaureate degree and who is a member of the professions.*

☐ *Skilled and unskilled workers:* skilled workers with at least two years' training or experience, and unskilled workers whose skills are in short supply in the United States. Note that US embassies do not keep a list of these professions.

☐ *Special immigrants:* certain religious workers and ministers of religion, certain international organisation employees and their immediate family members, qualified and recommended current and former employees of the US government, and returning residents.

☐ *Investors:* persons who will create employment for at least 10 unrelated persons by investing a minimum of US$1 million in a new commercial enterprise in the United States.

Full details of all US immigration visas can be found by contacting the Consular Information Unit, United States Embassy, 24 Grosvenor Square, London W1 1AE, or by contacting Surekha Kukadia at BDO Stoy Hayward on (+) 020 7893 2430, e-mail: sue.kukadia@bdo.co.uk

Useful information

Shopping hours: 10.00 am to 9.00 pm, with later shopping one or two evenings a week. All shops are open on Saturday and most on Sunday.

Electricity: 110–120 V, 60 Hz ac. Flat three-pin plugs are normal.

Driving: Driving is on the right. An international or UK licence is valid for one year, but it is advisable to get a US licence from the State Department of Motor Vehicles – after a test. Most highways and super-highways have several lanes, and lane discipline is very strict, as is the enforcement of speed limits. In 1995 the government repealed the national speed limits. Some states now have no restrictions.

Many expatriates buy a new or used car locally and resell it when they leave. The American Automobile Association (AAA) is an extremely helpful organisation for motorists.

Transport: Americans have taken to the air as naturally as our great-grandfathers took to rail. Flying is the most efficient and speedy (and relatively cheap) way of getting round this vast country. All the main cities are connected by internal flights and there are frequent 'shuttle' services between some cities (eg New York to Washington, New York to Boston, and San Francisco to Los Angeles). Helicopter services are often available, as well as private plane hire.

There has recently been some revival of the railways. Long-distance coaches (usually air conditioned) are the cheapest way of travelling, if you can stand the boredom. Americans are also used to travelling long distances by car.

There are underground trains or 'subways' in New York, Boston, Philadelphia and Washington. The famous cable cars in San Francisco are now back in service. New York city bus services are regular and frequent – you need the exact fare.

Health care: Medical treatment is of a very high standard, but is extremely expensive. If possible, people are advised to get full medical insurance for themselves and their families before departure, even for a short stay. However, many European insurance companies no longer offer cover for expatriates and their families in the United States; instead, they advise that insurance should be arranged with a US company such as the Blue Cross.

Education: Nursery school groups can be found in most centres. All children between 7 and 16 must attend school. The school year lasts from September to June. The system comprises public schools – there are about 90,000 in the whole country with over 50 million pupils – and there are 12 grades, 1–6 elementary, and 7–12 in secondary or high school. After the 12th grade the pupils will probably go to college. Schools are operated by boards of education and are free.

There are fee-paying private schools and a number of boarding schools, modelled on the UK pattern, where tuition and boarding fees are usually fairly high. There are International Schools in New York (the United Nations) and Washington. The UN School takes children from kindergarten to high school age and sometimes can take in children whose parents are not UN officials. Instruction is in English and French.

Useful contacts:

British Embassy, 3100 Massachusetts Avenue, NW, Washington DC 20008, tel: 1 202 588 7800, website: www.britainusa.com/embassy

United States of America Embassy, 24 Grosvenor Square, London W1, tel: 020 7499 9000

United States Information Service, 24 Grosvenor Square, London W1, tel: 020 7499 9000

Expatriate contacts:
www.britishinamerica.com

PERSONAL TAXATION

These details are as at January 2005.

Residence

In order to be resident in the United States for tax purposes, a foreign national must meet one of the two separate residency tests: the green card test or the substantial presence test. Tax residents are taxable on their worldwide income in the same way as US citizens.

The green card test

A green card, or an alien registration card, is given to a foreign national who is granted lawful permanent resident status, according to US immigration laws. A foreign national is regarded as a US resident from the first day he or she is present in the United States, while in possession of a green card, and residency continues as long as the green card is held.

Substantial presence test

In order to be regarded a resident in the United States for tax purposes, a foreign national must meet the substantial presence test for all or part of the tax year. This test is based on the number of days a foreign national is present in the United States in three consecutive calendar years. To meet the substantial presence test, a foreign national must be physically present in the United States for at least 31 days during the current year, and 183 days during the three-year period that includes the current year and the two previous years, under the following formula:

current year = number of days × 1
first preceding year = number of days × 1/3
second preceding year = number of days × 1/6

If this test is satisfied, a person is resident from the first day present in the US during the current year, subject to certain *de minimus* presence.

Tax treaties and certain elections under domestic law afford flexibility in selecting a residency status in some situations. Visa statuses also impact the determination of residency status.

Income from employment

US tax residents are taxable on their worldwide income, irrespective of where it is earned.

Non-resident aliens are taxable on all US-source income (and benefits in kind, unless they are specifically excluded under US tax law) and income effectively connected to US trade or business. Employment income is 'ordinary income', and taxed at regular graduated tax rates.

Investment income

Generally, US residents' worldwide investment income is taxed as ordinary income, at graduated tax rates. However certain qualified dividends may be taxed at 15 per cent.

Non-resident aliens are only taxable on investment income from US sources; however portfolio interest income is not taxable for non-residents. Certain investment income that is not effectively connected to a US trade or business is taxed at 30 per cent (or a lower treaty rate, if applicable). This tax rate is applied to gross income, without taking into account deductions.

Taxes on capital
Capital gains

Capital gains are distinguished as short term or long term (long term being gains on assets held for more than one year). Generally, long-term gains are subject to a maximum tax rate of 15 per cent (5 per cent for individuals in the 10 per cent or 15 per cent tax brackets), while short-term gains are included in ordinary income and taxable at regular graduated tax rates.

Capital gains and certain interest income of a non-resident alien are exempt from US taxation.

Treatment of capital

US residents are not taxable on the return of capital from investments. Foreign nationals are not liable to US tax on capital remitted to the United States.

Local income taxes

In addition to Federal income tax, separate states (and in some cases also cities) may impose tax at the local level. Each state has its own tax laws and tax rates, which can apply to both residents and non-residents of the state.

Double taxation treaties

The United States has a wide network of more than 50 comprehensive tax treaties. US and UK residents may utilise the protection granted by the UK–US double taxation treaty.

For further information on taxation and social security, contact:

Carol-Ann Simon, Expatriate Tax Partner, tel: 408-352-1975, e-mail: csimon@bdo.com

Asia

SOUTH EAST ASIA:
SOME NOTES ON ETIQUETTE

It used to be said that the UK and the United States were two countries divided by the same language: meaning that things which appeared similar were often very different under the surface. This is even truer of South East Asia, where the cities, at any rate, have an increasingly Western appearance that masks profound cultural differences between Asians and Europeans. The tendency is for expatriates to feel that these can be overcome by observing the ordinary niceties of social behaviour, Western-style, but these do not always translate themselves readily. In the West, for instance, it has become customary for business dealings to be conducted relatively informally – indeed informality has become almost a style in itself. In the East, a good deal of ceremony is still observed and the more important the negotiations, the more ceremony will be attached to them. This is related to what people in the East would call 'face'.

The notion of 'face' is prevalent throughout Asia and it is a difficult term to translate. It may be, as in the instance above, the dignity of an occasion or it may be, more often, simple human dignity. The reluctance to violate your own sense of 'face' may cause a subordinate who disagrees with you to disobey your instructions, having apparently agreed to follow them. The way to deal with such a situation is not to take issue with him or her in public but to sort it out in circumstances where no loss of face is involved for either party. This has to be done with a great deal of tact – the Western notion of frankness is largely unknown to people in the Far East, who are apt to regard it merely as rudeness.

Another rich area of potential misunderstanding lies in the use of body language. As in the Middle East, it is generally considered impolite to take or offer things with the left hand, though at meals dishes can be passed with the left hand, provided it is supported by the right. Oriental people are also very wary of effusive displays of affection. Even old friends should be greeted with a certain amount of gravity and reserve. Those same qualities should also mark your relations with subordinates – pointing at people with your finger or beckoning them by use of the finger is regarded as the height of bad manners. Indeed, many finger gestures are regarded as obscene, as is making points by pounding the open palm with the fist.

The Asian culture, wherever you go, is in fact one that is very nervous about familiarity and treats as familiarity many modes of behaviour that we would regard as fairly normal. (An excellent account of this whole issue is given in *Culture Shock*, by Jo Ann Craig, published by Times Books International of Singapore.) This also extends to the use of Christian (or proper) names. The Chinese style, incidentally, is for the surname to come first, the middle name second and the equivalent of the Christian name last. Thus a Chinese man by the name Liu Ming Shan would be Mr Liu, not Mr Shan.

Another way in which Asian culture differs from ours is in the importance attached to luck. Again it is important to respect this because to dismiss it as superstition would be a grievous offence against the concept of face. It can, of course, work in your favour; for instance, it is considered bad luck if the first person into a shop each day leaves without making a purchase. In those shops where bargaining is part of normal transactions, this can lead to the often-heard 'special price, just for you' indeed having some meaning. Normally you will find that after prolonged bargaining you have ended up paying about the same as in a department store.

A further point about shopping: Asians are, in general, slighter than Europeans, so you would be well advised to stock up on clothes before you leave.

BRUNEI DARUSSALAM

The economy

Brunei has one of the highest standards of living in South East Asia. Almost all its wealth comes from oil and gas, but the government has encouraged the use of oil money to foster the development of secondary industries and services such as fishing, agriculture, education and communications. The main trading partner is Japan, followed by the UK and Malaysia.

Working conditions

Entry and exit visas are not necessary for UK nationals entering for a period not exceeding 30 days. People entering to take up employment must arrange with their employers to obtain an employment pass prior to their arrival. Spouses and children under 18 years of age are required to obtain dependant's passes. Passes are not usually difficult to obtain for UK nationals.

Useful information

Electricity: 230 V, 50 Hz ac, with both round and square three-pin plugs.

Climate: The vegetation, climate and general atmosphere of the country are typical of tropical regions of South East Asia, with high humidity and a temperature that rarely falls below 70°F and rarely rises above 90°F.

Transport: You will need a car and a good choice is available locally. Japanese cars are cheaper than British and much cheaper than European models. A Toyota Corolla costs around B$27,750. Taxis, including water-taxis, and self-drive vehicles are freely available. Petrol is cheap.

Health: Generally, health standards are extremely good. Inoculation requirements are minimal – cholera and yellow fever are advised.

Health care: Charges are made for state medical services but most companies employing expatriate workers provide medical insurance. Standards are reputed to be high, but there are also private medical facilities for those who prefer them. Nursing care is poor.

Education: Most expatriate children of secondary school age go to boarding schools in the UK, though facilities for secondary education do exist in Brunei. There are several good nursery schools, as well as three good primary schools, of which the International School is the most popular.

Alcohol: Although alcohol is banned, 12 cans of beer or two bottles of wine or spirits may be brought in on first arrival and subsequent visits.

Special note: Women should observe the Islamic dress code.

Media: The *Borneo Bulletin* is the main English-language newspaper. The government-published *Brunei Darussalam* and *The Straits Times* are also available. A range of Australian, British and US programmes are shown on television.

Useful contacts:

British High Commission, 2101 2nd Floor Block D, Kompleks Banunan Yayasan, Sultan Haji Hassanal Boliah, Jalan Pretty, PO Box 2197, Bandar Seri Begawan 1921, tel: 673 2 222231

Brunei Darussalam High Commission, 19–20 Belgrave Square, London SW1, tel: 020 7581 0521

PERSONAL TAXATION

The public sector employs about 50 per cent of the workforce. Salaries are good and government jobs usually carry such fringe benefits as subsidised or free housing, an education allowance for children, paid home leave, free medical attention, a car or an interest-free loan to buy one, and an end-of-service bonus. There is no personal tax in Brunei. There is also no restriction on remittances.

THE PEOPLE'S REPUBLIC OF CHINA

The economy

Continuing economic reforms since 1979 have brought the country step by step into line with other economies. Sustained foreign investment has enabled the construction of an industrial and communications infrastructure. In November 2001 China finally gained accession to the World Trade Organisation and committed itself to a firm programme of tariff reductions. Since then, China has enacted and amended many new laws in compliance with its WTO obligations. Many of the former barriers to investment and trade have been removed, with new standards of transparency. There are two stock markets, in Shanghai and Shenzhen, and Shanghai has emerged strongly as China's financial centre, although most of the large successful state-owned enterprises have preferred public flotation in Hong Kong.

The economy has been growing steadily at more than 8 per cent (more than 9 per cent in 2003, 2004 and 2005), with higher exports every year and soaring foreign investments. The coastal provinces, particularly, are booming and inflation has been contained (1.9 per cent recorded for January 2006). At the end of 2005 foreign reserves stood at US$818 billion, much of which is invested in US bonds and securities. The current account balance has grown even more strongly since WTO entry as tariff barriers and quotas against Chinese goods have been brought down, but imports have also grown rapidly as a result of the demand for raw materials, oil and steel to fuel China's buoyant industrial production. The current account surplus for 2005 is estimated at 5.5 per cent of GDP against 4 per cent in 2004, a significant achievement in a year when real GDP grew 9.9 per cent.

In 2004, China gained international recognition of its growing status as 'the workshop of the world' and in 2005 became the world's fourth largest economy, overtaking France and the UK.

Working oonditionc

Office accommodation is scarce and very expensive. Many foreign companies still have their offices in hotels. It has been estimated by the *China Business Review* that it costs a company around £400,000 to keep a small, one-person office in China. Business hours are from 8.00 am until midday and 2.00 to 6.00 pm. Expatriates require a work permit to work in China. The employer must have permission in the form of a licence to employ a foreign individual. However, job opportunities in the mainland for Chinese-speaking managers are likely to increase as the restrictions on foreign investment in service sectors such as banking, insurance and retailing are removed from 2007 under the terms of China's WTO admission.

For further information, contact:

Surekha Kukadia at BDO Stoy Hayward, 8 Baker Street, London W1U 3LL, tel: 020 7893 2430, e-mail: sue.kukadia@bdo.co.uk

Useful information

Transport: Both imported cars and spares are still subject to high rates of duty, although reductions are scheduled. However, there is now a good choice of cars manufactured in China, mainly through joint ventures with European, Japanese and US automotive multi-nationals. Taxis are often the preferred mode of transport.

If you have a car it is becoming increasingly possible to get around. You need a permit to travel but this is generally granted without difficulty.

Health: Cholera and yellow fever inoculations are advisable. An AIDS test may be required.

Health care: Good medical care is available, although the equipment may not be the most modern, and proprietary medication may not be in full supply.

Education: There is an International School in Beijing and American Schools in Guangzhou and Shanghai. The British International School Shanghai, in the Pudong area of Shanghai, is also recommended.

Accommodation: International-standard living accommodation can now be rented or purchased by foreigners in major cities, particularly Beijing, Shanghai and Guangzhou.

Useful contacts:

British Embassy, 11 Guang Hua Lu, Beijing 100600, tel: 861 06532 1961

Chinese Embassy, 49–51 Portland Place, London W1, tel: 020 7299 4049

Chinese National Tourist Office, 4 Glentworth Street, London NW1 5PG, tel: 020 7935 9787

www.cnto.org (US website)

PERSONAL TAXATION

These details are as at March 2003.

Residence

The People's Republic of China (China or the PRC) imposes individual taxes on the basis of residence and domicile. An individual is regarded as being domiciled in China if he or she usually or habitually resides in China due to family relationships or because he or she is a registered householder with a personal residence record. An individual who lives abroad for reasons such as education, employment, work assignments, visiting relatives, or touring, and who thereafter must return to China, is regarded as being domiciled in China. The extent to which individuals who are not domiciled in China are liable to income tax depends on their period of residence in China.

Taxation of personal income

Personal income is liable to individual income tax (IIT). Individuals domiciled in China are liable to IIT in respect of their worldwide income. After five consecutive years of residence in China, a foreign individual will be subject to IIT on his or her worldwide income in the same way as a PRC domiciliary, starting from the sixth year. Subject to the approval of the tax authorities, foreign individuals who have resided in China for between one to five years will be taxed on their PRC-source income and non-PRC-source income borne by a PRC establishment. Foreign individuals who have resided in China for less than one year are liable to IIT on their PRC-source income only. A foreign individual who works in China for less than 90 days (or 183 days if from a tax-treaty country) during a calendar year is exempt from IIT if his or her income is paid by a foreign entity and is not borne by a PRC establishment. There are different categories of income which are subject to PRC IIT including:

- [ ] wages and salaries – 5 to 45 per cent;
- [ ] income from personal services – 20 to 40 per cent;
- [ ] business income from sole proprietorships, contracting and leasing – 5 to 35 per cent;
- [ ] interest, dividends, royalties and other income – 20 per cent.

Income is computed separately for each category of income and IIT is levied at the appropriate rate on taxable income of each category after deducting allowable expenses. The tax year is the calendar year, but tax returns must be filed and tax paid monthly.

Income from employment

Taxable income from employment includes wages and bonuses. Housing allowances are also taxable. Although the law provides for the taxation of benefits-in-kind, in practice these are not taxed if certain conditions are satisfied.

There is no deduction allowed for specific expenses. However, a general allowance of CNY 800 per month is deductible by PRC nationals from taxable employment income (in some locations, such as Shanghai and Shenzhen, the amount is greater). Foreign expatriates are entitled to an additional allowance of CNY 3,200 per month, in which case their total allowable deduction per month is CNY 4,000. Bonuses, however, are accounted for separately, with no deduction.

A system of withholding tax from employee earnings is operated.

Investment income

Interest and dividends are taxable with no allowable deductions. The rate of tax is 20 per cent.

Income from real property is taxable, after deduction of a standard 20 per cent of the gross income, in respect of expenses. There is no income attributed to owner-occupiers.

Taxes on capital

Capital gains

Capital gains derived by an individual are categorised as 'other income' for PRC IIT purposes. They will be taxed at 20 per cent as indicated above.

Wealth tax

There is no wealth tax in China.

Double tax treaties

China has over 60 comprehensive treaties in force with other countries for the elimination of double taxation on income, including treaties with the UK and the United States.

For further information on tax and social security, contact:

Katherine Yeung, Tax Partner, BDO McCabe Lo and Co, tel: + 852 2853 1428, e-mail: katherine_young@bdo.com

HONG KONG

The economy

On 30 June 1997 the sovereignty of Hong Kong passed from Great Britain to the People's Republic of China, when the former Crown colony became a Special Administrative Region of the mainland. Through no fault of the Chinese government the 'one country, two systems' formula failed initially to maintain Hong Kong's former prosperity. The temporary stagnation of Hong Kong's economy was largely attributable to the territory's failure to integrate with the vibrant local industries of the Pearl River delta during the pre-handover period and to relocate uncompetitive manufacturing and service industries over the border. The Hong Kong property market, once the mainstay of the economy, collapsed; residential values fell by about 40 per cent. In the medium term, when the Chinese currency becomes fully convertible and the mainland stock markets mature, it seems likely that Shanghai will assume Hong Kong's former role as the fourth great financial centre after New York, London and Tokyo. Meantime, the Hong Kong Stock Exchange enjoys a continuing flow of flotations and active trading.

Nevertheless GDP growth revived to 8.2 per cent in 2004 and is estimated at 7 per cent for 2005. Inflation is running at a modest 1.5 per cent and tight management of the budget maintains the deficit ratio at less than 1 per cent of GDP. Hong Kong now has a negative trade balance but the current account balance rose in 2005 to an estimated 13 per cent of GDP.

Working conditions

There are no exchange controls in Hong Kong and money can be remitted into and out of the former colony. In the halcyon days before the handover, an expatriate employee in the private sector could expect to be earning 40 to 50 per cent more than his or her gross UK pay. On top of this, an expatriate employee could expect to get free or heavily subsidised accommodation and medical and dental attention, an education and holiday visits allowance for his or her children, and possible further fringe benefits such as a car, servants and a good gratuity at the end of the contract. Since 1997 job opportunities for UK expatriates have dwindled as multinational corporations have moved their regional head-quarters to Beijing or Shanghai. Public sector positions are no longer open to UK nationals.

Hong Kong's largely Chinese population (98 per cent) is impressively intelligent, skilled and hard-working, so opportunities for expatriates are limited. A work permit is required for all foreign nationals in Hong Kong. However, they are hard to come by, and it is the policy of the Hong Kong government to recruit locally wherever possible. Employees living and working in Hong Kong for more than 180 days must have a Hong Kong identity card and carry it at all times.

Useful information

Special note: The feature of Hong Kong life that strikes a newcomer most forcibly is the population density, impressive even by Asian standards. The population density for Hong Kong Island is 5,380 persons per sq km, including barren areas (three-quarters of the whole). So Hong Kong is no place for people who feel the need for wide open spaces or who are bothered by crowds.

Climate: The climate of Hong Kong – warm and humid for most of the year but with a brief cool winter – makes air conditioning and some heating facilities a necessity.

Electricity: 200–220 V, 50 Hz ac.

Driving: There are very few straight roads in Hong Kong and distances, in any case, are short, so a big car is a status symbol that attracts a higher rate of registration tax and annual licence fees. UK driving licences are valid for a stay of up to a year, but can be exchanged for a local licence without a test. Bringing a new car into Hong Kong is hardly cheaper than buying one locally; a first registration tax is charged. However, good second-hand cars are reported to be readily available.

Transport: Public transport and taxis are inexpensive but apt to be overcrowded, and most expatriates have cars, which in many cases are not provided as a perk that goes with the job.

Education: Education in Hong Kong can be a problem and expatriates are advised to make arrangements for schooling as soon as they get there, or before. Prior to arrival it is worth notifying the Education Department (9–16th Floors, Wu Chung House, 197–221 Queen's Road East, Wanchai, Hong Kong), or the English Schools

Foundation (43b Stubbs Road, Hong Kong) to ask about places. This is because most of the schools cater for the predominantly Chinese population, so the medium of instruction is either Chinese or, if in English, with the emphasis on English as a foreign language. There are several independent schools offering a UK curriculum, at both primary and secondary level.

Media: Hong Kong has two TV stations and two main radio stations providing services in both Chinese and English. There are two English TV channels and three English radio channels, two of which combine, from midnight to 6.00 am, to provide a 24-hour service; there is a BBC World Service relay on another channel at night. Satellite television offers a 24-hour global news service and a cable TV channel carries locally produced programmes.

Useful contacts:

British Consulate General, No 1 Supreme Court Road, Central, Hong Kong PO Box 528, tel: 852 2901 3000, website: www.british consulate.org.hk/

Hong Kong Government Office, 6 Grafton Street, London W1X 3LB, tel: 020 7499 9821

Hong Kong Tourist Association, 6 Grafton Street, London W1X 3LB, tel. 020 7533 7100, website: www.hkta.org; www.hkta.org/usa/(US website)

PERSONAL TAXATION

These details are as at March 2003.

Residence

The Hong Kong tax system adopts a source concept on taxability of income, and residence is therefore not relevant. However, for the purpose of the personal assessment option (see below), the terms 'permanent resident' and 'temporary resident' are defined as follows. 'Permanent resident' means 'an individual who ordinarily resides in Hong Kong'. 'Temporary resident' means 'an individual who stays in Hong Kong for a period or a number of periods amounting to more than 180 days during the year of assessment, or for a period or periods amounting to more than 300 days in two consecutive years of assessment, one of which is the year of assessment in respect of which the election (of personal assessment) is made'.

Taxation of personal income

Hong Kong does not have a general income tax. Rather, those sources of income liable to taxation are each subject to a separate tax. An individual may be subject to salaries tax on employment income; profits tax on business profits if he or she carries on a trade, profession or business in Hong Kong; and property tax on rental income from real property situated in Hong Kong.

The tax year runs from 1 April to 31 March.

Income from employment

Taxable income comprises income from Hong Kong and offshore employment, 'any office or employment of profit' in Hong Kong, and pension income from a Hong Kong pension fund.

Income from employment includes salaries, allowances, bonuses, leave pay, commission, and benefits-in-kind that can be converted to cash, and so forth. All income from Hong Kong employment is taxable, wherever the duties may be performed. However, if certain conditions in relation to the employment contract are fulfilled and the individual provides services outside Hong Kong during the tax year, a portion of income attributable to the offshore services is exempt from Hong Kong tax. This exemption does not apply to income derived from any office, such as directorship, or employment of profit.

Housing reimbursement is not taxable as such, but where accommodation is provided rent free or where rent is reimbursed, it is taxed as a notional benefit of 10 per cent of total income from the employment.

Expenses incurred wholly, exclusively and necessarily for employment, and charitable donations, are deductible. Mortgage interest paid on a property used as the taxpayer's principal residence is deductible, with an upper limit of HK$100,000. As a temporary measure of relief, the cap is increased to HK$150,000 for the years of assessment 2001/2 and 2002/3.

Salaries tax is calculated at the lower of, a) the amount computed at progressive rates starting from 2 to 17 per cent *after* deduction of certain expenses and allowances; or b) the amount computed at a standard rate of 15 per cent *before* deduction of allowances.

There are a number of personal allowances, depending on the taxpayer's personal circumstances. For example, there is an allowance of HK$108,000 for a single person; HK$216,000 for married couples; and a child allowance in respect of children less than 18 years old of HK$30,000 for each first and second child and HK$15,000 for each third and ninth child.

Individuals are separately assessed for salaries tax, but a married couple may elect for joint assessment, where this is advantageous.

Investment income

Dividends and interest

Dividends and interest income from bank deposits are not taxable in Hong Kong, whatever their source.

Income from real property

Rental income from real property situated in Hong Kong is subject, after a statutory deduction of 20 per cent on gross rental income, property rates (local property tax) if borne by the property owner and irrecoverable rent, if any, to property tax at a flat rate of 15 per cent. Mortgage interest on let property is not deductible for property tax purposes but deductible if the individual elects to be taxed under personal assessment (see below).
There is no income imputed to owner-occupiers.

Taxes on capital

Capital gains

There is no capital gains tax in Hong Kong. However, net gains derived from trading of real property are subject to profits tax at 15 per cent.

Wealth tax

There is no wealth tax in Hong Kong.

Personal assessment

An individual may elect for personal assessment if he or she: a) is of or above the age of 18; *and* b) is, or whose spouse is, either a permanent or temporary Hong Kong resident (see definition of residence above).

Under personal assessment, tax on the individual's total income (ie employment income, rental income and profits from business) is calculated at the rates applied to salaries tax, and mortgage interest for financing any real property generating taxable rental income is deductible.

Double taxation treaties

Hong Kong has not entered into any treaty in respect of personal tax. There is, however, an arrangement with the remainder of the People's Republic of China for the avoidance of double taxation on income. This is applied to individuals working both in China and Hong Kong under the same employment.

For further information on tax and social security, contact:

Katherine Yeung, Tax Partner, BDO McCabe Lo and Co, tel: +852 2853 1425, e-mail: katherine_yeung@bdo.com.hk

INDIA

The economy

In the recent decade, India has emerged as an engine of economic reforms in the international arena. This is well reflected through persistent growth in India's share in real GDP, which has risen to more than 8 per cent for 2005. Inflation has fallen to 5 per cent and per capita growth has recorded an impressive increase from 3.8 to 4.3 per cent. Structural reforms of the country have made Indian industry internationally competitive, reflected in the growth of merchandise exports followed by growth in the service sector such as information technology, telecommunications, transport services and tourism. However, imports are also rising rapidly and the current account deficit for 2005 is estimated at 1.9 per cent of GDP.

In brief, the Indian economy has exhibited a strong performance in an environment of macroeconomic and financial stability through higher GDP growth, lower inflation, a resilient external sector and a strong financial sector. Like China, Asia's other giant growth economy, India is now set firmly on the path to prosperity.

Working conditions

The working environment in India is very congenial. Anybody coming to India to take up employment needs a valid passport, a visa application form completed and signed, along with the necessary formalities for a work permit.

The working week is usually from Monday to Friday, 9.30 am to 5.30 pm, Saturday until 2.00 pm. However, in some offices, there is a five-day week.

Useful information

Time zone: India is five and half hours ahead of GMT.

Geography: India is the largest country in South Asia and the seventh largest in the world. India, a peninsula, is a natural subcontinent flanked by the Himalayas in the north, the Arabian Sea in the west, the Bay of Bengal in the east and the Indian Ocean in the south. The Andaman and the Nicobar Islands in the Bay of Bengal and the Lakshadweep Islands in the Arabian Sea are part of the territory of India.

Language: India has 16 officially recognised languages of which Hindi is the official language of the Republic. English is extensively used and understood almost everywhere.

Population: India is the second most populous country in the world, with over 1 billion people, which is about 16 per cent of the world population. Twenty-three cities have a population of over a million. Mumbai, the largest city in India, has a population over 12.6 million.

Education: Education in India is of international standard. There are international-standard schools, colleges and universities. Various types of scholarships and loan facilities are provided. Government has also introduced employment exchange programmes all over the country to facilitate the recruitment of deserving candidates into various sectors.

The literacy rate in India is 65 per cent with a vast degree of regional variation.

Climate: Due to the enormity of the country and differences of altitude, there are various climatic zones in the country. However, India has three main seasons in the year:

Rainy	mid-June to mid-October
Winter	mid-October to mid-March
Summer	mid-March to mid-June

Political set-up: India is the largest democracy in the world and has adopted a parliamentary system of government with a federal structure. The central government in Delhi has exclusive juris-diction over all matters of national interest, and comprises a Council of Ministers headed by the Prime Minister. The country is administratively divided into 29 states and six union territories. The state government has primary responsibility for matters like law and order, education, health and agriculture. The parliament comprises of two houses, the lower house – the Lok Sabha, and the upper house – the Rajya Sabha.

Currency and banking: The Indian rupee (INR) is the country's currency. Transactions on capital account are still regulated but the rupee is convertible on current account.

The country's banking system is monitored and controlled by the Reserve Bank of India. The primary functions of the RBI are issuing currency, and regulation and supervision of Indian banks and banking. The commercial banking system in India is fully developed and most of large banks are state owned. Private and foreign banks also participate in the Indian banking sector.

Judiciary: India has a well-established and independent judiciary system. The Supreme Court of India is the highest court of appeal, in New Delhi. High Courts in the states, along with supplementary district courts enforce the fundamental rights of citizens that are guaranteed by the constitution.

Transport: All modes of public and private transport are usually available across India at reasonable rates.

Accommodation: India is witnessing increased urbanisation. International-standard living accommodation can easily be rented or purchased by foreigners in major cities in India.

Health and health care: Generally, health standards are extremely good in India. Government and private bodies have set up various hospitals and private nursing homes. These hospitals provide international-standard facilities at competitive costs. Various types of medical insurances are also available in India. Medical insurance for employees and their families is also provided by employers through a group insurance or for each individual.

Media: Media is widely spread and is operated both by government and private organisations. There are radio and TV stations such as All India Radio (AIR), Doordarshan News and the Press Information Bureau providing 24-hour service and offering global news through satellite links.

PERSONAL TAXATION

Individuals who earn more than a specified amount of annual income are liable to pay income tax under the Indian Income Tax Act. The tax liability of an individual in India depends upon the individual's residential status. An individual can have any of the following three types of residential status:

1. resident and ordinarily resident;
2. resident but not ordinarily resident;
3. non-resident.

An individual is said to be resident in India if he or she satisfies either of the following basic conditions: a) he or she stays in India for a period of more than 183 days; or b) he or she stays in India for a period of 60 days or more during the previous year and 365 days or more during the four years immediately preceding the previous year.

If he or she satisfies the two following additional conditions then an individual becomes resident and ordinarily resident in India: a) if he or she is resident in India for at least 2 out of 10 years immediately preceding the previous year; and b) he or she is present in India for at least 730 days during the seven years immediately preceding the previous year. An individual is said to be non-resident if he or she satisfies none of the basic conditions.

The fiscal year in India runs from 1 April to 31 March.

Types of income

An individual's income can be divided under the following headings:

☐   income from salary;
☐   income from house property;
☐   profits and gains from business or profession;
☐   capital gain;
☐   income from other sources.

Tax rates

Tax rates are fixed by the annual Finance Act. Tax is levied on the 'total income' of an individual in accordance with the provisions of the Act, which are:

Net Income Range	Income Tax Rates
Up to Rs 1,00,000	0 per cent
Rs 1,00,000 to 1,50,000	10 per cent on the balance of the total income
Rs 1,50,000 to 2,50,000	Rs 5,000 plus 20 per cent of the balance of income
Rs 2,50,000 to 10,00,0000	Rs 25,000 plus 30 per cent of the balance of income

If an individual's net income exceeds Rs 1 million, there is a surcharge of 10 per cent on the total income. There is also an education cess of 2 per cent on the total tax and surcharge thereon.

Fringe benefit tax

The Finance Act 2005 has imposed a new tax known as Fringe Benefit Tax (FBT) on the employer on the value of benefits provided or deemed to be provided to the employees with effect from 1 April 2005. The employee is not taxed on these benefits/perquisites; the tax is paid by the employer and cannot be recovered from the employee.

Investment income

Dividends are tax-free for shareholders in India. Shareholders pay tax on interest income as per the rates mentioned above.

Capital gains

The income earned by an individual from investments in India could be in the nature of a short-term capital gain arising from the transfer of a short-term capital asset, or a long-term capital gain arising from the transfer of long-term capital asset.

For these purposes a short-term capital asset would ordinarily mean a capital asset held by the transferor of such an asset for not more than 36 months immediately preceding the date of its transfer. In the case of a share held in a company or any other security listed in a recognised stock exchange in India, a capital asset held for not more than 12 months by the transferor would qualify as a short-term capital asset. Any capital asset that has been held by the transferor for more than the foresaid period would qualify as a long-term capital asset.

Income by way of short-term capital gains earned would be subject to tax at the rate of 10 per cent plus surcharge and education cess, provided such short-term capital gains arise from the transfer of qualifying securities. Any other short-term capital gains will be chargeable to tax at the normal rate for individuals as shown in sable above.

In the case of long-term capital gains a deduction for cost inflation index (CFI) is available, whereby the costs of assets sold are adjusted in the same proportion that CFI for the year in which the assets are sold bears to the CFI in which the assets were acquired. These are declared by the authorities every year. Income earned by way of long-term capital gains would be chargeable to tax at the rate of 20 per cent plus surcharge and education cess. Long-term capital gains arising on transfer of securities are subjected to tax at different rates. Income earned by way of long-term capital gain from the transfer of qualifying securities would be exempt from long-term capital gains tax and only a securities transaction tax will be payable on such a transaction. In the case of other securities, if the costs of inflation indexation benefits are taken, the gains would be subjected to tax at a normal rate of 20 per cent. Where no indexation benefits are taken, then these would be taxed at 10 per cent.

Wealth tax

Wealth tax is levied on individuals only in respect of specified non-productive assets. Debts incurred for acquiring the specified assets are deductible in arriving at net taxable wealth. Net wealth up to Rs 1.5 million is exempt from wealth, and net wealth in excess of this amount is taxable at a flat rate of 1 per cent.

Double tax treaties

There are double taxation avoidance agreements with over 65 countries, resulting in a stable and relatively lower tax cost for foreign companies doing business in India.

Indirect tax

Several types of indirect taxes and duties are levied by the various authorities in India like VAT, Excise, Custom, Service Taxes, etc. Among these, Service Tax, which has been recently introduced, is the effect of massive growth in the service sector and is increasingly becoming a significant source of revenue for the government.

Note

This information has been prepared based on details available to the public and the sources are believed to be reliable. Though due care has been taken to ensure accuracy, no representation is made that it is accurate and complete. The material is meant to provide general information and should not be acted upon without first obtaining professional advice tailored to the particular needs of the reader. For further information, contact:

R P Singh, Partner, rpsingh@bdolodha.com, Prashant Khandelwal, prashantkhandelwal@bdolodha.com, tel: 91 33 2248 1111, fax: 91 33 2248 6960

JAPAN

The economy

Despite Japan's almost total dependence on imported energy, the country remains one of the world's economic superpowers. Until recently Japan's readiness to adapt to new technology had been one of the secrets of its success. However, after a period of economic growth in the 1980s, since the end of the 1990s Japan experienced the worst economic crisis in its recent history. The banking industry, in particular, came close to disintegration but is now stabilised. In 2004, GDP growth rose for the second year in succession to 2.6 per cent and is expected to maintain that level of growth through 2006. The budget deficit has been reduced to 6.5 per cent of GDP, and the current account balance maintained at about 3.5 per cent of GDP. Although modest inflation is forecast for 2006, consumer price deflation continued through 2005 at 0.2 per cent, and unemployment remains rather high, for Japan, at 4.4 per cent.

Japan is a highly industrialised country; only 14 per cent of land is cultivatable. Fish rather than meat is the main source of protein in the diet. Rice is the staple food. Heavy investment in subsidiary manufacturing abroad has led to the peculiarity of Japan importing Japanese goods. Japan maintained a strong trade balance of US$94 billion in 2005 with a current account surplus at 3.5 per cent of GDP expected to continue at that level through 2006.

Working conditions

An expatriate executive will need double his or her UK salary to live at a normal standard, entertain as his or her job will require, and provide UK schooling for any children. Tokyo has consistently been one of the world's most expensive cities, and a senior expatriate executive should strive for US$180,000–$230,000, plus 15–20 per cent overseas loading. Japanese indigenous salaries, once relatively low, are also now in the upper quartile and well above UK levels. It is advisable to arrange for some salary to be paid elsewhere to ease the tax burden and facilitate the transfer of funds to the UK.

The majority of expatriates working in Japan are employed by foreign companies, particularly as representatives; otherwise, the main source of employment is as an English language teacher. EFL teachers are likely to be recruited by Japanese language schools. Bona fide students in Japan can appeal for permission to work a limited number of hours per week (teaching EFL); pay is from £16 to £25 an hour. Some language schools underpay their full-time staff. Even a primary school teacher should be earning at least £16,000 a year, bearing in mind the cost of living.

A person wishing to enter Japan for the purposes of employment, training or study, must apply for a visa. Requirements are: a valid passport; one visa application form completed and signed; one passport-sized photograph; and a certificate of eligibility (original and one photocopy). The certificate of eligibility is issued by the Ministry of Justice in Japan. It is provided by a future employer or sponsor in Japan. In certain cases additional support documents may be required.

Employment patterns in Japanese firms differ from those in the West – recruitment is on traditional paternalistic lines from families with loyalty to the company – and a knowledge of Japanese would be a prerequisite.

Holders of UK passports require no visas for tourist visits less than 90 days, which period may be extended to a maximum of 180 days at the discretion of the authorities. A work visa is required by those who have already obtained a post. To obtain a work visa you must first have a definite job appointment in Japan. Your employer should then apply to the Ministry of Justice for a Certificate of Eligibility. Once this is received you must submit, in person, a visa application to the Japanese Consulate, together with the

Certificate. Provided the documents are all in order a visa can normally be issued fairly quickly. Information is available from the Visa Section, Consulate General of Japan, 101–104 Piccadilly, London W1V 9FN. Temporary work is not permitted but, if when visiting as a tourist you receive a written offer of a permanent post, a working visa may be obtained by leaving the country and applying from outside (Korea, for example).

   Booklets outlining Japanese business practices and attitudes are available for business people from JETRO London, Leconfield House, Curzon Street, London W1Y 8LQ, and may be useful for other visitors. For points on etiquette and survival tips, three useful publications for intending expatriates in Japan are *Living in Japan*, *A Consumer's Guide to Prices in Japan* and *Finding a Home in Tokyo* published by the American Chamber of Commerce in Japan, Bridgestone Toranomon Building, 3–25–2, Toranomon, Minato-ku, Tokyo 105, tel: 03 3433 5381, fax: 03 3436 1446.

Useful information

Commercial organisations: Office hours are usually 9.00 am to 5.00 pm; many companies operate a five-day week.

Banking hours: 9.00 am to 3.00 pm Monday–Friday, 9.00 am to 12.00 pm on Saturday.

Shops: Shops and department stores are usually open on Sundays and public holidays, but most other businesses are closed then. There are public holidays throughout the year.

Electricity: 100 V, 50 Hz ac in eastern Japan, including Tokyo, and 60 Hz in western Japan, including Nagoya, Kyoto and Osaka. Hotels generally provide sockets for both 110 and 220 V.

Special note: Expatriate wives may find life difficult because of the position of women in society, where they are expected to be self-effacing. A wife's role might be confined to formal entertaining at home, of which there is a great deal, to promote her husband's interests.

Duty: The expatriate who will be staying longer than a year may bring in household effects, including a car and/or boat, duty free within limits considered reasonable by the customs authorities. The car (or boat) sales receipt must be presented to show that it has been in use for more than one year before its arrival in Japan.

Driving: An international driving licence is valid for one year, after which a Japanese licence must be obtained. This involves both practical and written tests, which may be taken in English. Traffic drives on the left, and tolls are payable for motorway use. The volume of traffic is immense, but Japanese drivers are patient and disciplined, and accidents are consequently few. Signposting is inadequate (supposing one can read them) and a compass might be useful.

Transport: All the usual forms of public and private transport are available.

Health care: Medical insurance for employees and their families is provided either by a government-managed scheme or a health insurance society. There are a number of English-speaking doctors in major cities, and Western brands of drugs are available.

Education: There are many schools for English-speaking children but they are not geared to UK education. Most expatriates leave their children to be educated in Britain.

Media: Four English-language newspapers are published daily: the *Japan Times*, the *Yomiuri Daily*, the *Asahi Evening News* and the *Mainichi Daily News*.

Useful contacts:
British Embassy, No 1 Ichiban-cho, Chiyoda-ku, Tokyo, 102–8381, tel: 813 5211 1100, website: www.uknow.or.jp/
Japanese Embassy, 101 Piccadilly, London W1V, tel: 020 7465 6500
Japan National Tourist Organisation, website: www.seejapan.co.uk

PERSONAL TAXATION

These details are as at March 2004.

General outline of tax system

The direct taxes most likely to affect the expatriate executive coming to work in Japan are individual income tax, inhabitant tax, and gift and inheritance tax. For individual income tax purposes, the fiscal year is the calendar year. The inhabitant tax is a local tax, levied at the prefectural and municipal level, and consists of an income-based element and a per capita charge. The National Tax

Administration administers national direct taxes; the municipalities administer inhabitant tax.

Treatment of the family

Husbands and wives are taxed separately. There is no option for joint filing.

Nature of income tax

Income tax is levied at progressive rates on the aggregate income of an individual from one or more of 10 sources:

1. income from employment;
2. capital gains;
3. interest;
4. dividends;
5. rental income from real property;
6. income from a business;
7. occasional income;
8. miscellaneous income;
9. forestry income; and
10. retirement income.

Residence

The extent of an individual's Japanese income tax liability depends on the individual's residence status. A permanent resident is liable for tax on worldwide income; a temporary resident is liable for income tax on Japan-sourced income and foreign-sourced income to the extent that it is paid in or remitted to Japan; non-residents are liable on Japan-sourced income only.

A permanent resident is an individual who is either 'domiciled' in Japan, or has lived in Japan for at least one year and is not a 'non-permanent resident'. A non-permanent resident is an individual who has been living in Japan for less than five years and has no intention of residing permanently in Japan. Most visiting executives are likely to fall into this category. An individual is domiciled where he or she has his or her permanent home or principal base of life.

Special rules are applicable to years of arrival and departure. An individual is regarded as becoming resident (whether temporarily or permanently) from the day of arrival in Japan if he or she comes to take up an appointment that requires the individual to live continuously in Japan for a period of at least one year. If the assignment lasts into a sixth year, the individual becomes a permanent resident from the end of the fifth year.

Upon departure, residence ceases immediately if it is apparent that the individual will be working abroad for more than one year.

Taxes on capital

Capital gains

Capital gains from the disposal of real property and of shares are subject to separate rules. The tax rates vary depending on the types of securities and the length of time held.

Wealth tax

There is no wealth tax in Japan.

Double taxation treaties

Japan has concluded over 40 comprehensive tax treaties, including those with the UK and the United States.

For further information on tax and social security, contact:

Paul Nakamura, BDO Sanyu & Company, 1–24–1 Nishi-Shinjuku, Shinjuku-ku Tokyo 160–0023, tel: 03–5325–1635, e-mail: pnakamura@bdo.or.jp

MALAYSIA

The economy

Malaysia is a fertile country. Its economy has traditionally been associated with palm oil, rubber and timber and these are still important products, particularly because of the impact of oil price rises on the synthetic rubber industry. Malaysia is also one of the few remaining sources of tropical hardwoods, grown mainly in East Malaysia. Oil palm is the most rapidly expanding new crop and Malaysia is now the world's leading exporter of oil palm products. Food crops are also grown extensively and the country is 90 per cent self-sufficient in rice. Recoverable gas reserves, however, have been found on a very large scale and these have spurred industrialisation at a growing pace.

The other resource with which Malaysia is traditionally associated is tin, and though facing competition from synthetic substitutes, Malaysia is the West's leading supplier of this metal. The exploitation of natural gas reserves is growing in importance.

The most rapidly expanding sector of the economy has been manufacturing, which provides 70 per cent of exports, including electronics, office equipment, cars and consumer goods. Malaysia is enjoying comparatively strong growth by European standards at 4.6 per cent for 2005, forecast at the same level for 2006. With a continuing surplus on its foreign trade current account, estimated at 12.6 per cent of GDP in 2005, and a positive trade balance, the outlook remains favourable. Foreign reserves stood at US$69.9 billion at 2005 year-end. Inflation was at 3.2 per cent in January 2006 and the budget deficit ratio to GDP is expected to improve to 3.2 per cent for 2005 and lower for 2006.

Working conditions

No one may enter Malaysia to take up employment without a work permit and this can only be obtained by the employer. Dependants need a dependant pass and must also obtain permission from the immigration authorities if they wish to take up any kind of paid employment. Separate passes are issued for peninsular Malaysia, Sabah and Sarawak and they are not interchangeable. Sponsorship and a guarantee may be necessary.

The working week is usually Monday to Friday, 8.30 am to 5.00 pm, Saturday until 1.00 pm, but in some states the Moslem week, Saturday to Wednesday, or Thursday morning, is kept.

Useful information

Electricity: UK electrical equipment is suitable for Malaysian supply (230 V, 50 Hz ac), but perhaps not for the climate.

Climate: The climate is tropical, hot and humid, varying little (except in the highlands) from a mean of 80°F (32°C). Seasons are more related to rainfall than to temperature. Rain, averaging about 2,300 mm a year, falls in short, drenching thunderstorms: about 60 per cent of it from November to March.

Driving: A private car is considered a virtual necessity and the general opinion is that it is better to buy one of the makes that is locally assembled than to import a car: spares are easier to get hold of, mechanics are more familiar with the cars, and they are better suited to local conditions. Moreover, there is an import duty of 100–350 per cent on cars. With effect from 1 January 2004, changes were made to the import duties and excise duties on cars under the ASEAN Free Trade Area (AFTA). In light of this, employers should be prepared to supply a company car, and as an expatriate employee you can reasonably expect that a car will go with the job. Petrol is cheaper than in the UK. It is advisable to take out a comprehensive insurance policy because local driving standards are poor. You will need to have a Malaysian driving licence eventually but an international driving licence is valid for one year.

Transport: Scheduled coach services and long-distance taxis are cheap and efficient. A small car can be hired for around RM110 a day.

Health: Malaysia's climate is obviously apt to present health problems for those who cannot take long spells of uninterruptedly hot, humid weather. However, the principal disease hazard, malaria, has been largely eliminated, though it still exists in some rural areas. (Yellow fever injections are required before you enter the country, and your doctor will advise you on other precautions.)

Health care: Most expatriates receive free medical treatment in some form or other, either as government employees or as part of the remuneration package. Otherwise, this is a potentially major expense to be budgeted for or insured against. First-class hospital accommodation alone – apart from actual treatment – costs up to RM850 a day.

Special note: Malaysia is very strict about drugs, and trafficking in hard drugs carries the death penalty. If you are bringing medicines with you, make sure they are prescribed and labelled.

Education: The schools situation in Malaysia is awkward for expatriates. It is difficult to get into state schools because Malaysian children have priority, and in any case the curriculum is designed for the indigenous population. There are a number of fee-paying schools catering for expatriate children, although only one, the Uplands School in Penang, offers boarding and a UK curriculum.

Useful contacts:
British High Commission, 185 Jalan Ampang 50450, Kuala Lumpar, tel: 603 2170 2200

Malaysian High Commission, 45 Belgrave Square, London SW1, tel: 020 7235 8033
Tourism Malaysia, 57 Trafalgar Square, London WC2N 5DU, tel: 020 7930 7932, website: www.tourism.gov.my

PERSONAL TAXATION

Broadly speaking, an expatriate should expect to be earning about 50 per cent more than his or her gross UK salary, taking the value of fringe benefits into account. Free or subsidised accommodation and medical care, a car, financial assistance with education and paid home leave every second year are usually provided. There are no restrictions on non-residents bringing in any amount of foreign currency and/or travellers' cheques. Declaration in the Arrival/Departure Card issued by the Immigration Department is only required for amounts in excess of the equivalent of US$2,500.

Tax is levied on a PAYE basis on any income accruing in or derived from Malaysia; benefits-in-kind, excluding free medical treatment and the payment of passages home, are counted as part of chargeable income. Deducted from chargeable income are a broad range of allowances for a wife, dependent children, contributions to pension schemes and part of the cost of educating dependent children. The rate of tax begins at 2 per cent and reaches a maximum of 28 per cent. The government is encouraging companies to establish their South East Asian headquarters in Malaysia, and expatriates employed in their regional office for a short period (60 days or less) are exempt from Malaysian income tax. Most tax treaties exempt non-residents from tax if they are employed for 182 days or less, subject to other conditions.

SINGAPORE

The economy

Singapore has no natural resources other than its natural harbour, its well-developed infrastructure and the skills and industry of its people. Despite the inherent disadvantages of a small domestic economy and lack of natural resources, Singapore has established itself as one of the best business destinations. It is recognised as one of the world's most competitive economies, supported by an increasingly globally competitive workforce.

International banks, insurance companies, ship operators, traders and professional consultants are an integral part of Singapore's business environment. The Republic is also a leading financial centre with a strong and stable currency, no exchange control restrictions, low inflation and low interest rates.

The success of the economy is the result of the government's timely implementation of a policy of industrialisation and diversification. The economy has been restructured to place emphasis on higher technological applications and skill-intensive, capital-intensive industries, and to promote Singapore as an important centre for such activities as international trading, warehousing, financial and business services, medical, dental and computer services.

As the economy matures, Singapore is finding it increasingly difficult to maintain the same rates of high growth experienced in the 1980s and 1990s. Manufacturing and services continue to be promoted as the twin engines of growth for the future. GDP growth in 2005 was in excess of 6 per cent and inflation has been contained at under 2 per cent. There is a surplus on the public sector budget.

Singapore's main trading partners are Malaysia, the United States, Japan, Hong Kong and China. Singapore has maintained massive foreign reserves at US$120.2 billion in January 2006 and is now investing actively in other high-growth economies in Asia in order to balance the more modest domestic growth rate. The foreign trade current account remains comfortably in surplus, running at about 24 per cent of GDP in 2005.

Working conditions

The British expatriate community is quite large – between 7,000 and 8,000. Jobs are advertised in the appropriate sectors of the overseas press and are usually on a contract basis with a salary plus fringe benefits, as indicated in the personal taxation section, below. The major Singapore professional bodies are affiliated to, or otherwise closely connected with, their UK counterparts. People going to work in Singapore must have an employment pass, which has to be obtained by the prospective employer. Dependants must also obtain a pass that has to be applied for by the employer. There are various immigration schemes for those with proven technical, professional or entrepreneurial skills.

Useful information

Climate: Singapore is less than 137 km from the equator and is hot and humid for most of the year.

Electricity: 230–250 V, 50 Hz ac. Three square pin plugs are common.

Transport: The importing of cars is discouraged, and there is a duty of 45 per cent on imported cars on top of a basic additional registration fee of 150 per cent of the value of any new car, imported or otherwise. Thus it is not advisable to bring a car into Singapore from abroad, even though buying one locally is very expensive. Second-hand cars are advertised for sale in *The Straits Times*. The government is trying to limit car ownership on the island, both by fiscal policies and by placing restrictions on the use of cars in the central business district. On the other hand, both taxis and public transport are correspondingly inexpensive, and indeed are among the world's cheapest.

Health: Singapore has a good health record and the government wages a somewhat draconian cleanliness campaign, which includes hefty fines for dropping even a bus ticket in the street.

Health care: There are no free medical facilities, but treatment in government clinics is very cheap, though most expatriates prefer to use private doctors, who charge between S$25 and S$50 (specialists S$45–$80), depending on their qualifications and what sort of treatment is involved. Surgeons' and obstetricians' fees start at around S$2,100 and a private room in a hospital costs about S$180 a day. Medical fees, or insurance premiums to cover them, are often, in the case of expatriates, met by employers.

Education: As with many other jobs overseas, education can be a problem, and arrangements to send children to local schools should be made as soon as possible. Government schools are very cheap, with only nominal fees for the children of Singapore residents. There are three good English private primary schools. The Singapore American School takes all ages up to 18, and there is also the United World College of South East Asia, which has facilities for A-level teaching. There is an excellent university in Singapore, at which the standards of entry and the level of the courses are equivalent to UK universities. Fees vary depending on the nature of the course being taken.

Useful contacts:

British High Commission, 100 Tanglin Road, Singapore 247919, tel: 656424 4200, website: www.britain.org.sg/

Singapore High Commission, 9 Wilton Crescent, London SW1, tel: 020 7235 8315

Singapore Tourism Board, 1st Floor, Carrington House, 126–130 Regent Street, London W1R 5FE, tel: 020 7437 0033

Expatriate contacts: www.expatsingapore.com

Information on Singapore tax: simonpoh@bdo.com.sg

PERSONAL TAXATION

Managers of medium-sized companies might expect to earn £40,000–£50,000 a year plus fringe benefits such as free or subsidised housing, home leave, free medical treatment, school fees and a car. There are no restrictions on the amount of money that can be taken out of the country. However, job opportunities for UK expatriates are not as robust as in the 1980s and 1990s.

Individuals resident in Singapore for tax purposes are liable to Singapore personal income tax charged on a sliding scale on income derived in or remitted to Singapore. Accommodation provided by the employer and certain benefits in kind are taxable, but not capital gains. Tax is levied at progressive rates from 0 to 22 per cent. There is tax relief for up to three children, but none thereafter – part of Singapore's policy of keeping down family numbers.

Employment for a period or periods that together do not exceed 60 days in a calendar year is exempt from tax.

SOUTH KOREA

The economy

South Korea is the world's 10th biggest economy in terms of GDP. Korea's GDP, a measure of economic size, was $667.4 billion in 2004, up from $605.2 billion in 2003 when Korea ranked 11th in world, a real growth in GDP of about 5 per cent. Per capita GNP was $14,100 in 2004, up from $12,000 in 2003. Considering the growth rate of per capita GNP in the past, the country could enter an era of $20,000 in 2008. Korean exports were ranked 12th in 2004.

If transit exports are excluded, Korea is the world's ninth biggest exporting country ahead of The Netherlands, Belgium and Hong Kong. South Korea remained the world's best in ship orders and shipbuilding in 2004. Korea is the world's fifth-largest steel producing country, and sixth in world car production in 2004. The country's sales of semiconductors were second in 2004. In particular, South Korea is believed to have topped the world in thin film transistor liquid crystal display (TFT LCD) output, sales of dynamic random access memory (DRAM) and sales of fresh memory. Foreign reserves were US$216.9 billion in January 2006. Korea consistently runs a surplus on its foreign trade current account, estimated at 2.3 per cent of GDP for 2005.

Consumer price inflation in January 2006 was at 2.8 per cent, while the deficit on the public sector budget for 2005 is estimated at 1.6 per cent.

Working conditions

Significant reforms to improve the flexibility of the employment market have contributed to employment stability. Part-time and contract employment have increased, accounting for 56 per cent of the total and so weakening the strength of labour unions. Increased labour flexibility has greatly contributed to the recovery of corporate earnings, resulting in greater job creation and reduced unemployment. In response to the rapidly changing economic environment and labour market conditions, the government adopted a five-day working week starting with government, financial institutions and companies with more than 300 employees. The move aimed to create new jobs, plus raise labour productivity and the general standard of living. The government expects that the adoption of the five-day working week will raise the standard of living for working people, which in turn will stimulate the creation of more jobs in the service industries, thereby lowering the unemployment rate further.

Obtaining a visa for business or work purposes for Korea is quite straightforward, but the rules are tight. A visa is not required for most tourist, transit, or non-remunerative business stays of up to 30 days. For longer stays for work, research, teaching, or extended family visits, longer-term work or other specified purposes, a visa must be obtained prior to arrival in Korea. To obtain a work visa, one must first obtain a work permit from a Korean employer.

Useful information

Commercial organisations: Office hours are usually 9.00 am to 6.00 pm; many companies operate a five-day week.

Banking hours: 9.30 am to 4.30 pm, Monday–Friday.

Shops: Shops and department stores are usually open on Sundays and public holidays, but most other businesses are closed then. There are public holidays throughout the year.

Electricity: 220 V for both residential and industrial purposes.

Driving: An international driving licence is valid for one year, after which a Korean licence must be obtained. This involves both practical and written tests, which may be taken in English. Since 1 July 2003, foreigners from countries that recognise Korean driver's licences have been able to drive in Korea with his or her country's driver's licence. However, a foreigner from a country that does not accept Korean driver's licences needs to take a test to drive in Korea. He or she can obtain a Korean driver's licence upon passing the test.

Transport: All the usual forms of public and private transport are available.

Health care: Medical insurance for employees and their families is provided either by a government-managed scheme or a private insurance company, including many reputable international insurance companies. There are a number of English-speaking doctors in major cities, and many high-quality general hospitals.

Education: There are some international schools in the Seoul metropolitan area.

Media: Some English-language newspapers are published daily, and international TV channels , such as the BBC, CNN and NBC are available through satellite TV.

Useful contacts:
British Embassy, Taepyeongno 404 Jeong-dong Jung-gu, Seoul 100–120, tel. 82–2-3210–5500

PERSONAL TAXATION

Personal income tax

The current Personal Income Tax Act classifies personal income into four categories: global income, retirement income, timber income and capital gains.

Global income

Global income comprises wages, interest, dividends, property leases, business income, temporary income, pensions and miscellaneous income. Deduction of necessary expenses and income deductions from the aggregate amount of the above sources of income produces the taxable amount, upon which the global income tax is imposed at 8 to 35 per cent. Incidentally, exempted from the obligation to file a global income tax return are, a) interest income, dividend income and miscellaneous income that are subject to separate withholding taxes; and b) wages and salaries where the obligation to pay personal income tax are fulfilled by monthly withholding and filing a year-end tax return.

Tax base (W000)

Not exceeding	Tax on lower amount	Rate on excess (%)	Rate on excess (%)
	10,000		8
10,000	40,000	800	17
40,000	80,000	5,900	26
80,000		16,300	35

Taxes on capital gain

Tax on capital gains derived by foreigner from the disposal of real property or shares are subject to tax treaties and income tax law. The taxability and tax rates vary depending on the types of assets, the length of time held, and equity ratio.

Wealth tax

There is no wealth tax in Korea.

Double taxation treaties

Korea has concluded tax treaties with 62 countries, including the UK and the United States.

For further information on tax and other matters, contact:

C S Kim, Partner, BDO Daejoo Accounting Corporation, Dongha Building, 6th Floor, 629, Daechi-Dong, Kangnam-Ku, Seoul 135–281, tel: 82–2-2263–2868, e-mail: cskim@bdodaejoo.co.kr

Australasia

AUSTRALIA

The economy

The outlook for the Australian economy is for continued growth, with low unemployment and moderate inflation. Economic growth is forecast to be increase from 2.5 per cent in 2005 to 3.1 per cent in 2006. The recovery in exports has been delayed by global conditions; however, exports are set to expand with the current account deficit ratio to GDP reducing from 5.9 per cent in 2005 to 5.3 per cent in 2006. The Australian government expects another budget surplus in 2005/6 at the level of 1 per cent of GDP, with substantial surpluses projected for the next three years. Unemployment was reported as 5.3 per cent in January 2006 and consumer price inflation is expected to increase modestly from 2.7 per cent in 2005 to 2.9 per cent in 2006.

The government maintains a cautious line on immigration policy. Preference is given to people with direct and close family connections, skilled and business migrants, and others accepted under refugee or special humanitarian programmes. A points system is used in some of the categories to determine a person's eligibility based on factors such as age, health, education, occupation and the level of skill required to undertake that occupation in Australia. All non-nationals must obtain a visa beforehand. Additional information can be obtained from the Australian High Commission in London or the Australian Consulate in Manchester.

Working conditions

Leave entitlements

At executive and professional levels, international standards and conditions of work apply. Holidays are normally four weeks a year and some firms pay a holiday bonus. There is also often a form of sabbatical leave after 10 years' service with a company. Flexible working hours are quite common in Australia, particularly in the public sector.

The chief difference in working conditions between Australia and other countries is that the concept of status related to specific jobs – and even more, social and workplace behaviour associated with it – has to be discarded. Any tendency to 'give yourself airs' is fatal!

Recruitment

Australian employers will not usually recruit from a distance, but it is possible to get a good picture of the sort of employment opportunities available from Australian newspapers and particularly from the Australian migration authorities. In general the demand is for specific skills and professional or managerial qualifications. Most British professional qualifications are recognised in Australia; however, accreditation from the appropriate licensing board may be required for certain professions.

Entry visas

There are a number of business visas available for individuals or companies wishing to set up a branch or representative office in Australia or to engage in business activities. The following is a brief summary of some of the more commonly used visas.

Business visit visa (456)/Electronic Travel Authority (ETA). The business visit visa/ETA allows for a visit of up to three months – no extensions can be made while the visa holder is in Australia. No work may be undertaken on this visa. The purpose is to attend meetings, hold discussions, participate in short-term training, etc. Nationals of certain countries can apply on the internet or through travel agencies or airlines for the ETA. Non-ETA eligible nationals need to apply for the 456 visa through the nearest Australian diplomatic mission.

Business long stay visa (457). This temporary visa is granted for up to four years and can be renewed or extended. It is commonly known as the work visa as it provides visa holders with permission to work – but only for the sponsoring company.

This visa is commonly used by companies overseas looking to send staff to Australia to set up and run a branch or representative office, or to establish a company in Australia, for the purposes of engaging in business. This visa is also used by companies already operating in Australia who wish to bring in specialist staff from overseas.

There are three stages to obtaining a 457 work visa:

1. Sponsorship – an overseas-based company must first apply for approval as a sponsoring company. Assessment looks at company background, financials, and proposed activities in Australia.
2. Nomination – this involves assessing the position that is to be filled by the visa applicant. The position must relate to an occupation on a list of skilled occupations. The salary for the position must meet minimum thresholds.
3. Visa – assesses the visa applicants and whether they have the formal skills and qualifications for the position.

Occupational training visa (442). A temporary visa for up to two years which allows an Australian company to sponsor someone from overseas to undertake work-based training. A formal training programme is essential.

Employer nomination visa. This is a permanent residence visa. It requires a company to sponsor someone and is similar to the 457, although the visa application requirements are different. Requires the sponsoring company to be established and operating in Australia.

Business skills visas. There are a number of these visas – most are temporary visas for four years, not renewable. They require visa holders to establish or purchase a business in Australia (a small business is usually sufficient) and manage that business. If that business achieves certain business outcomes in terms of turnover, equity, staffing, etc, then the visa holder may apply for permanent residence.

These visas target people who have successfully run their own businesses over the last few years, or who have had very senior executive positions in large corporations (non-government), or who have themselves actively managed a portfolio of investments over a number of years and who have a high net worth.

For further information on Australian visas and entry rules, contact:

Harriet Mantell, Registered Migration Agent No 9901517, BDO Migration Services Pty Ltd, 563 Bourke Street, Melbourne VIC 3000, Australia, tel: +613 9615 8747, e-mail: harriet.mantell@bdomigration.com.au

Surekha Kukadia, Immigration Manager, BDO Stoy Hayward LLP, 8 Baker Street,

London W1U 3LL, tel: +44 20 7893 2430, e-mail: sue.kukadia@bdo.co.uk

Useful information

Financial year: The Australian financial year runs from 1 July to 30 June.

Electricity: Electrical goods should be checked with the maker to see if they would work in Australia, because the voltage systems differ (220–250 V, 50 Hz ac). Gas appliances are particularly tricky because of differences in pressure and gas composition. British TVs and video recorders do not function in Australia because of different signals and need to be professionally converted to be compatible with the Australian system.

Driving: A car, essential in Australia, is best bought there. If you import a car you will have to make sure that it meets the safety regulations of the state to which you are going. You can drive on a British licence for the first three months. After that you will have to take a local test, but this will only be an oral one if you already hold a British or international licence.

Transport: Interstate transport is usually by aeroplane, although there is also a large railway network.

Education: Education begins at the age of 5 or 6 and is compulsory up to age 15 or 16 (depending on the state). The school session starts early in February, not September as in the UK. It must be remembered that, in the southern hemisphere, the seasons are reversed, hence the Australian Christmas is in mid-summer. Tuition is free in government schools, but parents generally have to provide uniforms, books and other materials. As many as 25 per cent of pupils, however, attend private schools, particularly in the latter years of secondary education. Fees are reasonable because these schools are aided by government grants. Allow A$5,000–8,000 a year for private secondary school tuition fees.

There are small tuition fees for university-level education, which is very well provided for in all states. Most Australians take a pass degree rather than honours. Standards are similar to those in the UK.

Useful contacts:

British High Commission, Commonwealth Avenue, Yarralumla, Canberra, ACT 2600, tel: 612 6270 6666, website: www.uk.emb. gov.au

Australian High Commission, Australia House, Strand, London WC2, tel: 020 7379 4334

Australian Tourist Commission, tel: 020 8780 2229, websites: www.aussie.net.au, www.australia.com

PERSONAL TAXATION

Residence

Australian tax residents are taxed on their worldwide income, while non-residents are taxed only on Australian-sourced income, subject to the operation of double taxation agreements, which override domestic tax law.

An individual will be an Australian resident for taxation purposes if he or she ordinarily resides in Australia or if any of the following tests is satisfied:

☐   the individual's domicile is in Australia and he or she does not have a permanent place of abode elsewhere;

☐   the individual has physically been present in Australia for 183 days or more in the financial year (1 July to 30 June) and does not have a usual place of abode outside Australia; or

☐   the individual is a member of certain Commonwealth government superannuation schemes.

A place of abode is the place where the taxpayer adopts a habitual mode of living. Where an individual is a dual-tax resident, double taxation agreements may apply to demarcate the taxing right of each country in respect of the income derived.

Income from employment

Gross cash remuneration, which includes wages, commissions, allowances (excluding living-away-from-home allowance, which is subject to fringe benefits tax), and bonuses, is assessable at his or her marginal rate. Individual tax rates are progressive and range from 0 to 47 per cent (see below for 2005/6 tax rates).

Non-cash remuneration is generally subject to fringe benefits tax (FBT), which is taxable to the employer, not the employee. FBT is levied at an effective tax rate of 48.5 per cent on the grossed-up value of benefits provided.

Lump sum payments due to termination of employment are subject to a maximum tax rate of 31.5 per cent, while bona fide redundancy payments are tax-free up to a certain limit.

Superannuation lump sum payments are subject to a maximum tax rate of 21.5 per cent. Termination payment received in excess of a Reasonable Benefit Limit (RBL) is subject to a higher tax rate. The excessive component (the amount over the RBL) is taxed at 38 per cent, if payment is from a superannuation fund, or 47 per cent if the payment is directly from the employer.

Australian residents are liable to pay a medicare levy at the rate of 1.5 per cent of their taxable income, although non-residents are exempt.

Special taxing rules apply to shares and rights issued under an employee share scheme.

Tax-free threshold

The annual tax-free threshold for most Australians (and some other residents) is $6,000. This means that, unless your circumstances are different from the majority, your first $6,000 of income is not taxed. When your taxable income exceeds your tax-free threshold you pay tax on the excess. The 2005/6 rates are:

Taxable income	Tax on this income
$0–$6,000	0
$6,001–$21,600	15c for each $1 over $6,000
$21,601–$63,000	$2,340 plus 30c for each $1 over $21,600
$63,001–$95,000	$14,760 plus 42c for each $1 over $63,000
Over $95,000	$28,200 plus 47c for each $1 over $95,000

Lodging an Australian tax return

Individuals must lodge a tax return if they are an Australian resident for tax purposes, and if any of the following applies: a) they paid tax during the year, or b) their taxable income exceeded certain amounts (for example their income is more than the tax-free threshold (see the tax rate table).

The due date for filing 2006 income tax returns is 31 October 2006; however, if you have a tax agent preparing your tax return, your due date for filing may be extended.

Tax file number

A tax file number (TFN) is a unique number issued by the tax office. It is not compulsory to have a TFN; however, if you do not have one you may have more tax withheld than is necessary or be unable to receive government benefits you are entitled to. A TFN will help you to:

- ☐   lodge a tax return;
- ☐   ask about your tax affairs;
- ☐   make or receive payments under the pay as you go (PAYG) withholding system;
- ☐   when you start or change jobs;
- ☐   join a superannuation fund.

If you have never had a TFN, you will generally need to complete and lodge an application form. Permanent migrants and temporary visitors to Australia can apply for a TFN online at www.ato.gov.au, or through Centrelink.

Superannuation schemes

Australia has in place a superannuation guarantee scheme which is administered by the Australian Taxation Office (ATO). Under this scheme, Australian employers are required to provide a minimum level of superannuation support for their employees. For the 2005/6 year this level of support is 9 per cent of the employee's salary. The level of support required in relation to an individual employee is measured on a quarterly basis and in the event that an employer fails to make an appropriate contribution to a complying superannuation fund, a charge is levied on the employer. The employer is required to make the appropriate superannuation contributions within 28 days after the end of each quarter. Importantly, the superannuation guarantee scheme applies to all employees whether they are employed on a full-time, part-time or casual basis.

Investment income

Gross investment income of residents is assessable to an individual at his or her marginal tax rate. Australian-sourced franked dividends (that is, paid from profit already subject to corporate tax) are assessable to resident shareholders, who are assessed on the grossed-up dividends (inclusive of franking credits which represent the company tax paid). Resident taxpayers in receipt of such dividends are entitled to offset the franking credits against their tax liability.

Dividends, interest and royalty income paid to non-residents from an Australian source are subject to withholding tax, which the payer is liable to withhold. Such withholding tax is a final tax and amounts that have been subject to withholding tax are not included in the Australian assessable income of non-residents.

An exemption from withholding tax applies in the case of franked dividends paid to non-residents. Unfranked dividends are generally subject to Australian withholding tax imposed at the rate of 30 per cent unless the dividend is paid to a resident of a country with which Australia has a double tax agreement. In such cases the rate of with-holding tax is reduced to 15 per cent. In certain other cases, an unfranked dividend paid to a non-resident of Australia may be exempt from Australian withholding tax where such a dividend consists of a 'foreign dividend account declaration amount'. Certain other specific exemptions from dividend withholding tax may also be applicable.

In regards to interest and royalty withholding tax, the rates of withholding are generally 10 per cent and 30 per cent on the gross payment respectively, although such rates may be modified by a double tax agreement.

From 1 July 2004, additional withholding obligations have been imposed on certain payments made to non-residents. Specifically, from that date withholding (currently at the rate of 5 per cent) is required from:

☐   payments for operating or promoting a casino junket tour;
☐   payments made to sportspersons and entertainers in addition to certain payments made to the support staff of such individuals;
☐   payments made under certain contracts for the construction, installation and upgrading of buildings, plant and equipment and related activities.

Australia has in place a regime that adopts a 'substance over form' approach in classifying interests in a company as debt or equity interests. Where a 'dividend' is paid in respect of a 'non-equity share' it is treated as interest for withholding tax purposes. Likewise, where a payment is made to a non-resident in respect of an equity interest (eg a non-share equity interest), the payment may be subject to dividend withholding tax.

Taxation of capital

Capital gains

The net capital gain from the disposal of assets acquired after 19 September 1985 is included in taxable income and taxed at the individual's marginal tax rate. A 50 per cent discount may apply if the asset has been held by the individual for at least 12 months. A capital loss may be carried forward indefinitely and can only offset a capital gain.

Certain assets that have a necessary connection with Australia are subject to capital gains tax, regardless of the owner's residency status, including Australian real estate, shares in Australian private companies, interests in Australian partnerships and trusts, interests of 10 per cent or more in Australian public companies and unit trusts, and Australian business assets.

Non-residents who become resident in Australia are taken, for the purposes of the Australian capital gains tax regime, to have acquired their assets for market value on the day that they become resident.

Australian residents who become non-residents are required to either calculate capital gains on all assets that they own that do not have the necessary connection with Australia as if they disposed of those assets for market value on the date that they ceased residency; or undertake to lodge Australian tax returns every time they dispose of assets with the necessary connection with Australia in the future. Certain assets are exempt from capital gains tax, including:

☐   an individual's main residence;
☐   motor vehicles;
☐   assets for which depreciation is allowable as an income tax deduction.

Wealth tax

There is no wealth tax at either the federal or state level.

Double taxation agreements

Australia has double tax agreements with a large number of countries, including both the United States and the UK.

For further information on tax and social security, contact:

Stephen Healey, National Expatriate Tax Leader, BDO Kendalls, Level 18, 300 Queen Street, Brisbane, QLD 4000, tel: +61 3 9615 8500, fax: +61 3 9614 4963, e-mail: shealey@bdokendalls.com.au

Cameron Allen, BDO, 563 Burke Street, Melbourne, VIC 3000, tel: +61 3 9615 8500, fax: +61 3 9615 8700, e-mail: Cameron.Allen@bdomel.com.au

Chau Tran, Senior Expatriate Tax Manager (Australia Desk), BDO Stoy Hayward, 8 Baker Street, London W1U 3LL, tel: +44 20 7486 5888, e-mail: chau.tran@bdo.co.uk

NEW ZEALAND

The economy

Economic reforms have changed the economy from being highly regulated and protected to one of market economics. Deregulation, privatisation and the removal of subsidies have brought great changes. The now-independent Reserve Bank has a contract to keep inflation between 1 and 3 per cent; the welfare state has been largely dismantled.

Agricultural products continue to form the core of the economy, primarily in dairy products, cattle and sheep. Fish, timber and wood pulp are increasingly important. Natural gas is the most successful resource export. Almost all power is provided by hydro-electricity. Manufacturing is being actively encouraged, but tourism is the fastest-growing sector. Main trading partners are Australia, Japan, the United States and the UK.

New Zealand recently enacted a law removing the Privy Council in London as the nation's highest court of law. This has been replaced by a new Supreme Court based in Wellington.

In 2005 GDP growth fell away from the 4.4 per cent registered for 2004 to an estimated 2.6 per cent and is forecast to fade further to 2.3 per cent in 2006. Inflation rose to 3.2 per cent in 2005 and is expected to remain at about that level though 2006. Encouragingly, unemployment continued to decline to 3.4 per cent in 2005, although it is expected to return to about 3.9 per cent in 2006 as the economy slackens. However, exports grew by only 1 per cent in 2005 while imports increased by 8 per cent, so that the current account deficit rose to 8 per cent of GDP.

New Zealand maintains a budget surplus and the ratio to GDP was a healthy 5.3 per cent in 2005.

Working conditions

Applications for work permits must be supported by an offer of employment from a New Zealand employer and must be submitted at least four weeks prior to intended departure from the UK. Accommodation guarantees may be required. Further information may be obtained from the New Zealand Immigration Service, New Zealand House, Haymarket, London SW1Y 4TQ, tel: 020 7973 0366. There are no restrictions on taking money into or out of the country. Visitors from the UK, and many other nationals, do not require a visa but those intending to stay for longer periods must apply for a residence permit. Consideration is generally only given to applicants with skills on the Occupations List.

In general, rates of pay are slightly lower than in the UK, while deductions are at about the same level. The cost of living, however, is less, so that the net result is very similar to working in the UK. Most employees receive at least three weeks holiday. The 40-hour week is universal.

Useful information

Electricity: 230 V, 50 Hz ac. Most UK electrical equipment will work in New Zealand, but some items may require a transformer to reduce voltage. British TVs have to be adapted as frequencies and line systems differ. However, in some instances it is possible to buy a suitable export model. A VHF modulator is required for video viewing on a normal New Zealand TV set.

Driving: People entering New Zealand to take up permanent residence for the first time may bring in a motor vehicle free of duty and Goods and Services Tax (GST; similar to VAT) if certain conditions are met (a leaflet is available from New Zealand House). UK driving licences are accepted for the first year of your stay, after which you have to take a test (which has written and oral parts) to obtain a New Zealand licence. Although New Zealanders drive on the left and road rules are essentially the same as in the UK, it would be advisable to check out the New Zealand road code – there are differences, especially in the 'give way' rules.

Transport: Travel by internal airline is very popular, and often the best option to more remote parts.

Health care: Widespread means-testing has been introduced throughout the welfare state, so that only the very poor now receive free or subsidised health care and other benefits. Under a reciprocal arrangement with the UK, health care (including hospitalisation) is available to residents who go to live in New Zealand and have made the necessary National Insurance Contributions here. Visits to the doctor, prescriptions and hospital outpatient visits are all charged in relation to the patient's ability to pay.

Education: Primary school education begins at 5, but there is also an excellent network of pre-school education for 3-year-olds upwards. Education is compulsory from 6 to 15 and tuition is subsidised. Parents are expected to pay some fees and for uniforms, the wearing of which is customary in secondary schools. There are also private schools, mostly conducted by religious bodies. University entrance qualifications correspond to those in the UK and tuition is subsidised for those who reach top-level entrance qualifications. There are university scholarships for the brightest students. There are seven universities.

Useful contacts:

British High Commission, 44 Hill Street, Wellington 1, tel: 644 924 2888

New Zealand High Commission, 80 Haymarket, London SW1Y 4TQ, tel: 020 7930 8422

Tourism New Zealand, 80 Haymarket, London SW1Y 4TQ, tel: 09069 101010, website: www.purenz.com

PERSONAL TAXATION

Residence

New Zealand tax residents are taxed on their worldwide income, while non-residents are taxed only on New Zealand-sourced income, although the liability may be reduced by the provisions of an applicable double taxation agreement.

An individual will be a New Zealand resident for taxation purposes if either of the following tests is satisfied: the individual has a permanent place of abode in New Zealand, even if a permanent place of abode is also maintained overseas; or the individual has physically been present in New Zealand for 183 days or more in any 12-month period. The individual would be New Zealand resident from the first day within that 12-month period that he or she was present in New Zealand.

A permanent place of abode is determined with reference not only to the availability of a dwelling in New Zealand but also to the extent of financial and social ties with New Zealand. Where an individual is a dual tax resident, a double taxation agreement may apply to demarcate the taxing right of each country in respect of the income derived.

Non-resident individuals working in New Zealand are subject to the same marginal rates of tax as residents, but only on their New Zealand-sourced income.

Taxation

Tax is deducted on a pay as you earn (PAYE) basis in respect of income from employment. The basic rates of income tax are progressive and range from 19.5 to 39 per cent in respect of individuals; both corporates and trusts have a flat tax rate of 33 per cent. Self-employed individuals and contract workers are generally responsible for their own tax affairs and are invariably subject to provisional tax and, in some instances, withholding tax obligations exist. In addition, there is a GST of 12.5 per cent.

Income from employment

Cash income from employment

Income derived from employment is generally defined as monetary remuneration and is assessable to the employee at his or her marginal tax rate. Monetary remuneration includes wages, employment-related allowances, bonuses, other emoluments, expenditure by an employer on account of an employee, certain benefits received from employee share plans, and benefits provided to the employee in respect of free or subsidised accommodation.

Non-cash income from employment

Non-cash remuneration is subject to fringe benefit tax (FBT). FBT is payable by employers on fringe benefits provided to employees at the rate of 49 per cent or 64 per cent of the taxable value of the benefit depending on the nature of the benefit provided.

Superannuation schemes

New Zealand does not have a compulsory superannuation regime. Employer contributions to a registered scheme (superannuation fund) are subject to a specified superannuation contribution withholding tax of 33 per cent. Employer contributions to a non-registered superannuation scheme will be subject to FBT. In most instances, payments from a New Zealand superannuation fund are not taxable in the hands of the recipient. However, in limited circumstances, certain withdrawals from a superannuation fund may have a tax consequence.

Investment income

Income derived from investments is also assessable to the taxpayer at his or her marginal tax rate. Investment income may include interest, dividends (including attached imputation credits and withholding tax) and rental income.

New Zealand-sourced imputed dividends (that is, paid from profit already subject to corporate tax) are assessable to resident shareholders, who are assessed on the grossed-up dividends. The imputation credit is offset against the taxpayer's taxation liability. Where imputation credits exceed the taxpayer's tax liability, a refund of the excess imputation credit is not allowed; however, it is carried forward as a credit against future income in respect of individuals. Excess imputation credits received by corporates and trusts are converted to a loss at 33 per cent and can be carried forward to future income years provided certain ownership thresholds are maintained. Dividends that have no imputation credits attached to them will be subject to resident withholding tax (RWT) at a rate of 33 per cent. Interest income is also subject to RWT at varying rates depending on the taxpayer's marginal tax rate.

Dividends paid to non-residents of New Zealand are subject to a withholding tax by the payer (non-resident withholding tax).

However, non-resident shareholders may indirectly benefit from dividend imputation under the foreign investor tax credit regime. Interest income paid to non-residents is subject to non-resident withholding tax.

Income derived from rental properties is subject to income tax. However, expenses incurred in relation to that property are allowed as deductions.

Taxation of capital

New Zealand does not possess a capital gains tax regime. However, where property (both personal property and real property) is acquired with the intention of resale or as part of a business of trading in that property (such as a dealer in shares), then that property will be subject to income tax upon its eventual sale.

Generally speaking, a company registered under the Companies Act 1993 can make distributions of capital tax-free to its domestic shareholders, provided certain criteria are met.

Gift duty

New Zealand maintains a regime for gift duties. Under current gifting rules, a taxpayer can distribute an amount up to NZ$27,000 tax-free in an income year. New Zealand does not have any estate or death duties or regional and state taxes.

Double taxation agreements

New Zealand has a large number of double tax agreements with other nation states, including the United States and the UK. The New Zealand–UK double tax agreement has recently been amended by a protocol updating certain of its provisions and allowing for the better exchange of information between the treaty partners.

For further information on tax matters, contact:

Craig Lamberton, Tax Partner, BDO Spicers, tel: +64 9 373 9605, e-mail: craig.lamberton@akl.bdospicers.com

PAPUA NEW GUINEA

The economy

Until fairly recently, the economy was based almost entirely on agriculture with no cash economy. Most of the population is occupied in this sector. Commercial crops include copra, cocoa, coffee, rubber, tea and sugar. Exports of tropical wood is a mainstay – PNG is one of the few remaining countries in the region exporting unprocessed timber, but restrictions to preserve the forests have recently been imposed. The most important natural resources are copper, gold and silver. The Panguna Copper Mine in Bougainville used to provide nearly half of PNG's national income until closed by rebel action. Large-scale mining has been encouraged elsewhere. Large oil and gas reserves have also been discovered. Other industries are small-scale or absent altogether.

GDP growth in 2005 is estimated at 2 per cent and is forecast to rise to 2.8 per cent in 2006. Inflation rose to 7.3 per cent in 2005 but is expected to moderate to about 4.5 per cent in 2006. The budget deficit ratio in 2005 was 1.5 per cent but is expected to fall to less than 1 per cent in 2006. Papua New Guinea maintains a foreign trade current account surplus, which has fallen from a peak of 15.2 per cent in 2001 to 1.7 per cent in 2005, although both exports and imports have grown steadily over the period.

Working conditions

It is necessary to hold a work permit in order to gain permission to reside in the country. This is obtainable before arrival, either through the Department of Labour and Industry or through the employer. In addition, all foreign nationals must have a valid passport and visa before entering Papua New Guinea.

Many expatriate posts in the country are in government employ, and are well advertised in the UK, typically in *The Guardian*. Salaries are quite high, but the qualifications and experience demanded are equally so.

Useful information

Climate: The climate is typically tropical and cool cotton clothes are normal year-round wear. The Highlands are cooler. Port Moresby has a dry season from May to November, the opposite of Lae's.

Health and security: Malaria is a problem in many areas, although Moresby is now relatively safe. Health problems have been replaced by domestic and personal security concerns. Violent crime is a particularly serious issue and houses should be well protected. Assaults on women are also a serious problem in the major cities. Curfews are not unknown.

Transport: Travel within the country is usually impossible by road (except from Lae to the principal Highland towns). Consequently, air is the normal medium for transport and Air Niugini flies to all the major centres and to many small towns; other carriers include Talair, Douglas Airways, Bougair and several other charter firms. Hire and radio cars are available in the main towns, but bus services are still inefficient. There are some scenic highways, of various quality.

Communications: The telephone service is excellent but all mail must be addressed to PO boxes.

Special note: There is no mains gas supply.

Education: The education system is good, and there is a university with 3,000 students at Port Moresby and a University of Technology at Lae. The language of instruction is English. There are a number of International Schools which follow a broadly New South Wales, Australia, curriculum, but many expatriates send their children abroad for their education.

Useful contacts:
British High Commission, PO Box 212, Waigani, NCD, Papua New Guinea, tel: 675 325 1677
Papua New Guinea High Commission, 14 Waterloo Place, London SW1, tel: 020 7930 0922

PERSONAL TAXATION

Wage-earners with only one source of income have tax deducted automatically from their pay, after deductions for dependants. Tax rates go up to 35 per cent.

There should not normally be any problems with remitting currency from Papua New Guinea.

Part Six:

Website Directory of Useful Contacts

The websites listed are those identified at the time of going to print. Due to the dynamic nature of the internet, variations in content and changes of address might occur. The publishers cannot take responsibility for the content of the websites listed but have tried to ensure, where possible, that the material is of a suitable nature. However, an exemplary illustration of what can be found on the internet is the *Electronic Telegraph's* expatriate website, Global Network, which offers advice, links and country profiles. It can be found at www.telegraph.co.uk or www.global-network.co.uk.

INTERNET DIRECTORIES AND SEARCH ENGINES

Alta Vista
http://uk.altavista.com
Britannica Internet Guide
http://www.ebig.com
Excite Search
www.excite.com
www.excite.co.uk
Google
www.google.com
Google Groups
http://groups.google.com
Search tool for finding news groups.
HotBot
www.hotbot.com
The Lists/Topica
http://www.lists.com
Search tool for e-mail discussion groups and e-mail publishing.
Regional Directory
www.edirectory.com
Listing of regional web directories.
UK Directory
www.ukdirectory.co.uk
Who Where
www.whowhere.com
Directory of e-mail addresses to help you keep in contact with friends, family and organisations.
Yahoo!
www.yahoo.com
http://uk.yahoo.com

JOB OPPORTUNITIES
Internet resources

America's Job Bank
www.ajb.dni.us
Extensive database of current vacancies in the USA.

Cadremploi
www.cadremploi.fr
France's leading management career site.
Career Builder.com
www.careerbuilder.com
Provides regional breakdowns of salary information.
Career Resource Centre
www.careers.org
Index of US and Canadian careers-related websites, with more than 8,000 links to related sites.
CareersInsite
www.careersinsite.org
US university site with over 1,000 links to job searching sites.
Cool Works
www.coolworks.com
Provides links to details of 'cool' jobs with the emphasis on the USA. For example, jobs in national and state parks, ski resorts and ranches. Visa restrictions are problematic for Europeans, but it is worth having a look at this site.
JobHunters Bible
www.jobhuntersbible.com
Reviews of US guidance sites with links to them.
Job Site
www.jobsite.co.uk
Directory of major UK and European recruiters, mainly in IT and human resource management.
The Monster Board
www.monster.com
Invaluable resource on international job opportunities and country-specific information. Sites in Canada, Australia, Belgium, The Netherlands and the USA.
Prospects Web
www.prospects.ac.uk
Careers information for graduates with overseas sites offering vacancy information.
The Riley Guide to Employment Opportunities and Job Resources on the Internet
www.rileyguide.com
Worldwide vacancies with emphasis on the USA.
Sciencejobs.com
www.sciencejobs.com
International scientific employment opportunities.
SYO-Guiden
www.syoguiden.com
Swedish site with links to career guidance sites worldwide.
TV Jobs
www.tvjobs.com
US TV companies offering intern or work experience or placements.

Media

BioMed*Scientist*
www.biomedscientistjobs.com
International life science and medical recruitment site. Vacancies from *The Scientist* and *BioMed* journals.

British Medical Journal
www.bmjcareers.com
Medical vacancies.

Careers in Construction
www.careersinconstruction.com
Vacancies from *The Architects' Journal*, *Construction News* and *New Civil Engineer*, updated weekly. Links to other sites of specialist journals.

The Daily Telegraph
http://www.telegraph.co.uk
Online version of full paper with recruitment vacancies worldwide.

Emap
www.emap.com
Publishers of a wide range of trade and specialist magazines with recruitment sections.

E&P Directory of Online Newspapers
www.editorandpublisher.com
Reference resource including newspapers on the web and proprietary online services. Listed by country with search facilities for specific publications, locations or attributes. Also provides a career centre which boasts an extensive job search facility.

Expat Network
www.expatnetwork.co.uk
Publishes *Nexus* and offers support service for expats and a register of those looking for work abroad which is sent to recruiters.

Financial Times
www.ft.com
Finance- and business-related vacancies.

The Guardian Unlimited
http://jobs.guardian.co.uk
Vacancies in wide range of occupational areas.

Inkpot Newspaper Links
http://inkpot.com/news/majint.html
Links to international newspapers by country and region.

Irish Times
http://www.irishtimesjobs.com
Searchable site for jobs in Ireland.

Nature
http://www.nature.com/naturejobs
International science job listings, updated weekly.

Overseas Job Express
http://www.overseasjobs.com
Newspaper carrying 1,500 job vacancies and information about working abroad every two weeks.

Physics World Jobs
http://careers.iop.org
Part of the UK's Institute of Physics site with job and research opportunities.

ResortJobs
http://www.resortjobs.com
Also produced by Overseas Job Express, a database of worldwide resort jobs. Includes ski and snowboarding resorts, national parks, cruise ships, hotels and restaurants.

Summer Jobs
http://www.summerjobs.com
Also produced by Overseas Job Express, a database of seasonal and summer jobs.

Recruitment consultancies and employment agencies

Au pair JobMatch
http://www.aupairs.co.uk
Search by country and nationality of families for worldwide au pair vacancies.

Crewseekers International
www.crewseekers.co.uk
Work found for amateur crews for leisure sailing, cruising and racing.

Engineering Production Planning Limited
www.epp.co.uk
Agency with offices in Europe, Singapore and the USA. Specialises in vacancies in aerospace, oil and gas, water, power generation, nuclear engineering, production, defence, communications, chemical processing, civil engineering and manufacturing.

Hays International
www.hays.com
International vacancies.

Malla Technical Recruitment Consultancy
http://www.malla.com
Specialising in engineering placements worldwide.

Michael Page International
www.michaelpage.com
Offices in The Americas, Australasia and Europe, specialising in accounting, banking and finance.

Pilot Select
www.pilotselect.com
Matches pilots with airlines looking for crews.

Reed
http://www.reed.co.uk
Vacancies, careers information and links to career resources worldwide.

Reed Finance
http://www.reed.co.uk/finance

Robert Walters
www.robertwalters.com
International accounting and finance recruitment agency.

Veterinary Locums Worldwide
www.vetlocums.com
Site for vets looking for short-term work in practices, wildlife projects or with exotic animals.

Professional Associations

British Medical Association
www.bma.org.uk
Information and advice on working abroad for BMA members.

Institute of Physics
www.iop.org
Physics-related vacancies.
Royal College of Nursing
www.rcn.org.uk
Information and advice on working abroad for RCN members.

Organisations

The British Council
www.britishcouncil.org
Teaching opportunities and voluntary work overseas. Recruits EFL teachers for its own Language Centres.
Committee on the Status of Women in Physics
www.aps.org/educ/cswp
Arm of the American Physical Society. Information on dual-science-career jobs.
Council on International Educational Exchange
www.ciee.org
Work experience, short-term jobs and worldwide exchange programmes for students and recent graduates.
Doctors without Borders
www.doctorswithoutborders.org
Opportunities for medically trained personnel to work in developing countries.
European Commission
www.cec.org.uk/work/index/htm
Commission's current vacancies for English-speaking candidates.
The International Health Exchange
www.ihe.org.uk
Health personnel for programmes in developing countries.
Search Beat
http://www.searchbeat.com/energyjobs.htm
Worldwide jobs in the petroleum industry.
United Nations
http://unjobs.org
Vacancy board for UN departments worldwide.

Teaching English as a Foreign Language

The British Council
See Organisations.
The Centre for British Teachers
www.cfbt.com
Teaching vacancies in Brunei, Oman and Turkey and educational specialists in Eastern Europe, Africa, Asia and India.
Council on International Educational Exchange
See Organisations.
ELT Job Vacancies
www.jobs.edufind.com
Teaching English as a Foreign Language posts worldwide.

International House
www.ihlondon.com
Recruits teachers for 100 schools in 26 countries.
i-to-i
www.i-to-i.com
i-to-i provides language courses, such as TEFL, for travellers along with volunteer placements around the world.
TEFL
www.tefl.co.uk
Teaching English as a Foreign Language courses.
TEFL.com
www.tefl.com
Teaching English as a Foreign Language job database with links to worldwide employment vacancies.

Voluntary work

British Council
See organisations.
i-to-i
See TEFL.
Voluntary Service Overseas
www.vso.org.uk
Opportunities in 58 countries in education, health, technical trades, engineering and other fields.

International companies

BDO Stoy Hayward
www.bdo.co.uk/taxservices
A cohesive worldwide network of specialists providing immigration, tax and social security advice to expatriates and their employers.
Boeing
www.boeing.com
Aviation giant offers internships for college students at US institutions.
British Airways
www.britishairwaysjobs.com
Cabin crew, IT and sales vacancies.
GlaxoSmithKline
www.gsk.com/careers/joinus.htm
Access to both UK and US searches for current vacancies in this pharmaceutical company.
Hewlett-Packard
www.jobs.hp.com
IT giant with online application forms.
IBM
www.ibm.com
US site has links to global recruitment.

Integra Global
www.integraglobal.com
International medical insurance providers.

Lloyds TSB
www.lloydstsb.com
International banking.

Microsoft
www.microsoft.com/careers
Information vacancies at the company's different locations.

Shell International
www.shell.com
Superb website with access to expatriate information on its 'OUTPOST' (www.outpostexpat.nl) and Spouses Support Network websites (see expatriate websites).

Standard Bank
www.standardbank.com
International banking.

COUNTRY-SPECIFIC DATA

Political information

Foreign and Commonwealth Office
www.fco.gov.uk
Travel Advice Unit provides up-to-the-minute information on political upheaval, natural disasters and epidemics worldwide.

United Nations
www.un.org
Information on countries in the UN.

US Department of State Travel Advisories
http://travel.state.gov/travel
Up-to-the-minute information in the same vein as the Foreign and Commonwealth Office.

Economic data

Economics Departments, Institutes and Research Centers in the World (EDIRC – University of Connecticut)
http://edirc.repec.org
Index of economic institutions on the web.

CIA FactBook
www.cia.gov/cia/publications/factbook
Country breakdown with economic, political, geographic and demographic information available.

Financial Times Country Briefs
http://surveys.ft.com
Superb country surveys providing developments and detailed information on regions and countries, including economic indicators and company activity and performance details.

Union Bank of Switzerland
www.ubs.com
Produces comparative survey 'Prices and Earnings Around the Globe' detailing costs and earnings in 53 countries.

Business guides

Department of Trade and Industry Export Publications
www.dti.gov.uk/export.control/publications.htm
Publications aimed at businesses abroad and for intending expatriates.
Hong Kong and Shanghai Banking Corporation
www.hsbc.com/businessprofiles
Publishes 'Business Profiles' aimed at companies and private individuals and contains useful information on living conditions.

General information

The Centre for International Briefing
www.farnhamcastle.com
Cultural and business briefings covering all regions of the world. Also customised programmes and language tuition.
ECA International
www.eca-international.com
Relocation company with excellent resources and country briefings worldwide.
Expat Network
www.expatnetwork.co.uk
Among other services provides location reports to members.
Expedia
www.expedia.co.uk
Many links to other travel sites.

Continent-specific information

Africa

Africaonline
www.africaonline.com
Information on African countries.
AllAfrica.com
http://allafrica.com
African news and information on countries.
Commonwealth Institute
www.commonwealth.org.uk
Information on member states of the Commonwealth.
www.kenyaweb.com
General information on the culture, history and life in Kenya.
Yahoo!
http://travel.yahoo.com/p-travelguide-191500003-africa_vacations-i
Search engine directory of information on the region.

America

US Census Bureau
www.census.gov
US statistics with links.
Yahoo!
http://travel.yahoo.com/p-travelguide-191501863-united_states_vacations-i
Search engine directory of information on the region.

Asia

Commonwealth Institute
See above.
East Asia Business Services
www.shef.ac.uk/eltc/services/eabs
Tailor-made briefings for expatriates going to Japan, China, Korea or other East Asian countries.
School of Oriental and African Studies
www.soas.ac.uk
Briefing and language service, open briefings on Japan and China, two-day Japan Business Orientation programme.
Yahoo!
http://travel.yahoo.com/p-travelguide-191500005-asia_vacations-i
Search engine directory of information on the region.

Europe

European Commission
www.europa.eu.int
www.cec.org.uk
Factsheets and information on working and living in the European Union.
Yahoo!
http://travel.yahoo.com/p-travelguide-191500008-europe_vacations-i
Search engine directory of information on the region.

Middle East

ArabNet
www.arab.net
Yahoo!
http://travel.yahoo.com/p-travelguide-191500009-middle_east_vacations-i
Search engine directory of information on the region.

Language tuition

Berlitz (UK) Ltd
www.berlitz.co.uk
Language tuition.

EXPAT NETWORKS

British in America
www.britishinamerica.com
Expats in the US link-up.
Britnet
www.british-expats.com
International site for British living abroad.
Brits Abroad
www.britsabroad.co.uk
Diplomatic Service Families Association
www.fco.gov.uk
Promotes the interest and welfare of spouses of serving and retired diplomatic service officers. Provides a link between those at home and abroad.
Escapeartist
www.escapeartist.com
Superb website with links to expat forums, country-specific data, advice on relocation and much more.
Expat Exchange
www.expatexchange.com
Comprehensive information source on moving overseas, tax and finance plus much more. Runs an expat network.
Expat Forum
www.expatforum.com
Chat forums in 24 country-specific areas, along with other areas of interest to expats.
Expatica
www.expatica.com
Well-resourced website for expatriates living in Belgium, France, Spain, Germany and The Netherlands.
Expats in Brussels
www.expatsinbrussels.com
Interactive site for the expatriate community in Brussels.
Expat Network
www.expatnetwork.co.uk
Publishes *Nexus* and offers a support service for expats.
Expat Online
www.expat-online.com
Network for expats living in Belgium.
Federation of American Women's Clubs Overseas, Inc
www.fawco.org
OUTPOST
www.outpostexpat.nl
Shell International's superb expat website.
Spouse Employment Centre
www.incnetwork.demon.co.uk
Shell International's website providing information to partners who wish to work or develop their skills during expatriation.
TCK
www.tckworld.com

Website for parents of 'Third Culture Kids' (TCK – expat children) which aims to enable parents to understand the culture shock their children may experience whilst living abroad.

EDUCATION

British Dyslexia Association
www.bda-dyslexia.org.uk
Advice on the teaching of dyslexic children.

Cambridge Education Associates
www.cea.co.uk
Provides free educational advice as well as a comprehensive guardianship service.

Clarendon International Education
www.clarendon.uk.com
Offers guardianship services.

Department for Education and Skills
www.dfes.gov.uk
Information on maintained boarding schools.

European Council of International Schools
www.ecis.org
Details of 400 international schools and website access to International Schools Directory.

Gabbitas Educational Consultants
www.gabbitas.co.uk
Advice on a selection of suitable schools. Also offers guardianship services.

Gabbitas.net
www.gabbitas.net
Excellent site that contains a fully searchable directory of English-speaking international and special schools.

International Baccalaureate Organisation
www.ibo.org

OCR – Oxford Cambridge and RSA Examination Board
www.ocr.org.uk
Administers the AICE curriculum.

National Extension College
www.nec.ac.uk
Offers GCSE and A-level correspondence courses.

The New School, Rome
www.newschoolrome.com

Universities and Colleges Admissions Service
www.ucas.com
Central agency for all UK universities.

The World-wide Education Service (Home School) Ltd
www.weshome.demon.co.uk
Specialises in teaching children with special needs.

World-wide Education Service
www.wesworldwide.com
Information on overseas schools.

HEALTH ADVICE

AXA PP healthcare
www.axa-pp.co.uk
BUPA International
www.bupa.co.uk
Medical insurance worldwide.
Hospital for Tropical Diseases
www.thehtd.org
For access to Health Information for Overseas Travel.
International SOS Assistance
www.internationalsos.com
Provides emergency help in a time of crisis.
Medical Advisory Service for Travellers Abroad (MASTA)
www.masta.org
Offers health briefs on 250 countries.
Reuters Health
www.reutershealth.com/en/

ENTERTAINMENT

Books

Amazon Books
www.amazon.com and www.amazon.co.uk
Delivery of over 2 million titles worldwide.
Internet Public Library
www.ipl.org
Online access to various publications.

Newspapers

The Daily Telegraph
www.telegraph.co.uk
Almost entire content of daily newspaper.
The Guardian
www.guardian.co.uk
Selected cuttings.
The Sunday Times
www.sunday-times.co.uk
Full content.
The Times
www.timesonline.co.uk
Full content.

Sport

Skysports
www.skysports.com
News on a range of sports.

Sportsweb
www.sportsweb.com
As above.
Yahoo!
http://sports.yahoo.com
Comprehensive listings of websites covering every type of sport imaginable.

Television and radio

BBC News
www.news.bbc.co.uk
BBC Online
www.bbc.co.uk
Radio and World Service programmes online with audio versions.
CNN
www.cnn.com
Soap Digest
www.soapoperadigest.com
Keep up to date with your favourite soaps.

Music, DVDs and Videos

Amazon Music, DVDs and Videos
www.amazon.com and amazon.co.uk
Delivery of over 2 million new and used CDs, cassettes, DVDs and videos worldwide.
CD Wow
www.cd-wow.com
International music, DVD and games site that delivers worldwide.
MTV
www.mtv.com
Online music site.

USEFUL MISCELLANEOUS WEBSITES

Allied Pickfords
www.alliedpickfords.co.uk
International removals.
Cybercafe Search Engine
www.cybercaptive.com
Cybercafe locations worldwide to ensure internet access.
Department for Environment, Food and Rural Affairs
www.defra.gov.uk
Advice on the transportation of animals overseas.
Expatnetwork
www.expatnetwork.co.uk
Gift service to send gifts or flowers to friends and family.
Expedia
www.expedia.co.uk
Travel links.

Fedex
www.fedex.com
Website of Federal Express for your freight needs.
Foreign Languages for Travellers
http://www.travlang.com/languages
Phrases in many languages.
Going-There.com
www.going-there.com
International relocation company with offices based in the UK and abroad.
Kropla
www.kropla.com
Extremely useful site with worldwide electrical and telephone information. Details of electric plugs and voltages used.
Mastercard/Cirrus ATM Locator
www.mastercard.com/cardholderservices/atm
Find automated teller machine in your new location.
MonsterMoving
www.moving.com
Comprehensive array of moving-related services and resources.
VISA ATM Locator
http://visa.via.infonow.net/locator/global
Find automated teller machine in your new location.
Visa Service
www.visaservice.co.uk
Specialises in processing applications for business visas and passports.
Worldwide Holiday and Festival Page
http://www.holidayfestival.com
Public holidays throughout the world.
Worldwide weather forecasts
www.intellicast.com
Local weather around the globe.
XE.com
http://www.xe.com
Currency converter.

ADVERTISERS' CONTACT DETAILS

AXA PPP Healthcare
www.axappphealthcare.com
Badminton School
www.badminton.bristol.sch.uk
BDO Stoy Hayward
www.bdo.co.uk
British Council
www.trs.britishcouncil.org
Bupa International
www.bupa-intl.com
Chelstoke International
info@chelstokeinternational.com

Frankfurt International School e.V.
www.fis.edu
Help I am Moving Overseas.Com
www.helpiammoving.com/www.helpimmovingoverseas.com
Jobsearch-in-Canada.com
www.jobsearch-in-canada.com
Leaders the Rental Agents
www.leaders.co.uk
Leana Nel International Relocations
www.propertiessouthafrica.com
Lloyds TSB International
www.lloydstsb-offshore.com/international
Number One Health Group
www.numberonehealth.co.uk
Overseas Emigration Visas
www.overseas-emigration.co.uk
Oxford University Press
www.askoxford/languages
Rosetta Stone
www.rosetta.co.uk
Routledge Taylor and Francis Group
www.routledge.com/colloquials
Willis Brazolot
www.willisbrazolot.com

Index

Index of Advertisers